ORDE WINGATE

Orde Wingate: A Man of Genius, 1903–1944

This edition published in 2010 by Frontline Books, an imprint of
Pen and Sword Books Ltd., 47 Church Street, Barnsley,
S. Yorkshire, S70 2AS.

Visit us at www.frontline-books.com, email info@frontline-books.com
or write to us at the above address.

ISBN 978-1-84832-572-2

PUBLISHING HISTORY
Orde Wingate: Irregular Soldier was originally published in 1995
by Weidenfeld & Nicholson. This updated edition includes
a new introduction by Andrew Roberts.

CIP data records for this title are available from the British Library.

Printed in Great Britain by CPI Antony Rowe

ORDE WINGATE

A Man of Genius, 1903–1944

TREVOR ROYLE

Introduction by Andrew Roberts

Frontline Books, London

Contents

Illustrations

Between pages 116 and 117
Colonel George Wingate[1]
Ethel Wingate[1]

On his rocking horse[1]
The Wingate clan[1]
The newly commissioned subaltern[1]
At Woolwich[1]
Learning the rudiments of gunnery[1]
The horse-mad subaltern[1]
The young officer[1]
Peggy[1]
On leave from the Sudan[1]
On leave from Palestine[1]
Lorna[1]

Between pages 212 and 213
Leading his Patriots into Addis Ababa, May 1941[2]
In the scrublands of the Gojjam[2]
Emperor Haile Selassie re-enters his kingdom[2]
With Colonel Dan Sandford[2]
With the emperor in Addis Ababa[2]
Inspecting the 2nd Ethiopian battalion at Dambacha[2]
With Derek Tulloch[2]
Parachuting supplies to the Chindits[2]
Briefing aircrew of the 1st Air Commando at Hailakandi[2]
Operation Thursday[2]
With Colonel Philip Cochrane[2]
Field Marshal Slim[3]
Admiral Lord Louis Mountbatten with General Stilwell[2]
Planning for victory[2]
Wingate on board a mule-carrying Dakota transport[1]
The last photograph[1]

Photographic credits
[1]Author and Wingate family
[2]Imperial War Museum
[3]Illustrated London News

Acknowledgements

No book of this kind could have been written without the active help of the Wingate family and I was indeed fortunate in the support and kindnesses offered to me. Lieutenant-Colonel Orde Jonathan Wingate not only allowed me to borrow his father's personal papers over a lengthy period but he was also engagingly tolerant and understanding when faced by my many queries. I hope that this book has gone some way to repaying that interest and assistance.

Although Judy Wingate, widow of Granville Wingate, never knew her famous brother-in-law she was equally helpful and involved. I am grateful to her for allowing me to borrow many of her husband's papers and photographs and for commenting on the finished product. Also, I would indeed be blameworthy if I did not thank her for some splendid hospitality and for helping to make the research seem such fun.

Through her I was able to meet Enid 'Peggy' Jelley who was engaged to Wingate in the early 1930s. Her frank comments provided me with a better understanding of the man and his mind and I cannot thank her enough for being so candid about her relationship with Wingate.

I would like to make special mention of three writers who agreed to read the manuscript before publication. Brigadier Shelford Bidwell, historian of the Chindit campaign and author of many fine military studies, discussed Wingate with me before I started writing and then read the result. His comments were both encouraging and instructive.

Equally helpful was Lieutenant-Colonel Rex King-Clark who gave me the benefit of his experiences with the Special Night Squads in Palestine and who cast his expert eye on the chapters dealing with those operations. I am also grateful to him for allowing me to quote extensively from his excellent autobiography, *Free for a Blast*.

Wingate's friend and colleague Abraham Akavia was kind enough to read and comment upon the chapters relating to Palestine and Ethiopia. His help and advice were beneficial to my understanding of that period of Wingate's life. Of course, I alone am responsible for any errors or misjudgements which remain in the text.

I am also indebted to Brigadier Michael Calvert, Michael Elliot-Bateman and the late Brigadier Peter Mead for providing me with some keen insights into the Chindit campaigns of 1943 and 1944. I am also grateful to Brigadier Calvert and his publisher Leo Cooper for allowing me to quote from his autobiography *Prisoners of Hope*.

Lord Weidenfeld kindly gave me the benefit of his personal knowledge of Wingate's relationship with Chaim Weizmann and other personalities involved in the attempt to raise a Jewish fighting force during the Second World War. I am pleased to acknowledge his interest.

I was fortunate, too, in receiving help from the Chindits Old Comrades' Association. Through the good offices of Lieutenant-Colonel J. C. White and Captain Baden K. Wilson I was provided with a copy of the appreciation of Wingate's operations in Burma which contains much useful first-hand information about the two Chindit operations. It is indicative of the respect which Wingate commanded that so many Chindits were prepared to commit their thoughts to paper at a time when his reputation was under threat. Another former Chindit, Dr Leslie Wilson, provided me with some important clues about the circumstances surrounding Wingate's attempted suicide in 1941.

For their help in interpreting the Jewish missionary work of the Church of Scotland and the Free Church of Scotland I wish to thank my old friend the Rev David Ogston, minister of the Parish Kirk of St John the Baptist, Perth, and Professor Alec Cheyne, late of the Chair of Church History in the University of Edinburgh.

The task of understanding Wingate's career at Charterhouse and Woolwich was made easier by the assistance granted by Peter Attenborough and Shirley Corke, respectively Headmaster and Archivist of Charterhouse; Brigadier K. A. Timbers, Historical Secretary of the Royal Artillery Historical Trust; and Dr T. A. Heathcote, Curator, Royal Military Academy, Sandhurst. They all have my thanks.

Brigadier John Platt and Lord Margadale kindly answered my queries about the South and West Wilts Hunt and about the Larkhill garrison's links with the hunts in the area. I am grateful to them for their help.

Unravelling the events leading to Wingate's death in March 1944 would have been made more difficult without the pioneering work undertaken by Dennis Hawley. He kindly made an extended loan of his research papers and gave me early sight of his book, *The Death of Wingate*.

I also want to thank the following members of the Sudan Defence Force Dinner Club who responded to my requests for information about Wingate's posting in the Sudan: Duncan Campbell, Sir Douglas Dodds-Parker, W. L. Newell, Harold Skeeles.

For their professional help, advice and guidance I wish to thank the staffs of the Imperial War Museum Library, London; the John Rylands Library, University of Manchester; the National Library of Scotland, Edinburgh; and the Public Record Office, Kew. I also wish to thank Jane Hogan, Assistant Keeper (Archives and Special Collections) at the University of Durham, for guiding me through the Library's Sudan Archive and Dr Peter Boyden, Head of the Department of Archives at the National Army Museum, for his help with various aspects of the military careers of George and Orde Wingate.

Crown copyright material in the Public Record Office is reproduced by permission of the Controller of Her Majesty's Stationery Office.

Extracts from the interviews in the *Middle East: British Military Personnel* archive are reproduced by permission of the Department of Sound Records, Imperial War Museum. I am also grateful to Major-General H. E. N. Bredin for giving me permission to quote from his interview in the same archive. Similar thanks are due to Miss Mary E. Jelley for permission to quote from her correspondence with Major-General Derek Tulloch.

Every attempt has been made to contact copyright holders and I apologise for any accidental omissions. Due acknowledgement will be made in subsequent editions if the information is forthcoming.

Finally, for making sure that this book saw the light of day I should like to thank my agents, Gloria Ferris and Rivers Scott; my publisher Ion Trewin and my editor Morag Lyall.

Trevor Royle
Edinburgh
October 1994

Introduction

In the 1930s, when Orde Wingate was learning the soldier's craft, the legend of Lawrence of Arabia was nearing its height, and he drank deep of it. What could be better than to be a dashing young British officer fighting deep behind enemy lines, disrupting lines of communication in uncompromisingly harsh territory? What Lawrence achieved in the desert, Wingate would achieve in the jungle. It must have seemed almost Kismet when Wingate discovered that his maternal great-great-grandmother had been Laurence's aunt. Although Lawrence chose to lionise the Arabs and Wingate the Jews, close connectivity was undoubtedly there, not least in the high regard in which both men were held by Lawrence's friend Winston Churchill, who called Wingate 'this man of genius who might well have become a man of destiny'.

As this excellent book shows, Wingate was just as strange a personality as T.E. Lawrence, who used to cycle up hills and walk down them while at Oxford, rather than the other way around. Some of Wingate's habits, views, training practices and military decisions – let alone his suicide attempt in Cairo in July 1941 – might seem almost unhinged, fully justifying Royle's subtitle for the original edition of the book, *Irregular Soldier*. His irregularity made him an object of ridicule and derision, but occasionally also deep respect to his contemporaries in the British Army officer corps, and Trevor Royle ably demonstrates why.

Few people could be better qualified to write Wingate's biography than Royle, who has spent a lifetime immersed in the story of warfare with many distinguished works to his name. He was given access and help by the subject's family, who were understandably keen that the name of Orde Wingate should be rescued from the calumny that some soldiers and historians heaped upon it surprisingly soon after his tragically early death. Originally published in 1995, the author was also able to hear first-hand account accounts of the Chindit expeditions from Wingate's comrades who are sadly no longer with us. In that sense, this book could not have been written today, and it is far-sighted of Frontline Books to republish it.

There is a central problem about Wingate, which military historians have debated for decades and which this book successfully solves. Essentially the question revolves about whether he was a genius and hero who single-mindedly pioneered a new form of jungle warfare that beat the Japanese at their own game, or whether he was an egomaniacal maverick whose two great Burmese expeditions of 1943 and 1944 cost more Allied lives than their meagre military returns were worth. Trevor Royle's conclusions are unambiguous, convincing and backed up with first-rate historical research.

Wingate made a fair number of enemies in the 14th Army in building up his command from a brigade to a division, but for all the sometimes bitter criticisms of him he was undoubtedly one of the true originals. On 31 August 1940, lunching at the War Office, 'He said he had acquired quite a taste for boiled python, which tasted like chicken,' the Director of Military Operations' Major General John Kennedy recorded. 'His men kept remarkably fit – he thought chiefly because they knew they would fall into the hands of the Japanese if they didn't. He is a man of great character, a good talker and a very good writer too.' A naturist who frequently wore only a pith helmet and fly-whisk in camp, someone who never bathed but instead cleaned himself by vigorous scrubbing of his body with a stiff brush, Wingate ate raw onions for pleasure. Small wonder he was controversial.

The fighting that Wingate's Chindits had to undertake, and the appalling conditions they had to contend with in the jungle, made their two expeditions far behind Japanese lines amongst the great military feats of the Second World War, whether one ends up admiring Wingate as a military strategist or not. A passage from Major-General Bernard Fergusson's war diary dated 30 March 1943 underlines the harshness of the situation by the end of the first expedition:

Party now consists of 9 officers, 109 other ranks, of which 3 officers, 2 other ranks wounded. All weak and hungry in varying degrees. Addressed all ranks and told them: (a) only absolute discipline would get us out. I would shoot anybody who pilfered comrades or villages, or who grumbled (b) Anybody who lost his rifle or equipment I would expel from the party, unless I was satisfied with the excuse (c) Only chance was absolute trust and implicit obedience (d) No stragglers.

Sentries who fell asleep could expect to wake up to a flogging.

Consider the conditions the Chindits faced on campaign: monsoon rain that could turn a foxhole into something approaching a Passchendaele trench in minutes; constant attacks of diarrhoea, malaria and any number of other tropical diseases; ingenious booby traps and the ever-present fear of them; highly accurate enemy mortar and sniper fire; inaccurate maps; leeches; bad communications; reliance on village rumours for intelligence; sick and obstinate mules; low-nutrition food and bad water; miles upon miles of thick jungle in which it could take an hour to cut through one hundred yards; the abandonment of the wounded and stragglers: these are the factors in Chindit warfare that crop up time and again in the memoirs of survivors.

For those who question the value of the two Chindit Expeditions, however, it is worthwhile recalling that it proved that Allied troops could survive long periods in the jungle just as well as the Japanese, which was a crucial psychological factor. The Chindits therefore helped to dissolve the myth of the invincible Japanese superman, a necessary precursor to building up the high morale and self-belief necessary for eventual victory.

Like much else about his life, Wingate's death at the age of only 41 is surrounded with mystery and controversy. In that he also mirrored his hero, distant cousin and alter ego T.E. Lawrence. In my view, Royle's account is the most convincing explanation of this great wartime tragedy.

This combination of Orde Wingate, Trevor Royle and Frontline Books is a fortuitous one. Wingate's story is fascinating, Royle's research and writing are superb, and Frontline are already proving themselves a very fine imprint. I salute all three.

Andrew Roberts, 2010

Prologue

The day that he tried to kill himself in Cairo, Major Orde Charles Wingate was finally convinced that he had been born to achieve great things.

As the faces around his hospital bed came into focus his first thought was that they must be devils sent to torment him for his wickedness. Concerned voices tried to calm him but in his anguish he could only repeat over and over again that he was damned to eternity, that hell-fire would consume him, that God had withdrawn the benison of his blessing. Neither the ministrations of the Scottish doctors and nurses nor the words of comfort uttered by the hospital chaplain could ease his misery. Not only had he let himself down as a man and a soldier but he had betrayed God's sacred trust.

But then there was a miracle of sorts. A Catholic chaplain hurried into the room to help him salve his soul.

'Am I truly damned?' asked Wingate.

'No,' came the reply. 'God will forgive you.'

Like the first ray of light at daybreak the words brought the promise of a new beginning. Wingate relaxed. He was saved. God still meant him to carry out his wishes: he was indeed destined for greatness. Whatever man might do to frustrate his efforts Wingate now understood that he had a mission in life and that God would shield and protect him.

High summer in Cairo in 1941 was not the best of times to come to that realisation. In the desert to the west General Erwin Rommel's Afrika Korps had advanced into Egypt with terrible swiftness; Crete had fallen and the Germans had entered Athens; the Germans had launched a massive armoured assault on the Soviet Union. The British high command was attempting to wrestle with the problems of global warfare and, following setback after setback, it looked as if the war might go on for ever.

And yet, despite the growing uncertainty, Wingate felt strangely elated. In the previous month he had enraged his superiors in high command by submitting an intemperate report about his personal worth. He had lost his patron General Archibald Wavell who had been sacked by Churchill for his failure to stop Rommel's advance. He had reverted to the middling rank of major and his attempted suicide had cast doubts on his sanity and his military ability. But he had reached a crossroads.

Behind him lay a career which by any standards had marked him out as being different from other soldiers of his generation. In the 1930s he had encouraged the Jewish settlers in Palestine to defend themselves during the Arab Revolt and had emerged as an inspiring leader of low-intensity military operations. When war had broken out with Germany in 1939 he was considered too temperamental and difficult for regular command but by creating his own luck he had been appointed to lead a guerrilla group in the harsh mountainous country of western Ethiopia. Charged with the responsibility of focusing a Patriot rebellion on the Emperor Haile Selassie Wingate had achieved a childhood dream that one day he might return a king to his rightful throne.

With life now stretching out in front of him and with God's renewed blessing Wingate knew that he could only advance. In the months to come he would put the seal on his military reputation by proving to unbelieving superiors that his radical long-range penetration tactics, used in conjunction with regular operations, could defeat a superior enemy and turn the tide of the war. The chance came in Burma in 1943 when he raised and led a special force of ordinary men deep into the jungle to sow confusion behind enemy lines. Known as Chindits, they proved that the Japanese soldier was not a superman and that properly trained soldiers could survive the difficulties of jungle warfare. Within a year, the Chindit forces had been expanded and Wingate stood at the pinnacle of his military career only to be robbed of complete success when his aircraft plunged into a hillside in Assam.

Between his suicide attempt in July 1941 and his death in March 1944 Wingate travelled further than most men in his quest to prove himself. During the course of that short but meteoric career he managed to combine the best elements of such contrary military leaders as Stonewall Jackson and Lawrence of Arabia, to whom he was distantly related, his maternal great-great-grandmother and Lawrence's father being sister and brother. Like them he was possessed of a strong personality, like them he inspired the troops who served him and like them, too, he dazzled his political masters. Churchill, Roosevelt, Wavell and Mountbatten were all agreed that Wingate was one of the few men of genius to emerge during the Second World War.

There was, though, a darker side to his character: his suicide was occasioned by cerebral malaria but exacerbated by depression and a fear that God had abandoned him. Deeply religious and aware of his own sense of destiny, Wingate attracted conflicting absolutes throughout his life. Most close friends and colleagues admired him immensely and warmed to the uneasy mixture of professionalism and iconoclasm he brought to the military life. To them, Wingate's unbounded confidence was an inspiration. Others, mostly those who had not met him or knew him only fleetingly, thought him little more than a charlatan, a flamboyant attention-seeker who came to believe his own publicity. Still more disliked him personally for his impassioned espousal of unpopular causes, but admitted a grudging admiration for his methods, many of which were innovative and unorthodox.

Wingate was a mass of contradictions and the passing of the years has done little to resolve them. After he died at the early age of forty-one disapproving official war historians played down his exploits, hinted that his Chindit operations were flawed and prompted by personal ambition and discredited his use of long-range penetration tactics in the hard fighting against the Japanese. Professional jealousy was one reason for their disapproval; dislike of Wingate's methods another; but their animosity was also fired by a belief that Wingate was an outsider who owed everything to carefully nurtured political connections and little to actual military ability.

There was also more than a touch of anti-Semitism involved in these variegated opinions. Wingate's pronounced Zionist views, his service in Palestine and his close friendship with Jewish leaders such as Chaim Weizmann all combined to give the impression that he was a Jew, a rumour given further substance by his dark aquiline looks. Not so; Wingate was of Anglo-Scottish stock and was raised on strict fundamentalist principles. His enthusiastic attachment to Zionism came from a desire to help the underdog and from a much broader admiration for the Jewish race and their religious beliefs, but it did him few favours at a time when young officers were expected to be orthodox and seemly.

Wingate was certainly a maverick with a reputation for eccentricity, yet he used the estimation as a cloak, because, being a zealot in a conformist society like the army, nothing would be expected of him, provided that he did not break the basic rules. More than that, throughout his life, he was a man of extremes who brooked no middle way. With Wingate it had to be all or nothing.

One

FATHER TO THE MAN

Through his family background and, later, by personal inclination Orde Charles Wingate was destined to be a soldier. His father George was an officer in the Indian Staff Corps, having been commissioned originally in the 19th Foot (The Green Howards) and his brother Alfred served with the Indian Cavalry. On his mother Ethel's side, the Orde-Brownes were of Gloucestershire county stock who had provided generations of soldiers and administrators for the service of the empire. His great-grandfather had commanded the 9th Lancers and his grandfather Charles Orde-Browne had seen action with the Royal Horse Artillery in the Crimea. In the nineteenth and twentieth centuries it was not unusual for sons to follow their father's profession and some regiments of the British army took immense pride in its officers' family connections.

However, it was not so much his family's military and imperial background that first influenced the young Orde Wingate as their religious beliefs which were uncompromisingly fundamentalist. The Wingates were originally a Lowland Scottish family with roots in Stirlingshire and Glasgow where they enjoyed close links with the Presbyterian Church of Scotland and later with the breakaway evangelical Free Church of Scotland; while on his mother's side the Orde-Brownes had long been stalwart members of the Plymouth Brethren. The mixture of public duty in the armed forces and of missionary service to the poor and the dispossessed was to have a lasting effect on the course of his life and career and were to have a major influence in shaping the man. It was the crossing of the Bible with the sword.

He was born in India on 26 February 1903 at Montrose House in Naini Tal, the summer capital of the United Provinces in the north of India. It was a pleasant hot-season residence, or hill station, with a boat club beside the lake and several imposing bungalows and hotels; some people in British India preferred it to the better known Simla or Oota-camund. During the hot season – roughly from April until September – Naini Tal was the official retreat for the officials and administrators of the state secretariat who escaped the fire of the plains by decamping with their families to the cooler weather in the hills. Only those men in essential work, and this included soldiers, remained behind to toil in the heat and dust.

Escaping the hot season in the hills was an annual exodus and it became part of the mythology of the British Raj. With their tennis parties and picnics, their fancy dress dances and amateur theatricals, the hill stations offered a shrill and hectic social round and holiday atmosphere which was very different from the normal run of life in British India.

Not that the Wingates would have allowed such trifles to interfere with their own lives. To begin with, they were in Naini Tal out of season because their two eldest children, Rachel and Sybil, were suffering from mumps and had to be kept in quarantine because their mother was pregnant. Even if the season had been in full swing, though, it is doubtful if the Wingates would have thrown themselves into it. Being Plymouth Brethren they eschewed such vanities and in keeping with the calling's strict tenets led plain and modest lives devoted to the service of God.

In this vocation they were not alone. Throughout the nineteenth century a strong evangelical strain existed in the British and Indian armies, many of whose senior officers believed Divine Providence had taken them to India and that it was their solemn duty to convert heathens and unbelievers to Christ's Truth. Known to their brother officers as 'serious' or as 'Blue Lights', these men took a fierce pride in their convictions and genuinely believed that it was their duty to convert their Indian men to Christianity.

Soldier heroes as different as John Nicholson and Gordon of Khartoum were imbued with a strong sense that they had been chosen by God to do his great work. Indeed, during the first years of his conversion to the Plymouth Brethren, Wingate's maternal grandfather Charles Orde-Browne had joined Gordon in his missions for destitute boys in Gravesend between 1865 and 1871 before establishing his own mission in North Woolwich. While the inordinate public piety of men such as Gordon marked them out as being different from their brother officers and at times bordered on moral exhibitionism, other evangelical officers, such as George Wingate, lived quieter lives devoted to the creation of 'a new heaven and a new earth, in which dwelleth righteousness'.

He had been brought up a member of the Free Church of Scotland in which his father William was both a well-known minister and a committed missionary to the Jews, first in Pest in Hungary and then in London. Born on 21 November 1852, the fifth child and second son, George was commissioned into The Green Howards on 23 September 1871 shortly after they had returned from fourteen years' service in India. From then until 1875 the regiment was stationed in Aldershot and the north of England, a period which gave the junior subalterns few opportunities to engage in real soldiering. Not being particularly wealthy and anxious to fulfil his ambitions, George decided to transfer to the Indian Army which provided the benefits of a higher income and fewer expenses and, above all, the chance to see some action. On 7 September 1875 he was posted to the Indian Staff Corps which provided a general list of British officers for appointment to regimental or staff positions in the Indian army.

Quite early in his career in India he underwent a religious conversion which impelled him to join the recently founded Plymouth Brethren, a Calvinistic faith whose members interpret the Bible quite literally and believe in the second coming of Christ. His faith was reinforced by his relationship to the Orde-Browne family whom he had met in 1878 while on leave in London. At the time they were living at Plumstead near their slum mission in Woolwich and there is little doubt that George was dazzled by them at first meeting. Not only did he greatly admire Charles Orde-Browne both for his piety and a wide range of enthusiasms which embraced model soldiering and astronomy, but he also fell in love with his twelve-year-old daughter Ethel.

Astonishing as it might seem – he was fourteen years her senior – it was immediately understood by the Orde-Brownes that the serious-minded young army officer would one day marry their daughter. Indeed, Charles encouraged the match because he believed 'it would be interesting to see the offspring of a marriage between two so definitely marked yet widely different characters.'

Convergence of religious interests was another reason for the match, as was the spirit of the age. During the latter years of the century there was a vogue for older men to engage in sentimental relationships with younger girls, tasteful postcards began to appear of cherubic pink-cheeked girls whose rosebud bodies betrayed no burgeoning signs of maturity and it was quite common for older men to accompany young girls on visits to the theatre and other public places. The most famous of these was the Oxford scholar, the Rev C. L. Dodgson, who wrote under the name of Lewis Carroll. He saw nothing wrong in his relationships with young girls – many of whom he photographed naked – and even went so far as to enquire of their parents if he could be 'on kissing terms' with them.

While it is unlikely that George failed to comprehend the impulses which led him to idolise Ethel Orde-Browne while she was still a young girl, the episode is interesting in that Orde Wingate was destined to fall in love with his future wife in 1933 when she was a sixteen-year-old schoolgirl and he an officer thirteen years her senior. They married two years later. However, George had to wait twenty years, until September 1899, before he and Ethel could get married. By then he was forty-six and she was thirty-two.

From the very outset of their marriage she threw herself into George's missionary work at Mardan in the North-West Frontier Province where, from his own funds, he employed two missionaries to run a centre for propagating the Christian faith.

Such solemnity need not dent an officer's career prospects; on the contrary, provided that it does not interfere with his professional work, commitment to a particular faith, even eccentricity, has never been a bar to advancement in the British army. When George Wingate sat down with a sadhu, or holy man, in the fierce heat of the midday sun and attempted to reason with him, few eyebrows were raised in the mess. Even when he refused to break the Sabbath by moving his men on a Sunday during the Naga Hills Expedition in 1879, his decision did not provoke the anger of the force's commander, Major-General William Gatacre. Indeed, at the end of the short campaign which was aimed at curbing King Thibaw of Burma, he was mentioned in despatches.

As well as following his own religious principles by converting to the Plymouth Brethren, Wingate was also treading in a family tradition. His father William had suddenly given up a prosperous partnership worth £800 a year in the family shipping business in Glasgow to train for the ministry of the Church of Scotland. It was as sudden as Saul on the road to Damascus. As a boy at Glasgow High School and then as a student at Glasgow University William Wingate had been widely admired as a beau-ideal who combined scholarship with athleticism and who was as much at home on the back of a hunter as he was on the dance floor. The untimely death of his wife Jessie in childbirth in 1838, when he was only thirty, was one reason for his unexpected conversion, but it is also true to say that even before that he had been caught up in the wave of evangelism then sweeping through Scotland.

The evangelicals were led by men of stature such as Thomas Chalmers and Dr Alexander Black of Aberdeen and, like the seventeenth-century Covenanters, they believed that society had to be transformed in preparation for the creation of Christ's kingdom on earth. For them personal salvation could only come through Jesus Christ and the principle of bringing people to his throne. According to his biographer Gavin Carlyle, it was a period of Scottish history when religion became an intense reality.

At that time the carrying out of the Lord's great command to preach His gospel to every creature, beginning at Jerusalem, was realised by the Church to be a great, solemn and responsible work. The cry, 'Who is able for such things?' went through the length and breadth of Scotland. In most congregations special meetings for prayers for divine guidance were organised and greatly blessed with tokens of the Saviour's presence. In the public worship of the Church ministers brought the scriptural duty of seeking the salvation of 'the scattered nation' before the people.[1]

Although the fundamentalists' enthusiasm for religious reform was directed mainly at the Scots themselves – between 1828 and 1841 over 200 new churches were built in Scotland by the Church Extension Committee – there was also a growing interest in missionary work overseas. In 1825 the first Church of Scotland missionary was sent to India in the person of one Rev Alexander Duff but it was not long before the more forward-looking ministers were eyeing the scattered Jews of Europe as a more promising people ripe for conversion to Christianity. It was hardly a new idea, for as early as 1809 the Church of England's evangelical wing had founded the London Society for Promoting Christianity among the Jews, but in Scotland it struck a deeper chord. Not only did the more zealous ministers believe that it was their duty to convert everyone to their religion but they also felt a special affinity with the people of Israel.

Both alike had a love of the Old Testament; both had an ardent and consuming affection for their own land, combined with a capacity for settling in other lands and making money in them; both alike had simplicity of worship, a somewhat similar church government, and a veneration of the Sabbath. These were all felt to be elements which would make a near approach to the Jews possible. Besides there was a renewed interest in Old Testament prophecy.[2]

William Wingate was one of the evangelicals who believed that if scriptural prophecy were to be fulfilled, then the Jews had to be converted to Christianity. Shortly after his wife's death he became an elder of the Tron Church in Glasgow whose minister Robert Buchanan was a cousin from the Stirlingshire branch of the Wingate family. Through him he was introduced to a small but important group of ministers who had formed a Jewish Mission Committee with funds given to them by the Hon Mrs Smith of Dunesk, daughter of the eccentric lawyer and wit Henry Erskine. These included Dr Moody Stuart, Wingate's old rival at school and university, Robert Wodrow, descendant of the Church historian, Horatius Bonar, writer of rousing hymns, and, above all, Dr R. S. Candlish, the influential minister of St George's in Edinburgh. Then, in 1843 William married Margaret Wallace, the step-daughter of John Duncan, another notable evangelist minister. Between them all they were to change the course of Wingate's life.

Despite pressure from his family to stay in Scotland he went to Berlin to study German, Hebrew and Church history and on his return to Scotland his path to the ministry was eased by Candlish who persuaded the General Assembly, the Church's governing body, to abridge his divinity course in recognition of his fine record at school and university. By 1842 William Wingate had been ordained and a year later he had joined the Church of Scotland's first mission to the Jews in Budapest which had been founded with the support of the Archduchess Marie Dorothea. But no sooner had he arrived than Wingate's life was to take another turn as he and his fellow missionaries were forced to take sides in a schism which split the established Church into two camps.

Known as the Disruption, it created the Free Church of Scotland which amongst other measures would henceforth depend on voluntary funds to pay its ministers' stipends instead of relying on patronage – one of the reasons for the secession. The Free Church quickly acquired a character of its own, reserved, serious and enthusiastic in its missionary desire to transform society so that the individual's path to God could be an easier one. Amongst the many hundreds of ministers who gave up easy livings to join this new puritanical Church was William Wingate: to a man the missionaries in Hungary crossed over to the Free Church and carried on their work, first in Pest and then in Jassy. Having broken with his family he could not return to Glasgow; instead he settled in London and continued his missionary work amongst the Jews. Never completely successful, he still enjoyed close links with Jewish society in London until his death on Christmas Eve 1899.

His decision to join the Free Church had been as sudden as his original conversion and it finally broke the family connection with shipping and the textile trade that had made his father Andrew a rich man. William's brother, also an Andrew, stayed on and lived in nearby Port Glasgow but the family was already beginning to break up and lose its connections with the west of Scotland. By 1852, the year of Andrew's official retirement, the family's business concerns had passed into other hands. William's three sons were all in India – Andrew, the eldest, was to become a senior and much-respected member of the elite Indian Civil Service – and brother Andrew's son Reginald (F. R.) Wingate later became governor of the Sudan after a notable career in the army. Like many other Scots, it was their destiny to serve the empire as soldiers or administrators and although they were to retain a sentimental regard for their homeland, the ties that had bound them to Scotland for over 800 years were gradually severed.

With their house in fashionable Blythswood Square, though, the Wingates had been an established and easily recognisable Glasgow family, wealthy, confident and with a wide range of social connections amongst the city's burgeoning middle class. Their wealth had been built on the back of the cotton trade which had come to Glasgow at the end of the eighteenth century and which, at the height of its boom, employed 20,000 people in some sixty factories. Merchants like the Wingates, who served the industry, lived well off it and in turn they became important patrons, paying for civic innovations and building solid and imposing new houses as the city expanded westwards.

They also took great pride in their ancestry which they traced back fervently, if mistakenly, to King Robert the Bruce. Another forebear was thought to be Ninian Winzet, a resolute opponent of the Reformation who was one of the few Catholics of his day able to stand up to the Scots reformer John Knox. Even their name had a northern ring. Derived from Old English 'windgeat', it meant a spot where the wind howls through a narrow pass and it is found in place-names as far apart as Derbyshire, Durham and Scotland. In the days of his fame, Reginald Wingate employed an Edinburgh antiquary, James Mackenzie, to research the family tree and to attempt to discover the links between the English and Scottish branches but, as he told Mrs Dalrymple of Gargunnock, he had been forced to admit defeat.

I have the full details of the English branch of the family dating back from the eleventh century, but even there it is difficult to establish an actual point where the Scottish and English branches separated; and then again we have an American branch, which appears to me to be of undoubtedly Scotch origin, though of course the English family was apparently the English stock.[3]

It is probable that the Wingates were originally a Norman family who came across to Britain in the eleventh century and that one branch eventually settled in Scotland. Before setting up in business in Glasgow, the Scottish Wingates had their home in Stirlingshire where two distinct branches of the family had lived at Craigengelt and Gargunnock in the nearby Flanders Moss and both enjoyed close links with St Ninian's Church in the town of Stirling.

Apart from wearing the family's Douglas kilt as a young boy Orde Wingate was to know little of his Scottish background. Instead, he was brought up in a traditional English middle-class family; he considered himself to be a gentleman by birth, was sent to public school, was commissioned into a good regiment, enjoyed hunting and field sports and was never considered an outsider in English society. Nevertheless, his Scottish connections were destined to cast a long shadow over his life and to make him the man he became: resolute, god-fearing, occasionally intolerant, conscious of his own sinfulness yet self-consciously aware of a sense of destiny, not unlike the seventeenth-century Covenanters, extreme Presbyterians, who took to the hills of Scotland to protect their religious principles following the Restoration. Despite the savage harassment of their field conventicles – services held in remote areas in the open air – and the execution of their leaders, those men of the Covenant displayed nothing but steadfastness and self-discipline and many went to their deaths in a mood of religious exaltation.

One further character trait was inherited from grandfather William. As a minister of the reformed Free Church of Scotland he believed that the Old Testament was the inspired word of God, that every moral matter was clear-cut, that man was predestined to eternal bliss or to everlasting fire and that to attempt to compromise was to bargain with the devil. As Orde's sister Sybil put it later in life, the Wingates had behind them 'a long line of Scots Presbyterian ancestors who were full of the belief that salvation was a matter of the wrestling of the individual soul with God and that no earthly authority, however august, must be allowed to come between'. It was an austere belief – it was meant to be – for salvation had been immutably decided in advance by the divine election of a chosen few who were destined to escape hell's torments. In return for such grace the elect were expected to devote themselves to God's wishes, to read his word as it appeared in the Old Testament and to keep the Sabbath, otherwise they could not be sure if they really had been counted amongst those whose salvation was preordained. Any who had the temerity to disagree with this premise were themselves damned.

The mood is caught in a letter which George Wingate wrote to his mother-in-law a week after Orde's birth. So alarmed had he been that Ethel might die after giving birth – she had suffered multiple haemorrhage and had lost a great deal of blood – that distressed telegrams were sent to both families in England requesting prayers for her salvation. Acknowledging that these had obviously been heard, George said that his grateful response had been to read Psalm 30 to his stricken wife.

Hear, O Lord, and have mercy upon me: Lord, be thou my helper.

Thou hast turned for me my mourning into dancing: thou hast put off my sackcloth, and girded me with gladness.

To the end that *my* glory may sing praise to thee, and not be silent: O Lord my God, I will give thanks unto thee for ever.

With these sonorous supplications, young Orde Wingate was brought into the world; as his father said, not without pride, 'an unusually fine large baby weighing nine pounds'.

Two

FIGHTING THE GOOD FIGHT

With the arrival of the hot season proper the Wingates left Naini Tal for England on six months' leave. They stayed in rented rooms in the London suburb of Blackheath to be close to the Orde-Brownes but when they returned to India in February 1904, Rachel, Sybil and Orde remained behind to live with their grandparents in their imposing home at 11 The Paragon, part of an elegant crescent of three-storeyed pairs of houses linked by stuccoed colonnades which looks out over the common and towards Greenwich Park.

It was not an uncommon arrangement. Wives had to choose between remaining with their husbands in India or living with their children in Britain, as home leave with assisted passages was usually granted only every five years. Before the First World War few European children over the age of five remained with their parents in India; instead they were sent home to stay with relatives and attend boarding schools in Britain. Children sent home could grow up to be strangers to their parents with only regular letters to keep them together. That Ethel was unhappy with the arrangement, yet aware that it was part of a grander plan, can be seen in her letters to her children.

My own precious little children,
    You don't know how perpetually Mummy is thinking of you, nor how often she says to herself, now they are going out for a walk, now they are having tea, now they are going to bed ... How you will enjoy going away to the seaside again, to the beautiful house Grand-mama is taking you to. My babies, how I wish I were going with you. The old black minister who comes and preaches to the servants every Sunday afternoon always prays so nicely for Ray and Tibloo and Ordey-boy that the Lord will bless and take care of them.

Fortunately for the young Wingates the separation was to be short as, in October 1905, father George was placed on the Supernumerary List: this was one of the ways in which the British army culled its older officers when employment could no longer be readily found for them.

By then he was a full colonel, having reached that rank on 21 September 1901, and was a veteran of several campaigns. In addition to the Naga Hills Expedition he had also served with the Chitral Relief Force in 1895 and the Tochi Valley Force in 1897 when he was the chief commissariat officer. Both forces were raised as part of numerous British attempts to pacify the North-West Frontier during local tribal uprisings and the fighting was more or less continuous, if rarely conclusive. For his role in the Tochi Valley campaign George was mentioned in despatches and in 1901 was made a Companion of the Order of the Indian Empire (CIE).

In other words he was a reasonably successful officer but he had failed to reach a rank sufficiently senior to avoid the army's constant reappraisal of its manpower needs. Being placed on the half-pay list was the usual solution for retaining promising officers for whom no suitable appointment could be found but being somewhat older George was offered this chance of early retirement. His age helped him in another important way. Having entered the army in the last days when commissions could be purchased – at a cost of £450 in The Green Howards – he was something of an anomaly and this allowed him to retire early on full pension.

After thirty years spent in the service of the Indian Army George Wingate brought his wife back to live in Britain and they set up house in Worthing on the Sussex coast, close to Brighton but also within striking distance of his in-laws in London. During a number of subsequent peregrinations the pattern remained the same: in 1908 they moved to Orpington in Kent and finally in 1914 to Godalming in Surrey where they bought a large Victorian house called Summerhill in Charterhouse Road. By then Orde was eleven and the family had expanded to seven children: four daughters (Rachel, Sybil, Monica and Constance) and three sons (Orde, Nigel and Granville). To the family he was always Ordey or Ordey-boy; nicknames abounded: Constance, the youngest girl, was known as Tossie, Rachel was Ray Baba and Sybil was Tibloo.

The Wingates were a close, home-loving family, outwardly not very different from many of their neighbours in the old wool town of Godalming. Never conspicuously wealthy, but certainly not poor, they settled into the comfortable existence enjoyed by the professional middle classes on the eve of the First World War. Indeed, Godalming seemed to have been tailor-made for their benefit. Until the end of the nineteenth century a bustling industrial town – the railway arrived in 1849 and in 1881 it became the first town to have electric street lighting – Godalming changed its character in 1872 when Charterhouse School moved into its imposing Victorian buildings and parklands on the north-west outskirts of the town. In its wake came the new suburbs to the south and on Frith Hill to the north as families like the Wingates moved into the town to take advantage of the new educational facilities, while the rail con-nections allowed husbands to become commuters to their work in London and the City.

With his army pension George Wingate was relatively well off – income tax still stood at one shilling in the pound – and Ethel enjoyed a private income from the Orde-Brownes. From her uncle, Benjamin Browne of Benwell, Newcastle-on-Tyne, she received £8,000 worth of shares in the Hawthorn Leslie engineering works and in 1903 these yielded £515. Although Ethel was pleased to receive the money she was always somewhat ashamed of her family's links with trade – her children claimed that she was inclined to snobbishness – and when her uncle was knighted she always referred to him as the Nightmare.

However comfortable were his family's financial arrangements, though, a tendency towards religious philanthropy meant that George was destined always to be short of money. Not only did he contribute substantially to a number of missionary societies but, more or less single-handedly with his wife, he also ran and supported the Central Asian Mission which had been founded in 1902 as the Central Asian Pioneer Mission. Its headquarters were in rented offices at Sardinia House in Lincoln's Inn Fields. According to its constitution the mission had been formed 'under the profound sense of the spiritual needs of many millions of people resident in the countries of Central Asia. The Mission seeks to carry the gospel to these as the way opens up for Missionary endeavours and acknowledges dependence upon God alone to provide workers and means in answer to prayer.'

All would have been well had the founding fathers relied on divine omnipotence but the mission was frequently short of funds and the Wingates contributed large sums of money to keep it in being and help the foundation of missionary centres in the society's chosen areas: north-west India, Afghanistan, Russian Turkestan, Chinese Turkestan and Tibet. In 1911, at his own expense, George travelled to the North-West Frontier Province in India to report on conditions facing Christian missionaries amongst the local Muslim community. Just as his father had attempted to draw the Jews of Europe into the Christian faith of the Church of Scotland, so too did George Wingate and his wife work long and hard to promote their interest in converting the Muslims. This meant arduous hours of labour preparing papers and budgets, coping with correspondence and distributing and posting an endless stream of circulars publicising the society's activities. Here the children were called to help and from an early age they were made well aware of their parents' commitment and sacrifice to the cause.

This covenant also meant that money would often be a problem and that the children would have to economise or use their wits to get by. As head of the household their father sanctioned all expenditure and paid all bills and, according to Sybil, he was secretive and frequently mean in his financial dealings. (When Granville was at Oxford he often had to wait for his allowance simply because his father did not have the money. Orde, then a subaltern, would usually help out, sending £5 or £10 with the request that it need not be repaid.) Their parents' piety also meant that the Wingates ran an intensely devout household which was dominated by the scriptures and adherence to an unyielding moral code. Sundays were kept as the Sabbath, the children learned long tracts of the Old Testament, devotional books were much in evidence and there was a strict religious emphasis on both education and play. They were also required to attend the Brethrens' prayer meetings at which their father often spoke. Not having ordained ministers, any baptised male could lead the meeting and George spent a good deal of time preparing his talks in advance. (For this he was considered 'unspiritual' by stricter members who believed that prayer leaders should speak as the Spirit moved them.)

On one level such an existence was not unusual for the period. In most parts of the country a universal silence fell over the towns and cities at the time of Sunday church services and in some areas it would last from dawn to dusk. For most religious families Sunday was indeed the Lord's Day of Rest and was celebrated accordingly. Meals would be prepared the day before, dark clothes were obligatory and the family would troop to church as one, while the rest of the day would be taken up with sedate walks and readings from the scriptures or other good works such as Bunyan's *Pilgrim's Progress*. To a more secular age such a description might sound like parody but despite persistent evidence of a drift away from church attendance, in 1914 the British Sunday was still a sign of the Church's control over its flock.

On that score the Wingates' private devotional activities were unremarkable. What kept them apart from other families in Godalming was their adherence to the Plymouth Brethren, whose strict tenets cautioned against children having much contact with the outside world. While the rule was enforced for the good reason that relationships with non-believers could be corrupting, it did mean that the seven Wingate children were thrown back on their own devices and came to depend heavily on one another. The older children, Rachel, Sybil and Orde, took it upon themselves to look after their younger siblings and their relationships with each other were close and intense; often, almost by a process of osmosis, they would know what the others were thinking or what they wanted before they were even asked.

Later in life, in an essay in the *Spectator* of 29 May 1959, Sybil described the childhood years as having a 'somewhat apocalyptic atmosphere' largely because the parents adopted a literal view of Christian doctrine which had been fired by a fundamental need to reform English religious life.

When we, as children, repeated the 96th Psalm, 'Let the field be joyful and all that is therein: then shall all the trees of the wood rejoice before the Lord, for He cometh to judge the earth: He shall judge the world with righteousness and the people with His truth,' it was the field outside the window that was to be joyful and the trees at the bottom of the garden that would clap their hands. And when we sang:

> O brothers stand as men that wait,
> The dawn is purpling in the East,
> And banners wave at Heaven's high gate,

we watched the banners waving in the clouds of the sunset and wondered if the army of the Lord was even now setting forth.

And sing they did, for the learning of the scriptures and the psalms of the Old Testament was a vital part of the children's early education, so much so that proficiency was rewarded with the presentation of a Bible. It had a lasting effect on Orde: throughout his life his colleagues were astonished by his ability to recite chunks of the Old Testament and the language of his written prose was often enriched by his knowledge of the King James' Bible. During the war he would end many of his papers with apposite quotations from the Old Testament.

According to Sybil the time devoted to the Bible was not just a matter of learning by rote. Together with their parents' radical approach to religious reform it left them with a lasting belief that righteousness could be transmuted beyond Christianity to affect society in general and that virtues like justice, mercy and common human decency should always triumph over discrimination, intolerance and impropriety. As she herself admitted, it was a heady feeling to believe that the reign of Christ was expected on earth not in the distant and unimaginable future but within one's own lifetime.

For the more literally minded Orde, though, the teachings were not so comforting. At the age of ten he came to the conclusion that he was inherently sinful and that, come the Day of Judgement, he would be left to rot in hell while his family enjoyed the fruits of salvation. This was not an idle fantasy. As he told his wife later in life, so terrified was he that death would claim his parents and siblings – whom he perceived to be full of grace – that he would 'wake up in the silent house and creep out to listen at his sisters' door for their breathing, trembling that he should be left alone, the only sinful member of the household'. The fear was heightened by the dark house which Nigel later described as a 'temple of gloom': one of George Wingate's economies was to switch off the electricity at ten o'clock every evening.

A terrible nightmare which recurred at regular intervals throughout his childhood seemed to epitomise his awareness of evil. Although it took several forms, it always involved the threat of damnation and it always ended with the devil entering the soul of the young Orde. Even in maturity the dream would haunt him: the devil would appear in the garden of Summerhill, 'unspeakably evil and horrifying' and would threaten to carry off Sybil. As she resisted him, he turned into a poached egg which she was about to eat. After a moment of indecision, Wingate would seize the egg and swallow it. 'Now Sybil is saved,' he would say. 'But I have the devil inside me. I am the devil.'

Not that night fears and gloomy religion over-dominated the children's early education. Their mother was a cultivated woman, fluent in French, much interested in music and literature and generally considered to be her husband's intellectual superior: there is little doubt that her promptings and encouragement to play the piano and to read the work of Malory, Grimm, Scott and Tennyson greatly added to the children's intellectual curiosity. 'Throughout our childhood Mother was a bright light in the darkest moments, as well as a source of entertainment and fun,' remembered Monica in a short memoir of her childhood. 'Her naturally happy temperament was a reassurance in itself, and did a good deal to counteract the severer side of the evangelicism in which she, like my father, had been brought up ... She gave us that most essential element in children's upbringing, the knowledge that they are loved.'

From their father they were given gifts of a different kind. Although a remote and somewhat austere and elderly figure – he was fifty-one when Orde was born – he encouraged independence and fortitude and, despite frequent and painful attacks of arthritis, he was a great believer in developing physical stamina. Family walks were popular activities but these were rarely polite Sunday afternoon strolls. Instead, even while his children were still young, George Wingate took them on red-blooded cross-country hikes through the open countryside of the Wey Valley in which Godalming sits. To the south there were walks to the hillside plantations of Winkworth Arboretum with its views over the North Downs and, further still, expeditions to distant Hambledon and Hydon Ball, the highest point on the Greensand Hills. For the children the walks were enlivened both by their father's animated interest in observing nature and by his stalwart refusal to take detours to avoid trespassing on private property. Above all, the outings were only counted a success if something useful had been learned.

The same asceticism accompanied their summer holidays when the entire household, including domestic servants, would decamp to rented accommodation in a resort on the Channel or Norfolk coast. If the atmosphere was more liberal, in keeping with the freedom bestowed by any holiday, there was little change in domestic arrangements. The children were encouraged to go to the beach and to spend long hours in the open air, but there had to be a useful end to their activities. Sun-bathing was frowned upon, but shrimping in rock pools would be approved provided that it was accompanied by some modest scientific enquiry. Sailing in dinghies was also encouraged and the children often embarked on lengthy excursions which might appear foolhardy in today's more safety-conscious world. (In time Granville was to become an accomplished sailor.) Certainly the young Wingates remembered their childhood holidays as a time out of life when they were allowed a freedom to be together, often, as they got older, without adult supervision.

If it sounds an idyllic, though precious and highly charged, life then on one level it was. There was a curious blend of discipline and tolerance, of repression and intellectual curiosity and of independence balanced by melancholy and restraint. Peculiarities of personal behaviour were tolerated, provided that they were not destructive, and little thought was given to niceties of dress with the result that the young Wingates looked different from other children. Before they were sent to school, Orde and his siblings cared little about such idiosyncrasies and in later life admitted that they never regarded their family as being unusual, merely different.

There was, though, a darker side to their childhood. George Wingate could be a remote and intolerant father, much given to gloomy musings on man's inherent wickedness. Being retired, he was usually at home and because he regarded the whole house as his domain, he appeared without warning in the children's playroom where he demanded, and received, total obedience. According to Sybil, who left several vivid accounts of her childhood, George was a gloomy patriarchal autocrat who believed in the benefits of corporal punishment. Spankings were common, so much so that Wingate later confided to his wife that he doubted if he would ever be able to withstand physical torture if captured by the enemy.

More often than not the children did not understand why they were being punished; usually it was done for the 'good of their souls' or some other godly reason and it was the older children who suffered most. They came to accept it as the norm in much the same way that they learned by heart the tracts from the Old Testament. In any case, as Sybil admitted, they knew so little about what other children did that the chastisement meted out by their father was not considered unusual and was balanced by their mother's gentle good humour.

The regime might have been harsh, even cruel, but it was suffered equally and that knowledge strengthened the bonds which had grown up between the children. Besides, before the First World War, discipline was tough and beatings still common in English public schools anxious to promote what was generally known as 'school spirit', a heady brew made up of virtues such as self-reliance, composure, responsibility, perseverance and patriotism.

Although the Wingate children had received a substantial part of their elementary education from their mother and from various tutors who visited Summerhill, it was always understood that they would eventually have to be given a formal schooling. This was especially important for Orde who was a late developer: according to Sybil, 'his mind did not fully wake up to the worlds of the intellect until he was in his late teens or early twenties.' Formal education at school and later at the Royal Military Academy, Woolwich, was to be something of a trial for him and despite his mother's promptings he later admitted that he had no real feelings for English poetry until he had the 'exciting and profound' experience of reading Wordsworth in the wastes of the Sudanese desert when he was in his late twenties. 'Poor George,' other members of the

Wingate family would say at that time. 'His daughters are clever and his sons stupid.'

Given their social background formal schooling would normally have meant a boarding-school education for the boys and a private day school for the girls. However, the prospect of sending his children away to school did not appeal to George Wingate who feared that they would fall under the sway of high Anglicanism, then the pervading religious influence at most of England's principal public schools. For that reason alone, Godalming was a good choice as it offered the opportunity of sending Orde and his brothers to Charterhouse as day boys so that they could be given a traditional public-school education without enduring any moral temptations. At the same time the youngest girls were sent to St Paul's School in London, travelling back and forth each day by train and thereby avoiding the school's extracurricular activities. The rule was later relaxed for Nigel and Granville who won scholarships to Cheltenham and Brighton.

Before entering Charterhouse at the age of thirteen, in 1911 Orde was sent to a local private preparatory school in Godalming called Hill Side whose headmaster, James Douglas, had played cricket for Middlesex as an amateur. As in many schools of that type the aim was to 'lick the boys into shape', to conform before they went to the more demanding atmosphere of their public schools. Games were all-important while academic work was considered to be useful only as a means to an end and pretensions to scholarship could lead to accusations of 'showing off'. Instead of encouraging the boys to develop a sense of individuality, the masters felt they were failing in their responsibilities if they did not instil the significance of loyalty to the house, to the school, to the country and to the empire; in that order.

Inevitably, the insistence on shared values and communal experience emphasised the importance of team spirit and played down any tendency towards displaying individuality. If a boy refused to conform he would be singled out and ridiculed by masters and boys alike until he decided to fit in. Eccentricity was only encouraged if it were amusing and the whole atmosphere was geared towards creating corporate pride in the school, especially on the sporting field. Because boys from Wingate's background spent nine months of each year at boarding school between the ages of eight and eighteen it is hardly surprising that school could be a more lasting influence than parents or family.

This turned out not to be the case with Wingate, or Winguy as he was quickly nicknamed. Not being a boarder helped because he could escape Hill Side at the end of each day's schooling but, from the outset, it was clear to his fellow pupils that he had no intention of observing the school's arcane rituals. For a start, he was not good at organised team games like football or cricket; a cardinal sin. Then he let it be known that, although slow at formal learning, he liked reading and enjoyed music, interests he shared with another boy, Jossleyn Hennessy, who recalled in a BBC radio broadcast on 20 April 1959 that whereas he was terrified of appearing different, Wingate was quick to retaliate if provoked.

He wasn't good at doing what he was told simply because it was what he had been told to do. He was the type whom the conventional schoolmaster automatically pitched into – as a mere reflex action. He was the sort of boy who used to be kicked from one end of the school to the other, for the good of his soul. Nobody, however, ever kicked Wingate. He feared no one. Whether it was a mob of boys of his own age or a group of high and mighty seniors, Wingate, lowering his head like a bull, would charge at his tormentors, his arms flailing like windmills.[1]

Because physical and moral courage was generally admired, Wingate escaped excessive bullying at Hill Side, although his nickname was soon changed to Stinker and other boys remembered him as being something of an outsider. It is easy to see why. According to Hennessy, Wingate presented himself to the school as being dour, unsociable, even unlikeable: the sort of boy who would have been a red rag to the more old-fashioned type of schoolmaster, of whom there were many in the enclosed world of English private education. (During the First World War, Hill Side's younger masters all joined the armed forces, leaving the school staffed by older men.)

The change to Charterhouse hardly improved matters for Wingate. By the time he went there in September 1916 for the Oration Quarter (first term) most of the 600 pupils were boarders and day boys were considered to be if not unusual then at least different because they could not participate fully in the school's life. Although they were made members of one of the school's ten houses – Wingate became a Saunderite in the headmaster's house – it was impossible for them to be an integral part of the ethos so carefully developed by masters and pupils alike. His clothes were different, too. He wore the regulation black jacket and striped trousers but the materials were of poorer quality and, as he later revealed to his mother-in-law, he was forced to wear boots while the other boys wore shoes. The deprivation was keenly felt for dress was a matter of some importance at Charterhouse: boys were expected to wear hats and carry walking sticks when walking in Godalming, and a visit to London meant hat, gloves, and rolled umbrella.

There were also arcane rules and regulations about dress and a new vocabulary had to be learned. Big Ground was where the 1st XI played football; Etceteras were the third house cricket or football teams; Godge was Godalming, a basher was a hat and a shagger was the starched collar which was not abolished for normal school wear until 1918. Not only were the 'new bugs' expected to master the terminology during their first term but they were then tested on their new-found knowledge and beatings were the fate of those who failed badly. Throughout Wingate's stay at Charterhouse physical punishments were common and his contemporaries have admitted that school life was dominated by a Spartan code and that the accommodation was often austere and uncomfortable.

On its ridge to the north-west of Godalming, the spires and pinnacles of Charterhouse presented a noble prospect – Osbert Lancaster likened it to a 'rural St Pancras' – but on closer inspection the buildings themselves left much to be desired. The plumbing was erratic, the boys' studies were cold in winter and hot in summer and the dormitories were cramped. Only in the Long Rooms, or house common rooms, was there a degree of communal ease. Much of the discomfort was an echo of Charterhouse's previous existence near St Paul's Cathedral in London where it had abutted the noisome Smithfield meat market. But there was, too, a prevailing belief that English public schools should be forbidding places in order to foster 'manliness' and a sense of asperity so that the boys could cope with anything which life might throw at them. In that sense Charterhouse was neither better nor worse than any other similar institution of that time.

Other than occasionally recalling the slights he received at Charterhouse, Wingate chose not to recollect his schooldays with any affection and he never felt the nostalgia for his old school shared by so many others of his generation. One reason was that he was a genuine outsider; an exact contemporary, W. H. Holden, admitted in a volume of reminiscences about life at Charterhouse that he had 'no memory of him at all nor any idea now what he looked like'. Not only was Wingate a day boy who wore odd clothes but his adherence to the faith of the Plymouth Brethren was unusual in a world where to be middle class, white, Anglo-Saxon and Anglican was everything. At his father's insistence he was excused attendance at chapel: instead, he and five other boys were permitted to form a 'Christian Union' which held Sunday afternoon prayer meetings at Summerhill.

His exclusion from mainstream school life also placed him in the same predicament as the Jewish boys who attended Charterhouse in relatively large numbers. Unlike Clifton or Cheltenham, Charterhouse did not have a separate house where Jewish boys could practise their own faith – they were merely excused chapel – but they were treated differently within the school's prevailing ethos of excellence at games and disdain for scholarship. With its tradition of being a City school Charterhouse had always attracted a wide range of boys from the merchant classes, many of whom were Jews, and the tradition continued after the move to Godalming. Although anti-Semitism was not a problem at Charterhouse, several of Wingate's contemporaries later remarked that many of the Jewish boys were openly hostile to the concept of organised team games and this 'failing' made them unpopular. As for Wingate, who shared their dislike of football and cricket, he told his future mother-in-law that the presence of the Jewish boys at school was something of a revelation. 'He said that it was at Charterhouse that he saw a Jew for the first time. A small pale, nondescript-looking boy was pointed out to him. Orde said, "I looked at him with the greatest interest and I thought, how extraordinary! There is somebody who is a descendant of David!" '[2]

Another reason for Wingate's contempt for his schooldays was his refusal to take part in house or school team games although he took part unwillingly and unsuccessfully in swimming, boxing and rifle shooting, the latter being encouraged by the school's Officers' Training Corps. Never more than a lance-corporal – a relatively minor rank – Wingate became a member of the corps as soon as he went to Charterhouse and in November 1920 obtained the 'Certificate A' which would allow him to join the army. Although he enjoyed it he was never a particularly good cadet and failed to distinguish himself in the regular shooting competitions. (Writing about Wingate in the *Dictionary of National Biography*, Earl Wavell claimed that Wingate was a good shot and excelled at swimming and tennis: this is not borne out by the school's records.)

During the First World War the corps had assumed a new importance and according to W. W. S. Adams, another contemporary of Wingate's, it had 'ceased to be a joke and had become a duty, one of the accepted things'. Commanded by a former officer called Colonel F. W. B. Smart, who insisted that the boys live up to his surname, it was central to school life and, though officially a voluntary organisation, membership was in fact obligatory. Most English public schools had raised rifle corps in the

1860s during a nationwide craze for establishing volunteer units for home defence but these were transformed into quasi-military operations in 1908 as part of the government's plans for establishing Territorial Army reserve forces.

Training took place once a week, there were two field days a year and exercises on Salisbury Plain. As was the case in other public schools, there was a serious military reason for the corps's presence: as part of Lord Haldane's reforms of the army, from June 1908 school rifle corps were to be regarded as a junior officer training corps. Many senior soldiers and public figures supported the move because they believed that war in Europe was a probability – Field Marshal Lord Roberts was the most outspoken on this count – and that Britain should prepare itself by raising strong and well-trained volunteer reserve forces to support the regular army. The War Office also believed that the public schools could help Britain's defence needs by training the kind of boy who would be offered an immediate commission in time of war. So it proved. Old Carthusians paid for that concept between 1914 and 1918; there are 686 names on the school's roll of honour.

Masters, too, assisted in the running of the corps, most notably S. H. Langton, housemaster of Gownboys. A curious combination of dandy and martinet, he had charge of the boys in the Army Class who were destined for the Royal Military Academies at Sandhurst or Woolwich, and he was well known for his trenchant establishment views. By 1918 Wingate was under Langton's tutelage in the school's Army Division which prepared boys for sitting the army's entrance exams to Sandhurst or Woolwich. His reasons for deciding on an army career are clear-cut. There was the influence of his father and the family tradition of soldiering. Not being particularly bright at school – his marks placed him near the bottom of every class he attended – he had not been encouraged academically and university was out of the question. Money, too, entered the equation for it had been made clear to him that he would have to earn his own living and could not rely on his parents to support him.

There was one other spur. In the last year of the war a master called A. W. Tressler, unusual in being a socialist and a pacifist, invited Gilbert Murray to talk in Godalming about his ideas for the formation of a League of Nations which would guarantee world peace. The quietly spoken Oxford professor of Greek left a lasting impression on the boys who heard him. 'It seemed impossible that everyone, the whole world, would not realise the common sense of it all,' remembered Adams. 'I came out of the Town Hall in an excitement which lasted several days.

Later, believing I was serving the cause of peace I stayed a private in the Corps in silent protest, although I was then Head of House.'

With the war in its final stages and with evidence of the heavy casualties a dreadful reality, Murray's message was persuasive. International co-operation in the cause of peace and disarmament had a heady ring and by 1918 unofficial plans were at an advanced stage: over 3,000 people supported the League of Nations Union, founded with the object of promoting 'the formation of a World League of Free Peoples for the securing of international justice, mutual defence and permanent peace'. Politicians such as Balfour, Asquith, Lloyd George and Edward Grey became honorary presidents and Murray, whose son Basil was at Charterhouse at that time, was the first chairman of the Executive Committee.

With his family's religious interests, Wingate might have been expected to support the League's objectives, but Murray's talk did not affect him in the way that it had touched Adams. Instead of being enthused – Murray was a persuasive speaker – Wingate noted that as the proposed League of Nations would not be backed up by military forces it would be powerless to stop another major international conflict. That realisation was a major influence in his decision to become a soldier.

Of course, there was one other reason: money, or the lack of it. He knew that he could never hope for a commission in a cavalry or a smart infantry regiment, both of which expected their officers to have private incomes. For that reason it would have to be the engineers or the artillery as both corps anticipated that their officers could live off their pay.

Choosing that option meant applying to the Royal Military Academy, Woolwich, which trained both engineer and artillery officers and preparing for the army's entrance examinations. These were held twice a year and were tests of some complexity. Eight subjects were obligatory: English, English history, geography, elementary mathematics (arithmetic), intermediate mathematics, French or German, physics, chemistry; and one subject was optional, depending on what had been taken in the first group: a choice of French, German, Latin, Greek or higher mathematics. A total of 14,000 marks could be scored overall but to scrape through the candidate only had to score 33 per cent in all subjects except arithmetic where the pass mark was 75 per cent. The papers were relatively straightforward and there were no trick questions. In Wingate's examination the English paper asked: 'What is a sonnet? Name any great writer of sonnets in English and give some account of his sonnets.' Other questions in history and geography were equally bland and, overall, the army seems to have been looking for clear thinkers who could communicate logically and precisely. The general introduction to the examination left no candidate in any doubt about what was expected: 'Irrelevance will be regarded as the most serious fault in any essay but incoherence, obscurity, needless repetition, diffuseness will also be regarded as grave defects. Bad grammar, the incorrect use of words and phrases, and serious errors in punctuation will be heavily punished.'[3]

Today the examination would be regarded as a rigorous test of general knowledge in the arts and sciences and Wingate was well prepared for it, having had the syllabus drummed into him by the masters in Charterhouse's Army Division. (Such careful preparation did not always bear fruit: the examiners later reported that in answers to the English paper H. G. Wells was described twice as a boxer, once as a cricketer.) However, as the family feared, Wingate did not gain particularly good marks: out of sixty-nine successful candidates he passed into Woolwich sixty-third, an important consideration for his future career. The low marks were followed by a confusing message from the War Office that Wingate had passed into Sandhurst and would be expected to pay full fees. These were steep: £60 for the son of a serving officer, £100 for others. A worried father immediately contacted the War Office and the mistake was corrected to allow his son to enter Woolwich at the reduced rate of fees. While it was enough to have scraped through the first hurdle, academic achievement determined a Gentleman Cadet's future career: those with the highest marks at the end of the four-term course were allowed to enter the corps of their choice and most opted for the Royal Engineers or the Royal Field Artillery while, generally speaking, those with lower marks were allotted to the Royal Garrison Artillery.

Wingate entered Woolwich on 3 February 1921 and like most other cadets he was somewhat dismayed by the spartan appearance and its warren of buildings, all looking much gloomier in the mirk of an overcast winter's day. The academy had opened in 1741 as the cadet training establishment for army officers commissioned into the Artillery, the Engineers and, later, the Signals. Known to generations of soldiers as the Shop, it was a tough down-to-earth institution which demanded high standards of learning and discipline. It produced fine soldiers too: other notable alumni of Woolwich included Gordon, Kitchener, Ironside, Alanbrooke and Glubb Pasha. At one point during the war the courses at Woolwich had been truncated to six months and the main thrust was to train officers as quickly as possible and to place them with formations already serving on the different fronts. (Later the folly of force-feeding cadets was recognised when examinations were reintroduced and the course extended to twelve months.)

However, there was little time for any of the cadets, or snookers as they were known in their first term, to feel sorry for themselves. During the first nine weeks they were 'on the square' and their days were dominated by a strict regime of drilling and inspections under the gaze of sergeants drawn from the Brigade of Guards. It was not until they had satisfied their mentors and passed off the square that they were more fully integrated into the life of the academy. Other lessons took longer to learn. Daily cold baths were obligatory and punishments, known as hoxters, were common. Anything from a speck of dust on a rifle to leaving out a comma on an official form could lead to the Gentleman Cadet appearing on the early morning defaulters' parade. Dress was important: service dress with breeches and puttees during the day; slacks and a jacket could be worn in the evening and formal wear was a blue patrol jacket and overalls. There was, too, a noticeable public-school atmosphere in the place with an emphasis on games, ragging, spit and polish, and a delight in practical jokes. Indeed, most of the cadets were ex-public school boys, the post-war list being dominated by Cheltenham, Wellington, Clifton, Marlborough, Winchester and Charterhouse.

With the end of wartime conscription the army was gradually reducing its size and becoming once more the small professional force it had been before 1914. Woolwich, too, was keen to return to peacetime soldiering and under its commandant, Major-General Sir Webb Gillman, Royal Artillery, the staff was keen to brush away the hustle and bustle of the wartime years and to get back to the familiar pre-war routine of turning out sound young officers and gentlemen. To achieve the first aim the syllabus included a broad range of military subjects including tactics, military law, map-reading, riding and horsemanship, drill, hygiene and organisation and administration. The day began at 6.15 a.m. with reveille, then chapel and breakfast; the first parade was at 8.30 followed by instruction and drill until 12.30. After lunch there would be games or further instruction until 4.30 p.m. Evenings were reserved for study with lights out at 10.00 p.m.

Riding was still an important part of the curriculum, all cadets having to endure the Chief Riding Master's course at Woolwich's Riding School. The instructors, all Royal Horse Artillery, were merciless in their treatment of Gentleman Cadets who could not ride and were scornful of those who could not sit properly or whose horses showed their teeth. The ultimate sin was falling off the mount. Not having

ridden before, Wingate might have been expected to kick against such
a strict system but he rose to the challenge and, despite many falls, soon
became a passionate and committed horseman.

On paper it was a disciplined and orderly nursery but there was
another side to life at Woolwich, one which was bound up with the
need to make sure that the young officers were also gentlemen. As more
than one former Gentleman Cadet has testified, the system at Woolwich
was designed to break the toughest cadets and then to mould them into
a recognisable pattern. To underscore the seriousness of this intention
each new intake was addressed by the Senior Under Officer who read
out a list of prohibitions before telling them: 'You may have thought
yourselves pretty hot stuff at Eton or Wellington or wherever you've
come from. Well, here for the next six months we regard you simply as
dirt.'

Most of the boys were well used to the strict discipline, which they
had already endured at boarding school, and were prepared to put up
with it for the good reason that they would not be snookers for ever and
in time would graduate to the privileges enjoyed by the seniors. Not so
Wingate. Shielded from the system by being a day boy at Charterhouse,
he was at first bewildered then angered by the unfamiliar environment.
His own behaviour did not help matters. Never interested in his clothes,
he looked scruffy and did not take kindly to the rules which insisted on
at least nine changes of uniform during the working day. He was also
indifferent to washing and was naturally untidy: his notebooks were
scarred by cigarette burns and he was careless with his belongings, a
cardinal sin in the cramped barrackrooms shared by three snookers.
These failings could not go unnoticed in Woolwich's deeply conformist
society and he was constantly ragged, or teased, by his fellow cadets who
were not a little shocked by his 'refusal to conform and to accept any
form of imposed discipline'.

Matters were made worse at the end of the second term when he
missed his examinations, apparently through illness, and was forced to
drop a term. Not only did this put him back by six months but it meant
that his intake would therefore be in a position to discipline him. To
protect himself, Wingate decided that the only way to survive was to
fight back and to refuse to be cowed.

Much of the long history of tough disciplinary behaviour at the Shop
was simply crude bullying practised by the seniors on the new cadets to
lick them into shape. A near-contemporary of Wingate's writing in 1954
remembered that their intake was perhaps fortunate in getting off 'lightly

with nothing worse than sprains, a broken leg and a broken wrist'. Cadets could also have their rooms smashed up for speaking out of turn, boasting, showing signs of pomposity or simply not fitting in. Rioting was common, indeed encouraged, and the prevailing ethos was designed to make sure that cadets knew their place. To this kind of behaviour the commandant and his staff generally turned a blind eye, doubtless because they felt it was manly behaviour and part of the general learning curve.

Humiliation was also part of the process and there was no greater mortification than the Snooker Dance which was held every Friday night. While the military band played a selection of dance tunes seniors would turn up resplendent in their formal clothes to take their partners from the motley collection of snookers clad in white vests and flannels. Everyone had to dance but in Wingate's day terpsichorean ability was not the only reason for these farcical events.

After each dance the snookers were herded into a crowd and organised to perform various antics for the benefit of the onlookers. These varied from ludicrous to rough and usually a certain number of cadets sustained minor injuries. At the end of the session the snookers had to run the gauntlet of the other terms on the way back to their houses.[4]

Although Wingate gave as good as he got during these affairs and fellow Gentlemen Cadets remembered him as a tough down-to-earth scrapper, one episode was to have a lasting effect on his attitude to military life. This was the infamous time when he was 'run' by his fellow officer cadets. Like the rioting, this, too, had a long and dubious history at Woolwich – earlier it was known as toshing – and it was considered to be the ultimate sanction at the disposal of the senior term whose members were almost entirely responsible for cadet discipline.

It was a particularly unpleasant form of chastisement, the aim being to mortify the victim by punishing him both physically and mentally. The first stage was to arrive in a baying pack outside the victim's room and announce the sentence; failure to accept this was unknown for although the punishment was strictly unofficial it had been sanctified by use and custom. Then the wretched fellow was taken to the rugby pitches behind the academy, told to strip naked and then forced to run the gauntlet between two lines of seniors armed with knotted towels or swagger sticks with which to lash him. The reprimand ended with the victim being tossed into one of the nearby water tanks. No one ever died or had any great injury done to them after being run but it was an embarrassing and much-feared punishment. In a volume of memoirs another Gentleman Cadet, John Bagot Glubb, remembered a dark winter's evening five years earlier when he heard the seniors arrive to run someone in his block.

In a few seconds, a deafening pandemonium was raging outside the door of my room. For several moments my heart stood still. Then the screaming torrent went on up the stairs to the floor above. The victim was in the room immediately above mine. There is something terrifying in an excited crowd which inspires more fear than shells of bullets. I have been involved in various battles since those days, but I doubt if I have ever again been so frightened.[5]

Wingate was similarly treated in his third term although he dealt with the situation in a way quite unlike any other Gentleman Cadet. According to the evidence of his friend Derek Tulloch, a fellow cadet and one of the seniors who ran him, this was one of the key moments in Wingate's development. So deeply did Tulloch feel this that he agonised for several years over whether or not to include the full story when he came to write his own account of Wingate as a military leader. Like Wingate, Tulloch had passed into Woolwich with low marks and never shone as a cadet but unlike him he had decided to conform even though that meant involving himself in an action about which he was to be considerably ashamed.

The underlying reason for Wingate's punishment was his personal unpopularity. Many of the seniors disliked his 'surly manner' and the Senior Under Officer at the time, a cadet called Whitman, wondered 'why the Shop's authorities didn't get rid of him'. Not fitting in is a cardinal sin in the army and through his truculent and unconventional behaviour Wingate had probably upset not a few of the more conformist seniors. However, the decision to run him came as a result of Wingate's own foolhardiness in continuing to break rules which he thought stupid.

Having won his spurs – the last of his term to do so – he was given the privilege of hunting with the Woolwich Drag Hounds or enjoying an additional day's riding while other cadets played team sports. It was the custom for the select few to present themselves on parade at the academy's stables before selecting their mounts. This Wingate consistently refused to do and he enraged his fellow cadets by arriving early to choose the best horse and then by keeping it out longer than was allowed. From his point of view the matter was clear-cut. He had developed a burning enthusiasm for riding and wanted to indulge it whenever possible even if that meant breaking the Riding School's rules. At that stage of his life Wingate was not a particularly social animal and as his idiosyncratic childhood meant that he was unused to conforming to the needs of a social group he could not see that he was offending his fellow cadets. What he regarded as the pursuit of his instincts, they considered boorish behaviour and as a result they decided to punish him.

According to Tulloch in *Wingate in Peace and War*, running was not just an aid to the better enforcement of discipline, it was also meant to be a salutary warning that 'the cadet's own term considered him guilty of disgraceful conduct'. However, in Wingate's case his term was not involved and the punishment was decided upon by the seniors under Whitman who took the decision after discussing it with his junior under officers and Woolwich's adjutant, Major G. A. Pinney, RA. If the procedure were somewhat unusual, according to Tulloch what followed next was electrifying. Instead of accepting his fate and getting it over with as quickly as possible Wingate decided to confront his tormentors. Stripped naked, he turned the humiliation to his own advantage. 'Orde walked very slowly the whole way down the line, with a dangerous look in his eye which I have frequently had cause to recognise since. Few of us could bring ourselves to even apply the knotted handkerchiefs and many of us came away feeling very ashamed of the part we had played.'

Wingate then completed the performance – no other word describes it – by diving into the cold water tank and then returning to his rooms. Woolwich was soon awash with stories about his behaviour; his own term rallied to his cause and revenge was taken on the seniors by smashing up the room of one of the ringleaders.

If anything, Wingate emerged with his reputation enhanced by the running, which had a lasting effect on him, not all of it detrimental to his future career as a soldier. On the credit side it made him realise that he could exert his authority over his fellow men and that through the strength of his own personality he could overcome pettifogging indignities. It also gave him an insight into the nature of power and how to use it to his own advantage.

However, on the distaff side, the punishment increased his distrust and horror of military blimpishness and although that is no bad lesson for a young officer to learn, the knowledge was not acquired without some damage to his own self-esteem. Always aware that he was out of the ordinary, he now understood the penalties which faced the outsider from a jealous establishment. And for all that he had behaved well under stress, it had been a demeaning experience: to Tulloch he later vowed that he would never again allow such indignities to be meted out to him.

One immediate effect of the running was a distinct improvement in his personal performance at Woolwich. Summoned to an interview with the commandant, Wingate was told in no uncertain terms that he had not shown sufficient aptitude and that unless his performance improved he would never become a regular officer. Tulloch was convinced that Gillman's warning, plus the running, had a salutary effect on Wingate.

At the time he was a voracious reader of the more sensational detective fiction. He realised that knowledge was power and from that day he never read another book of that type but threw himself wholeheartedly into the task of improving his mind and gaining a wide knowledge. He took a deep interest in Tolstoy and Karl Marx and also studied military tactics right down the ages. He could give full tactical details of most of the battles contained in the Bible, which he knew almost by heart.

While it was hardly a case of throwing away his crutches, Wingate's final term at Woolwich was a Lourdes of sorts. He turned his energies to his studies and read voraciously. According to Sybil, 'his mind had suddenly wakened and was crying out for food': whenever she wanted to know what he was thinking she would check with the Bomb Shop, a bookseller at 66 Charing Cross Road at which he kept an account, and ask, 'When was my brother last here and what books did he buy?'

In the end, though, the last spurt did little to improve his chances and he passed out of Woolwich on 11 July 1923 fifty-ninth out of the seventy of his new batch. As a result of this relatively poor performance he was gazetted to the Royal Garrison Artillery and posted to 18th Medium Battery, 5th Medium Brigade, which was based at Larkhill on Salisbury Plain.

Three

OFFICER AND GENTLEMAN

The army which Wingate joined in 1923 as a commissioned officer was little different in tone from the one which his father had known in the latter part of the nineteenth century. The great military machine constructed for fighting the First World War had been dismantled, the conscripts had been demobilised and the old professional soldiers were getting back to what they fondly imagined to be 'real soldiering'. For the officers this meant that an army career was often little more than an opportunity to indulge in an agreeable social and sporting life while for the rank and file it usually represented an escape from the dole queue. All too often, too, regiments took an exaggerated interest in smartness on the square and strict etiquette and custom in the mess. Cleverness was frowned upon and the tactical and strategic awareness produced by the war was reduced to policing the empire or fighting limited campaigns in places like Iraq or the North-West Frontier of India.

The army's horizons had shrunk in other ways: it was a much smaller organisation, having come down in size from 3.5 million men in November 1918 to 370,000 in 1920. The War Office committee responsible for establishing the post-war army's complement estimated that a small professional force could cope with Britain's immediate imperial defence needs and that in the event of a major European war conscription could once more be introduced.

But the decline was also economic. In 1919, at the instigation of Winston Churchill, the War Minister, the government adopted the Ten Year Rule for defence spending. This rested on the assumption that there would be no large-scale war for ten years and as a result defence expenditure was reduced in every year between 1919 and 1929. Not only was there little or no investment in new equipment but there were massive cutbacks in manpower and a savage paring of the army's

cherished regimental system. Under the terms of the Geddes Axe of
1922 – Sir Alexander Geddes had been charged by Lloyd George with
the task of cutting public expenditure by £86 million – the army was
reduced by 50,000 officers and men, the infantry lost five of its Irish
regiments and ten regular battalions and, by way of amalgamation, sixteen
famous cavalry regiments were reduced to eight.

Because the army was a much smaller place and because there were
so few chances to see active service, promotion was slow and senior
soldiers stagnated. The changes and the lack of public interest in the
army had other drawbacks. A military career was not regarded with
much sympathy, other than as a pleasant way of spending a few years,
and original thinkers or creative minds were rarely attracted to it. (There
were exceptions such as J. C. Fuller and B. H. Liddell Hart.) The neglect
was to lead to immense difficulties in 1939 when Britain once again
went to war in Europe but in the immediate future it condemned the
army to a backwater of British life, complacent, amateurish and comatose.

Wingate's posting to Larkhill took him to the heart of the Royal
Artillery's establishment. Situated on Salisbury Plain it had been acquired
in 1897 as a range for gunnery practice and within two years it extended
to 22,000 acres. Before it came into operational service the artillery had
made do with ranges at Shoeburyness and Okehampton and before Irish
independence the regiment also had the use of Glen Imaal in Ireland. It
was a busy, sprawling, yet unlovely place, and a contemporary remembered that, like other garrisons in Britain, Larkhill had also suffered from
the post-war cutbacks: 'a straggling sprawl of huts on both sides of the
Parkway, many in obvious need of repair, gave Larkhill the appearance
of a rather seedy, down-at-heel shanty town ... it was not exactly a prepossessing sight.'[1]

The centrepiece of Larkhill was the School of Artillery but there was
also a survey company, which linked the guns' fire control, and a Field
Brigade and a Medium Brigade. Wingate had been posted to 18th
Medium Battery, one of 5th Medium Brigade's four six-gun batteries
which were equipped with the obsolescent five-inch sixty-pounder gun.
An artillery brigade was similar in size and formation to an infantry
battalion but the battery was considered to be the focus of loyalty and
therefore an important element in building and sustaining morale. For
example, Wingate's battery took great pride in the fact that their gun
teams were horse-drawn – sixteen Suffolk Punch heavy draught horses
supplied the traction – and, indeed, they were the last medium battery
to be mechanised during the slow process of post-war modernisation.

Rivalry between batteries was encouraged – the 19th Battery had changed over to four-wheel-drive trucks – but all officers lived together at the brigade's mess on the Parkway. It was there that Wingate renewed his acquaintance with Derek Tulloch who was serving with the 19th Medium Battery. Soon a close friendship grew up between the two men, each blossoming in the carefree existence of life as an artillery officer at Larkhill. Tulloch recalled:

I do not wish to suggest that he neglected his military duties, but in those days these were not of a very arduous nature. The system of carrying out all fatigues and camp duties by combatant soldiers, coupled with the shortage of men through continual finding of drafts for service overseas shattered the military ardour of many a young officer.

Not that army life for an officer was without interest or amusement. Field training was kept to a minimum and was hardly ever strenuous; there was much emphasis on bull and drill and the officers were encouraged to adopt an easy-going, almost amateurish approach to soldiering. Apart from the brief summer training season the day ended after morning parade and inspection and it was considered bad form for a young officer to appear too serious about his work by being seen in the battery or company office after lunch.

With time hanging heavy on their hands young subalterns were expected to make good use of it and were encouraged to participate in all kinds of field sports. Hunting and horse-racing were popular pastimes and some regiments considered it a matter of pride to excel at horsemanship. There were two reasons for this insistence. First, good horsemen would only bring credit to the regiment; they would also attract invitations to ride with the best hunts, usually at a reduced subscription. This was certainly true of the artillery officers at Larkhill who were made welcome by the South and West Wilts Hunt whose Master of Fox Hounds, Isaac 'Ikey' Bell, was considered to be one of England's most knowledgeable huntsmen. Up to forty gunner officers would ride with the hunt and according to John Morrison (now Lord Margadale), who lived nearby, 'they enjoyed their hunting, and they all behaved impeccably and had a good go at what was offered.' Second, many older officers were convinced that hunting was an important part of military training: riding to the meet gave an officer a good eye for the lie of the land and the hunt itself provided endless opportunities for showing dash and initiative. In short, as the poet William Somervile had it, hunting provided the army with the 'image of war without its guilt'.

Shortly after he joined his battery Wingate took up hunting on a regular basis with the South and West Wilts and quickly earned a reputation as a daring and frequently madcap rider to hounds. The liking for horses which had been nurtured at Woolwich developed into a passion at Larkhill and whether hunting, riding or tent-pegging, with Tulloch as a constant companion, it consumed most of his free time between 1923 and 1926. The social prominence of the horse meant that the army provided him with a charger and a groom for his own use but he was also expected to keep another horse out of his own funds, no easy matter when his pay as a gunner subaltern was only £17 a month. Here he was helped by a legacy of £1,800 which unexpectedly came his way from his mother's Browne relatives.

The additional funds not only allowed him to improve his standards of living, they also revealed a quixotic and generous streak in his nature. Impecunious fellow officers were helped with loans which he did not expect to be repaid and he sent additional funds to his brothers and sisters: Monica was at Newnham College, Cambridge, and Nigel at Pembroke College, Cambridge. This was never done ostentatiously: a typical letter would include the offhand comment, 'Here's a fiver. I don't want it back.' Money never meant much to him – although he was given to checking and questioning all bills submitted to him – but like many other generous spirits he always believed that funds were there to be used. Fortunately, too, his first legacy and later family bequests meant that he never had to worry overmuch about his personal finances.

He then decided to buy a decent mount for point-to-point racing. The normal course of events would have led him to take local advice but that meant delay and possible procrastination. He wanted the horse immediately. Hearing that a fellow gunner had an uncle in Ireland who bred horses and had a suitable mare for sale, Wingate summoned his groom and sent him across to Baronston in the great Irish hunting county of West Meath with £100: £80 for the horse and the remainder for expenses. Despite the light-hearted nature of the purchase, it was a good buy and the horse, an eight-year-old bay mare called Tatters, duly repaid Wingate's optimism by winning for him the South and West Wilts members' race at Kingston Deverill in the spring of 1925.

He also bought a car, a somewhat dilapidated white Scrips-Booth sports model and was taught to drive by Tulloch. Although the frequent loss of the clutch turned it into something of a liability the car had style and speed, both of which were much admired by Wingate throughout his life. Above all it gave the two friends mobility and allowed them to get to hunt meets in some style; like other gunners at Larkhill they were permitted to stable their horses at Pyt House, the home of Colonel Jack Bennett Stanford. Standing on the hill looking south towards Knoyle Windmill, Pyt House was a regular haunt for army officers hunting with the South and West Wilts and Stanford's hospitality to man and beast was legendary.

His friendship and help with stabling was also a matter of some importance to Wingate and Tulloch because medium gunners were not supposed to ride with smart hunts and the pair had to put up with some criticism, not all of it good-natured, from the haughtier officers in the Field Brigade who believed that their privileges were being usurped.

A younger Wingate might have kicked against the slights but his experiences at Woolwich seem to have chastened him, albeit temporarily. Instead of sulking or objecting, he kept his peace during meets and picked up the arcane lore of the huntsman by watching and listening. 'We were doubtful of how to make any hunting cries, which sound so different to the way they are written, so we wisely refrained until we had listened carefully and then practised for some time.' Tulloch also remembered that their hunting dress was 'Mr Moss's second-best' but this is not entirely borne out by the photographs from that period. Both men wore black coats and white breeches and both had good top boots, all perfectly acceptable for young officers who wanted to fit in and not draw attention to themselves. They were also helped by the discreet purchase of Major-General G. H. A. White's *Hunting Notes for Beginners* which the Royal Artillery had produced for use by its young officers.

That the policy worked can be seen in the young men's acceptance by their fellow huntsmen. After a day's hunting they would be asked to dine with Ikey Bell at Motcombe and Wingate soon made a name for himself through his fearless behaviour in the field. Faced by high hedges or the obstacle of a resolutely closed gate, he would invariably choose to jump, even if it meant damaging his horse or risking a fall. By 'going straight' and following his own line he won nothing but plaudits from the older huntsmen who put a high premium on a rider's dash and courage.

Wingate continued to show the same attributes during the autumn of 1925 when he and Tulloch rode with the neighbouring Portman Hunt in Dorset. And just as he had caught Ikey Bell's eye with his youthful enthusiasm and bold horsemanship, so too did Wingate make his mark with the Portman's master, Colonel William Browne. Later in life he told Tulloch that he remembered Wingate as a charming and lively young man, full of fun and high spirits, just like many of the other carefree young officers who rode with the hunts in the area. Indeed, there is much in this period of Wingate's life which contains irresistible echoes of Siegfried Sassoon's *Memoirs of a Foxhunting Man*. When Tulloch recalls the delights of hacking back with the hounds towards Blandford on a crisp winter's evening or eagerly refilling a racing cup with champagne in the mess – 'more than once' – it is impossible not to be reminded of young George Sherston.

I can see the pair of us clearly enough; myself, with my brow-pinching bowler hat tilted to the back of my head, staring, with the ignorant face of a callow young man, at the dusky landscape with its glimmering wet fields . . . I can hear the creak of a saddle and the clop and clink of hoofs as we cross the bridge over the brook by Dundell Farm; there is a light burning in the farmhouse window, and the evening star glitters above a broken drift of half-luminous cloud.

Just as Sassoon gloried in the pastoral elegy of his own sporting years before the First World War so too did Wingate fall more than half in love with his existence as a carefree young officer at Larkhill. There were guest nights in the mess, often 'fairly rough affairs', followed by scraps with the Field Gunners and games of high-cockalorum. On one memorable occasion, recalled by Tulloch, Wingate led the subalterns in a moonlit steeplechase in full mess kit: 'I would like to be able to add that we sped round the course in style, but alas somewhat of a shambles occurred; only two of us got over and one of the others took a nasty toss. We decided that there was more in moonlight steeplechase than met the eye and returned to stables somewhat chastened.' There were also hunt balls which Wingate enjoyed immensely and he had a wide circle of friends amongst the young men and women who hunted in the surrounding counties.

Wingate had grown up and was maturing into a self-sufficient and capable young man. He had taught himself how to hunt and had perfected his horsemanship; he had learned how to drink and how to enjoy himself in any company; he had grown to like decent clothes and although he could still be scruffy and dirty, he went to a good tailor, Holts of Sackville Street, and bought his shirts at Sulkas of Bond Street; he had smoothed off some of his rougher edges and had taken on the complexion of a typical officer and gentleman of the period. On a personal level, for all his success as a horseman, he was entirely without conceit – no young officer could be both popular and big-headed – and he threw himself into all the brigade's many social activities.

In so doing he had also begun to move away from the pull of home. He still visited Godalming and presented his riding cups to a somewhat bemused mother who feared that his successes were but one step from a fall from grace. 'My darling boy,' she wrote to him early in 1925. 'Do not wax confident and give up fearing God – that is a danger that fills me with dread whenever I think of it – and I pray God to keep you from the two special sins that are as a rule associated with success in horsemanship.' But the close, almost suffocating, childhood relationships had gone for ever. With his father he now enjoyed a different kind of intimacy, based on mutual respect and tolerance in place of the uneasiness which had suffused his childhood years. Once a figure of paternal authority the colonel was now on more equal terms with his soldier son and, judging from their letters to each other, both took pleasure from their mutual interest in things military.

Wingate blossomed in other ways. To the surprise of his brother subalterns for whom excessive studying was suspect, he continued to read voraciously, not just military history but also philosophy, political theory and even books on birth control. (A diary entry on 22 February 1925 reveals that he found *Candide* 'delightful in its way but coarse and disgusting' and its author, Voltaire, 'extremely plebeian'.) Having read *Das Kapital* he flirted for a time with Marxism although Sybil noticed that he was too committed a Christian and a believer in God ever to become a communist. While it was true that his formal ties with the Plymouth Brethren had slackened at Woolwich and had been finally loosened at Larkhill he was still an immensely religious young man who felt God's presence as a pure wind of reason, perhaps something beyond understanding.

Only once had he questioned his faith from an intellectual point of view. Throughout 1924 he had convinced himself that he was really an agnostic and that he would be better off renouncing his parents' strict religious tenets. When he confided his doubts to Monica he was astonished to discover that she shared them and that during her time at Cambridge she had begun to question her faith. However, there was a difference. Whereas Wingate was fascinated by the possibility that he might be an agnostic, Monica was thoroughly alarmed and had taken steps to retrieve the situation.

Her confidant was Dr Claud Fothergill, a Harley Street consultant who also ran prayer meetings and Bible study groups to help young people in their spiritual development. Each winter he took groups of young people to Kandersteg in Switzerland, principally for winter sports – he was a well-known mountaineer – but also for intensive Bible study and end-of-day prayer sessions. The atmosphere was a mixture of muscular Christianity and religious revivalism and not even the strong-willed Monica could resist his message. When she accompanied Fothergill's party in the winter of 1924–25, this time to Cheglio in Italy, she was sufficiently convinced by his arguments to renounce her agnosticism.

The news infuriated Wingate who had been invited to join the next expedition to Kandersteg and he penned an abusive letter to Fothergill admonishing him for interfering in Monica's affairs.

Forgive me if I hurt your feelings but do let us be sincere and not be always trying to replace the powerful revolutionary teaching of Christ with the emotional dogmas of the churches which call themselves by this name. I think myself that the strong religious feeling, which, to a greater extent in the past and to a lesser extent in the present, has always, and will probably always, move mankind, has little or nothing to do with true morality or the teachings of Christ.

Before posting it, Wingate sent the letter to Sybil who warned against his further involvement with Fothergill whom she believed to be 'as incapable of understanding anyone's point of view as his own as an amoeba is of appreciating the 9th Symphony'. Despite this forthright advice, Wingate sent the letter to Fothergill who immediately lost all interest in winning him back from his temporary agnosticism. In his autobiography Fothergill claimed that Wingate's letter was 'so abusive and insulting that one felt very definitely that he was trying himself to fight against God's Holy Spirit'.[2] This could have been true: Sybil ended her letter to her brother by reminding him that 'God made us not for happiness but for suffering, struggling and falling to rise again with him.' In future, she advised, he should keep his religious views to himself or 'confide them to the first stone you see on the road' and that he should lose his doubts in his horsemanship.

In fact, his new-found skills were helping him in other ways. In January 1926 he was selected for one of the much-coveted vacancies on a five-month course at the Army School of Equitation at Weedon in Northamptonshire. This was a singular honour as only thirty cavalry and artillery officers and fifty non-commissioned officers were admitted to the bi-annual courses and the training was conducted on strictly formal lines. Once again Wingate attracted attention to himself through unorthodox riding style and by his boldness in the hunting field. Officers from Weedon were much in demand at the winter meets and were expected to hunt three times a week. Although Wingate cut a less than elegant figure amongst the scarlet-coated grandees his dash and courage made him a popular figure in the county's hunting community. Even such eccentricities as discussing Marxism in the mess at Weedon did not discomfort the more languid cavalrymen who believed that as long as a man rode well it mattered little what he thought. They also forgave him when his dog, an Alsatian bitch called Lorraine, whelped in his quarters.

In July the course came to an end and Wingate received the army's certificate of a qualified instructor in equitation and skill at arms. Asked by the commandant what he hoped to do next, Wingate replied, 'Have a bath and wash off the smell of horse manure.' The reality was less enticing. His battery had moved from Larkhill to what Wingate called 'the swamp' of Fort Brockhurst near Gosport in Hampshire and after a short leave this was to be Wingate's home for the rest of the summer. It was also to be another milestone in his life, for while staying there he met the first real love of his life, a spirited girl, Enid Margaret Jelley whom he always knew as Peggy.

Their coming together was pure serendipity. During a visit to the officers' mess her father, a retired army officer, had informed the commanding officer that he would be happy to invite young officers to his family's tennis dance parties and Wingate was asked to return the call. Never a good tennis player – his brother officers claimed that he used his racquet like a spoon – Wingate was happy to make up numbers and soon became a regular visitor with his brother gunner officers at Hawkstone in Fareham, the Jelleys' home. To begin with it was Peggy's older sister Mary who was most attracted by him and his sudden enthusiasms: 'I thought him such a strange young man, half humorous, half morose.' But it was with the younger, more serious, dark-haired Peggy that Wingate fell in love; by autumn a strong relationship had developed between them.[3]

By then he had started giving serious thought to his future career as a soldier. In 1925 he had been promoted a full lieutenant and had started studying for his captain's exams. Much as he had relished his untroubled life as a footloose subaltern on Salisbury Plain, he knew it could not go on for ever. And it was entirely within his religious convictions to believe that it was wrong, perhaps even sinful, to enjoy himself so completely, that sooner or later there had to be a reckoning. His next posting would be crucial and he was determined to make the right move. Like many other successful men, Wingate was well aware that he could not sit back and allow events to carry him forwards: he had to make his own luck.

Here he was fortunate in having influential family connections. His father's cousin Sir Reginald Wingate was perhaps the most potent – although his own uncle Sir Andrew Wingate had made a name for himself in the Indian Civil Service – and it was to 'Cousin Rex' that Orde Wingate turned. As Kitchener's Director of Military Intelligence during the Sudan campaign which culminated in the defeat of the Mahdists in 1898 Reginald Wingate had become a household name. Not only was he a superb intelligence officer who understood the Sudanese desert and its people but he was also a popular author who had translated Rudolf Slatin's influential account of ten years' imprisonment by the dervishes and was himself the author of several books about the Anglo-Egyptian Sudan. At the end of Kitchener's campaign Wingate had been appointed Governor-General of the Sudan and Sirdar, or commander, of the Egyptian Army, and became one of the great British gubernatorial servants. During the First World War he was High Commissioner for Egypt, a post he held with less success – he was effectively sacked in 1919 after failing to deal adequately with Egyptian nationalists – but his name was still indelibly associated with his service to the Sudan.

Indeed, it was true to say that Cousin Rex had acted as the uncrowned king of the country during his period as Governor-General. He revelled in the social side of his work and turned Khartoum into a fashionable winter resort for minor European royalty and wealthy aristocratic travellers. Levees, balls and formal dinners were regular features of life at Government House and he took pains to ensure that he was treated as King Edward VII's representative in the Sudan. Precedence was all-important and whenever he went on tour he surrounded himself with a huge entourage and he expected his officials and guests to maintain high standards of behaviour and comportment. Given the strength of this proprietorial affection for the country and its people, it was not really surprising that Cousin Rex should have encouraged his young kinsman to follow in his footsteps.

Because the policing of the British Empire was one of the army's duties after the First World War, it was not unusual for a young officer to want an overseas posting to escape the tedium of regimental life in Britain. India was the obvious choice: it provided a garrison of 60,000 British soldiers, and Wingate's father had served there with distinction and through his missionary work retained links with the North-West Frontier Province. However Wingate never considered this possibility; perhaps it was too transparent a choice. According to Tulloch, once Wingate had begun corresponding with Cousin Rex in 1924, he never examined any other prospect than service in Egypt or the Sudan. Even when his life was taken up with fox-hunting and other delights, at his father's prompting, Wingate had started bending his mind to the study of Arabic, an obvious requisite if he were to live for any time in the Islamic world.

However it was not until the summer of 1926 that Wingate was to make the move which changed the course of his military career. Having successfully completed the prestigious course at Weedon he was in a good position to apply for one of the army's language courses at the School of Oriental Studies in London University which the War Office organised for officers bound for overseas postings. An earlier application, made in May 1925, had been turned down and at this second attempt Lieutenant-Colonel Crawford, his commanding officer, was still dubious about the proposal but, prompted by the evidence of Wingate's willingness to knuckle down to difficult tasks, he backed the application. In September 1926 Wingate sold off his horses, said farewell to Tulloch who was bound for a field battery in India and went up to London to begin the five-month-long intensive course to become an army translator in Arabic. At that stage he still had little idea where it might lead him; Cousin Rex had suggested that he should finish his education with a further six months in Egypt and the Sudan but any future move depended on the army granting him the necessary leave of absence and it was by no means certain that this would be forthcoming.

It was a winter well spent. Having enrolled at the school on 5 October Wingate settled down to the life of a student, sharing a flat in High Holborn with two fellow gunners from Larkhill, James Woodford and G. T. N. Bellamy. As their fees had been paid by the army and they were entitled to draw allowances from London District, the young men were reasonably well off and they were determined to have a good time, perhaps compensating for the university years which had been denied them by their army careers. All three were different. Bellamy was a stolid Yorkshireman who shared Wingate's love of horses, while Woodford was an urbane charmer who first shocked, then amused his flatmates by enquiring of any woman of their acquaintance, 'Is she bedworthy?' Woodford's seductions became the stuff of legend and in later life Wingate always spoke of him with amusement and affection, one reason being that he had emerged as his principal academic rival in the intensive Arabic course.

The classes were supposed to give the young officers a rapid introduction to spoken and written Arabic and to prepare them for life in an Arabic-speaking environment. Much of the work was learned by rote and Wingate's notebooks show a methodical mind at work. Vocabulary was listed and memorised and the complexities of grammar and syntax were carefully delineated and logically expressed. Whereas Woodford had the ability to assimilate information intuitively and exactly, Wingate had a more pragmatic streak and believed that learning had to be based on reason and hard work.

Wingate enjoyed student life. At that time the School of Oriental Studies was situated in a large eighteenth-century building (long demolished) at Finsbury Circus and it had a vaguely bohemian atmosphere, a mixture of Levantine exoticism and undergraduate liberalism. Arabic was taught by the distinguished oriental scholar Sir Thomas Arnold and spoken language classes were taken by Sheikh Goma'sa Muhamad Mahmud, 'a sturdy, brown, genial person' who was later to become Iraq's consul in Jerusalem. Once more Wingate found that his family name was no disadvantage.

Whenever he could he spent weekends at Fareham with Peggy who was becoming an increasingly important part of his life. Not that he did much to impress her parents who had come to dislike him as 'that rude young man' who had taken up with their daughter. According to Mary Jelley her father 'loathed' Wingate and her mother only tolerated him because she understood the strength of Peggy's feelings for him. Much of the dislike was caused by Wingate's refusal to display simple good manners or to conform to the Jelleys' middle-class standards of behaviour. They were particularly infuriated by his tendency to throw cigarette ends wherever he pleased and to read the daily newspaper at breakfast before offering it to Colonel Jelley; it was considered 'bad form' to do this and Wingate compounded the disgust by leaving the paper in an untidy condition or stuffing it down the back of a chair. This was hardly venal behaviour but it discomforted the Jelleys who wondered what had possessed their daughter to involve herself with such an untidy young man. When he was challenged about his unconventional behaviour Wingate simply replied: 'If you're in the army you have to do something extraordinary to be noticed.'

None of this bothered Peggy who had fallen deeply in love with Wingate. Not only did she offer him devotion and affection but she also became the main confidante of his hopes and fears. So different from him in temperament – friends remember her as a serene and intelligent girl – she understood his moods and as time went by was able to help him come to terms with his remaining uncertainties about life, religion and his career in the army. 'If you fear God you are free to love,' he told her. 'But if you love God, you are just loving yourself.' Other elements in his philosophy were equally severe. Peggy noticed that he was never completely at ease in company and had a tendency to be combative in conversation. When she took him to task he responded that he was giving people the opportunity to be themselves, not what they thought they should be. 'None of us knows ourselves completely,' he said. 'We have to be shown by others.'

Partly at Peggy's bidding Wingate moved out of his flat in the spring of 1927 and into lodgings in Campden Hill Road. Although it was a somewhat eccentric establishment run by a landlady called Mrs Bowler who was little disturbed by Wingate's sloppy habits, it gave him the necessary stability to concentrate on the academic demands made by his course. That it worked can be seen in the result: in March 1927 he passed the formal exams, obtaining 85 per cent and coming second to Woodford. For someone who had been written off at school it was a considerable achievement.

It was one thing to have passed his first exams with high marks but quite another to persuade the army to grant him extended leave; after all, he had been commissioned for less than four years and the War Office usually demanded at least five years' service before its young regular officers were allowed to make a serious change of direction in their careers. To Wingate's horror his request for leave was turned down on grounds of youth and inexperience and on 14 March 1927 he was ordered to return to his battery at Fort Brockhurst.

His reaction to this setback was a significant pointer to the way he would behave in the years to come. Instead of throwing in the towel he decided to use what political influence was available to him and asked Cousin Rex to help him. Here he was not disappointed as Reginald Wingate was a constant intriguer in the corridors of British power and maintained an influential set of contacts at court and in the Foreign and War Offices. His long service to the British Empire and his earlier association with great men such as Cromer and Kitchener meant that politicians listened to him and Cousin Rex made full use of that advantage. As he grew older, his constant interference and proffering of advice were less cordially received by a younger generation of civil servants but in 1928 he was only recently retired and his voice was still heeded. Having listened sympathetically to his young relation's difficulties he made the necessary enquiries and when Wingate reapplied for leave in June it was immediately given.

The next stage was to decide a plan of action and in September

Wingate went north to Scotland, to Cousin Rex's windswept house of Knockenhair in the East Lothian seaside town of Dunbar, a rare visit to his native soil. Under his kinsman's tutelage it was decided that Wingate should spend six months in the Sudan where he would further his studies at the language classes of the Sudan Agency which was responsible for the administration of the country. At the same time steps would be taken to get him a posting to the Sudan Defence Force which had come into being in 1925 and was still looking for suitable British officers to lead and train its men. Only two difficulties stood in his way. Any officer seconded to the Sudan Defence Force had to have served for at least five years in a British regiment. This Wingate had not done: of his four years' service to date only three had been spent on regimental duties. Second, the Sudan Defence Force was most fastidious in its choice of officer. As one officer of the same period remembered, selection depended almost entirely on the old-boy network: 'Nearly always the officer serving in the SDF knew of someone (usually in his British regiment) whom he thought would get on well with SDF life, and if his friend would like to apply for secondment he would recommend him. It was not easy to get selected if you did not know somebody serving, or someone who had just finished serving in the SDF.'[4]

Wingate failed to score on both points but these were but trifles to Cousin Rex. Not only was he one of the best-known names in the Sudan but he knew Huddleston Pasha, the Kaid, or commander of the SDF, and he wrote to him strongly recommending his young kinsman for service in his army. With backing of that kind it would have been most unusual had Wingate not been seconded and so it transpired. The lesson was not lost on him. In the years to come he was to use to full advantage whatever political influence was available to him and he always made certain that he cultivated the friendships of men in positions of power or those whose star was in the ascendant. This had little to do with knowing important men and women for their own sake; rather Wingate cherished his contacts for their ability to cut through administrative red tape. As he said to Cousin Rex in a letter written from the Sudan, 'From my own experience I believe that little service of value is to be expected from officers who do not possess executive authority.' Even at this early stage – he was still only twenty-four – he had discovered one of the critical secrets about gaining access to political power: that it can rest almost entirely on an ability to influence or impress the person who wields it.

The rule about five years' service was conveniently forgotten and

Huddleston agreed to see Wingate when he arrived in Khartoum; he was certain that anyone bearing such a resonant name would have little difficulty fitting into his little army. With a recommendation of that order there was also no need for Wingate to be known to anyone serving in the SDF. Although to modern ears the need to fit in might smack of a closed shop or private club, this was an important qualification. The SDF was a compact organisation and its small band of officers had to work harmoniously in remote areas, usually without the amenities of modern life. In Darfur Province alone there were only twenty-three British civilian and military personnel to govern and control an area of 192,000 square miles, four times the size of Britain, with a population of 1,005,000. Unless the newcomer was prepared to accommodate himself to the local conditions life for everyone else would have been intolerable, hence the insistence on personal recommendation.

There were other conditions. All officers were expected to ride and to play bridge, both necessary requirements in postings where entertainment had to be home-made. Three months' leave was granted each year and this had to be spent outside the country, preferably in Britain or Europe; a wise condition given Sudan's enervating climate. In addition each new officer had to have learned enough rudimentary Arabic to understand his men. Above all, they had to be single. No officer serving with the SDF could get married until after he had completed four years of service and no one was permitted to become engaged until he had reached the age of twenty-seven. This was less draconian than it first appears. Most British regiments followed this rule but in the Sudan it was deemed to be absolutely necessary. Apart from Khartoum, which had been modernised under Kitchener's direction, life in the out-stations could be tough, unyielding and, more than anything else, dominated by men. As most were bachelors who regarded duty and uncomplaining endurance as tenets of their faith and who looked for little reward other than personal satisfaction in their service, they were unlikely to welcome a married woman into their monastic society.

The rule presented no problems to Wingate as he and Peggy only had the loosest of understandings about their future together and despite their growing intimacy were not to become engaged until 1932. Like other girls from her background she understood that Wingate's career had to come first and that long separations were inevitable. It was certainly not unusual for couples to wait several years before they became officially engaged and many had to wait until the man reached a position of suitable seniority before they could marry. Long engagements or 'understandings' were also supposed to be good for the relationship as most marriages in the empire had to endure lengthy periods of separation. Besides, Wingate had made it clear to Peggy that they could not announce their engagement until he had completed his five years in the Sudan.

Having laid his plans with Cousin Rex, Wingate returned to Godalming to take his farewells of his family and to start on the first big adventure of his life. Never having travelled abroad before Wingate might have been expected to take the conventional route to Egypt – normally overland by train to Marseilles and then by ship to Alexandria – but Wingate had other plans. He would travel by bicycle and train across Europe to Genoa and catch a ship there. It was an audacious decision for a young man travelling abroad for the first time in his life, but it was by no means unique. Young officers were encouraged to show their initiative when travelling to overseas postings – leave could be refused if it resembled a holiday – and by the 1920s several officers had already travelled overland to India by car.

None the less, Wingate's mode of travel in September 1927 was nothing if not strenuous. Having made the crossing from Harwich to the Hook of Holland he pushed through the Netherlands into Germany and continued south through Czechoslovakia and Austria into Yugoslavia. By the time he reached Trieste, his first goal, he reckoned that he had travelled 600 miles by bicycle, averaging seventy miles a day. It had not been without incident. In Prague he had been robbed by a seemingly friendly Jewish pedlar, the police had arrested him as a vagrant in Vienna and by the time he reached Yugoslavia he was so short of money that he considered the possibility of working as a labourer to earn some much-needed cash. However, luck was on his side: a 'good Samaritan' bought his bicycle for £5 and he was able to take the train from Trieste to Venice. As he told his father, it was an entrancing moment.

I like three things about Venice. The silence due to the waterways. The San Marco Square. And lastly the delightful habit the people have of coming out at about six o'clock and walking up and down the square in twos and threes until ten. Most of them are Venetians – at any rate in October – and I cannot believe that Beatrice was more beautiful or Dante more romantic than some of these superb creatures.

Other discoveries were less congenial. On the boat from the Grand

Canal to San Marco he met an instantly recognisable couple: the retired Englishman abroad with his 'faded, querulous wife'.

I have come to the conclusion that I never met an Englishman until I left England. [He wrote in the same letter to his father] English people abroad are so much more English. Usually for some unexplained reason they have the appearance, views and habits of the Victorian era ... off the beaten track one meets English people with the outlook of 1890 and the appearance of having stopped at about that date and not been wound up since.

While it is not unusual for young people travelling abroad for the first time to be disconcerted by the appearance of their fellow countrymen and to avoid their company, Wingate's attitude to the old colonel and his wife is revealing. Having made it clear to them that he too was English – he revelled in the wife's 'powerful curiosity' – he engaged an Austrian in conversation and entered into a loud and spirited discussion about the current political situation in Europe. This was done less for the interest he took in the subject than for the chance to embarrass his fellow countrymen. In other words he was playing to the gallery and enjoying every minute of it.

I pointed out to the Austrian what a mess Lloyd George and Clemenceau had made of Central Europe. I drew his attention to the fact that a reckoning was inevitable and that no right-minded man could wish to prevent it. I deplored the French nation. I admired the Germans. And I was gratified at the look of incredulous horror and loathing that crept over the faces of my fellow countrymen.

Wingate's views were not particularly radical. He always believed that the League of Nations was a broken reed and that another European war was inevitable and it was fashionable in the British army to prefer the Germans to the French. None of this mattered: what concerned him at the time was to shock the inoffensive couple by drawing attention to himself. On one level his behaviour was little more than a case of *épater les bourgeois*; on another he was simply being rude and thoughtless, but the incident does offer a clue to his future behaviour. Under normal circumstances Wingate used his considerable charm to good effect with older people and felt at home in any society, but he also understood the value of making an impact by standing up for his own point of view.

As he had little money and had to be in Genoa by 6 October to make sure of catching his ship, he only spent one day in Venice and caught an overnight train south. There he embarked on the *Italia*, a liner of the

Italian Sitmar Line, where he found himself sharing a cabin with 'a Gypo doctor, an Austrian hairdresser (dames), a German secretary [and] a Levantine'. Also travelling with him was a fellow gunner called Blunt whom he had met hunting with the South and West Wilts. The two young officers quickly made themselves at home.

We took charge of the cabin between us and did pretty much as we pleased, with due consideration for our fellow passengers' feelings. Filthy habits, such as turning off the fan at night, shutting the port-hole, except in a rough sea, smoking in the cabin etc, we could not permit. We further discouraged others from getting up at the same time as ourselves which would make movement difficult.

Although travelling third class Blunt and Wingate had little difficulty in spending the day on the second-class deck where the British married couples normally travelled. (First class was reserved for 'millionaires, Jews, Greeks and others of that kidney'.) On a British liner plying between India and Britain this would have presented difficulties as passengers travelled according to their social position and the classes were strictly demarcated; social divisions in India were maintained on board ship and on board P & O liners in particular the protocol of the cantonment ruled shipboard life. None of this held good for Wingate's four-day voyage on the *Italia*. Both men knew that their accents, bearing and 'superior manner' would forestall any awkward questions from the stewards and that their fellow British passengers were unlikely to complain to an Italian crew. What the other passengers in their cabin felt about the two subalterns' overweening behaviour Wingate did not relate but even as late as 1927 young men bound for the heavenly commands of imperial service still felt that they were a cut above the rest of the world. In his innocence, and travelling abroad for the first time in his young life, Wingate was no different.

He arrived in Alexandria on 10 October and took the train to Cairo where he was met by Jim Woodford, his flatmate from High Holborn days. Employed as a translator at the British Residency, Woodford had a palatial apartment at 1 Sharia Walda Kasr el Dubara. So too did Blunt and a new acquaintance called Boulanger, the manager of the National Bank who insisted that the three young men should take all their meals with him during Wingate's stay in Cairo. This was a godsend as Wingate was slowly running out of money and was finding some difficulty in making ends meet. Before leaving Britain he had promised his father that he would live off his subaltern's salary of £40 a month, including overseas allowances, but there had been problems in accrediting the money to his account. Meanwhile he had the expense of buying suitable tropical clothes, including two white duck suits and a sun helmet, and he still had to pay for his passage to Khartoum. For all those reasons he was desperately keen to be seconded to the SDF whose officers were paid at twice the rate of pay and were not obliged to pay income tax.

There is little doubt that Wingate enjoyed the ten days he spent in Cairo. He visited the pyramids and other tourist sights, had a drink at the world-famous Gezira Sporting Club, dined at Shepheard's Hotel and paid a call on the British headquarters at the Kasr-el-Nil garrison. He also took care to follow the letters of introduction supplied by Cousin Rex and dined with the Sudan Agent in Cairo who acted for Sir John Maffey, Sudan's Governor-General. By far the most important introduction was to Ibrahim Bey Dimitri, Cousin Rex's former Arabic secretary, who introduced Wingate to his circle of influential Egyptian and Syrian politicians and businessmen in Heliopolis. Wingate was much taken by their company and insisted that they spoke to him in Arabic: as he told his father, he felt that if he could stay in Cairo he would make rapid strides in his ability to speak the language.

However, Wingate knew that he had to get to Khartoum to further his claims for a posting to the Sudan and at the end of the month he left Cairo by train in the company of one of Ibrahim Bey Dimitri's friends who lived at Kassala in the eastern Sudan. At Wadi Halfa they transferred to river boat for the last stage of their journey up the Nile to Khartoum. There he met A. L. W. Vicars-Miles who had served in the Sudan Political Service since 1922 and who was returning from leave to his post at Rashad in the Nuba Mountains in the Kordofan Province.

The older man was able to help Wingate in two ways, giving him painkillers for a painful mouth abscess and offering some well-meant advice about British life in the Sudan. Khartoum was to be avoided at all costs, he warned. There were endless balls and dinner parties, most British officials stopped work at midday and few were prepared to have much contact with the Sudanese. As a result it was difficult to find native Arabic speakers and the exigencies of the season meant that the Sudan Agency would only be manned by a skeleton staff. (Following the lead given by Cousin Rex most senior officials were only in Khartoum between December and June; summers were spent on leave in Britain and October and November were reserved for Cairo.) Under the circumstances, counselled Vicars-Miles, it would be more sensible for

Wingate to live up-country and to that end he would be happy to welcome him in Rashad.

At first inspection Khartoum was indeed a disappointment. He had to stay in the stuffy Sudan Club which was not only expensive but was full of older officers and civil servants who ignored all new arrivals, whatever their name. (This too was not unusual: in the smarter British regiments young officers were not allowed to instigate conversations until they had served for at least six months.) And as Vicars-Miles had warned, with the Sudan Agency's Arabic classes on holiday, it was almost impossible to find anyone with whom to speak Arabic. There was also a complication over his posting to the SDF. Although he had dined with Huddleston Pasha who had promised to find a vacancy for him, this could not take place until 1 April 1928 and would depend on Wingate's papers coming through from his regiment. Under normal circumstances this was not a problem but at the end of October Colonel Leech had committed suicide before he had the chance to deal with Wingate's papers and there was an inevitable delay in completing the administrative arrangements.

With time to spare Wingate remembered Vicars-Miles's invitation and wrote asking if he could take up the offer, both to give him something to do and to help him improve his colloquial Arabic. Agreement was freely given and in January 1928 Wingate set off for Rashad in the Nuba Mountains, travelling up the White Nile by boat and then completing the final part of the journey overland by camel. Like most other outposts in Sudan Rashad was small, self-contained and self-sufficient and the political officers had to make do with life as they found it. With a handful of men living and working in close proximity in an isolated area tolerance was a prime virtue and visitors were also expected to exercise a considerable amount of restraint in their personal behaviour. This Wingate was not always prepared to do and within days of his arrival he had made himself disagreeable by his refusal to wash or change his clothes regularly. He also demonstrated a tendency to espouse unorthodox and eccentric views on a wide range of subjects.

Although Vicars-Miles was willing to be tolerant – he only displayed rage when Wingate took a pot-shot at his pet gazelle – his guest's behaviour discomforted the other officers and not for the last time in his life Wingate found that he was considered an outsider in a strictly regulated male society. Much of what he said was innocent enough and was no more radical than the views he expressed in his letters to his father. That was not the problem: it was that he had the temerity to advertise them. Amongst men who valued the 'stiff upper lip' – keeping one's thoughts to oneself, containing personal emotions and maintaining strict standards of protocol – Wingate's behaviour appeared boorish and offensive. One of his contemporaries, E. A. Balfour of the Sudan Political Service, remembered the prevailing public-school ethos as a necessary evil. Although it was obvious that amongst his colleagues, 'this one had a tendency to pomposity, that one lacked humour; this one was conceited, that one was weak', it was essential to maintain the illusion that everyone was either 'an awfully good fellow' or 'a splendid chap'.[5]

Wingate did not see it that way. To him, 'good form' for its own sake seemed to be a despicable pretence and he was now determined to stand up to those whom he felt were stupid or foolish; Sybil described it as a growing refusal to have a rational respect for all constitutional authority. Partly his behaviour resulted from a late-maturing intellect and he was inclined to show off his newly gained knowledge. At school and Woolwich he had been considered dull and it had taken him time and effort to re-educate himself through a wide programme of reading. This was one reason why Vicars-Miles could never be angry with him for long; whereas the younger officers regarded Wingate with disdain he saw a young man in a hurry.

There was also a more fundamental reason for this change of demeanour. As he matured intellectually Wingate became more aware of himself and what he wanted from life. It was not enough to make pretences: there had to be a cause and, if necessary, it had to be defended and succoured against all opposition, whatever the personal cost. For Wingate this meant turning away from prevarication, upholding principles no matter how unorthodox or unpopular they might be and accepting a willingness to drive himself and others to the limits of their possibilities. This was entirely in keeping with his personal religious beliefs which insisted that a man must act within the precepts of his compact with God and that his own sense of destiny had to take precedence over unnecessary temporal constraints. Later in life his unwillingness to compromise over important issues was to become a hallmark of Wingate's behaviour. According to the evidence of Peggy Jelley and Vicars-Miles and others in the Sudan Defence Force, the transformation seems to have taken place at this time as he slowly began to grapple with an inner certainty that he might be different from most other men, that within him were the seeds of greatness. In a telling letter to Peggy he admitted as much, 'I cannot be a nobody. I cannot be nothing!'

It is also possible that his abrupt behaviour masked a fear that he was undeserving and that God would turn his face against him unless he constantly strove to attain a state of grace. At times like that he was once more back in the night-time world of Summerhill listening out for the steady sound of his sisters' breathing. To combat the morbid depression which accompanied his apprehensions he would take refuge in the conviction that he had been called into the world to do great things. The struggle was real enough and it led to frequent bouts of melancholia which were so acute that he was able to recall them in minute detail several years later when he was happily married.

It is impossible to describe the kind of horror that engulfed me at these times. It was not the horror of any particular fate or any one fear; nor was it concerned with general ideas of sin or suffering. It was much worse because it was without form or limit and it swallowed up the whole of existence. After I had two or three of these attacks I hit on a sort of formula which I said to myself as the waters closed over my head and went on repeating. 'God is good,' I used to say over and over again. It had to be something simple because my anguish prevented any thought process and it had to be something comprehensive that I really believed or it would have been no good to me. These words summed up my whole belief and when I hung in the abyss, they were all that I had the strength to utter.

One cause was homesickness. Despite the camaraderie of Vicars-Miles's establishment he missed England and imagined himself to be dispossessed in the desert places, far from family and friends. 'When Allah made the Sudan he laughed,' ran the Arab proverb, a light enough jest for a difficult terrain. At night it was bitterly cold, during the day a scorching sun beat down from a cloudless sky and the desert itself, rocky in places, scrub and soft sand in others, sapped the energy of all but the most hardy. In time Wingate learned to respect the austerity of life in the country but in the early days at least, he admitted more than once, 'I would sometimes lie in bed at night with tears in my eyes as I thought of a damp spring morning in the ploughlands of the Blackmore Vale.'

His own mental condition, though, was the underlying reason for these fits of depression which were as disabling as any physical sickness. To medical science he was suffering from cyclothymia, a mild form of manic-depression characterised by marked swings of mood and behaviour. This accounted for the extremes of humour which first became apparent in the Sudan and which would remain with him for the rest of his life. In the 'manic' state Wingate would be hyperactive, talking excessively and intemperately and brooking no interruption; the 'depressive' state would be marked by melancholia, despair and a terror of failure. Both left their mark on his character and help to explain why he could be dazzlingly inventive or pushy and aggressive one day and prone to despair the next. The condition also accounts for Wingate's conviction that he had been born to greatness and the mixture of charm and boorishness which was an unavoidable part of his personality.

Wingate's mental make-up and the effect it had on his career and reputation was first investigated fully after his death by the military historian Shelford Bidwell.[6] He takes the view that although the condition was chronic it did not mean that Wingate was mad or that he could not distinguish between the real and the imaginary. On the contrary, he argues that the 'hypermanic phases were purposeful, his torrents of words were not gibberish but contained a flow of ideas which held his listeners riveted and his aggression was directed towards specific rational goals'. Bidwell also believes that Wingate's cyclothymia had its genesis in his childhood experiences. This was certainly the view taken by Wingate's wife after his death.

The origins of his suffering are not wholly to be uncovered. The rudiments of his forefathers imbedded in his brain, his parentage whose elements so unlike were mingled in a heat that brought about the new substance that was Orde; his youth in a house where God was always an inmate, dwelling in thick darkness, and eternity outside the window-pane; all these things may be called upon to explain why he suffered as other men do not.

Sudan was only the beginning. For the rest of his life Wingate had to wrestle with a condition which he and those who came into contact with him only half understood: the frequently frightening contrast between intellectual frenzy and the black dog of depression.

Fortunately for his immediate future, though, the attacks became less chronic as he got into his stride in the Sudan and he learned to control them by imagining that he was two people, one suffering and the other strong. 'I used to talk to myself and say, "It's all right, don't worry. You're going to be all right. Have a hot bath and a whisky and soda. You need not write any letters tonight, you can read *Jane Eyre* instead."' Work was the other antidote and, as he was to discover, there was to be no shortage of that once he joined the Sudan Defence Force. At the end of February 1928 he received orders from Huddleston Pasha to report to Khartoum during the first week of April. A contradictory order arrived from the War Office instructing him to proceed to the Sudan Agent in London but this could be safely ignored.

As he wrote to his father on 25 February 1928, all was well: his personal finances had been assured, he was speaking enough Arabic to pass the first-class certificate and he had grown a moustache, 'partly because it's less trouble, and partly because the Arabs pay more attention to one wearing the appendage'.

Four

SOLDIERING IN THE SUDAN

It is not difficult to understand why British army officers enjoyed serving in the remoter parts of the empire in the years before the Second World War. Far away from the rigid discipline and protocol which surrounded regimental life at home or in the cantonments in India, they could develop their own ideas and interests and were able to exercise authority well beyond their age and experience. A young subaltern could find himself in charge of around 200 men in an isolated area where conditions might be crude or dangerous. If communications were primitive and the chain of command flexible — as was the case in the majority of places — he was supposed to show initiative, and survival was frequently a matter of forgetting the rule book and acting according to local conditions. In short, it was what the more adventurous officers called 'real soldiering'.

The Sudan Defence Force offered all this in abundance. For a start, when Wingate joined, the organisation was still in its infancy. After Kitchener's defeat of the Mahdist forces at Omdurman in 1898 and the resultant Condominium of the Anglo-Egyptian Sudan the country was garrisoned by the Egyptian army which was largely commanded by British officers to company commander level and manned by Egyptian and Sudanese troops. The GOC, or Sirdar, was also British and he included the governor-generalship of the Sudan amongst his responsibilities. (This was the post formerly held by Cousin Rex.) However, in 1924, following a spate of Egyptian nationalist agitation which culminated in the assassination of the Sirdar Sir Lee Stack, all Egyptian units were withdrawn and a new Sudan Defence Force was formed from the five all-Sudanese units which already existed.

In the following year, 1925, these were re-established as the Cavalry and Mounted Rifles (later the Sudan Horse), the Eastern and Western

Arab Corps, the Camel Corps and the Equatorial Corps. In addition
there were logistic and supply units in the shape of the Engineer Troops,
the Animal Transport and Supplies Unit, the Mechanical Transport Unit
and the Stores and Ordnance Department. The post of Sirdar came to
an end and the new force's commander was given the title of al'Kaid
al'Amm or General Officer Commandant. His was a small self-contained
all-volunteer force never more than 4,500 strong and although it did not
possess modern first-line equipment it demanded high standards of
service and commitment from its small cadre of British officers. After
initial training most of these were thrown in at the deep end, posted to
command a company of 300 men 'somewhere in the vast Sudan' where,
according to J. H. R. Orlebar, the historian of the SDF, he was forced
to combine the attributes of a military commander and a colonial
administrator: 'He had to be a man of spirit, initiative, reliability and
resourcefulness: above all he had to be an energetic type with a good
sense of humour, for he was on his own now, with no CO, no other
Company Commander, Adjutant or Quartermaster with whom to
discuss his problems or to guide him.'[1]

While it was a daunting proposition it was also a challenge, made
somewhat lighter by the knowledge that in the remote areas of the Sudan
it was possible to learn from one's mistakes without attracting immediate
retribution from on high. Company commanders were also responsible
for running training programmes, recruitment, maintaining the local
defences, handling stores and equipment and all disciplinary matters. In
return he was given the rank of bimbashi, or major, and if he were a
fluent Arab speaker he was awarded an additional allowance of £120 a
year. All this was to come Wingate's way within a year of joining the
Eastern Arab Corps at its headquarters at Gedaref in the Kassala Province.
In June 1928 he took over command of number 3 Idara (company),
Eastern Arab Corps, based at Kassala near the border with Eritrea.

Typically perhaps, Wingate almost destroyed his chances before his
service in the Sudan had even got under way. Displaying all his old
impetuosity he indulged in prolonged outbursts of verbosity, brooked
no interruption and refused to take the hint that his brother officers at
Gedaref were intensely annoyed by his behaviour. His subject matter was
also taboo: politics, especially Marxism, and religion. He also tended to
say too much about himself and his hopes for the future, another cardinal
sin in a young officer. Wingate was guilty of breaking a basic, though
unwritten, army rule and it did not take long for his commanding officer,
Lieutenant-Colonel Paddy Walsh, to warn him about his behaviour.

'You've been talking too much: a subaltern of your age should be seen and not heard,' he told him. 'I don't like the things you say and I don't like you, but I will give you a choice. Either you shut up and keep your ideas about communism to yourself or I shall have you returned to your regiment with a black mark against you.'

Wingate's first reaction was to protest that Walsh was being unfair and that it was mere blimpishness to dictate what an officer should or should not discuss. It seemed to be Woolwich all over again. But on this occasion Wingate was an older and more experienced soldier who had no wish to return to Britain in disgrace. Swallowing his pride, he agreed to Walsh's request and long afterwards came to respect the plain-speaking nature of the warning. ('It's no good talking a language people cannot understand,' he told friends in Palestine ten years later. 'In fact you insult a man just as much by talking to him on an intellectual level higher than his own as you do by talking to him as though he were a fool.')

The episode affected Wingate in other ways. Instead of offering his opinions so frequently and so definitely, he took care to moderate them. He also said rather less about himself and his ambitions. The belief that he had been born to greatness burned strongly within him but he was careful to whom he expressed his thoughts. A letter written to his father on 13 June 1928 shortly after taking his first command gives some idea of his impatience to give substance to his ambitions.

It is satisfactory to find myself in command of 275 men but as this is the rain season there's little to be done unfortunately. However I'm setting seriously to work at Arabic in order to put that behind me and turn my attention to promotion exams and the Staff College.

I doubt very much whether the Sudan will be useful to me for longer than five years at the outside. There's no future for a soldier in the Sudan, but the responsibility (not to mention the pay) is most valuable to a young soldier like myself. I want to go to the Staff College as soon as may be. I daresay if I made a dead set at it and fortune favoured me, I might become Kaid el Amm [sic] here one day, but I feel disposed to attempt something bitter. However, man proposeth, God disposeth.

Having decided to be more circumspect about his behaviour Wingate found to his surprise that he quite enjoyed listening to what others had to say. As he began to relax he also made the discovery that his brother officers rather liked him and were prepared to welcome him into their company. Eccentric he might have been – he was never tidy and wore his hair somewhat longer than expected of the typical young officer of the day – but at least he was interesting and determined. His horse-manship helped in this respect and he took up polo to become a brave, though never entirely skilful player.

The fits of depression which became a constant companion during his time in the Sudan he kept to himself or confided only to Peggy. Sometimes they were so severe that he believed himself to be close to death: 'I have been in such a state of nerves during the last week or two that I have read an omen of death into everything,' he told Peggy in a letter written on 12 April 1931. 'The tree that blew down outside my house, a worm-eaten tree; the owl that visited my garden each night and hooted at me; the skeleton I've just seen in a landslide; the crows that have been cawing over my head just now – all are omens of approaching death.'

At first he thought that the 'nervous melancholia' – his description – was due to poor diet and that its onset was caused by simple biliousness. On the same occasion, while out on trek with his Idara, he felt so depressed and out of sorts mentally that he was forced to take to his bed.

The effect on my mind was indescribable. It followed a course which I afterwards grew to be familiar with and to measure, which was a great relief in itself. The first time I had nothing to hang on to, not even the knowledge of when it would end. For two or three days I suffered fits of depression each one longer than the last and then blackness clamped down on me and I could think of nothing else until after the appointed time, usually about two days, it began to lift and passed off slowly as it had come. During the early stages it was possible for me to be distracted for short periods and to go about my business and make decisions, but when I was in the middle of a nervous attack, I reacted in the same way as one does to physical pain. I felt deathly cold, my teeth chattered and I became very pale. No stimulants had any effect, or at least none of those to which I had access, such as tea or coffee or alcohol; nor did anodynes do me any good, nor sedatives. I could do nothing but sit by myself and hold on to my reason as best I could.

It must have been a terrifying experience. The onset of a fit of clinical depression is bad enough at any time but in the depths of Sudan's wilderness, bereft of contact with his fellow Europeans and only his bewildered men for company, Wingate must have felt that he was in a living nightmare. Because he refused to consult the SDF's medical staff he held the condition to him like a shroud and, apart from his letters to Peggy, refused to discuss with it anyone. Even had he consulted a medical officer it is unlikely if much would have been done to help him. Psychiatric care was in its infancy and in the army, with memories of

First World War shell-shock still strong, it was practically non-existent. As late as 1945 an experienced officer, Brigadier G. W. B. James, was able to claim in the *Lancet*: 'The doctors of Empire, no matter where they trained, were with few exceptions bewildered by the psychiatric casualty; they looked upon him with distaste and were quite unable to deal with him effectively.'[2] Had Wingate chosen to seek medical help, more likely than not he would have been told to pull himself together, take more exercise and lose himself in his work.

To a certain extent he did just that. During his first year at Gedaref and later at Kassala he continued learning Arabic by getting to know the men of the Sudan Defence Force and spending time in their company. Armed with a notebook he would jot down everyday words and phrases and commit them to memory; in the evening he set aside time for reading and studying in preparation for the second part of his examination at the School of Oriental Studies. This he sat and passed during his first leave in the summer of 1929 and he returned to the Sudan in September.

It was an uncomplicated yet deeply fulfilling existence and the days were rarely short of incident. All officers had a personal servant, a cook, a houseboy and a groom, thus relieving them of domestic tasks and allowing them to concentrate on their military duties. A typical day's service would begin at 5.30 a.m. in the hot weather and an hour later in the cold season; lunch was taken late and during the heat of the afternoon everyone rested. In the early evening there would be time for recreation – riding, polo, tennis or squash – before dinner when it was the custom to change into white silk shirts and slacks. Evenings were spent listening to the gramophone, reading or playing cards. Wingate never excelled at bridge, the most popular pastime, but he proved to be an excellent and successful poker player. 'Poker is like life itself,' he would say, 'it is ruled by chance and skill, but bridge calls for nothing but a good memory and a power to work out combinations and permutations.' Only if the occasion were formal would a dinner jacket be worn but most stations eschewed this kind of convention unless visitors were present.

The accommodation in most company stations was fairly basic. Some were forts, Beau Geste-like in appearance, but the typical SDF station consisted of a collection of buildings which included the headquarters office, guardroom, stores, barrackroom for single men and mud huts or *tukls* for the married men and their families. The self-contained complex was usually protected by an outer barbed-wire fence and inner wall and above the buildings flew the Union Jack and the flag of Egypt.

Because there were always more applicants than vacancies, the quality of the men in the SDF rarely varied and was always high. No British officer who served in the Sudan doubted that it was a privilege to command them and the enthusiasm was caught by one of Wingate's fellow officers, Hugh Boustead. 'The family atmosphere of the company, the manliness and intense fun of the Sudanese soldiers and his complete reliance on his officers produced a feeling of affection between the British company commander and his men which formed one of the main charms of African service with an irregular corps.'[3]

Wingate was similarly affected by the men under his command who represented the multiplicity of types to be found in the SDF: Sudanese Muslims, Baqqara Arabs and pure-blooded negroes from Somalia. 'They were delightful people,' he said, 'and I should have been perfectly happy to concern myself with their affairs indefinitely.' It was for that reason, the tendency for British officers to become over-attached to their postings, that company commanders were only allowed to serve for a maximum of five years in the Sudan, provided, of course, that they survived the first two years' 'apprenticeship'. There was, too, a sound military reason for this rule: the British army insisted that five years was long enough for an officer to be absent from regimental duties otherwise he would lose touch with military innovations.

Because it was part of the bimbashis' duties to be answerable for the total welfare of the men under their command, and because the SDF allowed married men to keep their wives and families with them on the station, Wingate soon discovered that the role also had patriarchal responsibilities. On the military side these amounted to little more than making sure that the men received their pay and that they were well fed: there were no central messing arrangements and the cooking was usually done in the tukls by the womenfolk. On another level, though, most bimbashis discovered that, sooner or later, they had to deal with domestic problems involving the men and their families. Sometimes these amounted to little more than disagreements over personal property or long-standing grudges brought into the force from civilian life; at others, those involving women, they found that they needed the judgement of Solomon.

In fact, the bimbashi was well equipped to deal with most problems: it was the interpretation of the rules which counted. The Code of Military Law in the Sudan was the same as that of the Egyptian Army and in turn was based on the Indian codes of military law. Although similar to British military law, the powers of punishment available to a company commander were far greater than anything in the British army.

For example, depending on the seriousness of the crime, he could punish a private soldier by awarding fourteen days confined to barracks, twenty-eight days' detention or twenty-five lashes with a rhinoceros-hide whip. In the British army this was limited to seven days confined to barracks: anything more severe had to be referred to the commanding officer. One reason was racial: the colonial authorities were prepared to treat their native troops more severely than their British counterparts. The other was expediency: such were the distances between corps head-quarters and company stations that it would have been impossible to handle justice quickly and effectively unless the bimbashi had additional powers vested in his command. This was especially true of the domestic cases which required quick solutions to stop them getting out of hand.

In his time in the Sudan Wingate had to deal with two crimes of passion. The first, at Gedaref, involved murder when a soldier accidentally killed his rival during a quarrel about a woman. Realising that it was a case of mischance Wingate decided not to send the case up to corps headquarters because he knew that the man would probably be imprisoned for manslaughter. He also realised that the culprit was already suffering severe remorse for what he had done. As he said later, his reasons were quite clear-cut.

Here is an ignorant Sudanese peasant, his mind is quite uncomplicated, all his reactions are those of a normal, primitive creature in excellent health and good spirits. Since he is a man, he is capable of showing great virtues, as I have reason to know, and he is capable of suffering mental distress. He never intended to kill the dead man, but for this mishap he will be put in prison for a number of years. To inflict on such a man the hardship of such a punishment, to shut him away from his natural surroundings, would be in my opinion a crime greater than this particular manslaughter.

While there is a degree of lofty paternalism in Wingate's reaction – revealed by his vocabulary – he was also impelled by an intense dislike of imprisonment as a punishment. 'Living at King George's expense', he called it. Far better, he reasoned, to deal with each case on its merits and to secure a form of correction which did not entail imprisonment. This did not mean that he was not prepared to use corporal punishment. On the contrary, although he was sickened by it, he believed that the short sharp shock of a beating was far better than confining a man in jail. In the second serious domestic case, at Kassala, he sentenced a man to twenty-five lashes for attempted rape and told him that it should have been treble that amount, such was the savagery of the attack.

In this case, as in others, Wingate took care to be present when the sentence was carried out. 'If one accepts the responsibility of punishing a man,' he said, 'it is one's common duty to take the trouble to see that the punishment is properly carried out and that he is neither victimised nor favoured.' Not that he ever found it an edifying spectacle. The victim was spread-eagled on the ground, his back covered by a silk sheet to prevent the twelve-foot-long whip breaking the skin and the beating was done by the bash shawish, or sergeant-major. Wingate noted that, almost invariably, the man would take the punishment silently and when it was over he would pull on his shirt, stand to attention and salute before returning to his lines. With his memories of childhood beatings Wingate always insisted that he himself would never be able to remain silent under physical torture: none the less, later in his military career in Palestine, Ethiopia and Burma, he insisted on a strict code of punishment, including beatings, for the men under his command.

Wingate also came to the conclusion that his men would be more content if they were kept busy. With his second-in-command, a native Sudanese officer, or *yuzbashi* (captain), he maintained a busy training programme and instituted a weekly competition with the prize of a sheep for the platoon which unloaded and assembled its Vickers machine-gun in the shortest time. Each Idara had three rifle platoons and a support section. He also stimulated their interest in marksmanship by creating a realistic moving target in the shape of a man on horseback followed by a naked runner carrying a spear. Made out of sheet metal and mounted in a wooden frame it would be drawn across the desert by a lorry and gave Wingate's men no end of pleasure.

There was also a serious side to the soldiering. In support of the civil authority SDF patrols were used whenever there were outbreaks of trouble which could not be contained by the civilian District Commissioner and his local policemen. Wingate undertook one such patrol in 1931 and the reports from these incidents provided the SDF with an intriguing record of its activities in the pre-war years. Without fast roads and with few cars or lorries able to operate in desert conditions, the patrols had to rely on camels, donkeys and the men's own fitness to get into any area suspected of being troublesome. Only rarely were shots fired; the most serious incident of this period took place in 1928 when an SDF Idara of the Equatorial Corps put down an insurrection by the Nuer tribe following the murder of the local District Commissioner, Captain H. V. Ferguson.

Each Idara was also supposed to carry out a number of treks during the autumn and winter to show the flag in the remote areas of the country. These could last a week or more and during that time the men had to be entirely self-sufficient: each man carried with him his own supplies of *dura* flour and salt for making bread and it was up to the bimbashi to augment the rations by shooting the copious amounts of game which could be found in the rolling uplands and forests of eastern Sudan. Not only was he responsible for feeding his men, he also had to make sure that at the day's end he brought them to an adequate water supply. In this respect, the use of water, Wingate operated strict rules. For himself he restricted his intake to half a pint a day: 'My urine was the colour of strong tea,' he told his father. The men under his command were more fortunate. Two mugs of water were supplied at breakfast but no one was allowed to drink again until evening; to stop their mouths drying up during the march the men were encouraged to suck date stones. Experiments with his own diet were another feature of the treks. While his men ate meat he would often content himself with dates and unleavened bread spread with cod-liver oil. Personal hygiene was also a matter for experimentation. Washing and shaving were forbidden and it was during these treks that Wingate developed the habit, which he never lost, of cleaning his body with a stiff brush.

The Dinder country which was his territory is a mixture of desert scrubland and thick thorny forests split by dry river beds and small streams. Much of it had not been explored and the maps were rudimentary enough for each trek to take on the aspect of an adventure. Setting off in the cool morning – in the cold season temperatures could be as low as 2°F – the men would swing into the march, lu-luing their rhythmic tribal songs. Ahead lay a long slow trek in the ever-growing heat, broken at midday, until the shade of evening brought a welcome rest for the night. A *zeriba*, a temporary fortification cut from thick thorn bushes and sage brushes, would be constructed for the Idara's protection, a campfire would be lit and dinner prepared as darkness fell. The night air would be alive with a mixture of sounds: the soft padding of the camels as they walked into the lines, the steady thumping to restore the beasts' circulation after the day's march and, later still, the chatter of the men laughing and joking around the campfires. Beyond the *zeriba* the immensity of the hills stretched in darkness and a silence so intense that it was impossible not to hear the slightest sound. And overhead the sky was covered with the sharp brightness of African stars.

If the scene is touched by romance then on one level it was a fabulous existence: Wingate felt that he had tasted the salt of life and its savour

would never leave him. Even the dangers helped to mould his character
and he had several brushes with injury or death. Once, on trek, his men
were alarmed by the sudden appearance of a large snake and after chasing
it into the cover of nearby rocks summoned Wingate to kill it. It
presented a difficult target and the first shot missed, leaving the snake
free to retaliate. As Wingate took aim again the snake, a spitting cobra,
lurched at him and sprayed venom into his face. Fortunately he was
wearing sunglasses, otherwise he would have been blinded. On another
occasion his horse was almost pulled from underneath him by an attacking hyena which he was able to shoot with his revolver. Again, the
experience had a lasting effect on him.

He fell back heavily onto the ground and I saw that he must have been hit in
the spine because his hind legs were useless. He began to drag himself away and
I followed to make an end of him when I saw something very remarkable. Two
more hyenas rushed out and confronted me and then took up their place on
either side of their wounded comrade and began to shoulder him along. I
followed them for a little way, but except for looking back now and then and
snarling at me, they concentrated all their attention on getting the cripple back
to the bush. They did it in a most businesslike way and all three disappeared
after a couple of minutes.

Here, beyond the reach of artificial civilising influences, life could be
clean and uncomplicated and he and his men were bonded by the ideals
of service to a common cause. However, the experience of trekking
would leave a lasting effect not just on his personal development; it
would also influence the way he viewed soldiering. Alone with his men
in the wastes of the Dinder country he learned a number of useful
lessons. The first was that, properly trained and motivated, small groups
of men could learn to survive in a hostile environment. Second, they
could operate in isolation far from home base provided that they were
properly led and had faith in their commanders. Third, they had to be
kept up to the mark and galvanised by constant training, the more
realistic the better.

An opportunity to test himself and his men came early in 1931 when,
at the request of the local District Commissioner, he led a long patrol in
the Dinder and Gallegu country in pursuit of Ethiopian poachers who
had been killing animals in the game reserve. By SDF standards it was a
common enough operation but for Wingate it gave him the first opportunity to handle a small body of armed men under what amounted to
active service conditions.

The two sections of men were drawn from number 2 Idara, Eastern Arab Corps, then under Wingate's command at Singa on the Blue Nile. Because news of the patrol was common knowledge before the men set out in the early morning of 11 April 1931, Wingate let it be known that his first destination was the town of Roseires to the south. The ruse worked. Instead of following the normal route through Abu Hash his patrol set off across country towards the River Dinder where the poachers were reported to be operating. There they found several tracks of men and mules which, although several days old, gave them a vital lead; throughout the operation Wingate was to be impressed by the poachers' ability to scatter and re-form whenever they felt threatened.

At Umm Orug island Wingate had another piece of luck when local traders told him that around forty Ethiopian poachers with mules had been seen in the area a few days earlier. They had then scattered after being buzzed by a patrolling RAF aircraft. This incident irritated Wingate and in his report he concluded that aircraft were useless for hunting poachers because they 'associate the appearance of aircraft with the approach of soldiery and are on their guard'. However, tracks there were aplenty in the vicinity but it was not until the late morning of 19 April near the Gallegu River that the patrol made its first sighting of two poachers with a camel. Although they made off to the north, Wingate and one of his men gave chase on horseback and were able to capture them after a headlong dash over two miles. It was to be the first of several arrests and one, a former SDF trooper, was given a pardon on condition that he told Wingate where the main body of poachers was operating.

During the next phase of the operation Wingate had his first experience of violent death when a party of nine poachers resisted arrest near Ras Amer. They had been drying the meat from the carcasses of the game they had shot and were taken by surprise when Wingate's patrol surrounded them. One, an old man dressed in the blue jersey of the SDF, stood his ground in a nearby ravine and started shooting his ancient Remington rifle. Fearing for his life, one of Wingate's best soldiers, Onbashi Omar Et Tigni, returned fire and killed him with a single shot to the head.

'I turned his body over on its back and a feeling of extraordinary sadness and of regret came over me,' remembered Wingate later.

Here was a man who had nothing much to lose in this world except his life. He gained a meagre living at a dangerous trade, he had never harmed me and yet I had taken from him his chief possession. His was the first dead body I had ever seen. He was an outlaw and an alien. I might have accounted his death as less to me than a beast's and yet I felt a sympathy with him which was greater than the sympathy I felt with the living. At that moment he looked to me truly noble, in his ragged clothes with his dead face turned up to mine.

Most soldiers experience a variety of conflicting emotions after encountering their first enemy casualty or killing a man in battle. For some it is indifference. Wingate's future commander in Burma, Field Marshal Sir William Slim, remembered 'the most intense satisfaction' of shooting a Turkish soldier in Mesopotamia in 1917. This was the acme of all his training on the ranges, the proof that skill in marksmanship was essential to the soldier's trade. Others have echoed Wingate and have written about their intense sadness and uneasiness at the loss of human life. For them it is a reminder of their own mortality.

The killing of the old poacher was a turning point of sorts because later Wingate found that it could so easily have been him. His sergeant, Shawish Magdoub Mohd Ali, had also taken aim at the old man and was about to shoot when his commanding officer appeared in his sights in the field of fire. Henceforth, as Wingate admitted to Peggy in a lengthy letter-cum-diary written during the expedition, he would always treat death as a simple fact of life.

Darling, I have I think loved mercy and justice but I have yielded too much to my own desires and lusts and because I wanted to. And to this extent my house is built on the sands of self, the dread of whose destruction frightens me. These thoughts have given me great comfort because I feel I can now cast aside this self-love – and that should it please God to take my life I shall know that my love for his creation lives on, and that my own self is a small part of me.

The letter, along with others, was not posted but was kept in a sealed bundle, marked: 'In the event of my death please send this packet to Miss Peggy Jelley, Hawkstone, Fareham, Hampshire, England.'

It was not to be the patrol's last incident. The following day they marched to the Gallegu and then on to Ain Es Shems on the Dinder, where they caught two poachers in the act of preparing a heavy animal trap. The biggest haul came in the late morning of 21 April when the patrol surrounded eleven poachers busy loading half a dozen camels with dried meat. Despite repeated appeals to them to surrender there was another fire-fight in which one poacher was killed and another injured. There was further action later in the day when Wingate and his groom gave chase to a young poacher and shot him in the foot. As Wingate reported, the tally could have been higher but for the hard going. 'As our horses were dead beat and we had four rounds left we gave up the pursuit and sat down in the river bed to wait for the section.'

Convinced that the poaching gang had dispersed, the patrol returned to Singa on 26 April. It had been a reasonable haul: eleven prisoners, seven camels, one donkey and three tons of dried meat and hides, the greater part of which had to be burned. The patrol had also captured three rifles, one of which was a Remington made in the USA during the 1860s. Used by the Egyptian Army, large numbers of them had fallen into Arab hands after the Mahdist annihilation of General William Hicks's expedition into Kordofan in 1883. The most important result of the patrol, though, was the convincing evidence that the Ethiopian poaching gangs did most of their recruitment on the Sudanese side of the border and that many of their most capable men were former soldiers of the SDF.

The report was well received by the Governor-General, Sir John Maffey, who praised it for the 'very interesting narrative of a most successful expedition conducted with great dash and judgement'. The accolade was well deserved for Wingate had shown considerable military flair and determination in bringing the patrol to a successful conclusion. Faced by offensive action – albeit from untrained men equipped with obsolete weapons – he had not panicked and had put his men's own training to good use. He had also demonstrated tactical skill at the Gallegu by extending the section and surrounding the poaching party. In short, he had proved to himself and to his superiors that he could lead small groups of men in action; no bad experience for a twenty-seven-year-old officer.

Later, in 1939 when he was at a low ebb mentally following his service in Palestine, Wingate was to over-emphasise both the importance of the patrol and its significance to his development as a soldier. Also, demonstrating to the full the feelings of persecution which accompanied his worst depressions, he came to believe that he had been given no recognition and received no credit for planning and carrying out 'a wide sweeping march through country held to be impassable and never previously traversed, which resulted in complete surprise of numerous groups of Abyssinian and Sudanese bandits for the first time since the war'. This was not strictly true but, as we shall see, it was brought forward as evidence of his military ability at a time when Wingate was engaged in a lengthy battle with the War Office to clear his name after receiving an adverse report from his superior officers in Palestine. At the time, in 1931, it was enough that he had proved himself to be an above-average officer in the SDF.

Because physical conditions were harsh in the Sudan and because their officers were expected to work hard during the cycle of treks and patrols which culminated in annual field manoeuvres, the SDF granted their officers three months' leave of absence. This was usually taken in the summer and it allowed the men to return to Britain to recharge their batteries or to travel further afield in search of fresh adventures. (Wingate's colleague Hugh Boustead was a noted mountaineer and spent one of his leaves taking part in an attempt on Mount Everest in the Himalayas.) Invariably Wingate spent his leaves in England, visiting his parents and spending as much time as possible with Peggy at Hawkstone. Although they were opposed to the match the Jelleys had reconciled themselves to the fact that their daughter would eventually marry 'that rude young man' but the engagement was not announced until 2 September 1932 as Wingate's final period of service in the Sudan Defence Force came to an end. Even then Wingate managed to cause further offence to the Jelleys by offering Peggy the choice of an engagement ring or buying a car which they could both enjoy. Typically, Wingate solved the problem by buying both and Peggy was presented with a handsome eternity ring.

One of the problems faced by the couple was finding time to be with one another without the interference of their respective parents. Wingate's mother in particular showed a tendency to be possessive and felt that he should spend more time at home during his leaves. Not that she disliked Peggy, but she believed that he should not impose himself on the Jelleys' hospitality. On more than one occasion, as Wingate admitted in letters to his brother Granville, there were 'family storms' if he overstayed his time at Hawkstone. Left to themselves, away from the social round – they often visited friends of Peggy's in Devon – the couple spent much of their time planning their future and talking earnestly about Wingate's ambitions. He also told her about the worrying depressions which had darkened his time in the Sudan, describing them, in the language of the day, as 'attacks of nerves'. Peggy proved a good listener and more than once Wingate admitted that her calm nature and happy disposition countered his gloomier nature in much the same way that his mother had acted as a foil to his father. They made an intense and serious-minded couple and the relationship gradually became more intimate. To the free-thinking Sybil this came as something of a surprise but not because she herself was being prudish for her brother's sake: 'Ordey, although he could indulge at times, was in general pretty abstemious in such things as drink, smoking and sex.'

For most of their engagement, though, the relationship had to be kept alive by correspondence and throughout his time in the Sudan Wingate also took pains to keep in touch with his family. Never a voluminous letter writer, he was consistent and affectionate, however short the letter. When Granville went up to Oxford he wrote to congratulate him, and to warn him against mistaking 'dreams for actions, the common fault at universities'. At other times he would send a cheque and, with typical generosity, arranged for Granville to buy a dinner jacket on his personal account at his tailor, Holts. Monica was sent three guineas for a new ball dress and all five siblings received odd amounts of money with the customary injunction that it need not be repaid. And, whenever he could, he sent funds to his parents' Central Asian Mission, as well as to other deserving charities.

This generosity extended to helping those in need and, even while he was in the Sudan, he was never slow to come to the assistance of the men who had served with him at Larkhill. When one, Sergeant Evans of 18th Battery, was invalided out of the army with deafness in his left ear, Wingate responded to his call for help and did his utmost to find him civilian employment. At the time Evans had been serving in India with 5th Brigade and was ensconced in the military hospital at Netley but Wingate still did what he could to help him by sending him money for rail fares and other expenses. Another gunner asked for support in buying himself out the army because his father was seriously ill and once again Wingate was prepared to help. His mother, alarmed about the possibility of falling victim to debt, warned against such generosity but Wingate always replied that while he served in the Sudan he was well paid and could afford to be liberal with his funds.

The Sudan offered other experiences. For the first time in his life he flew in an aircraft, a Fairey IIIF biplane of 47 Squadron based in Khartoum. Aircraft had been used in operations in the Sudan as early as 1916 when the Royal Flying Corps had helped to suppress a rebellion mounted by Ali Dinar, the Sultan of Darfur, and in the early 1920s they had been deployed as part of the Air Ministry's policy of 'air control'. The creation of Hugh Trenchard, the founding father of the RAF, this new strategic concept was based on the use of bomber aircraft, supported by armoured cars and men on the ground, to police the more remote areas of empire where communications and usable roads were few and far between. At first the deployment was only meant to be temporary but in 1928 aircraft helped the SDF to suppress the Nuer uprising in support of the prophet Gwek Wonding; declaring himself to be 'greatly impressed' by the performance, Sir John Maffey lent his support to the permanent stationing of a squadron in Khartoum.

The aircraft were also used on communications duties and Wingate had his first flight when he was taken from Kassala to Khartoum. At first he enjoyed himself – the pilot took the aircraft down to treetop level over the jungle and Wingate was entranced by the huge herds of elephants – but they soon ran into turbulence. 'I had no hesitation about what to do,' said Wingate. 'I leaned over the edge of the plane and was violently sick, when to my horror a powerful air eddy caught the contents of my stomach and plastered the face of the unfortunate pilot, who turned round and looked at me with a reproachful expression.' The incident notwithstanding, Wingate greatly admired the pilots and their courage but he never overcame his fear of flying. During the war he was forced to fly frequently on operational duty and although he grew accustomed to the routine he admitted that he never felt entirely happy in an aircraft.

Other Sudanese experiences were more pleasurable. Because SDF officers were supposed to supplement their men's rations with game, Wingate was given a game licence and soon became a proficient shot. Hunting was also an important part of SDF culture – another officer, Wilfred Thesiger, reckoned that he shot fifty lions during his service – and, as with polo, expertise with the gun added greatly to an officer's stature within the service. Towards the end of his career in the Sudan, on 8 December 1932, he shot a bull elephant in Khor Gallegu and brought the tusks back for sale to the agents in Khartoum. On another occasion he shot a buffalo and sent its head back to England to be mounted. Unfortunately it was forgotten until, alerted by an 'unpleasant smell', his mother threw out the box and its mouldering contents. (The only other time she broke the family rule of non-interference was when she threw out her son's collected works of George Bernard Shaw, because she believed them to be immoral.)

Although the days of the classic big game hunter were at an end British personnel serving in the Sudan still took a keen interest in the pursuit. None went so far as the distinguished Scottish hunter Walter Dalrymple Maitland Bell who sawed open a dead elephant's skull in order to discover the exact position of the brain because he believed that a successful head shot would prevent the rest of the herd panicking, but several SDF officers developed their own theories about hunting lore and practice. Wingate was no exception and one of his favourite and most-voiced theories was that a hunter could escape a charging buffalo by running at it and diving aside at the last minute. The chance to put theory into practice came when he was hunting with a fellow officer whose first shot missed the target and caused the herd to panic. With the nearest shelter 200 yards away, Wingate picked up his rifle and ran.

'I had no time to think or feel,' he said later. 'It was all over in a few seconds. I ran as fast as my legs would carry me towards the buffalo and gave a sharp spring to the right a moment before we collided. As I sprang I turned half left and fired my rifle in the animal just behind the shoulder as it swept past.' Just as his natural courage on the hunting field had won him plaudits in Britain so too did his hunting exploits attract favourable notice in the Sudan. Certainly there is nothing to suggest that, apart from his untidiness and occasionally eccentric habits, he was anything other than a typical young officer on attachment in a remote and exciting part of the empire.

Even the attacks of depression were put down to experience: 'If I had to choose whether to go through that appalling misery again or to forfeit the experience, I should certainly choose the misery,' he wrote in 1937. 'To go through it and come out on the other side still holding on to one's faith and one's reason gives one something of the utmost value. I mean a knowledge of the depths; after that, the ordinary terrors of life are as nothing.'

Something of that fortitude, of the need to test himself, can be seen in his last months in the Sudan when he determined to round off his service with a desert expedition. It was not an uncommon decision. British army officers have been, and still are, doughty desert travellers and the period between the two world wars offered them the opportunity to venture into the remaining uncharted areas of Africa and Arabia. As Wingate was fond of saying, advances in transport systems were making the world a smaller place and there would soon be few opportunities to find areas unsuited to the internal combustion engine. After much thought he fixed on the Sea of Sand, the huge and variegated desert of Libya. Not only was it relatively near at hand – he only had six weeks' leave – but, being largely in Egyptian territory, there would be no political problems obtaining permission for an expedition. Also he was experienced in handling camels, his preferred form of transport.

At first he had toyed with the idea of finding the lost army of Cambyses, the vast force of 50,000 Persian soldiers who were supposed to have been swallowed up by a sandstorm in 525 BC. According to Herodotus, whose *Histories* provide the only evidence for this unlikely occurrence, the men were attempting to reach the oasis of Siwa and the fabulous temple of Jupiter Ammon when they were surprised and buried while taking their midday meal. The idea intrigued Wingate: 'Somewhere in the sand sea their bones, swords and armour await the arrival of the man who is destined to recall to a softer generation the memory of their heroic failure.' He was not the first British soldier to be excited by the idea – Gordon awaiting his fate in Khartoum in 1884 had pondered the mystery of the desert swallowing up an entire army – but it was too vague a notion to pursue without huge funds and equally large amounts of time to spare.

Instead, Wingate settled on a plan for searching for Zerzura, the lost oasis of fluttering birds, the so-called 'oasis of the blacks' which had been home to a race of beautiful black giants. The idea had haunted earlier travellers and it was every Libyan explorer's dream to discover the secret of this fabulous place where the water was supposed to be sweet and the air was thought to be thronged with huge flocks of song-birds. Although this was the stuff of legend it was not beyond the realms of possibility that such an oasis had at one time existed, only to disappear in the shifting landscapes and changing weather patterns.

Having discussed the idea with Dr John Ball, the Director of Desert Surveys in Egypt, Wingate started laying his plans in the early part of 1932. His first need was to get the necessary leave but this routine request turned out to be more difficult than he first imagined because the army was unwilling to underwrite a risky expedition undertaken by a relatively young subaltern. Once more he called on Cousin Rex to help and the War Office eventually gave grudging permission for the expedition to take place provided that Wingate signed a document excluding the British government from paying any benefits should he be injured or die during the expedition.

This caused him little heartache; rather more difficult was the matter of paying for the expedition and borrowing the necessary instruments. Again luck favoured him and a request to the Royal Geographical Society brought the grant of surveying instruments worth £118: these included a theodolite, a mountain aneroid and a chronometer, all vital for fixing his position and plotting his course in the desert's changing wastes. Fortunately these arrived sooner than expected and he was able to practise with them during several treks in November and December 1932. The actual costs of running the expedition he would have to meet himself and following some frantic estimating he reckoned that he could afford to hire the services of thirteen camels and four Arabs to mind them. Cars were already widely used as desert transport – other desert soldiers such as Glubb in southern Iraq had driven them and the British army had made lengthy motorised reconnaissance trips into Libya during the First World War – but Wingate was not convinced and decided to rely on the small and sturdy Egyptian hill camel for his expedition's transport. Finally, he computed that the expedition would take forty days, a suitably biblical number.

For his personal needs he allowed a staple diet of dates, biscuits, cod-liver oil, leavened by a small supply of chocolate, raisins, flour and tinned grapefruit. His clothes would reflect the terrain: on top of his bush shirt and shorts he would wear an Arab *gibbah*, or long shirt, and the outfit would be completed by open sandals and a turban. Finally, he wrote to his mother describing the journey as being in the nature of an essay and asking her to pray for his safety. Thus prepared he left Khartoum by train on 28 January 1933, bound for Dakhlat where the rest of his party awaited him.

Later he told the story of his expedition in a long essay which was published in the *Geographical Magazine* in April 1934 and although it is hardly a classic account of desert exploration it still makes an enthralling tale about a young man's first adventure. His companions are lovingly described: Es Senussi Abdullah, an experienced desert traveller who knew 'all the desert lore'; the honest Abd Er Rahman Saleh; the feline Abu Bekr Guweia; and the youthful Suleimen Foula, a mere boy 'with a craving for cigarettes'. Setting off westwards into the desert over 'a sort of dry sludge of fine sand and black stone' they soon found the going hard and the pace slow. Personal discomforts mounted. The days were hot and the nights bitterly cold and the unyielding desert sands caused Wingate's feet to blister.

It took four and a half days to reach the wells at Bir Abu Mungar where they left a supply dump before beginning the long climb up the Kufra road which led into the sand sea proper. Like other travellers Wingate also noticed that the desert was not a lunar landscape but a place of variety and endless fascination, rolling dunes here, limestone escarpments there. Here the party had to rely on dead reckoning and on the experience and sense of direction of Es Senussi Abdullah to guide them to the outer western reaches of the desert. This was the area thought most likely to hold the secret of Zerzura and the sudden onslaught of a sandstorm seemed a good harbinger: according to Es Senussi, 'it was due to the action of the Djinn who inhabited that spot.'

It was, of course, only a fond hope, and no trace of an oasis was found. But worse was to follow. As they made their way across the dunes on 18

February they saw a black object on the northern ridge. Hurrying towards it Wingate was appalled to find that it was 'a hated symbol of civilisation', a black Ford motor car belonging to the Desert Surveys of Egypt. The moment was not as shattering as Scott's discovery of Amundsen's flag at the South Pole, but it was still a heavy blow and seemed to mock all Wingate's 'labour and effort'. Because the engine started easily, its occupants were obviously near at hand but Wingate had neither time nor inclination to look for them. Instead he wrote a note and lashed it to the windscreen. Two days later the car and its owner, Patrick Clayton of the Desert Survey, caught up with them and Wingate was presented with irrefutable evidence that cars were already traversing ground which he and his little party had covered on foot.

Ahead lay the return route to civilisation which 'passed uneventfully enough in calm and pleasant weather'. On 6 March they spent their last night in the desert at the friendly oasis of Sheikh Maihub, Wingate once more indulging in reading Hume's *History of England* by candlelight. And then it was all over.

As we drove through the pleasant gardens of the oasis I recalled all the abortive effort, the vain expense of strength, of the enterprise, now rapidly receding into the past, and wondered whether I regretted it; whether I would do it again were the chance to offer. Before I considered it I knew that the experience was real, and that therefore I would always treasure it.[4]

This is the voice of the true desert traveller, of the man who swears never again to split his head in long glaring days on the march only to discover that a month of ease fills him with impatience to be back in the sands to inflict on himself the same torments once more. True, the expedition accomplished little – Wingate collected some specimens and proved that Zerzura did not lie on the Kufra road – but it proved to him that he had the inner strength to live and survive in an unforgiving environment. Later, he was to revise his opinion about the expedition's worth: on an annotated off-print of his essay in the *Geographical Journal*, he scored out the original title, 'In Search of Zerzura' and replaced it with 'An Abortive Journey'. In the months which followed, though, he was to be overcome with nostalgia for his desert journey, proving perhaps the old adage that you can take the man out of the desert but you cannot take the desert out of the man.

From Dakhlat Wingate returned to the main railway line and a few days later he was back in the bewildering civilisation of Cairo where he was able to recharge his batteries before returning to England. His weight had dropped to around nine stone, he was gaunt and weatherbeaten and his feet were so badly swollen that he had to have a new pair of shoes made for him. Friends hardly recognised him but he was filled with an inner contentment that not even a change in his travel arrangements could disrupt. Before leaving Khartoum in January Wingate had booked a return berth on the *Viceroy of India*, at that time P & O's largest and most modern liner on the Southampton–Bombay route. However, when he reached Cairo he discovered that he would have to travel on the *Cathay*, a smaller liner following on a few days later from Australia. It was another decision which would change the course of his life.

What followed next is difficult to decipher, so various are the accounts which have been left by the main protagonists. However, some facts are unalterable. Wingate joined the *Cathay* at Port Said where the liner halted after coming through the Suez Canal. His appearance immediately attracted comment amongst the liner's passengers, who could not help noticing the intense-looking young man with longish hair, unkempt clothes and rather odd over-sized yellow shoes. Amongst them were Alice and Walter Paterson who were returning to their home in Aberdeenshire with their sixteen-year-old daughter Lorna.

Walter Paterson was a typical product of the British Empire. Scots born and bred – he had attended the Edinburgh Academy – he had followed the family tradition of working in Ceylon and had retired in 1920 after a successful career as a director of the Aitken, Spence trading company. His wife Alice Ivy Wigmore had been born in south Australia but her childhood was spent mainly in London where she studied at the Royal College of Music. An accomplished attractive woman, she had married Paterson when she was eighteen and their only child, Lorna, was born in 1917 in Colombo, three years before they returned to Scotland to live in a house called The Place of Tilliefoure at Monymusk, Aberdeenshire. Had it not been for the illness and subsequent death of Ivy's mother, the Patersons would not have visited Australia; had they not done so, Lorna would not have met and fallen in love with Wingate. Shortly before the *Cathay* reached Malta they had contrived a meeting and were to be inseparable for the rest of the voyage.

Later in life, Lorna would always maintain that it was love at first sight: 'I marched up to him and said, you're the man I'm going to marry, we both felt the same way about it.' In her memoir of Wingate Ivy was equally insistent that there was a strong mutual attraction and that it seemed to be almost fated that her daughter would marry this 'obscure young subaltern'.

By the time we reached Malta, Orde seemed to have made up his mind. He and I went ashore together and at a small café we drank some chocolate and whipped cream, and this is what happened. It is all so vivid to me that it might have been yesterday. He said to me: 'If anyone had told me that this would happen to me with a girl of sixteen, I would not have believed them.' (He seemed to have forgotten that when his own father, then a young soldier of twenty-six, first met his mother and determined to marry her one day, she was even younger.) I told him, 'She has to go back to school when we arrive home.' He replied, 'Yes, I know, but if there is any chance for me, I will wait for her as long as I have to.' Feeling a little sorry for him, I then said something which was strange, but quite true. 'Well, you know, a fortune teller read Lorna's hand a few years ago and said she would marry a very famous soldier, so you never know – why, Mr Wingate, it might be you.'[5]

Even allowing for the romantic allure created by the passing of the years – Ivy wrote the account in the late 1950s – it is still an extraordinary tale. Wingate was thirty at the time and cautious of sudden enthusiasms; Lorna was sixteen and still a pupil at a prestigious girls' school, St Leonard's at St Andrews in Fife. However, both were strong-willed and independent spirits and both were aware of the powerful sense of mutual attraction. What Ivy's account fails to make clear was her own and her husband's opposition to the match which became more apparent after they returned to Scotland. They wanted Lorna to go to Oxford and were therefore not in favour of her marrying so young, before she had a chance to experience life. Not unnaturally the Patersons hoped it would be a short shipboard romance, although when they parted company at Marseilles it was reluctantly agreed that Wingate could continue to see their daughter.

There was no mention of Peggy who was waiting for Wingate in London. According to Mary, friends of the family called Morse had lent the couple their flat in Belgrave Square so that they could be alone together 'without incurring displeasure'. It should have been a joyous reunion but Wingate was forced to tell the hapless Peggy that he was in love with someone else and that he was unable to marry her. After days of painful discussion the engagement was broken off, much to the disgust of the Jelleys. Wingate's first biographer, Christopher Sykes, claimed that the incident passed 'without any feeling of rancour on her part'. The sorry fact was that Peggy was devastated and told her sister that Wingate 'had beaten to death an innocent dove'.

Eventually we were to learn of the anguish and bitter tears that were to follow. Poor Peggy, not only the ruthless end to the love of her life but the secondary pain of having to face the world without him. She acted with courage and dignity, but her family never forgave Orde what he had done to her. What man can be forgiven for having ditched a girl after all those years of keeping her tied to him with such a long engagement, including intimacy that should not have been unless marriage was to follow.[6]

It is not difficult to understand Peggy's pain. After five years of engagement to a man whom she wanted to marry, she had to acknowledge the fact that he had fallen in love with someone else. Suddenly all those months of separation and of holding a torch for him in the face of her parents' opposition had come to nothing. In her pain she hugged the grief to herself: 'My mind completely went. I was acting like a zombie. I went out and everyone saw me but my mind was blank.' Not that it was any easier for Wingate, but comforted by his belief that every moral question was clear-cut and that it was evil to compromise, he probably realised that, once he had met Lorna, he could never marry Peggy.

Sykes hints at another reason for the break-up. Wingate often told Peggy that he was disconcerted by her resemblance to his own mother, that she was too patient and forgiving and would not stand up to him and that he needed a more confrontational kind of relationship if he were to achieve his full potential. Certainly, according to Lorna, Wingate seemed to reassess his relationship to his mother at this time and came to the conclusion that by subjugating herself to her husband's will she had 'renounced her freedom of choice'. Moreover, he felt an angry distress when

he realised that, as a little boy, his mother's code made her a partner in his father's injustice towards him, and that his comfort was cut off at its natural source. He forgave the hard treatment, the remembered humiliations, the punishments and the perpetual criticism only with a smile of affectionate admiration for the old man who had meted them out; but he felt that his mother had failed him and his love for her never quite recovered.

The end of the affair was occasioned by Wingate's meeting with Lorna who was prepared to stand up to him and to treat him on equal terms, but there were obviously deeper reasons. As Peggy seemed to resemble his mother too closely – Mary remembered her as 'a loving, tender, often amusing intelligent girl' – then it seems likely that Wingate could never have been completely happy with her. Confronted by the memory of his mother's withdrawal of love and her complicity in the beatings he endured as a child, he would always choose the harsher, narrow, uncompromising path taken by his father.

As for Peggy, she forgave Wingate and, to her family's consternation, she continued to be loyal to him, carrying the memory like a flame for the rest of her life. She never married.

Five

IN THE LAND OF BEULAH

It was not an easy return for Wingate. Quite apart from the broken engagement, itself a traumatic moment for both parties, he had to accustom himself once more to regimental life. It also meant going back to subaltern's rank and pay: having been a temporary captain he was once more a lieutenant and had to put to one side the memory of being a well-paid company commander in the Sudan. After visiting his parents in Godalming he booked into his club, the Army and Navy, and waited for the War Office to give him his next posting. Like other officers who served overseas he was out of touch with many military innovations and although he had attended manoeuvres on Salisbury Plain with Hugh Boustead in 1931 the Royal Artillery was anxious to see him working once more with a modern artillery battery. Accordingly, he was posted to the 9th Field Brigade stationed at Bulford Camp near Amesbury in Wiltshire.

In a sense it was a return to the carefree days he had enjoyed on Salisbury Plain before going out to the Sudan. Derek Tulloch had returned from India and, now married, was living nearby at Larkhill. Come the autumn both men were back hunting with the South and West Wilts; Wingate was still entitled to an army charger, a dark bay horse called Hannibal, and he also owned Martrine, a sweet-natured mare which he had bought in Devonshire during his last leave from the Sudan. Once again both men were able to indulge to the full their love of hunting and racing but the light-hearted bachelor days of earlier years had gone for ever. Tulloch was married, Wingate hoped to marry Lorna in two years' time and both men were anxious to be promoted to a captaincy before they were much older.

There was also much new information to assimilate. Although the Artillery did not embark on a complete mechanisation programme until

1936 many units, the 9th Field Brigade included, had exchanged their draught horses for modern lorries and tractors and there was much experimentation with new and different types of artillery pieces. Although cuts in defence expenditure prevented a sustained and uniform introduction of new equipment, the Royal Artillery had an excellent director in Major-General H. A. Lewis who set his designers to work to produce excellent compromise weapons such as the 18/25-pounder gun which was towed by a Morris-Commercial tractor, better known as the Quad.

Welcome though these innovations were to the more forward-looking gunners, the steady shortage of funds had repercussions in the army's manpower. Not only was there a shortage of trained soldiers coming up through the ranks, there was a bottleneck in the promotion ladder with too many elderly captains and majors blocking the path of the younger subalterns. For that reason it was essential to win a nomination to the army's Staff College at Camberley which provided selected middle-ranking officers with intensive professional training in what might be loosely described as the function of command. For any officer aiming for the stars it was an essential prerequisite to have the initials *psc* (passed staff college) after his name in the *Army List* and entry to the courses was hotly contested. Once he had been promoted captain in 1935 Wingate began the lengthy business of applying; selection was by nomination and depended on first passing a formal examination, getting through an interview by a military committee and scrutiny of personal reports.

Until that time Wingate had to get back into the swing of regimental soldiering and he made a happy start by becoming the brigade's senior subaltern, a post which gave him certain privileges such as starting the day somewhat later than his fellows and ending it at lunchtime. As before, it was considered 'bad form' for an officer to be seen in the battery office after lunch. He also became the brigade's messing officer and attended a cookery course at Aldershot which he attacked with his usual enthusiasm. Just as he had experimented with diets during his time in the Sudan, attempting time and time again to find the best mixture of food and drink to match the body's needs, so too did he take considerable interest in his new-found knowledge. Instead of giving the men 'chocolate pudding and plum duff and sausages and mash all the year round' he advocated cutting down on meat and introducing more fresh fruit and vegetables. It was not a popular regime; it was not meant to be, but Wingate rarely allowed personal approval to stand in the way of his own thinking about military matters.

Being an efficient officer he did not attract any comment from the other members of the mess and he experienced little difficulty fitting in to the life and work of the brigade. He enjoyed life in the mess, 'with a guest night once a month at which nearly everybody got drunk and broke up the furniture', he went to parties given by senior officers and in the company of his fellow subalterns he drank beer and played poker. Books remained a delight in his spare time and he bought a small two-seater car which he handled with his usual disregard for driving skills or mechanical perfection. In short, he was not very different from any other youngish gunner officer of the period: involved in his work and the life of the brigade, living a quiet life on small means.

For a long time, though, he felt deeply nostalgic about his life in the Sudan. Not only did he miss the independence of commanding a company of men but he regretted leaving the country and its fantastic landscapes. Days spent in the saddle under a sweltering sun and the nights around the campfire in the desert places were but a lingering memory. His sadness was compounded by the sudden death of his sister Constance (Tossie) early in 1934. He also continued to be prone to attacks of depression which would strike him unawares and it was difficult to mask them in a camp which offered nothing in the way of privacy. While at Bulford Wingate shared a spartan quarter with three other subalterns but the walls were so thin that he could hear his fellow lodgers' every movement. Although he could shut himself away in his room complete seclusion was impossible and, once more, he fought his way through any attack by immersing himself in work.

In time, as he began to enjoy and appreciate his new surroundings, his longing for the Sudan became less acute. Like most people who enjoy field sports Wingate was at heart a countryman and like any other colonial servant he took immense delight in returning to England's greenness. Before the advent of modern farming's huge unbroken fields, suggestive of the North American prairies, much of Salisbury Plain was still dissected by thickets and copses of fir and hazel trees, waiting to be explored. It was all a stark contrast to the mean military camp at Bulford with its corrugated iron and brick barrack blocks and its simple wooden garrison church. A visiting overseas dignitary catching sight of the camp from the top of nearby Beacon Hill is supposed to have remarked to his military hosts, 'Ah, one of your penal settlements, I presume?'

Wingate also had to wrestle with the problem of his relationship with Lorna who was ensconced for the time being in her Scottish boarding school and working to get into Oxford. As a result her mother Ivy

Paterson became an intermediary and whenever she visited London Wingate made a point of meeting her and pressing his case. In her memoir Ivy makes it clear that she enjoyed these meetings which included visits to the theatre and concerts and that she was much attracted by the idea of an interesting young man like Wingate becoming her son-in-law. Although she admitted to being surprised when Lorna decided to give up Oxford for marriage, a decision which offended her husband because he had 'an old-fashioned attitude towards the obligations of husbands', the overall impression is that throughout 1934, when Lorna was in England preparing for the Oxford entrance examination, the relationship was allowed to develop smoothly and unhurriedly.

The reality was rather different. Not unnaturally, Ivy felt protective towards her daughter and wanted her to get the best out of life. Her husband was also concerned: he was a wealthy man and he wondered if a captain's pay would be sufficient for married life. When questioned on this point Wingate never hid the fact that he did not have a large private income but he always made it equally clear that he felt himself to be the Patersons' social equal. None the less, with Walter Paterson opposing the match on financial grounds and with Ivy insisting that Lorna should continue her education, an immediate marriage was out of the question and, at first, Wingate seemed to accept the fact. In the spring of 1934 he told the Patersons that he was prepared to wait until she had finished with Oxford before marrying her. However, he was sufficiently confident about the unofficial nature of their 'engagement' to confide the news to Sybil in a letter written on 15 April.

It may perhaps cheer you to hear that I am very happy in the discovery that Lorna loves me and the hope which has been strengthened, in the very personal and incommunicable sort of way in which such hopes are strengthened, that I shall one day be in a position to marry her and shall do so ... I have the strongest belief in the existence and goodness of God and I rejoice in the conviction that there is a plan in life for those that will believe it.

Sybil was all in favour of her brother marrying and throughout this period offered nothing but support. Wingate was also helped by Cousin Rex who wrote to Walter Paterson strongly recommending his kinsman as a suitable husband for Lorna. He also entertained Ivy when she was in London and revealed to her the family connection with Lawrence of Arabia with whom Wingate was often later compared. At that time the facts surrounding Lawrence's illegitimate birth were not widely known and Ivy was sworn to secrecy about this relationship: Lawrence's father changed his name from Chapman after abandoning his wife and setting up home with his mistress Sarah Junner. Chapman's sister Maria had married Thomas Browne, Wingate's great-great-grandfather.

Although she never doubted the fact that Wingate was a 'gentleman' and although she enjoyed his company in London – she was fascinated by his ease in female company – Ivy continued to insist that Lorna, 'a mere child', should not rush into an early marriage. However, during the autumn of 1934 Wingate and Lorna decided that they could no longer wait to get married: with both sides taking opposing points of view a collision was inevitable and when it came it settled the issue once and for all. The final disagreement was Ivy's insistence that the couple should not be allowed to spend too much time alone together, at that time an understandable objection given a social position which insisted such behaviour was 'not the done thing'. As so often happens, though, the flashpoint was caused by a minor altercation when Ivy strongly objected to her daughter being alone with Wingate in his car. There was a row, Wingate responded bitterly to the criticism and Ivy left in high dudgeon. The next day, 1 October 1934, Wingate wrote to Ivy castigating her for her lack of trust.

If I was rude I am sorry. If I hurt you, I am very sorry. The fact is that it was imperative that I should have a long uninterrupted talk with Lorna then and there and nowhere else and at no other time. We had no time as you must have reflected later to get out of the streets and what you suppose can be done in a car in lighted streets I can't think.

Ivy, if you really cannot trust us there is just as much danger in two hours out of your sight as in two hours in a car together – in fact more if we're devoid of decency. Such a supposition is so intolerable that we must regard you as an implacable foe if you persist in it.

Having established his main point – that he thought Ivy wrong to be angry with them for spending time alone together – Wingate proceeded to a more general criticism of the way in which the Patersons treated Lorna. It is an extraordinary document, nine pages long, which hammers home Wingate's belief that Ivy suffocated her daughter emotionally and stood in danger of damaging her psychologically.

Ivy as God made me I tell you I am frightened for her – you'll have on your hands a nervous breakdown before you know what has happened. If that happens Ivy I shall curse you from the bottom of my soul – and you will not escape that curse. May God judge you and may God render it to you again if you refuse to listen to me.

Acknowledging that many people would think him mad for writing to a prospective mother-in-law in such an openly critical way, Wingate excused himself on two counts. First, Ivy had insisted on candidness and honesty and he felt he was displaying both to a woman well able to accept his frank comments. Second, he loved Lorna and had her well-being at heart: the whole tone of the letter smacks of his devotion and of his refusal to be swayed by 'worldly euphemisms'. Having made his position clear he ended the letter by stating his intention to marry Lorna 'the sooner the better' provided that the Patersons would continue to give their daughter her allowance. On the same day Wingate wrote a shorter letter to Walter Paterson formally requesting his daughter's hand in marriage.

Both letters caused consternation in the Paterson household but at least the situation allowed everyone to concentrate their minds. Realising that their daughter was intent on marrying Wingate and that further opposition would only drive her away from them, the Patersons agreed to the marriage taking place early in the following year, 1935. Not that the agreement brought their problems to an end. As late as 13 January 1935, less than a fortnight before their wedding, Wingate had to entreat Sybil to postpone a visit to the Patersons because 'affairs are in such a state at present that your visit would almost certainly do harm'. So tense was the situation that the wedding was not announced beforehand and Wingate did not trouble to tell his brother officers, although a notice did appear in *The Times* on the Saturday following the marriage. When the time came he merely took some leave and returned to Bulford with his new bride.

The couple were married in Chelsea Old Church on 24 January 1935, the day before Lorna's birthday. It was a quiet affair attended only by the immediate family but Lorna displayed a fine degree of individuality by carrying a white vellum copy of *Wuthering Heights* instead of a Bible. The music, too, reflected their tastes: Bunyan's great hymn 'To be a pilgrim', the Pilgrim's Chorus from Tannhäuser and, as Ivy noted, 'prophetically, Parry's Jerusalem'.

After two weeks' honeymoon in Devon Wingate and Lorna took up residence in a married quarter in Somme Lines. Situated on the edge of Bulford camp overlooking the plain, it was hardly a prepossessing first house, having large bare rooms, but it was a start and Wingate revelled in the task of turning it into a home. Carpets and furniture were bought in nearby Salisbury, including a huge oak bookcase for Wingate's library, an eclectic collection which included at that time Doughty's *Arabia*

Deserta and Richard Burton's translation of *The Arabian Nights*. It took time to restore some order to the house but to the disgust of their servants, a batman and a cook, the Wingates were hardly a houseproud couple. Tulloch remembered one occasion when the servants were on leave and the Wingates simply ploughed their way through their wedding presents, allowing the dirty plates and cutlery to pile up unwashed in the kitchen.

There were other eccentricities. Acting on a whim of Lorna's, Wingate bought from Harrods' pet department a small Barbary ape with ginger hair and pale blue stomach and the creature, called Bathsheba, soon became well known around the camp. Wingate was not the first soldier to own an odd pet – as a young officer in Cyprus Kitchener had kept a bear – but it added to his reputation as an original free-thinking officer. While respecting his friend's tastes, Tulloch had little love for the beast and recalled one occasion when he was asked to look after it. 'I shall remember that fortnight to my dying day. The little brute made messes everywhere, but preferably in my nursery because she realised Nurse particularly hated her guts.' Guests, too, had to take their chance with the ape when they stayed with the Wingates for its cage was kept in the one spare room. Slightly less quaint was the Wingates' habit of sleeping outside on warm summer nights: a mattress would be loaded on to the car and off they would go on to the plain to spend the night in a remote spot.

Having been promoted captain Wingate started studying for the Staff College in 1935 but Lorna noticed that he lacked concentration and was all too easily diverted from his work. In addition to his military duties he continued to train and ride his horses and there was a steady round of dinner parties. When the mood took him he could be an exhilarating guest, holding forth on a wide range of subjects, often late into the night. Tulloch noticed that although Lorna looked disconcertingly younger than her years, she had strong views of her own: 'Consequently on occasions a duel would ensue which was both entertaining and frequently instructive, but never dull.' With the Patersons continuing to pay an allowance to Lorna they were secure financially and were able to lead a reasonably comfortable existence. Later, Lorna was to remember it as an idyllic time with parties, cocktails at the Haunch of Venison pub in Salisbury, weekends in London and a large circle of army friends.

The enchantment was broken in the autumn of 1935 when he was posted to Sheffield as the adjutant to a Territorial Army formation, the 71st (West Riding) Field Brigade, Royal Artillery. This was part of a scheme to provide the part-time soldiers with a small core of training officers and senior non-commissioned officers from the regular army who were seconded to the Territorial Army for three years, and there was a good deal of competition to be posted to a pleasant part of the country; with their hunting traditions the Yeomanry regiments of the English West Country were an obvious first choice and Wingate was disappointed to get an industrial northern town. When he first arrived in Sheffield Wingate was dismayed by the harsh landscape and told Lorna that he was depressed by the thought of living in 'this alien country amongst people whom he might respect or sympathise with but with whom he could never feel at home'. His sense of gloom was not helped by living alone in a cheap city-centre hotel without Lorna and whenever he returned to Bulford the contrast between the two areas only unnerved him further.

The year ended badly, too. With Lorna in Aberdeenshire with her parents, Wingate found that there was no room for him at Godalming at Christmas – his parents imagined that he would be making his own arrangements for the festive season – and he was forced to stay in a hotel in Bloomsbury. Such was his sense of being an outcast from his family that he sulked, spent Christmas Day by himself and returned to Sheffield earlier than necessary.

Matters improved early in the new year when Wingate found rooms for himself and Lorna in The Peacock, a pleasant pub in the Derbyshire village of Baslow close to the Duke of Devonshire's seat at Chatsworth Park. As Lorna told her mother, the arrangement, though quaint, was necessary because of the impossibility of finding suitable accommodation in Sheffield. The only available houses for rent were large semi-detached villas – 'too big for two people like us' – and the few flats in the city were 'very dark and dingy'. Ideally, they would have liked a cottage in the country, but of this kind of house 'there does not appear to be a single specimen'. Living in a pub had its advantages in that Lorna did not have to trouble with housework but it also meant parting with some of their possessions. Wingate sold his horses, and Bathsheba was presented to a local midwife who had taken a fancy to the beast; what luggage they needed was sent north and the Wingates settled down to a new and quite different regime.

Being an adjutant gave him a good deal of responsibility for the smooth running of the brigade and it was considered the most useful appointment for any officer aspiring to higher command. As the commanding officer's personal staff officer he dealt with disciplinary matters, manning and recruitment, personnel topics and all social occasions. Normally, in the regular army an adjutant's work is never done; he works the longest hours in the regiment and always has to be 'on call'. However, in a territorial regiment where the men were part-time soldiers the pace of life was different and geared towards evening training nights and weekend duties. As a result the pattern of Wingate's days began to change. Because most of his work was concentrated in the evenings the day began late. He would get up at midday, bathe, have lunch and then read or go for a walk before driving in to the brigade's handsomely proportioned drill hall, officially Norfolk Barracks, in Edmund Road, Sheffield. Following a three-hour training stint the officers would repair to the mess to talk and drink beer and it would be one o'clock in the morning before he got back to The Peacock. Even then sleep was impossible; he rarely went straight to bed and would sit in the snug with the landlord and one or two regulars to drink more beer and talk.

Although Wingate enjoyed his work and the life which went with it he seemed to realise that this was very much a dormant period. This can be seen in his attitude to his work. Efficient and well regarded he might have been but he never seems to have engaged himself fully in his vocation. One reason was that he felt Sheffield to be an alien place, quite different from anything he had previously experienced. He liked the people well enough – although he frequently despaired of their heavy drinking and male-dominated society and smiled at the provincial nature of the dances which were held each Saturday night in the drill hall – but he never warmed to his surroundings. Wordsworth continued to be an influence and he would tell Lorna that the men had been brutalised by their environment; that, although essentially decent and good, they had been beaten down by a system which exploited their labour for little return and left thousands of their number unemployed. It was always a surprise to him that they did not rise up in revolution against the society which oppressed them.

The other reason was his continuing awareness of his own potential. In the Sudan and earlier it had been a bright flame which sustained him in quiet moments; in Sheffield it was more of an ember. Whenever he felt the familiar doubts returning he would take to his bed and read voraciously. He also read in his bath, to the detriment of many of his books, but the long slow days at home allowed him to retire from reality into a world of his own making. Partly this was a necessity because he needed privacy to study for his forthcoming staff examinations but it was also a reclusive response to his predicament. Like many iron dreamers who see life in terms of action, he was stultified by his work in Sheffield and felt the need to store up his energies for the time when they would be needed. He had made this clear to himself as early as April 1931 in a journal he had kept about his experiences in the desert places of the Dinder country.

The present is in this sense a dream, as is the future and the past, to live rightly is to achieve a proper blending of the three, or rather two, for the present in this sense does not exist ... What I mean is that we cannot wholly live either here and now or in an imagined future, but we must have just that touch with the ideal that will enable us to work with a blessing upon reality.

Certainly, from Lorna's descriptions of life at Baslow it is clear that Wingate found temporary respite from his concerns about the relationship between dreams and the reality of action by cutting back on his bodily activities to the point of inertia.

Orde's physical life moved to a rhythm which was very much closer to the natural animal state than to the artificial civilised one; he alternated periods of great and sustained activity, sometimes very long periods, with days or even months of physical repose which amounted to lethargy. At these times he preferred to go to bed and stay there as long as possible, eating very little and drinking enormous quantities of weak tea; having two or three hot baths a day and going back to bed to sleep, wake up and talk or read for a few hours, and then throw down the book and go to sleep again. His mind never withdrew altogether from the conflict; he allowed it to relax, and was quite prepared to pull the bedclothes up to his chin and read sentimental novels, or talk nonsense of his own particular brand; but his mind slept with one eye open and an ear always lifted to the wind, and in a second it could start up and spring like a leopard on a vanishing thought.

Even allowing for the overwriting, bordering on fancy, this is a remarkable description of Wingate's predilections during this period of his life. On one level behaviour of this kind was symptomatic of his mental state; on another, his metabolic rate seems to have slowed down to such an extent that he was able to endure long periods of inactivity without injuring his health, for it is equally clear that he took little exercise while staying at Baslow. By way of compensation he ate very little and continued his experiments with diet in an attempt to find the correct level of nutrition needed to keep his body fit. At this time he became a firm believer in the value of eating raw vegetables – especially onions – and, to the surprise of fellow officers, he also started chewing oranges whole.

Behind his inactivity, though, lay a real fear that he would fail to get a nomination to Staff College. His first attempt at the written examination in February 1936 had ended in failure but he passed at the second attempt in June. Although he had 'qualified' for a course at Staff College he still had to be 'nominated' and it was on this point that his application ran into difficulties. The four competitive places open to gunners went to those who had the highest marks and Wingate was not amongst their number. He now had to rely on getting one of the eight places open to the remaining 'qualified' gunners who would be chosen on their past records.

Once again when confronted by a personal crisis, Wingate was assailed by doubt. He knew that around 100 gunner officers had applied for the course and he was far from certain that his record would give him an edge over rivals who had a solid record of service with operational artillery formations. To his mind everything would hang on his period in the Sudan where he had commanded the equivalent of an infantry company and on the successful outcome of his Zerzura expedition. Telling Lorna that he did not feel particularly hopeful, he decided to play the Cousin Rex card once more. On 10 June he wrote to him requesting his help and listing the reasons why he felt he should be nominated. It was hardly an unassuming document.

It would be false modesty in me to say that I have a poor opinion of my abilities. I have a very high opinion of them. Given the opportunity that is necessary to the use of my ability I see no reason why I should not reach the highest rank in the British Army. But if I fail now, in this my last chance, to get to Camberley, I shall not waste any more time in the Army. I shall regard it as a sign of failure.

This was not an idle threat – Lorna wrote to her mother at the same time saying that they dreaded three more years in Sheffield – and Cousin Rex took the hint. A letter of recommendation was sent to the Army Council at the War Office, but to no avail. On 24 July, while Wingate was with his men at their annual summer camp at Catterick he read in *The Times* that he was not amongst the officers to receive a nomination. It is possible that Cousin Rex's last-minute plea did more harm than good but without any evidence it is impossible to say if the Army Council were swayed by this obvious attempt at using family influence. More likely Wingate was beaten by rival officers with higher marks in the written examination and a stronger record of regimental service at home or in India. Whatever the reason it was a tremendous blow to his pride and it reawakened all his insecurities about the army's high command whom he now felt had victimised him on account of his secondment to the Sudan Defence Force. In high dudgeon he told Cousin Rex that he was going to make an official complaint to the Army Council and would enlist support from Sir John Maffey.

In fact there was no need for him to follow through this plan of action. On 3 August the new Chief of the Imperial General Staff, General Sir Cyril Deverell, visited Catterick to watch the Territorials' final manoeuvres and Wingate took the opportunity to confront him. Having introduced himself and made his position clear he presented the general with a copy of his Zerzura essay, asking at the same time if his expedition had been taken into account when his application was being discussed. This was a shrewd move as the elderly Deverell was chairman of the Staff College selection committee and Wingate felt entirely vindicated when the general confessed that there had been no mention of the expedition.

On paper Wingate's direct behaviour seems rude and pushy and many fellow officers would have been outraged by his obvious self-promotion but there was method to it. Wingate was merely taking a gamble that Deverell would regard it as initiative – good commanders encourage enterprise in their younger officers – and so it proved. Deverell promised to look into the matter and although the answer came back that he could find no reason to find Wingate a place at Camberley or at the Indian Army Staff College at Quetta, he promised to give him the first available staff job suited to his rank. This came sooner than expected and was related directly to Wingate's skills as an Arabic interpreter. On 7 September he was posted as an intelligence officer in the rank of captain, GSO3 'I', with the 5th Division which was stationed at Haifa in Palestine. The news came at a doubly good time, for he was still coming to terms with the death of his father who had died suddenly on 21 August, in his eighty-fourth year.

For an ambitious soldier it was an excellent appointment. In 1936 Palestine had been the scene of sporadic but fierce fighting between the Arabs and Jews and the British response had been to send two divisions – the 5th and the 8th – to contain the situation. Although they were in a difficult position, caught between the rival communities, the question of internal security had to be solved and it presented staff officers in both divisions with a wide range of opportunities. As it turned out, the military presence was only able to contain the violence, for the problem required a political solution, but it is interesting to note the number of prominent Second World War commanders who saw service in Palestine between 1936 and 1939. These included John Dill, Bernard Montgomery, Neil Ritchie and Archibald Wavell.

That Britain should have been involved in the country was due to a remarkable blend of imperial realpolitik and historical romanticism. After the First World War Britain had undertaken to rule Palestine through the mandate of the League of Nations, a form of trust by which the country was administered under the supervision of a Permanent Mandates Commission. Under its terms Britain had also included the Balfour Declaration of 1917, a wartime pledge of support for the creation of a Jewish national homeland in Palestine. The region contained a 90 per cent Arab majority – including the land on the east bank of the River Jordan – but at the time Britain had been anxious to receive, and to continue receiving, Jewish money and support for the war effort. (In fairness, it was not just a matter of good business: Balfour, the British Foreign Secretary, was as much moved by his reverence for the Old Testament as he was concerned with the need to create a British sphere of influence in the area.)

As a result of the Anglo-French carve-up of the Middle East at the end of the war the new country of Transjordan came into being under the control of the Hashemite ruler the Emir Abdullah and this was excluded from the terms of the Balfour Declaration though not from the mandate, much to the anger of the Zionists. However, although Transjordan was to influence the events of 1936, the flashpoint was provided in Europe where Hitler's Nazi Germany had begun persecuting the country's Jewish population. In November 1935 he had passed the Nuremberg Laws which deprived the Jews of German citizenship and under the terms of an agreement known as Ha'avara, the Nazi regime encouraged the emigration of wealthy Jews and their property from Germany to Palestine. The result was an upsurge of Jewish immigration into Palestine: in 1931 it stood at 4,075 but by 1935 the figure had shot up to 61,854.[1] As the rate increased so too was there a greater need to purchase land in Palestine and Transjordan: through the Jewish Agency Arab lands were sold off to the new settlers and in consequence many Arab smallholders were deprived of their livings.

To the Arabs it suddenly seemed all too likely that a Jewish state could be created in Palestine and that they would end up as the underclass. The response came on 15 April 1936 when the Arabs in Palestine began a general strike which quickly escalated into a series of vicious attacks on Jewish property. Two Jews were killed in Nablus, their murders setting off a chain reaction of further murders followed by retaliation, and by the end of the month there had been serious outbreaks of violence in all the main centres of population. The Haifa–Lyddah railway line was attacked; there were widespread demonstrations against the British authorities while, in country areas, attacks on Jewish property led to reprisals by Irgun Zvai Leumi, the Zionist defence organisation. In the north there was evidence of Syrian-inspired terrorism.

Initially the British responded by using minimum force to put down the Arab revolt and defend their interests. Not until the end of August, by which time they had reinforced the garrison, were they able to threaten the imposition of martial law as a solution to the problem. At the same time, in response to calls by Arab leaders to end the strike, the British government announced the formation of the Peel Commission to investigate the root of the problem in Palestine by taking evidence from the different factions. All this recent history had to be assimilated and understood before Wingate could take up his posting as an intelligence officer with one of the divisions responsible for maintaining internal security in the country.

After being suitably briefed at the division's permanent headquarters at Catterick, Wingate went out to Palestine in September 1936 still unsure if he had received a permanent posting. (Somewhat to his disgust the Royal Artillery had appointed a temporary adjutant to the 71st Field Brigade in Sheffield and it had been made clear to him that much would depend on his performance in Palestine.) On paper, though, everything was in his favour. He might not have passed the Staff College course but he had been given a staff appointment with a formation on active service. His experience of Arabic and his work as an interpreter would also stand him in good stead because in the troubled community of Palestine there was a marked tendency for the British to favour the Arabs, especially the Bedouin tribes of the desert.

Indeed, some British officials and soldiers, such as St John Philby in Saudi Arabia or Glubb Pasha in Transjordan, had committed themselves to the Arab world and considered themselves in some small measure to be more Arab than the Arabs. It was not an unusual stance for British imperial servants to take. District officers operating in the more remote areas of India tended to take a fierce delight and pride in the company of people they served; British colonels from the shires spoke with pride about their 'little Gurkhas' and affected to despise the argumentative Hindu lawyers and middle-class babus who clamoured noisily for independence. Their preference was for the martial races, Pathans or Punjabi Muslims, people who were loyal and trustworthy and whose demeanour seemed to mirror British values. In the Middle East they regarded the Bedouin people as a warrior race which maintained high standards of chivalry and courtesy, which disdained luxury yet was generous and hospitable, which regarded courage and personal honour as supreme virtues and despised meanness, cowardice and soft living. It was natural for Englishmen schooled in the classics and Arthurian literature to see such people as the true heirs of Saladin and to admire them for the apparent simplicity of the rules which governed their lives.

Had Wingate followed suit it would have been an entirely natural path to have taken and one which would have kept him in step with the majority of his brother officers. Instead, he took the other direction and espoused the cause of the Jews.

On one level there were well-grounded political antecedents for Wingate's decision. During the First World War the idea of a Jewish Palestine annexed to the British Empire was an attractive proposition: in addition to Balfour, the idea was supported by Prime Minister David Lloyd George, Lord Milner, Winston Churchill and an influential group of Foreign Office officials including the Middle East expert Mark Sykes. As a result of this support Chaim Weizmann and Nahum Sokolov, two leading lights in the World Zionist Organisation, had moved to London. By 1914 Weizmann was president of the Zionist Federation and enjoyed strong links with the British cabinet.

However, although much of the support was based on a sentimental attachment to the biblical concept of the Holy Land and on the need to secure British interests in the area, Britain was forced to link this policy to its traditional support for the Arabs, especially to its Hashemite allies in Iraq and Transjordan. Because successive cabinet members were themselves unaware of the strength of political Zionism – the concept of turning Palestine into a national Jewish state – they believed that immigration would be modest and therefore easily controlled. The creation of a politically powerful Jewish Agency in 1929 and the increase in Jewish immigration into Palestine in the 1930s changed all that.

On another, more immediate, level, Wingate's decision was unusual. His family background, including Cousin Rex's interests and career, should have made him more sympathetic to the Arab cause. After all, Wingate was a fluent speaker who had read the Koran. There was, too, a widely held, though never formally expressed, sense of anti-Semitism in the British army. This was never as powerful as the Dreyfus affair which had almost split the French army apart in the 1890s but there was an endemic antipathy towards the Jews in the upper echelons of the officer

class. Certainly, Wingate's support for the Zionist cause in Palestine did
not endear him to many officers serving with the 5th Division at that
time. Such hostility rarely troubled him. Lorna recalled that while
lunching with the Bishop of Jerusalem, an elderly lady told Wingate that
as he was so fond of the Jews he should become one himself. Modestly
casting down his eyes, Wingate replied, 'Alas, I am not circumcised.'

There are no easy reasons to explain why Wingate became such a
pronounced Zionist within months of his arrival in the country. So
strong were his beliefs by the beginning of 1937 that he was able to admit
to Moshe Shertok (later Sharett), a future Prime Minister of Israel, that
he had adopted Zionism 'as a religion'. Sybil was convinced that the
underlying reason was his deep knowledge of biblical history, particularly
as it is expressed in the Old Testament. In a letter to Derek Tulloch in
1962 she explained that this understanding 'which no one outside the
small dissenting sects can understand' provided a powerful impetus.
Knowing the text so thoroughly, the plight of the Jews came into sharp
focus during his first months in Haifa; even the names on the map were
powerful reminders of the Children of Israel, the Kingdom of David and
the ancient Judaism of the Law and the Prophets. When he saw Gath he
was reminded that David took refuge there after fleeing from Saul; at
Ein Harod Gideon raised his 300 to rout the Midianites and across the
Jordan were the lands where the tribes of Reuben, Gad and Manasseh
had pitched their tents and tended their flocks. For Wingate, the Old
Testament was not just a religious text but an inspiring history of the
Jewish people and an account of their national aspirations.

There is also much to be said for the argument bruited in Christopher
Sykes's biography, by Wilfred Thesiger and others, that Wingate preferred the Jews because he admired their resilience in the face of the
world's hostility and could relate it on a smaller scale to his own
experiences. Citing the bullying at his prep school, his non-acceptance
at Charterhouse and the running incident at Woolwich, he told Thesiger
that he understood what it was like to be persecuted. This would fit in
with the persecution complex which never entirely left him and coloured
his response to personal setbacks. Equally persuasive is the view that
Wingate would have supported Zionism for the good reason that most
of his fellow officers were pro-Arab: not for him the easy path of
conformity when other possibilities existed. It is also clear that, following
his experiences in Sheffield, Wingate had to have a cause to adopt and
defend and had found it in Zionism.

While there is a good deal of truth in all three explanations, they are rooted in the sense of mystical destiny which was promulgated around Wingate's name by his family and friends after his death. To them, Wingate regarded Zionism as a cause for which all his previous training and experience had prepared him; it was waiting for him when he arrived in Palestine. There were, though, other, more pragmatic reasons for Wingate's conversion. When he arrived in Haifa he did what any self-respecting intelligence officer would do on taking up a new posting. He studied the political background, spoke to as many local people as possible, picked up local gossip and attempted to reach some tentative conclusions about the current situation. He began learning Hebrew too, using the same system that had stood him in such good stead in the Sudan: writing down and memorising the vocabulary and listening to the language being spoken. Having settled in the division's temporary headquarters in Haifa's Savoy Hotel he set about the process of educating himself about the country and its peoples.

It was a hard regime but he relished it. He told his mother on 14 October that he began work at 8.00 a.m. and the day ended at 11.00 p.m.: 'I really have been working for once in my life and it is no idle excuse to say that when I have had a moment I had to spend it asleep ... one has to be careful what one says, especially in my job, or I could tell you some interesting things.' At the same time there was the compensation of getting to know the country: Nazareth, 'a lovely place among hills with many cypresses and high walls'; Tiberias, 'a beautiful little town projecting into the sea'; the hamlet of Capernaum and, above all, the striking image of fishermen pulling in their nets in the Sea of Galilee. In these country areas where 'the desert really begins to blossom like the rose', he began to admire the energy and commitment of the Jewish settlers to till the soil and to revolutionise a centuries-old system of agriculture. As Wingate saw it, these were ambitious hardworking people, preparing for future prosperity, and they were so different from the Arabs who cared little for the land other than as a means to an end.

His instincts were given further shape when he began to meet the Jewish community and found that he enjoyed being in their company. He particularly relished the society of David Hacohen, a businessman, and Emmanuel Wilenski (Yalan), an architect, both of whom had to overcome their natural suspicion that Wingate, a British intelligence officer, was nothing more than a spy. In this respect their doubts were allayed both by the passionate interest which Wingate took in all things Jewish and also by his friendship with another pro-Zionist officer, his colleague Roy Strange, the Special Service Officer for Haifa.

Not that Wingate disliked the Arabs – his knowledge of their language and religious culture was too strong for a simple division – but as he told his mother and Cousin Rex, he preferred the company of the more cosmopolitan Jewish political activists and the hardworking settlers in the country's kibbutzim, or collective farms. Almost as an antidote to his experience in Sheffield where he felt he had encountered the tail end of a moribund industrial tradition in which businessmen were past their prime by the age of forty-five, he believed that the Jews of Palestine had the energy and commitment to create a new homeland. Although written in 1939, at the end of his service in Palestine, the mood is caught in 'Palestine in Imperial Strategy', a paper he wrote for Field Marshal Lord Edmund Ironside, soon to become a short-lived Chief of the Imperial General Staff.

The natural character of the Jew is that of a creative individualist. He is obstinate but a tremendous worker capable of great enthusiasm. All over the world today are homeless Jews with not only excellent natural faculties but also a high degree of training. Skoda's [the Czech arms manufacturer] had many Jews in key positions. An arms factory allied to Skoda's was owned and run by Jews. Jewish chemists and mechanics are numerous. The proportion of trained mathematicians is very high. Every prophecy made by the British official [sic] regarding Jewish development in Palestine during the past twenty years has proved baseless. Lands that [Sir John] Hope Simpson [leader of the Royal Commission on Palestine, 1930] proclaimed uncultivable have long borne profitable crops. To judge the potential of a vigorous, intelligent and desperate people by that of the feckless and flaccid populations we are accustomed to deal with is a blunder.

By then Wingate had come to the conclusion that the new Jewish homeland, formed from Palestine and Transjordan, should be an integral part of the empire and a bulwark of British interests in the Middle East with its own Jewish armed forces, but the thinking had begun soon after his arrival in the country. In a letter written to Cousin Rex on 12 January 1937 he claimed, amongst other personal assertions about the shortcomings of Britain's policies in the Middle East, that he wanted to raise a Jewish Brigade 'to defend our interests in the coming war'. It was the first mention of what was to become a lifelong ambition.

Lorna's arrival in Haifa also quickened his interests in Zionism: in some respects she was to become a more perfervid supporter of the movement than her husband. She arrived in Alexandria in November and, after spending a short time in Egypt, they motored up to Jerusalem where Wingate had a new appointment as intelligence officer at corps headquarters. At first they stayed in the Hotel Fast but by April, and following a visit by Ivy, they had moved into a first-storey flat in the Christian Arab quarter of British Talbieh. As Wingate told Ivy, it was the ideal home for them.

The advantages are as follows:
1. It is situated in the best and airiest quarter of Jerusalem.
2. It is near my office and, in the event of disturbances, comes within the zone certain of protection by British troops at all times.
3. We can stay here, thus obviating the annoyance and endless difficulties of constant moves.
4. It is an exceptionally nice flat of exactly the right size and type.

As he also pointed out in a letter full of domestic detail, the flat came with the disadvantage of being unfurnished and that the landlord insisted on doing this for them. Here Lorna's forcefulness, obviously a family trait, came into its own.

It was really quite useless to fix a figure at which this was to be done since he would then have insisted on doing it from his own or friends' shops and could have provided as much or as little as he felt inclined. We therefore hit on the novel arrangement of leaving it to him and Lorna to thrash it out together. She has chosen everything and exerted herself with great success to prevent any weakening on his part. So far she has screwed him up to two hundred pounds and I don't think she will get him to go any further.

Soon Lorna was helping in other ways. She started learning Hebrew and threw herself into the local social life, British and Jewish. On first meeting her, many were taken aback by her youthful looks – Tulloch had thought she looked little more than a girl – but she was possessed of a maturity and social poise beyond her years. In an age when most middle-class wives were supposed to be comely and competent adjuncts to their husbands' careers – this was doubly true in the colonies – Lorna was held in considerable regard. But beyond the niceties of the social round she soon showed herself to be as determined as her husband to understand the country and its people. This was particularly true of the Wingates' friendship with Chaim Weizmann who was to cement their interest in, and subsequent involvement with, the Zionist cause and its main protagonists.

They first met in December 1936 at an official dinner at Government House given by the High Commissioner Sir Arthur Wauchope, to whom, naturally enough, Wingate had been introduced by Cousin Rex. Although, unfairly, Wingate did not rate Wauchope very highly – a retired soldier, he had been appointed to the post in 1931 and managed to steer a reasonably neutral course between Arab and Jewish interests – he and Lorna were mightily impressed by Weizmann and their meeting at Government House was the beginning of a long and mutually beneficial relationship. (Although no believer in the Balfour Declaration Cousin Rex proved to be the catalyst once again: he had met Weizmann in Cairo in March 1918.) By the 1930s Weizmann was at the height of his powers. Recognised as the spiritual leader and guide of the Zionist cause, he had been a key player in the creation of the Balfour Declaration and had been the driving force behind the evolution of the Jewish Agency. His early work as a scientist and the subsequent sale of patents had made him a wealthy man, financially secure and independent. Something of a dandy with dark good looks, he was also possessed of great charm which few could resist. Sir Isaiah Berlin called him 'an irresistible political seducer'; leaders such as Churchill, Truman and Lloyd George endorsed the judgement and it was no surprise that the Wingates were similarly entranced. In the same letter to Cousin Rex, Wingate described him as 'a truly great man, and, I am proud to say, our friend'.

Weizmann and his wife Vera were equally impressed with this intense young couple: later in the month they arranged for them to be included in their party when Toscanini conducted a series of concerts given by the newly formed Palestine Symphony Orchestra. In time Wingate and his wife were to become regular visitors at the Weizmanns' palatial mansion at Rehovot, some fourteen miles to the south of Tel Aviv: a nephew Ezer Weizmann, then a boy, remembered the sense of excitement which would accompany any mention of a forthcoming visit by the Wingates. There is little doubt that Weizmann was impressed by the sincerity of Wingate's passionate concern for the creation of a Jewish homeland in Palestine and he realised, too, that he could be of use to him. (Unlike those who had earlier doubted Wingate's sincerity, Weizmann was well aware that converts to the Zionist cause were often its most committed supporters.)

It is also probable that Wingate's fervour compensated for the lack of interest which Weizmann's two sons took in Zionism. Indeed, by 1936 both Benjamin and Michael Weizmann were in a state of constant rebellion against their father, having made it clear that they felt no concern for his beliefs. Although Weizmann remained reasonably close to Michael, the older boy Benjamin was a disappointment who had drifted away from the closely knit family circle. Shortly after meeting Wingate, in November 1937, Weizmann confided to his wife the dismay he felt whenever he considered his relationship with his sons.

Benji and Michael each one in their own way are witness to my defeat. I have in my own clumsy way tried to make partial amends, but it is no good. We speak different languages and we have different standards of values, we are strangers; they not only belong to another generation, but almost to another category. I am a lonely man standing at the end of a road, a via dolorosa. I have no more courage left to face anything – and so much is expected from me.[2]

Given the pain behind Weizmann's words Wingate's arrival in his life must have seemed like an atonement and he quickly formed a deep attachment to him. Here was a young man who was not only much the same age as Benjamin but who was also a true disciple. Certainly, throughout their friendship in Palestine and, later, in London Weizmann was to allow Wingate a latitude not always granted to his closest Jewish associates. Always neatly dressed himself, he tolerated Wingate's unkempt appearance and made allowances for his angry outbursts and occasional temper tantrums. (As we shall see, he wisely distanced himself from some of Wingate's wilder political ideas.) Through him, too, Wingate was introduced to the inner councils of the Jewish Agency and was soon on intimate terms with its leading personalities, men of substance such as Shertok, Eliyahu Golomb and Emmanuel Wilenski, both Haganah commanders, David Ben-Gurion and Abba Eban. By the beginning of 1937 there was no doubting the strength of Wingate's commitment to the Zionist cause.

Six

DEFENDER OF THE FAITH

Wingate's friendship with Weizmann began at a demanding time in Britain's handling of the Palestine problem. For the first time in their relationship the Zionist leaders started to believe that the British government was no longer interested in implementing the terms of the Balfour Declaration and preferred a compromise which would allow Jew and Arab to co-exist in Palestine. Most of its political supporters had retired or were dead and in the Foreign Office there had been a shift in mood towards appeasing the Arab princes whose appeal for peace had helped to end the 1936 Arab revolt. (Although the Colonial Office was responsible for administering Palestine the mainly pro-Arab Foreign Office had overall supremacy in evolving British policy in the Middle East.) To this end Jewish immigration was restricted to 29,727 in 1936, less than half the figure for the previous year. Also, little was done to curtail the activities of Haj Amin al-Husseini, the Mufti of Jerusalem and leader of the Higher Arab Committee, who organised the policy of Arab terrorism against British and Jewish targets.

Inevitably, the change of heart created a shift in the direction of the Zionist movement. Veterans such as the revisionist Vladimir Jabotinsky believed that a confrontation was inevitable and that the Jews would be forced to fight for, and then defend, their national home. This was in direct opposition to Weizmann's policy of *havlagah* or restraint which was now being questioned by younger and more radical Zionists. The change of mood was also to influence Wingate's attitude to the creation of a Jewish homeland and, more immediately, to the need to protect the Jewish settlers. At the same time, being aware of the drift in British thinking, Weizmann put his weight behind the policy of partition which was slowly gaining favour amongst the members of the Peel Commission which reported on the future of Palestine during the winter of 1936–37.

Headed by Lord Peel, a grandson of Sir Robert Peel, the commission took evidence from Jewish, Arab and Christian sources and, after meeting sixty-six times, it published its findings in July 1937. As expected, the members of the commission concluded that division of Palestine into separate Jewish and Arab areas was the only solution to the problem: 'Partition seems to offer at least a chance of ultimate peace. We can see none in any other plan.' The Jewish area would consist of a coastal strip from Haifa to the south of Beer-Tuvia, with Jaffa excluded and joined to Jerusalem by a land strip, together with the traditional lands of Galilee. A new mandate would be created for Jerusalem and separate treaties would be concluded between the Arabs of Palestine and Transjordan on the one hand and with the new Jewish state on the other. Other recommendations included a ceiling on Jewish immigration and a ceiling on land purchases.

Inevitably, during the commission's proceedings, the future of Palestine was a matter for intense discussion. Inevitably, too, Wingate had his own opinion which he confided to Cousin Rex in a rambling letter of 12 January 1937. Taken as a whole it is a naïve document which contains several misunderstandings. (Amongst other recommendations he wanted to encourage Transjordan to join the Arab revolt to 'provide the excuse for the removal of the corrupt and slovenly Abdullah and the reclamation of the country for Palestine'. At the same time, the Mufti was encouraging Syrian terrorists to destabilise Transjordan so that a greater Arab Palestine could be carved out of the territory on both sides of the River Jordan.) What makes it interesting is Wingate's insistence that the Jews – 'who never broke the law and remained loyal throughout [the Arab revolt]' – could provide Britain with a firm and committed ally in the Middle East, provided that it was given the means to create its own armed forces.

The Jews are loyal to the Empire. The Jews are men of their word – they have always been so – in fact it is the Gentiles' main complaint against them. There are 15,000,000 Jews in the world. Palestine will take over a million within seven years. You can have no idea of what they have already done here. You would be amazed to see the desert blossom like a rose; intensive horticulture everywhere – such energy, faith, ability and inventiveness the world has not seen. I have seen the young Jews in the Kvutsots [kibbutzim]. I tell you that the Jews will provide a soldiery better than ours. We have only to train it. They will equip it.

It was a radical point of view. At the time the British army tended to think that the combat arms of its native regular and irregular forces could only be drawn from the so-called martial races. In the Indian army this had been adopted almost as a creed with preference being given to Punjabi Muslims, Sikhs, Gurkhas, Rajputs and Pathans; in Transjordan, the British-led Arab Legion consisted of Bedouin Arabs; in Iraq the Iraq Levies were recruited mainly from Assyrian Christians and in Aden a similar force was based on the warlike Awlaqi and Awdhali tribes. This concentration was accompanied by a belief that races which had been subjected to modern industrial life were second-rate; a contemporary Indian Army instruction booklet warned that those Muslims who 'live in cities and owing to a life of ease and to inbreeding are an effete race'. For that reason Bengali Hindus and Madrasis were considered suspect in India (although they both made names for themselves as military engineers) and, similarly, in the Middle East it was generally thought that town-based Arabs and Jews would never make decent soldiers. In making the proposal for the creation of a Jewish army – an idea which was to occupy him between 1937 and 1941 – Wingate was flying in the face of received military opinion in the British army.

Wingate's instincts were given momentum by the failure of the Peel Commission's recommendations to gain the necessary support: they were opposed in the Middle East by most of the Arab world, in London by the Foreign Office and the War Office chiefs of staff, and in Palestine by radical Jews who now believed more firmly than ever that they would have to fight if a homeland were ever to be created. 'We shall bring into the country all the Jews it can contain; we shall build a sound Jewish economy,' wrote David Ben-Gurion to his son in July 1937. 'We shall organise a sophisticated defence force – an elite army.'[1] In that respect Wingate's proposals were not unique: what made them different was a written submission to Weizmann on 31 May 1937 in which he and an unnamed brother officer, his colleague Lieutenant Antony Simonds, Royal Berkshire Regiment, offered their services to the Jewish cause.

You may recollect my views regarding the role Palestine Jewry might hope to play in a future world war. The application of this to the problem of the formation of a Jewish Palestine Defence Force is that it must be efficient and organised in a special manner.

For this reason I conclude that you have considered the advantages of including in its ranks a small number of British officers. I know the possible disadvantages of doing so, but my knowledge of military science joined to what I have observed of the confusion and muddle that invariably follow the attempts of untrained, or partially trained, persons to conduct an undertaking, have convinced me that you will not get the forces you need without such support ...

I wish to offer you, as head of the Zionist Movement, our services in case you should wish to accept them. Should you wish to do so, then may I ask you further to inquire my views on this most important subject, as I have much to say? It is of paramount importance to look far ahead and avoid mistakes which cannot be corrected afterwards. I know that you could recognise the need of trained and friendly military advice.

At the time Weizmann was in London where he had been arguing the case for acceptance of the partition scheme before the meeting of the Zionist Congress in Geneva in July. So inflammatory was the letter that Wingate entrusted its delivery to his mother-in-law who was returning to Britain after a visit to Palestine. He was wise to do so for in making such a proposition he was breaking all the rules and could have landed in serious trouble with his military superiors; equally sensibly, Weizmann replied cautiously on 20 June – 'I am proud and happy about the offer you are making and naturally I accept it with the greatest pleasure' – and sent the letter through an intermediary in a heavily sealed envelope. He also suggested that any future communications should be made through Shertok when he came to Europe later in the summer. However, Shertok was concerned about the involvement of Simonds whom he regarded as 'a light-weight champion [who] did not possess Orde's personality, his profoundness and his spiritual background'.

We always treated him a little slightly, and he complained to me bitterly. 'It is not that I am exactly like Orde,' he said to me. 'Supposing Orde would suddenly come to the conviction that in order to save Jewish Palestine, it would be necessary to blow up the Suez Canal, he would do it, but I wouldn't. I would also think of the British Empire.'

Weizmann must have known that Wingate and his younger colleague Tony Simonds were treading on thin ice. Although the Zionist Organisation in London was assisted by leaked information from Westminster – the Minister for Health Walter Elliot was particularly helpful to them in this respect – indiscretion has always been part of British political life and Weizmann thrived on gossip from Westminster. However, the offer he received from Wingate, a serving army officer, was not just indiscreet; it was potentially dangerous for all concerned. (While British officers served other Middle East rulers in little armies like the Arab Legion and the Iraq Levies they had been seconded by the War Office: at the time there was no Jewish force in which Wingate could serve on similar terms.) If the British authorities had known about it there is little doubt that, at best, Wingate and Simonds would have been sent home in disgrace. It would certainly have put the British in a difficult position in Palestine where as the mandatory power the administration was supposed to be impartial, although it has to be said that if Wingate had been friendly to the Arabs no one would have commented on it. On the other hand, as a serving intelligence officer it lay within Wingate's interests to trade information with the Jewish Agency: he always insisted that his motives were grounded in the need to promote the cause of friendly Jewish–British relations.

Not that Weizmann wanted to close down the source altogether. After all, as an intelligence officer at military headquarters in Jerusalem, Wingate was privy to confidential information which could be of use to the Jews. He also knew the importance of maintaining his own personal security: because he worried about concealed microphones being used in his office at GHQ he insisted on meeting his Jewish contacts in his car, a dilapidated Studebaker convertible. That Wingate continued to help Weizmann and his colleagues by passing on clandestine information is made clear by Blanche 'Baffy' Dugdale, another influential British Gentile who supported the Zionist cause in the 1930s and 1940s. A niece of A. J. Balfour, she was Weizmann's friend and confidante – through her were channelled Elliot's confidences – and in her private diaries she proved to be a shrewd observer of contemporary British-Jewish relations. While visiting Jerusalem in 1938 she met Wingate with Vera Weizmann on 23 January and was both surprised and gratified by the willingness with which he passed on confidential information to them.

He told us that Ibn Sa'ud's London representative had wired to Ibn Sa'ud, in answer to a question, that he understood a joint memorandum from all the Arab Kings on the subject of Palestine would be acceptable to HMG. This confirms Chaim's conviction of FO intrigue against policy. Wrote to Walter [Elliot] about it. Moshe [Shertok] will see that the letter goes safely. Lucky for us that Wingate's fanatical Zionism gets the better of his sense of duty as Intelligence Officer. He is clearly one of the instruments in God's hand.[2]

On one level this was fairly low-grade intelligence. In the wake of the Peel Commission's recommendations the British government had formed yet another commission under Sir John Woodhead to work out the details of partition, to which Weizmann had already committed himself. At the same time a new Arab revolt had broken out during 1937 and Britain was keen to prevent the intervention of the Arab princes – Ibn Saud of Saudi Arabia, Ghazi of Iraq, Abdullah of Transjordan and

Iman Yahya of Yemen – all of whom had conflicting interests in the outcome. Ibn Saud detested Zionism but he also feared that following partition his Hashemite rival Abdullah would benefit from the creation of an aggrandised Arab Palestine. From a Foreign Office point of view it was imperative to keep him neutral while forestalling Abdullah's territorial ambitions. In keeping with its pro-Arab stance, therefore, the Eastern Department worked hard to persuade the princes to maintain a policy of non-intervention and throughout the 1937–38 revolt there was no concerted Arab action against Britain or the Jewish population in Palestine.

Even though the initiative would eventually have become public knowledge, Wingate's actions in passing on sensitive information do not place him in a favourable light and Blanche Dugdale's observation about fanaticism getting the better of his sense of duty is revealing. As a reliable source of communication between the British government and the Zionists and no mean gossip herself, she was used to dealing with confidential material but she was also surprised that Wingate behaved in this way. Later still, she was to revise her opinion about his commitment to the Jewish cause, which she thought was too intemperate to be of practical use, and began to think of him as 'a most ungovernable character' and 'an irresponsible lunatic'.

Wingate's excessive enthusiasm for their cause had already alarmed other Zionists such as Moshe Shertok. On first meeting him in 1936 the reaction had been immediate and favourable: 'I was very much impressed by his appearance, and his deep-set eyes and suppressed passion struck me right from the start. He displayed also a terrific concentration on something, which he thought to be the most important and essential thing.' Shertok was also impressed by Wingate's absolute willingness to assist the Zionist cause, no matter how trivial the occasion. When Shertok was granted an interview by Wavell, who was often painfully tongue-tied and given to sudden silences, Wingate coached him in the approach he should take.

Wingate advised me to take advantage of his nervousness, and be very stiff, even slightly discourteous. He told me to call him 'General' right from the beginning, and not 'General Wavell'. 'Don't give him much of a chance,' he said. 'And when you have done your talking, say "Goodbye, General" and walk out. Just get up and walk out, don't even look back. Choose your point for terminating the conversation and don't wait till he dismisses you. That's the way to treat him.' Wingate even typed out what he wanted to say.

Although the ruse worked – Wavell, ever courteous, invited his guest to sit down and discuss the problems involved in partition – Shertok was taken aback by the approach. As one of Weizmann's principal lieutenants – in 1937 he was head of the political department of the Jewish Agency – he understood the need to maintain high standards of discipline in the relationship with Britain and he, too, began to be concerned by Wingate's hot-headed approach to Zionism. As he admitted to Ivy Paterson in 1950, although he never doubted Wingate's genuineness, 'he had a passionate and violent affection, yes, his affection was overpowering'.

In time, too, that was Weizmann's conviction. While he was always interested to hear Wingate's military theories and encouraged him to develop his ideas for the creation of credible Jewish forces, he became increasingly uncertain about his political touch. Indeed, some of Wingate's more preposterous suggestions for dealing with the British government were not only embarrassing, but they could have damaged the Zionist cause; for example, at one point in 1938, at the time of the Czechoslovakian crisis, he suggested that the Jews should threaten to use force to achieve their political aims. To Weizmann, this was a case of a soldier dabbling in politics and he acted accordingly by distancing himself from Wingate's more extreme ideas. 'Much as I admired and loved Wingate,' he wrote in his memoirs, 'I did not think that his diplomatic activities in any way matched his military performance or his personal integrity.'[3]

In fact it was on his interpretation of the current military situation in Palestine that Wingate was on firmer ground and his papers on the subject showed frequent flashes of genius. At an early stage he decided that he would not be tied to his desk and he gave short shrift to the general rule that there is a dividing line between the collection of intelligence and the evaluation and analysis of the resulting information. Most of his insights came from the effort he put into his work for, whatever his faults in the political arena, Wingate never shirked his responsibilities at Force Headquarters in Jerusalem. On the contrary his immediate colleagues regarded him as an ideal officer who was prepared to question received opinion and was unafraid of arguing his own case. When he discovered that there were no Hebrew-speaking officers on the British staff he promised General Sir John Dill, the officer commanding Palestine, that by 1 March 1937 he would have mastered the language sufficiently well to be able to translate the local Jewish newspapers for the weekly intelligence summaries. At that time the work was entrusted to a Jewish agency and Wingate could never be certain if the translations were accurate. Typically he underlined the problem at the end of 1936 by deliberately omitting the Hebrew press summary and then marched into Dill's office to give his reasons.

Reading the local newspapers quickly became an important part of Wingate's work. With a Royal Army Service Corps corporal Ivor Thomas (later Lieutenant-Colonel I. G. Thomas) he began the pains-taking task of creating biographies of local personalities from information culled from the Palestinian press. (He translated the Arab papers, hence his concern for the Jewish translations.) At first his fellow intelligence officers were inclined to scoff at the amount of effort put into the task but as Thomas remembered, he and Wingate had the last word: 'By and large all the people who condemned it, later were coming to us and saying "Have you got anything on Ibrahim So-and-so?" And it was pretty obvious that we'd built up something which should have been done long before and which a lot of people coveted in its later stages.'

One reason was the accuracy of the information for Wingate proved himself to be a painstaking intelligence officer who refused to take short cuts in his work. When an intelligence report came in from Saudi Arabia with an illegible place-name he insisted that Thomas should scour the maps to find it. Although the maps officer had told Wingate that GHQ possessed no detailed maps of Saudi Arabia, Thomas discovered that there was one on the wall of Dill's office and on it found the correct name. The information enraged Wingate who accused the maps officer of lying to him and deliberately withholding information, both cardinal sins in Wingate's book. However, instead of letting the matter rest he asked Thomas why the general had the map. 'That's the way of generals, sir. Why shouldn't they? They shouldn't be generals if they haven't got everything. And if anyone's entitled to it he is.'

'Rubbish, rubbish, absolute rubbish,' stormed Wingate. 'Find out if the GOC is in.' Minutes later, he reappeared carrying the map. 'Bom-bardier, put this map on the wall, I've convinced the general that I'm more important than he is.'

Not unnaturally, perhaps, Wingate's cavalier attitudes towards the hierarchy were not always appreciated by his more traditionally minded brother officers. Although Dill allowed Wingate a fair degree of latitude because his work was first class, others thought him arrogant and con-ceited and it did not surprise Thomas to find that 'one or two people were gunning for him'. Professional jealousy played a part: many an officer would have liked to possess the nerve to walk into a general's office, few would have carried out the intention. So too did a general dislike of Wingate's growing and obvious attachment to the Jewish cause. By the beginning of 1937, according to Thomas, he was spending more and more time in the Jewish kibbutzim in the country areas near Tiberias.

I think there were one or two snide remarks being made in the branch about him going up there by the other officers. But, of course, it was quite legitimate that he should go up there. And they couldn't do very much about that because he was learning Hebrew. But I think at the same time, going to these kibbutz, it also infected him with a little bit at that time, perhaps not noticeable, with the Jewish cause.

Wingate's appearance did not add to his popularity. Although he kept himself scrupulously clean he was careless about his own clothes and uniform and frequently gave offence to the more regimentally minded officers who put a premium on their personal appearance. Arthur Dove, the brigade major with 16th Infantry Brigade, regularly came across Wingate wearing a uniform without badges of rank, dirty shoes, socks round his ankles 'and generally looking a bit dishevelled'. While he admired Wingate's professionalism, and conceded that he often had to sleep rough in the Jewish settlements, Dove could not help feeling that he was not 'particularly soldierly from a barrack-square point of view'. At the same time Wingate's lack of interest in his dress increased his standing with the British troops, like soldiers everywhere ready to be amused by an officer's eccentricities.

He mainly wore the khaki issue shorts, shirt and stockings. The shorts might well have been the same pair the whole time. They looked like it. During one spell, he wore one khaki stocking and one grey Army issue sock. This fascinated my Manchesters who would eagerly await their next sight of him. Then you would see them nudge each other and smile – and one might say to the other, 'Look! He's got sock on t'other leg today!'

Rex King-Clark served under Wingate in 1938 and respected him as a military leader but even at that early stage in his career – he was a twenty-four-year-old subaltern – he noticed the sense of deliberate eccentricity, bordering on showmanship, which characterised his appearance. While it was clear that Wingate did not particularly care what brother officers like King-Clark thought about his dress sense, he seemed keen to make an impression and obviously wanted to be remembered. 'Whether Wingate cultivated his untidiness to make his mark, I don't know. Perhaps he just allowed it to flourish.' During this period, too, he began wearing the distinctive and old-fashioned Wolseley sun helmet which was to become his personal trademark in Ethiopia and Burma.

Even out of uniform he caused eyebrows to be raised. His favourite civilian clothes consisted of a pale grey suit, blue silk shirt, brown suede shoes and a black Homburg hat which gave him a rakish European appearance. The whole effect was almost calculated to annoy and on one occasion while dining with Lorna in Jerusalem he nearly got into a fight with two drunk army officers who made loud sarcastic comments about his appearance when he entered the restaurant.

Those who knew him better and who visited him in the privacy of his home were also frequently taken aback by his attitude to nudity: Reuven Shiloah (Zaslani) was not the only member of the Jewish community to find him naked when he first met him to discuss tactics. On active service he continued the habit of not washing, preferring instead to scrub his body with a large brush. Brigadier John Evetts, his immediate boss in 16th Infantry Brigade in 1938, remembered seeing Wingate in his tent, covered in sweat and using what looked like 'a large toothbrush'. Throughout his life Wingate felt completely relaxed about not wearing clothes and seemed to be indifferent to what others thought of his behaviour.

Lorna said that he was only embarrassed once, in his first accommodation in Sheffield, which stood opposite a factory: 'Three or four windows were crowded with big strong girls in green overalls, who shook their glossy hair and roared with laughter and waved their bare arms at him. Orde did not care very much who saw him with nothing on, but he was slightly disconcerted by the force of their remarks.' Occasionally, British soldiers would be equally nonplussed by this habit: although their service conditions meant that they were no prudes themselves when it came to nudity, the fact that a man chose to wear nothing was considered slightly shocking. Like other facets of Wingate's behaviour his partiality for not wearing clothes was never forgotten.

Naked or not, Wingate made a lasting impression on the Jewish settlers whom he met in the kibbutzim in 1937 and the early part of 1938. Although many were initially reserved in the face of his obvious passion for their cause or still harboured suspicions that he had been planted by British intelligence, the more adventurous settlers were quick to see that he could be useful to their cause. According to Dov Yirmiya (Yermanovitz), who served with the Haganah, Wingate's sudden appearance at the exposed settlement of Hanita near the Lebanese border was typical of the way he operated and confirmed his growing use of dramatic gestures to cut a figure and thereby make his point.

One night a taxi came up to Hanita and a very strange figure alighted from it. It was then that I saw Wingate for the first time as he entered the courtyard. He carried two rifles, some papers, a Bible, a Hebrew dictionary and a copy of the Hebrew daily, *Davar*. We gazed at him with amazement, wondering how he dared to come here at night and even alone. We led him to the local commander and they talked for several hours.

As confidence in him grew, Wingate was given a nickname: Hayedid, or the friend. The encomium was not misplaced for as Shiloah pointed out, Wingate was not only a conduit for 'irregular dealings, taking out papers and revealing secrets', he was also openly critical of the British attitude towards internal security in Palestine. During his frequent visits to the settlements, therefore, Wingate threw himself into the task of understanding the problems faced by the Jews in defending their property and the necessity of finding a solution. The more exposed settlements were guarded by policemen while others employed armed watchmen but all acted in a defensive capacity and were open to attack at night.

By the end of the autumn of 1937 there was a degree of urgency because following meetings of Arab nationalists in Syria violence had broken out again in Palestine. The first shot was fired on 26 September 1937 when Lewis Andrews, acting District Commissioner for Galilee, was murdered in Nazareth. As the liaison officer with the Peel Commission he was an obvious target for Arab extremists and his death outraged British opinion. Although the Higher Arab Committee condemned the crime the British authorities reacted with a surprising degree of firmness. Warrants were put out for the arrest of HAC members, the Mufti was deposed and went into exile, first in the holy places of Jerusalem and then in Lebanon from where he continued to exercise a baleful influence over Palestine's affairs.

As part of the new policy it was announced that Wauchope would be replaced by Sir Harold MacMichael and that conciliation would be superseded by coercion. At the same time Dill was replaced as GOC by General Archibald Wavell, one of Britain's great military commanders and a man who was destined to cast a long shadow over Wingate's life.

In the wake of Andrews's murder Arab terrorists waged a long and bitter campaign to undermine British authority in Palestine. On 14 October the Jewish quarters in Jerusalem were set on fire and Lydda airport, then under construction, was attacked and destroyed. A large forest of 50,000 trees south of Nazareth was set ablaze. Lines of communication were also a target: telephone lines at Hebron were sabotaged, a passenger train at Lydda was derailed and the Iraq Petroleum Company's pipeline to Haifa was vandalised and set on fire with monotonous regularity. Attacks against Jews and moderate Arabs became commonplace and in most areas, except for Gaza and Beersheba, the predominantly Arab police offered little resistance.

In response to the anarchy military repression became the order of the day in the war against Arab terrorism: capital punishment was used against individual offenders and there were collective reprisals against villages or settlements which protected the terrorists. Sometimes this was done through fines; at others, as Hugh Foot recalled in his memoirs, sterner measures were used: 'When we thought that a village was harbouring rebels, we'd go there and mark one of the large houses. Then, if an incident was traced to that village, we'd blow up the house we'd marked.'[4] No one was safe, for the Arab terrorists not only attacked British positions and Jewish settlements; they also harried their own people and killed Palestinian Arabs who worked for the British administration. Much of the worst violence was orchestrated from Syria by an Arab terrorist leader called Fauzi al Kaukji.

It was a desperate time which called for extreme measures. Amongst these was the far-reaching decision to use Jewish paramilitary forces in the fight against the Arab terrorists. The first force to be created was the Jewish Supernumerary Police which had come into being in July 1936 mainly for general defensive duties. Useful though it was, it never numbered more than 3,040 men (plus 2,400 reservists) and even on that scale Foreign Office officials such as the influential Arabist Sir John Shuckburgh minuted that Britain might be guilty of taking sides.

The moral strength of our position as holding the scales between Jew and Arab would be undermined and we should be placed in the position of having allied ourselves with the Jews against the Arab population of Palestine. Such a course might be justifiable and necessary when once the boundaries of the Jewish state have been defined and approved by HMG but to enlist the active military assistance of the Jews before it has been decided whether partition is practicable would, I suggest, be a most dangerous move.[5]

While agreeing that limited use should be made of Jewish forces for self-defence, the Foreign Office always fought shy of supporting any policy which included arming and training Jews for offensive operations. In the face of Arab terrorism officials such as Shuckburgh cautioned that the revolt should be countered by British regular forces – by then reduced to eight infantry battalions and one cavalry regiment, backed up by air support from the RAF – working in conjunction with the Palestine

Police and the Transjordan Frontier Force. In Transjordan itself the battle
against terrorism was undertaken by the British-officered Arab Legion
whose Desert Patrol was responsible for protecting the Iraq Petroleum
Company's pipeline and for preventing terrorist incursions from Syria.

Although Shuckburgh had enunciated the official government view,
the British were prepared to co-operate with the illegal Haganah, the
Jewish self-defence force founded in the 1920s. It was here that Wingate
saw his chance to create an unorthodox force which would allow the
Jews to defend their own settlements and by so doing lay the foundation
of a Jewish army of the future. It also came at a time when a growing
number of radical young Jews were being attracted into the Irgun Zvai
Leumi, the underground Jewish terrorist organisation which believed in
taking the battle to the Arabs. In the summer of 1938 they demonstrated
their military effectiveness by killing seventy-four Arabs in a bomb attack
on Haifa after one of their members had been hanged by the British
authorities.

Wingate was never attracted by the revisionist beliefs of the Irgun,
which was later to wage a bloody and unrepentant terrorist war against
the British presence in Palestine. Instead, he put his faith in the Haganah
and persuaded his superiors that this organisation, though illegal, could
be a priceless asset in the war against Arab terrorism. In pursuit of that
objective Wingate wrote a succession of discussion papers, some for
GHQ in Jerusalem, others for Weizmann and his colleagues in the
Jewish Agency. As Wingate's thinking on the subject progressed he began
to embrace the possibility of founding a Jewish army, but the original
idea was to establish small units of fighting men to be used in offensive
operations against the enemy. Although Wingate never tired of discussing
the idea his theories are best expressed in a paper written in 1938 entitled
'A Desert Force for Palestine'. (The same words appear in his paper
'Palestine in Imperial Strategy', written in 1939 for the attention of
General Sir Edmund Ironside, Chief of the Imperial General Staff.)

Hitherto [1937] owing to so-called political reasons, we had made no attempt
to utilise the support of the loyal section of the population, the Jews. Hence it
was that every move of troops or police, living amongst Arabs, was known to
the rebels almost before they knew of it themselves. The rebels in a given area
knew to a T exactly what the government forces would do in any eventuality.
The rebels always moved at night, because they were certain of meeting neither
troops nor police anywhere, but on roads they could avoid. Nearly all the rebel
work was done by night, in fact, their watchword was 'Edh Dhulam'. It was
clear to me that were troops to seek the cover of Jewish colonies, widely

Colonel George Wingate, Indian
Army: 'Much given to gloomy
musings on man's inherent
wickedness he was a constant
presence in the children's lives.'

Ethel Wingate: 'She gave that most
essential element in the children's
upbringing, the knowledge that they
are loved.'

Destined to be a soldier. Orde Wingate on his rocking horse in the family home at Godalming.

The Wingate clan. Orde stands on the left of his brothers and sister wearing his Douglas kilt. 'Almost by a process of osmosis they would know what the others were thinking or what they wanted, even before they asked.'

The newly commissioned subaltern. Orde Wingate in Royal Artillery uniform shortly after leaving the Royal Military Academy, Woolwich.

Something of an outsider: unlike most other cadets of his generation Wingate was never nostalgic about his time at Woolwich.

Learning the rudiments of gunnery: Wingate (seated middle) with fellow cadets.

The horse-mad subaltern: 'Shortly
after he joined his battery Wingate
quickly gained a reputation as a
daring and frequently madcap
horseman.'

The young officer: 'A charming and
lively young man, full of fun and
high spirits.'

'The first real love of his life, a spirited girl, Enid Margaret Jelley, whom he always knew as Peggy.'

On leave from the Sudan and engaged to be married to Peggy.

On leave from Palestine, 1938, and married to Lorna Paterson.

Lorna Paterson, aged 15, at the time she met Orde Wingate.

dispersed as they are, were when necessary to dress as colonists, were to move in small squads across country by night, off tracks, on a plan drawn up by a commander in closest touch with the various sources of intelligence, then success in dealing with the gangs would only be a matter of time.

From this concept was born the military units which came to be known as the Special Night Squads. Their title explained their function. Wingate's starting point was the realisation that, while the British could maintain a semblance of order during the day, the night belonged to the Arab gang leaders who terrorised the people living within their areas of control. As a result police had orders to stay within their barracks and only the army ventured out on regular patrols. Even then, as Wingate pointed out in his discussion paper, they stuck to main roads 'which were worse than useless because they afforded an opportunity to the rebels to shoot them up from safe cover'. If authority was to be restored, especially in the troubled northern areas near the border with Syria, then the fight would have to be taken to the terrorists.

As part of his preparation – and as colleagues at GHQ such as Corporal Thomas noticed – Wingate spent as much time as he could visiting the Jewish settlements under threat. More often than not his trips were unofficial or taken during periods of leave but they were essential to his plans and preparations. However, they were undertaken with Wavell's approval: Wingate had engineered a meeting by stopping the GOC's car and telling him about the importance of his plans. Wavell, an educated and sympathetic commander, was sufficiently intrigued by Wingate to encourage the young staff captain to develop his unorthodox ideas. This support was crucial. Once again Wingate discovered the importance of powerful patronage and this 'protection' gave him the scope and authority which would have been denied, say, to an officer of similar rank in one of the infantry battalions based in Palestine at that time.

Less easy to win was the consent of the Haganah commanders whose top committee fought shy of contributing to Wingate's scheme. Not only was it a proscribed organisation but its leaders were still unsure about Wingate's motives. When Wingate approached Wilenski, head of Haganah intelligence in northern Palestine, with the request to place men at his disposal, he met with a cold response for the good reason that Haganah did not want the names of their men to fall into British hands. According to Shertok they only began to trust Wingate once he started his initial experimental operations in settlements such as Hanita and Tirat Tsevi and turned a blind eye to the illegal weapons which were used under the cover of the official arms carried by the Supernumerary Police.

The methods used by Wingate also helped to convince Haganah leaders that their personnel should contribute to the new self-defence scheme. At Hanita, for example, Wingate restored confidence after the murder of the settlement's leader by taking young Jewish settlers out on night-time patrols to the neighbouring Arab village of Basra to accustom them to moving silently and fearlessly in the open countryside at night. At other times, as Yirmiya remembered, 'he came, went out all alone and left again. Sometimes he stayed for a number of days, and our people were especially interested to know what he was doing in the evenings. They noticed that he was learning Hebrew, reading the Bible and Hebrew papers.'

He also spoke to the settlers and to top officials of the Jewish Agency for Palestine, such as Reuven Shiloah, who were critical of the way in which the security forces operated.

Before Wingate started his operations, General Dill brought out two divisions for what he called 'a combing operation'. These divisions combed the whole country from the Mediterranean to the Jordan. They marched over hills and valleys, and in the end emerged with some rusty Turkish pistols and a few empty rounds of ammunition. It was something to laugh at. It was all done in bright daylight, and the army's appearance was heralded in advance, some ten miles away. The Arab gangsters just hid their arms and mingled with the population of the villages. Not only did the huge British army find absolutely nothing, it discredited and ridiculed itself in the eyes of the whole population.

While it was true that, more often than not, the British army did employ cumbersome tactics, there had been innovations such as the well-tried use of RAF aircraft in support of military operations and the construction of the wire fence, known as Tegart's Wall, to prevent terrorist incursions from Syria. Commanders such as John Evetts had also used the army's experience of fighting on India's North-West Frontier to establish pickets on the high ground around Nablus. Although mainly static their presence denied the terrorists the use of many of the country routes used for arms smuggling. Evetts also introduced a system of 'mobile columns' drawn from the four infantry battalions under his command in 16th Brigade. Using lorries these patrols were able to cover considerable ground in the northern area and their movements were co-ordinated by wireless from brigade headquarters. Most columns took with them eight transport donkeys or mules in one of the lorries so that foot patrols could be deployed in the more inaccessible areas. However, according to Lieutenant John Gratton (later Colonel J. S. S. Gratton) of the 2nd Hampshires, it was almost impossible for the British soldiers to move silently over the terrain due to their unsuitable equipment.

If you wear long puttees, you cannot run. Your muscles swell up and you've simply got to stop. You can't move your feet any longer. And that's how amateurish we were. And after a space of time we had hobnailed boots which on rock or shale of course make a hell of a noise ... and when I look at the kit, I mean looking at that Wolseley helmet – and you had to have by day a spine pad tied on at the back.

Other initiatives included training sessions in elementary defensive tactics for Jewish watchmen which were arranged by the 2nd East Yorkshires.

In spite of these measures Wingate was convinced that the settlements could only be protected against terrorist attacks at night by using small bodies of well-trained and well-armed men: Jewish settlers reinforced by small numbers of British troops and led by British officers. Having arrived at that conclusion Wingate then had to convince the military authorities that this plan should be put into operation as quickly as possible. The first response came from Brigadier John Evetts, commanding 16th Infantry Brigade in Haifa, who showed a commendable degree of enthusiasm for this unconventional idea. Together with his brigade major, Arthur Dove, he encouraged Wingate to draw up a detailed plan, based on his experiences at Hanita and the other northern settlements, for the establishment of Jewish counter-insurgency units which would operate at night with the support of British troops.

The policy had the blessing of Force Headquarters in Jerusalem but because it was considered to be an irregular practice few papers ever mentioned it. Certainly, in the official correspondence between Jerusalem and London MacMichael never mentioned the Special Night Squads by name and merely noted that he had

sanctioned the employment of a small column of Jews and British troops operating under the command of a British officer in Galilee both to afford better protection to the pipe line and also when the occasion demands for ambush work in Galilee generally and in particular on the northern frontier which in its present state is very liable to attacks by foreigners from the Lebanon. [6]

The absence of detailed documentation was entirely in keeping with

Britain's policy of not wanting to upset Arab opinion by any suggestion that the Jews in Palestine were being armed and trained for offensive operations.

At this point his plans almost became unstuck because Wavell had been replaced by Lieutenant-General Sir Robert Haining, a gunner with considerable experience of intelligence work; his previous position had been Director of Military Operations and Intelligence at the War Office. Unfortunately for Wingate, Haining's own head of intelligence in Palestine, Wing-Commander A.P. Ritchie, RAF, was not enthusiastic about him or his unorthodox ideas. On 25 May 1938 Wingate was posted to Nazareth to run an intelligence centre which would be responsible for collecting and co-ordinating all intelligence from military, police and civilian sources and processing it for Force Headquarters. Other centres were established at Nablus and Haifa and Ritchie insisted that the military and police members should form 'a united body' working for the common good. At first Wingate kicked against the appointment. Not only did it mean working in a new team at a time when he was developing radical freelance theories, but the administrative work would deflect him from creating the Special Night Squads.

Fortunately, Nazareth came within the 16th Brigade area and Evetts permitted Wingate to use his brigade liaison officer for administrative work, thereby freeing him from all essential duties and giving him the cover to organise his small force. At the end of the month Haining gave permission for the three squads to be formed and Wingate established his headquarters at the kibbutz of Ein Harod in the Plain of Jezreel. For this purpose he was given thirty-six British infantrymen led by three young subalterns: 2nd Lieutenant Mike Grove, 2nd Royal West Kents; Lieutenant Rex King-Clark, 1st Manchesters; and 2nd Lieutenant H. E. N. 'Bala' Bredin, 1st Royal Ulster Rifles. The squads would be based at Hanita and later at Tel Amal (Grove), Aiyelet-hash-Shahar and later at Afikim (King-Clark) and Ein Harod (Bredin). Initially their task was to guard the Iraq Petroleum Company's pipeline but Wingate had immediate plans to extend their operations to protect the more isolated and less secure settlements.

The reasons for the creation of the Special Night Squads are contained in a lengthy paper which Wingate prepared for Force HQ Intelligence on 5 June 1938 on 'the possibilities of night movements by armed forces of the Crown with the object of putting an end to terrorism in Northern Palestine'. Subsequent papers gave details of the organisation and operational orders for the squads. They are coherent and well-argued documents, written in a lucid and uncluttered style, and they show that Wingate had a clear idea of his objectives. Just as importantly, they demonstrate Wingate's uncanny grasp of the fundamentals of counter-insurgency warfare.

In the first instance, Wingate defined the threat as the ability of the Arab terrorists to operate against the Jewish settlements at night and to attack them with impunity. Not only did this give them a tactical advantage but it also provided them with a priceless propaganda advantage. To counter the threat Wingate argued that the security forces should adopt a two-track policy: defensive operations to prevent the terrorists achieving their aims and offensive operations to root out the gangs. Both were designed to prevent the enemy from functioning.

What is needed, therefore, is to produce in the minds of the rebels the conviction that the armed forces are able to move at night as freely and as dispersed as themselves, without their being able to obtain, as heretofore, previous knowledge of such movement; that whenever they enter a village to prey it is more than likely that they will be surprised there; that, even when they move across country by the most isolated tracks, they are liable suddenly to be attacked – not by a distant exchange of shots, from which little is to be feared, but by bodily encounter for which they are totally unfitted. The rebels have shown that, while they are prepared to face attacks when occupying covered and previously prepared positions, they are quite unable to face any kind of charge or surprise onslaught.

To be able to operate in this way Wingate realised that his intelligence-gathering and security procedures had to be first rate. For this reason he insisted that his squads be accompanied on all operations by a senior Jewish supernumerary. Men like these had excellent contacts with the local community, knew the lie of the land and understood the rhythms of local life. More often than not they also enjoyed good relations with the indigenous Arab community who had equal reason to fear the terrorist gangs. From the very start, therefore, Wingate insisted that there should be a substantial Jewish contribution both to the manning of the Special Night Squads and to the overall planning of their operations. Wingate also insisted that his men should not operate out of police stations or military bases where their movements could be easily monitored; instead, they should be based in the settlements themselves and whenever possible they should disguise their presence.

Jewish supernumeraries, especially those drawn from colonies, are excellent material for our purpose. A Jewish Colony is at present the only place in

Palestine where one can discuss operations with the certainty that everything said will remain as secret as the grave. A British Night Squad, reinforced by two supernumerary squads, becomes three British Night Squads controlled by a British officer. All squads are highly mobile, know the theatre of operations thoroughly and contain members with a fluent knowledge of all three official languages. This would be true of no other possible combination of forces in Palestine.

On the operational side the squads were composed of ten British soldiers, a British non-commissioned officer and a British officer. To these were added ten trained Jewish supernumeraries, thus doubling the size of the squad; Wingate estimated that in the first three months he was able to train 115 Jewish volunteers, all of whom he described to Evetts as 'splendid fighters'. On operations the patrol divided into two sections under the command of the British officer and his NCO who were also responsible for all drill and weapons training. Wingate believed that all initial training could be completed in six days and his training programme called for intensive practice in moving silently, obeying signals and practice in close-quarter bayonet fighting and dummy grenade throwing. Like the other commanders, Rex King-Clark found that the Jewish supernumeraries were ready learners and that some of them had already seen military service in European armies. One member of his squad, Shim'on Koch (Avidan), later became a leading commander in the Israeli Defence Forces and won a notable victory in Gaza against the Egyptian army in 1948.

The standing orders and battle plans were equally forthright. On all operations Wingate demanded complete silence and introduced an elementary system of hand and torchlight signals. (He designed a special torch attached to a pole and hooded so that it was only visible in one direction.) A system of concealed moves was also introduced. Patrols would leave a settlement by lorry, move in a contrary direction and then march across country towards their intended target. Patrol commanders were also ordered never to march along tracks for more than a kilometre at a time and to use zigzag movements to counter the possibility of ambush. To prevent the possibility of clashing with friendly forces Wingate always provided 16th Brigade with detailed plans about his squads' patrols and was a regular visitor at Evetts's headquarters in Haifa: contrary to what some senior officers came to believe the Special Night Squads were not a 'cowboy outfit' but were fully integrated into the brigade's counter-insurgency policy.

On kit and equipment, Wingate recommended an absolute minimum, believing that 'a squad which does not march fifteen miles across country per night out is not doing its duty or exerting its proper effect.' Although standards varied, most squad members wore a blue police shirt or British army shirt and shorts and thick woollen stockings or puttees. Instead of the standard issue British army boot which Gratton had found so ineffective, they wore a variety of rubber-soled footwear, ranging from plimsolls to special rubber-soled boots made by Jewish cobblers from old tyres. At Afikim Rex King-Clark equipped his men with rubber and canvas hockey boots painted black. Weapons, too, varied. Because standing orders insisted that 'rifle fire loses a great deal of its value by night' he set a premium on the use of hand grenades and the bayonet. In each patrol there were two bombers equipped with hand grenades and a revolver. The rest of the squad carried the army's Short Magazine Lee-Enfield rifle complete with a bayonet covered by a dark cotton sleeve to prevent reflection at night. The section leaders carried Webley & Scott Mark VI revolvers although King-Clark bought a German Mauser 7.63 mm machine pistol and both Bredin and Grove always carried rifles. Ammunition was carried in a bandolier and each man had a water bottle. The officers had also been presented by the Jewish Agency with fine 7×50 Zeiss binoculars for night vision and Wingate insisted that, despite being cumbersome, they should always be used.

Wingate's plans and operational orders for the Special Night Squads were clear and precise. The next stage was to implement them, no easy task given the British army's inexperience in low-intensity operations of this specialised kind. None of the British officers knew what they were letting themselves in for when they were chosen to command the squads and all three admitted that they had to learn the necessary skills demanded by Wingate. When Bredin got the call he was serving with B Company, 1st Royal Ulster Rifles at Nathania, and his commanding officer's orders gave him little idea of what was expected of him. He was merely told to take his platoon by truck with a month's rations to a map reference some eighty miles to the north where someone would be waiting for him at five o'clock in the afternoon.

So I took my platoon complete with rations and ammunition and all the things that one knew one had to have with one ... and off we went. The map reference was quite near a Jewish kibbutz called Ein Harod in the Valley of Jezreel halfway between Afula and Beisan. And we got to this place, we got there early, half an hour before the time that I mentioned, and when we stopped a rather untidy looking officer came out from behind a hedge and said, 'You're

late. All right, follow behind my car.' That was my first meeting with Captain
Orde Wingate.

That night, following a meal in the kibbutz, Bredin and his men were
taken out by Wingate and given their first training in moving silently
during cross-country marches in the dark.

For King-Clark the shock of meeting Wingate was less severe: he had
already encountered him, 'under almost ludicrous circumstances', while
serving with his platoon (C Company, 1st Manchesters) at their position,
a newly built, but derelict, hotel on Mount Canaan above Safad. One
afternoon in May, King-Clark's men had picked up a suspicious-looking
civilian in the drive; his sergeant reported that 'the man claimed to be a
British officer and that, though he sounded like one, he didn't much
look like one.' Further inspection revealed that the man's car contained
a rifle and several hand grenades. As British officers were not permitted
to drive around the country in their own cars and wearing plain clothes,
the men of the Manchesters were within their rights to apprehend him
but Wingate did not see it that way. Demanding to meet King-Clark,
he angrily explained that he was a staff officer at GHQ and drove off,
threatening further reprisals.

(Commanding officers frequently test security by demanding to be
admitted without identity papers because their men know them.
However King-Clark admitted that 'a Semitic cast' to Wingate's features
'added weight to the picket's decision to bring him in'. Wingate would
not have been affronted by being taken for a Jew but it is not difficult to
believe that he would have been infuriated by the men handling him as
if he were one.)

Surprisingly, the incident was not mentioned when King-Clark met
Wingate again on 16 June 1938 at the settlement of Aiyelet-hash-Shahar.
He, too, had received the same bare instructions that had been given to
Bredin and, like him too, his men went straight to work.

He first introduced me to the Mukhtar [mayor] of the small colony, who
showed me the room in the hut in which I would be living, the accommodation
allotted to the men of my squad who had not yet arrived, our feeding arrangements and so on. Wingate then sat with me in my room telling me of his plans
for the squads ... 'We'll begin training tonight,' he said, finishing with that
somewhat wolfish grin I soon learned to recognise as an indicator that something
not altogether pleasurable was at hand.

After training at Aiyelet for a fortnight, King-Clark and his men
moved to the settlement at Afikim on the Beisan road, south of the Sea

of Galilee, which resembled 'the traditional frontier forts of the Wild West of America'.

For his part, Mike Grove was acting as the Royal West Kents' mortar officer and was told by his commanding officer to pick a sergeant and ten men. Because he was captain of the football team he knew that most of them would come with him. 'And they were all pretty fit. I knew it was going to be an awful lot of hard work and they were pretty tough chaps so I chose them.' An added inducement was the extra pay given to the Special Night Squads and his men took considerable pride in the knowledge that they were different and taking part in an operation quite unlike any other at the time in Palestine. Although based originally at Hanita, his squad was later deployed at Tel Amal in the Jordan Valley and at Geva near Ein Harod.

Being a career soldier in a good regiment, Grove admitted to being taken aback by Wingate whom he thought 'scruffy' and 'slightly mad'. However when operations began any doubts gave way to admiration for Wingate's methods. Not only did the squads receive first-rate intelligence but it quickly became obvious that Wingate's methods worked in practice. He also admired Wingate's courage. Going into action for the first time on the pipeline he was astonished to see that Wingate had not taken cover but was doing his best to encourage his men. 'There was bullets going all over the place and Wingate was walking along saying, "No, you point that way, and you point that way", just as if we were on an OTC field day or something. He took no notice of the bullets whatsoever at all.'

In that respect Wingate proved to have the characteristics which a commander needs if he is to conduct operations successfully, and it must be remembered that he had only had limited experience of command in the Sudan and had only been involved in minor operations. First, he had enormous physical energy which allowed him to keep in contact with his subordinate commanders and to encourage them at first hand. Not for him the temptation to direct operations from his headquarters. That dynamism was also mental and was abetted by the belief that he was doing God's work. Although a strict disciplinarian – Grove recalled that 'he used to get hopping mad if people didn't do exactly what he said' – his example helped to inspire the men under his command, especially the Jewish settlers.

Second, he possessed tremendous courage and, third, he had complete confidence in himself and his plans. Finally, he rarely lacked determination. His British troops and subordinate commanders might have been surprised by the strength of his Zionism and by his constant quotations from the Old Testament, but they realised that they were serving a spirited leader. 'Oh, I think he was a fine chap, marvellous,' remembers Corporal Fred Howbrook, King-Clark's second-in-command. 'He knew what he was doing. He knew what he wanted. And he knew how to get it. He was very strong-willed. And he stuck up for his men.'

With his base at Ein Harod where the 300 men of Israel were chosen to fight the Midianites, this latter-day Gideon went to war with a will in the Zionist cause.

Seven

GIDEON'S MEN

There is no doubt that Wingate was well aware of the biblical significance in choosing Ein Harod as the base for the Special Night Squads. It was by the well or spring of Harod that Gideon had chosen his 300 men at God's behest by selecting only those 'that lapped, putting their hands to their mouth' and Gideon himself used unorthodox methods to defeat the Midianites. One of these was the use of trumpets to discomfort the enemy in their camp: at one point Wingate thought that a similar ruse would destroy the confidence of the Arab gangs but he was unable to persuade Jewish religious leaders to part with their ceremonial horns or *shofars*. An experiment was made with British army bugles but these were found to have an uncertain tone and the idea was quietly dropped. More substantial was Wingate's decision to operate three night squads each of which would train and control three Jewish squads, just as Gideon had 'divided the three hundred into three companies'.

At Ein Harod Bredin's Ulster Riflemen were given a rapid introduction both to the tasks they would be expected to perform and to the routines Wingate wanted them to follow. Although, by their very nature, kibbutzim were communal settlements, Wingate did not anticipate that the British members of the Special Night Squads would be integrated into the local communities. On the contrary Bredin noticed that Wingate paid little personal attention to the British soldiers but chose instead to concentrate his attention and energies on his Jewish recruits. This did not mean that the British soldiers and Jewish settlers did not mix – they ate together and the conditions of their service forged long-lasting friendships – but, as Rex King-Clark noticed, the barriers were real enough. Not only were the British soldiers treated with some initial suspicion but there were also obstacles created by language and culture and the social organisation within the kibbutz was decidedly clannish.

Also the routine did not encourage much fraternisation: Wingate insisted that no squad should work more than one night in two and that a complete rest of four days every fortnight was 'essential to preserve efficiency'.

For all that it was a concentrated operation the men in the squads responded well to the conditions. One reason was the sense of belonging to a small and elite force – a concept encouraged by Wingate who at one point wanted it to be called 'Wincol' – another was the knowledge that they were involved in a new and different kind of warfare. There were also new lessons to be learned. It was difficult for the men to grasp the importance of moving silently at night. Not only did it take time to practise walking as quietly as possible – and as Wingate required – but the men were used to receiving spoken orders. As Bredin noted, 'the British soldier is an inveterate talker at night.' To overcome these short-comings and to train the men in his system of hand and light signals Wingate made the squads practise in daylight hours, then at dusk before perfecting the routines at night. His standing orders for the squads insisted on this requirement.

Complete silence is the rule in all cases. Members of squads should try to cut down their smoking with consequent coughing. Rubber soled shoes will be worn. The feet should be lifted at each step to avoid collisions with stones etc. The human voice should never be heard. The true quality of a whisper is that, while perfectly audible within a circle of five yards it is completely inaudible further off. The human voice, on the contrary, although almost inaudible at five yards, will nevertheless carry and attract attention as far as 1000 yards off. The average soldier feels self-conscious when whispering loudly and so tries to murmur. This feeling must be overcome by members of night squads.

As befitted a commander who led from the front, Wingate never asked his men to carry out tasks which he could not perform himself and he put considerable effort into improving his own performance before training sessions. Whether it was leading the men in practice moves over rough ground or teaching them to lay down their rifles as if they were made of glass Wingate worked long and hard to instil his belief that the squads' safety lay in their ability to outwit the Arabs at night. Not surprisingly with such novel methods, the infantrymen took time to assimilate the lessons and there were occasions when Wingate lost his temper with them. All three commanders remember occasions when they received a tongue-lashing and admit that Wingate did not suffer fools gladly, a failing which Bredin saw as a flaw:

When Wingate came up against somebody who didn't agree with him he merely felt that this chap was stupid. Now this I'm afraid happens with a lot of brilliant men, they think that anybody who's got a different view to themselves must be stupid. It's only an even more brilliant man who understands that there may be a second viewpoint.

With the Jewish settlers Wingate could be even more rigorous and several of the supernumeraries were treated with a casual brutality which would have been a criminal offence were it meted out to a British soldier. It was not an uncommon occurrence for Wingate to strike a man who made a mistake or who disobeyed orders when on operations; and not even his closest associates were immune from the treatment. Early on he singled out Israel Carmi for advancement and made him his first trans-lator. During an operation against Beshattwe nomads suspected of attack-ing the pipeline, Carmi was ordered to carry the patrol's wirecutters. Instead, he gave them to one of the men with the inevitable result that when they were needed to cut a fence they were at the rear of the patrol. Wingate took immediate retribution and slapped Carmi's face. 'I never forgot it,' said the future Israeli colonel. 'It was my first real lesson in army discipline.'

Faced by evidence of Wingate's severity Bredin warned him 'not to do any of that sort of thing to any of my soldiers because I wouldn't like to tell you what would happen if you did'. In fact, had Wingate struck a British soldier he would have faced court-martial and disgrace, and, prudently, he kept his temper within acceptable limits when handling British troops. With the Jews, though, he adopted more draconic methods: an NCO was punched when he drank before his men, another was slapped for being late on parade. Zvi Brenner, who served with King–Clark, remembered in his autobiography that there was a general acceptance of his methods because Wingate rarely spared himself.

Wingate maintained strong discipline, which he did not teach us by military phrases but by personal example and immediate responses. The guys knew that in the camp you could walk about in your underwear and not shave, but when you went out into the field there were no shortcuts. If you took something with you that interfered with the battle, you would be punished. If there was no bullet in your rifle barrel, you would be punished. If you kicked a stone you would be punished. If you fired without being ordered to do, that was the worst offence and in such cases Wingate was absolutely fanatical.

Wingate could have landed himself in trouble by handling his Jewish supernumeraries with such offhand injustice – as they were not under

British military law he would have escaped court-martial – but there was never an adverse reaction. Some of the men had experience of service in the Russian army during the First World War and were used to rough treatment; others regarded physical punishment as an essential part of military life. To Carmi, as to others, it was a short sharp lesson in military discipline and was considered to be a necessary ingredient of Wingate's methods. Many of the men belonged to the illegal Haganah and they were well aware that the Special Night Squads' training and tactics could be put to use at a later date. Besides, as an experienced recruit Nathan Shadni remembered later, the squads were not just defending life and property, they were fighting for the reconstruction of a Jewish homeland, and they understood that this factor was also recognised by Wingate. Like any early pioneers they were prepared to suffer in the cause.

Here we were on the soil of our fatherland, here we worked on our own fields. Our approach was entirely different. We all felt that we were realising a great idea. Many people who would never risk their life for defending other people and their property would willingly sacrifice their life for an ideal, and that is what we found in Wingate.

It also helped that Wingate spoke Hebrew and rarely appeared wearing badges of rank: as more than one squad member has recalled, they were always impressed by his scruffy appearance and by his ability to quote lengthily and accurately from the Old Testament. At a more senior level Wingate's behaviour was tolerated because he had the support of the Jewish Agency and it was well enough known that he was close to Weizmann, Shertok and Golomb. None the less, his unbridled temper and his harsh treatment of the Jewish supernumeraries is a reminder of the darker side to his character.

Although Wingate managed to avoid the nervous collapses which had left him debilitated in the Sudan, he was driven by intense nervous energy. To Lorna he confided the belief that 'no great man could be happy' and that it was only through suffering that his life could be consummated. Not only did this mean treading an appointed path, but it also entailed showing others how to follow, so that they, too, could become 'giant-killers'. Under such a regime he insisted that spiritual perfection was not just for him, it was the right of everyone under his command. For that reason everything was permissible provided that the means justified the ends; what was more, any compromise was intolerable.

Not that he did not drive himself, too. His diary for 1938 shows that he was rarely in Jerusalem and that although Haifa was his official base, he spent most of his time at Ein Harod or working with the squads in other settlements at Hanita, Tel Amal or Afikim. Throughout this period Lorna was on leave in Britain. She left Palestine at the beginning of March and spent most of her time with her parents in Aberdeenshire or in London where she was a frequent visitor at the Weizmanns' stylish house at 16 Addison Crescent. She did not return to Palestine until the beginning of December and her diary for 1938 reveals a busy social life: in addition to spending time with the Weizmanns she kept in close touch with other prominent Zionists such as the historian Lewis Namier and Wyndham Deedes, a distinguished soldier and diplomat who had given up public life to work amongst the poor in London's East End.

Because Bredin lived with Wingate at Ein Harod where they shared a room, he had first-hand experience of the unrelenting activity and determination.

We would come in perhaps from three or four days out in the hills, marching hard all night and lying up in hidden places by day [most patrols only lasted twenty-four hours], and we'd all come back to Ein Harod and all most of us wanted was a good drink, a bath and a lot of sleep. But he didn't. This dynamo which buzzed inside him kept him going; all he did was he'd eat a bunch of grapes and he would then get hold of some maps and, with the information he'd managed to arm himself with talking to Arabs and peoples where we'd been around, he'd then rush off to Haifa to brigade headquarters or to some Jewish settlement and make plans for the next operation. And only when he'd finished that, would he come back and then he'd absolutely drop and sleep for twenty-four hours.

Quite apart from the advantages his energy and commitment brought to the Special Night Squads, Wingate's behaviour mightily impressed the Jewish settlers. If he was prepared to drive himself so unforgivingly, like Carmi, they were obviously prepared to forgive the harsher side of his temperament and character.

The discipline also came into its own when the Special Night Squads went into action and the men realised that all the hard training bore fruit in the cut and thrust of battle. Although the actions were more skirmishes than pitched battles, the dangers were hardly trivial and the fear of death or injury was constant. Throughout June the squads maintained patrols on the oil pipeline and the men became accustomed to the long enervating marches. 'Most of the going was over dry, very stony ground, which was generally hilly, often steeply so,' recalled King-Clark. 'The dreaded jebel! I shall never forget the endless stones, large and small, covering, it seemed, every inch of Galilee ground, and making the going so tiring and frustrating.'

The first squads in action were Grove's at Hanita and Bredin's at Ein Harod. Although the operations were little more than routine patrols during which Arab terrorists were ambushed they instilled confidence by showing the men that Wingate's tactics worked. Bounded by Mount Tabor and the settlements at Beisan and Afula their operational area had a bad history of violence and sabotage but the SNS patrols had an immediate effect. In his first report to 16th Brigade Wingate was able to claim that whereas the pipeline had been attacked several times a week, by 14 June it had only been punctured once, near the hamlet of Danna. On that occasion the gang of saboteurs were captured – by Bredin's Ulster Riflemen – and two of their number killed. Three days later they were in action again, this time near Khirbet Jurdeth near the Lebanese frontier where Grove's West Kents and Jewish supernumeraries surprised a gang of Arab arms smugglers and inflicted several casualties. According to Grove, 'that shooed them off all right for quite a long time.'

As in any learning process, mistakes were made. Bredin was uncompromising in his attitude to the Arabs who attacked the pipeline and encouraged his men to follow suit. On 28 June a patrol led by a British corporal got into difficulties in the Jordan Valley after warning a group of Beshattwe tribesmen that further attacks on the pipeline would lead to their deportation to Transjordan. While delivering the ultimatum they came under enemy fire and were forced to retreat to Beit Yosef where they summoned help. In the subsequent counter-attack, led by Wingate and Bredin, the terrorists were engaged and ten of their number killed. (This was the occasion when Carmi was slapped by Wingate.) Although disaster had only been narrowly averted, and despite the fact that the patrol had behaved foolishly by not covering their move into the nomads' camp, Wingate was well enough pleased by the outcome. The Jewish squad members had not panicked when things went wrong and had responded to military discipline.

In his report to Evetts Wingate announced that his force was fully operational, a claim that was put to the test on 5 July when the squads had their first serious taste of battle at a hilltop village called Kaukab el Hawa, not far from the pipeline at Danna. Acting on intelligence that an Arab terrorist gang was operating in the area, Wingate laid plans to ambush them and determined on a double flanking movement towards his target. Early in the evening a patrol of four Ulster Riflemen and five supernumeraries led by Bredin had been driven by truck along the road

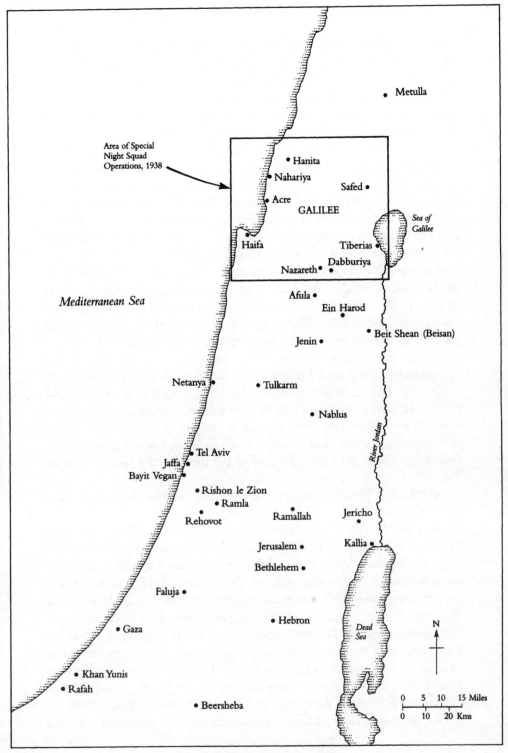

Special Night Squad Operations, 1938

between Gesher and Beit Yosef towards Wadi Kaman in the Jordan Valley.
At the same time Wingate led another patrol from the west with the
intention of cutting off the Arabs' retreat.

However, when Bredin's patrol reached the hill they found a large
number of Arab terrorists on the summit and were immediately involved
in a heavy fire-fight. 'They had apparently expected us,' said Dov
Yirmiya. 'We were in an open field, caught by surprise, but Bredin kept
calm. He ordered us to fire back and then to withdraw.' Undeterred by
the setback, Bredin divided his little force in two so that he and his
young Jewish bomber could attack the Arab position with grenades
while the remainder gave covering fire. In the counter-attack a rifleman
and a supernumerary were wounded but the ruse worked. Several Arabs
were killed in the explosions and the rest retreated.

Pushing eastwards towards the junction of the road and the pipeline,
Bredin's men established contact with Wingate's patrol who managed
to engage the retreating Arabs outside Kaukab el Hawa. At the same
time a patrol led by King-Clark had also encountered terrorists in a small
wadi in the slopes above Menahemiya but in the excitement of their
first engagement failed to prevent the Arabs escaping. 'It was a grand
opportunity missed and I feel a fool,' King-Clark noted in his diary.
'BLAST!' The knowledge that Bredin had enjoyed a more successful
patrol added to King-Clark's frustration but, as it transpired, the action
at Kaukab el Hawa only encouraged the Arabs to retaliate and led to the
first major encounter at Dabburiya, a village named after the prophetess
Deborah, which lies five miles east of Nazareth at the foot of Mount
Tabor.

Fortunately, Wingate had created a reliable field intelligence service,
using not just Jewish but also Arab contacts, and from his sources he
learned that the rebel leader Fauzi al Kaukji planned a strike in retaliation
for the setback at Kaukab el Hawa. All the information pointed to the
hilly area between Dabburiya and Ein Mahil where a terrorist group had
assembled under the command of Shayk Naif Zobi and was being
sheltered in Arab settlements in the neighbourhood. The problem facing
Wingate, though, was the conflicting evidence from 16th Brigade's
intelligence centre at Nazareth which suggested that the gang was using
Ein Mahil as a base, a conclusion Wingate was inclined to accept as
Dabburiya was close to a police post. To Evetts, Wingate signalled his
object: 'To find and destroy the gang responsible for the occupation of
Nazareth a few nights previously, and the attacks on the police there.'

Not without reason, Dabburiya has become an important name in the Jewish history of the Special Night Squads. It involved all three British-led squads plus a Jewish squad under Wingate's command; there was a fierce fire-fight during which both sides suffered casualties, one of whom was Wingate; and for many of the men it was their first real experience of concentrated fighting. None the less, the existing accounts of the battle are largely fictitious. Amongst earlier writers about Wingate both Mosley and Sykes over-emphasised the ferocity of the action and provided wildly inaccurate descriptions of the actual fighting: Mosley claimed the action lasted fourteen hours whereas the actual fire-fight was over in less than forty-five minutes. Surviving Jewish descriptions are equally exaggerated.

In fairness to Wingate, though, his subsequent report to Evetts is a model of restraint, but, perhaps understandably, he was keen to emphasise the importance of his tactics. His squad commanders were more blunt. Rex King-Clark called the operation 'a cock-up of the first water' and Bala Bredin concluded that, good intelligence gatherer and planner though Wingate was, he was liable to change his mind on the ground, causing chaos and disarray. On that score at least, the fighting at Dab-buriya did not go according to plan and there was a good deal of confusion which led to Wingate and others being hit by 'friendly fire' from their own side. (Some of the Jewish supernumeraries, such as David Gelbart, had imperfect English and later admitted that they were not fully aware what was happening.)

In essence at least, Wingate's plans were simple enough: to surround the village of Ein Mahil after nightfall and lure the gang into an ambush shortly before midnight. To this end the four units were deployed separately, each being dropped off by truck at different points and times along the road between Nazareth and Tiberias and each being given a different objective. At the same time the trucks, two of which were equipped with Lewis guns, proceeded to a position at Mahane Yisrael. Once again the ruse was used to confuse the terrorists about the squads' real target.

Once deployed, the squads proceeded along parallel routes to take up their positions around Ein Mahil. Wingate's men set their ambush north of the village, Grove to the east and the Ulsters under Corporal MacConville to the south-west. Meanwhile, King-Clark's patrol set off south by west for five miles towards a point known as Khirbet umm Jhebeil close to Dabburiya: 'an easyish walk and not too dark' he noted in his diary. It was at this point that things started to go wrong. According to the plan, King-Clark was supposed to fire two white Verey lights

which, it was hoped, would alarm the Arabs and bring them out of Ein
Mahil to investigate. As nothing happened when the lights were fired,
Wingate ordered his men to move southwards to take up position around
Dabburiya, with Grove's squad leading.

Shortly before midnight the fighting began. From his position near
Dabburiya, King-Clark heard 'a perfect fusillade of shots' coming from
behind the village; this was the Arab terrorists engaging Grove's men
who, according to Wingate's report, had gone in earlier than planned
and were replying with rifle-fire and grenades. During the action nine
Arabs were killed and one West Kent soldier seriously wounded in the
abdomen. Alarmed by the shooting, Wingate took his men towards
Dabburiya but while he was moving them through an olive grove 'a
burst of fire came from the rear again at close quarters, killing one
supernumerary, and wounding two soldiers, and myself.' According to
Dov Yirmiya, who left a colourful account of the battle, this came from
the Ulsters squad which was approaching from Iksal.

I heard a burst of automatic fire and saw Wingate crouching. He said something
I couldn't understand but I noticed that he was hit and rushed to him. He
crawled back to a heap of corn and as I bent down to help him he pushed me
away, saying all right, all right. It appeared that one of the Irish soldiers who
carried the Lewis gun had received the order to fire but the gun slid out of his
hands and a bullet went off and hit Wingate in his legs. When the others saw
what happened, they nearly lost their head. The soldier who had dropped the
gun was bewildered and almost got crazy. Wingate was wounded in both legs
but I did not hear him groan.

By this time, King-Clark's squad had reached the village at the time
ordered by Wingate but, unfortunately, 'after the excitement was over'.
Wingate was removed to what Fred Howbrook of the Manchesters
thought was a haystack – it was the village threshing floor – where,
despite having been hit five times by the Lewis gun, he remained calm
and ordered all the patrols to come in. It was half past three in the
morning and with dawn beginning to break the men collected their
wounded and went to the tiny settlement of Mahane Yisrael where a
Jewish doctor tended the wounded. The following morning Wingate
was removed by ambulance to Haifa and treated for gunshot wounds in
the RAF hospital at Sarafand, near Ramleh, where fellow patients were
Bredin and Wavell's son, Archie John, like his father an officer in The
Black Watch.

From hospital Wingate wrote a detailed and reasonably accurate report of the fighting and concluded that 'everything went without hitch':

We learned, however, that however unpleasant it may be for the enemy, village fighting at night is both dangerous and difficult. The difficulty of knowing what is happening is increased. More deliberation and care is called for than is suitable to an encounter in the open. All this is obvious but the personnel concerned have now learned it. Although none of the officers commanding squads had seen the country they were operating in before, no one got lost, late or made a mistake. This, I think, is to their credit, and it proves that such operations at night by infantry are perfectly practicable.

Although not written from an infantryman's point of view Wingate's report rings true. On one level, none of the squads made forced errors, each carried out its orders to plan and, despite the casualties – one Jewish Supernumerary Policeman and one West Kent killed (died of wounds) – no one had panicked badly during the fire-fight. However, in two vital areas, mistakes were made. First, Wingate had followed faulty intelligence backed up by his own hunch that the Arabs would always choose the more isolated Ein Mahil to Dabburiya. (In his operational notes for the Special Night Squads he encouraged commanders to follow their instincts: 'Never be swayed unduly by the opinion of the man with local knowledge. Go away from him and think it over and then follow the method you personally think best.') Second, no plans had been laid to prevent 'friendly fire', men shooting on their own side in the confusion of battle. (King-Clark noted in his diary that 'a situation I was anticipating occurred – firing on each other in the darkness.')

On the first point Wingate cannot be blamed entirely. Everything pointed to Ein Mahil as the terrorists' resting place; on an earlier occasion Wingate had visited Dabburiya with the local district officer, Mr Blackburne, and had found no trace of intruders. Where he erred was in not laying contingency plans and failing to take measures to prevent his men firing on their own side. Although 'friendly fire' is an unfortunate by-product of any close-quarter fighting, most commanders go to great lengths to prevent its occurrence. In this case Wingate had to be content with being wise after the event. On returning to Ein Harod he spoke to MacConville, the Ulsters' Lewis gunner, and quietly told him that a great many mistakes had been made during the action and that the important thing was to learn from them.

Then there was the matter of the two white Verey lights. Wingate reported seeing these but they were fired not by King-Clark but by his Jewish section which had become lost. The firing of the lights and the absence of any response led Wingate to give the order to move south towards Dabburiya where the action began. In turn, realising that he could not make the prearranged signal, King-Clark had sent Howbrook to collect the trucks but this was after the firing had ended:

He returned in a hurry and told me that one of our ghaffirs and five of the RWKs [Royal West Kents] were wounded, that Wingate had been hit five times in the arms and legs ... I went down and saw Wingate, who in spite of being literally riddled with bullets, was calmly sitting in the hay giving orders quite normally. He is the most extraordinary man.

Despite the fact that Dabburiya had not been a complete success – few battles are – King-Clark's view of Wingate was also shared by the military authorities. In the aftermath Wingate was awarded the Distinguished Service Order (DSO): in the gazette the action at Dabburiya and the earlier encounter at Khirbet Jurdeth were mentioned, as was his 'consistent and arduous' work in training and organising the squads. There had also been early praise from General Haining who had informed Dove on 28 June 1938 that he was 'much impressed with the results obtained by the SNS to date, and considers they reflect great credit on all concerned'.

There was little doubt, too, that Evetts and his staff in 16th Brigade were well pleased with Wingate's Special Night Squads, although it must be remembered that the resident infantry battalions were also carrying out similar sweeps and patrols at night. What made the squads different was the involvement of the Jewish supernumeraries and it was this factor, together with a traditional dislike of 'private armies', that led to a growing antagonism towards them amongst senior staff officers working for Haining in Jerusalem. Ritchie, for one, still entertained deep suspicions about Wingate's undisguised adherence to the Jewish cause and officials such as Hugh Foot were concerned that Wingate's methods had harmed the British army's reputation for 'fair play'. ('To be fair to the army and police,' remembers King-Clark, 'the antipathy they felt towards the SNS was justifiably aggravated by the fact that we did become rather swollen-headed about our imagined toughness and "killing rate".')

Wingate was once again in a familiar position. His tactics had been accepted and he had been rewarded but at the same time he had attracted enemies in the high command who were in a position to stymie his every move. For that reason he came out of hospital more determined than ever to improve the squads' performance and to expand their training and levels of manpower and equipment. Not that he had much time in hospital to dwell on his plans. He proved to be a difficult patient, unwilling to rest, and he left before his wounds were completely healed. Equally typically, he played down the incident when he wrote to his mother on 2 August, several days after he had discharged himself from hospital. 'Gunshot wounds is the War Office way of saying bullet wounds. They have to do it differently. These were only flesh wounds and healed at first intention – much to my surprise as they were caused by ricochets and the soil was filthy. However I must have pure blood or something.'

In the days following Wingate's return to Ein Harod on 30 July his fellow Special Night Squad commanders noticed that he was in tremendous pain and 'looked far from well'. Because he refused to allow himself sufficient time to recuperate properly, the wounds in his leg took longer to heal – despite his remonstration to the contrary in the letter to his mother – and during operations in early August they frequently broke down and had to be rebandaged with field dressings. When Grove mentioned Wingate's obvious discomfort, Bredin, who of all three commanders knew him best, replied: 'It's not his legs that cope with it, it's his mind.'

While it was true that Wingate possessed considerable reserves and refused to be daunted by physical pain, which he believed was a case of mind over matter, he was also driven by the fear that his absence could harm the cause of the Special Night Squads. Having completed five major and six minor engagements, during which up to seventy Arab rebels had been killed, he was anxious to maintain the momentum. In a memorandum to Evetts he made a case for expanding the squads by the addition of two more subalterns and twenty soldiers and increasing the equipment through the supply of eight more Lewis guns and 150 rifles and bayonets. Although these were modest requests, the high command hedged its bets and simply gave cautious permission for Wingate to extend his training programme at Ein Harod, provided that the funds were provided by the Jewish Agency. Typically, Wingate turned the snub to his own advantage. On the closing day he told the Jewish settlers that it was a course for training potential non-commissioned officers and reminded them that 'we are establishing here the foundation of the Army of Zion . . . If it fights it will achieve its independence in its land.' At the same time he changed his official translator and employed a young Jew called Abraham Akavia who was to become one of his closest friends and associates.

To consolidate his position Wingate also changed the tenor of the squads' operations. As King-Clark noted: 'The Jewish supernumerary strength at Ein Harod increased, almost surreptitiously, and our "patrols" tended towards becoming "night operations", combining all the squads. At the same time, they became less frequent but more tedious – and less popular – thought they remained just as physically demanding.' On 31 July all three squads were in action against a terrorist gang commanded by Hussein Ali Diab at Umm Mejaddaa, south of Beisan; eleven terrorists were killed and four taken prisoner, two of whom were later executed. August brought the same routine of irregular sweeps north of the Tiberias–Nazareth road in the hilly countryside which the squads had come to know so well. Operations were also undertaken in tandem with the 2nd Royal West Kents but as Wingate told Evetts, 'These had no results, the reason being that large combinations in this guerrilla fighting defeat their own object. This is a subaltern's war.'

Two further actions underlined the truth of Wingate's remarks: a counter-terrorist action at Khirbet Beit Lidd in the plain of Esdraelon to the west of Afula on the night of 3 September and a spirited riposte against an Arab gang which had committed one of the war's worst atrocities at Tiberias on 3 October. In both cases the squads were largely Jewish in composition and both achieved substantial results which, to Wingate at least, seemed to provide final proof that the Jewish supernumeraries could be turned into a regular defence force. Certainly, the action at Khirbet Beit Lidd had all the hallmarks of a well-planned and well-executed low-intensity operation and it resulted in the killing of Sheikh Tahir, a troublesome terrorist leader and one of Fauzi al Kaukji's principal lieutenants.

The incident came against the background of renewed attacks on the pipeline, the eastern end of which had become the responsibility of the Trans-Jordan Frontier Force. (According to Bredin, Wingate had little time for the TJFF which he described as 'just a lot of stupid Arabs who were commanded by probably a lot of stupid British officers'.) This decision made it impossible for the Special Night Squads to operate east of Danna but by then Wingate had lost interest in pipeline protection: he was more interested in taking the war to the terrorists and engaging the gangs which were operating in northern Palestine. The change of emphasis allowed the squads to mount a successful offensive operation in which fifteen terrorists were killed and large quantities of rifles and ammunition captured.

Once again, the outcome of the operation was dependent on reliable intelligence and in this case it turned out to be much more accurate than at Dabburiya. On learning that Sheikh Tahir's gang was staying in the

Bedouin encampment at Khirbet Beit Lidd, Wingate deployed his squads separately in a broad encircling movement so that they were on the high ground before dawn. At the same time Wingate ordered a Jewish truck to drive towards the east of the village and stop half a mile from it to drop two supernumeraries disguised as farmers. The object was to make the terrorists suspicious and bring them out into the open; unbeknownst to them, the lorry also contained a section of Ulster Riflemen equipped with a Lewis gun. Wingate hoped that the surprised terrorists would then beat a hasty retreat in the opposite direction where the squads would be waiting for them.

Everything went according to plan. As King-Clark's squad moved across the flat dusty ground into the encampment and heard the Ulsters' Lewis gun commence firing, they were treated to 'an extraordinary spectacle – more exciting even, than a movie!' From the black Bedouin tents rode a splendid figure on horseback, his checked *kheffiyah* headdress streaming out behind him. Alerted by the gunfire, he wheeled his horse dramatically and rode towards the village. It was Sheikh Tahir. When the Manchesters' squad entered the village they came across him again, firing at them with a rifle from behind a pile of brushwood. King-Clark immediately engaged him with his Mauser while Howbrook ran up to the brushwood and hit him with a single shot from his pistol, just as Sheikh Tahir was attempting to reload. The dead man was smartly dressed in riding breeches and leather boots and he carried a Luger automatic and a Lee-Enfield rifle. 'In one pocket was a tiny, handwritten and illustrated, copy of the Koran, bound in tooled leather,' remembered King-Clark. 'But I'm afraid it hadn't been much help to him.'

More importantly he carried incriminating papers which listed the names of local Arabs friendly to the terrorist cause and these enabled the squads to mount another operation two nights later when the *mukhtar*, or mayor, of Tantura was arrested for giving aid and assistance to the gangs by helping with gun-running. Although the arrest was botched – as the *mukhtar* attempted to escape he was shot and killed by a supernumerary – Wingate was sufficiently pleased with the outcome of the operation to highlight its significance in a report he wrote the following year in defence of the Special Night Squads.

This action had an important local effect, having regard to the state of the rebellion at that time. It should be remembered that a surprise of armed rebels by armed forces of the Crown which was not an equal surprise for the latter, was seldom gained during the rebellions of 1936–38. I can think of only one case when a gang was surrounded by deliberate action and completely surprised.

Gangs have been rounded up after drives carried out, usually for days, by large
Forces; small columns have bumped gangs unexpectedly, and more often been
bumped. But if a case strictly comparable to those of Umm Mejaddaa and
Khirbet Beit Lidd exists, I do not know of it. It becomes necessary for me, the
commander of the SNS to say this, owing to the attacks now made upon the
value of our work by those ignorant of what we have done.

The squads followed up their September successes with three more
operations which resulted in the final destruction of the terrorist gangs
led by Naif Zobi and Hussein Ali Diab, the latter being killed along with
eleven of his accomplices. Despite these achievements, though, Haining's
growing disquiet about Wingate's operations led to the first moves being
made to close them down. On 9 September he took Evetts into his
confidence and told him that, in view of the worsening security situation,
the time had come to reconsider the Special Night Squads. Palestine was
once more heavily garrisoned, with the equivalent of two divisions, and
the infantry component was already carrying out the type of operation
instigated by Wingate; on the same night as the Tiberias massacre units
of the 1st Royal Scots had successfully engaged terrorists at Tulkarm,
killing three and wounding eight. Quite apart from the political wisdom
of arming Jewish supernumeraries to fight the Arab terrorists, Haining
had come to the conclusion that the squads were surplus to requirements.
Having discussed the problem with Wingate, Evetts responded diplo-
matically to Ritchie three days later, on 12 September.

I think it would be a great mistake to break up this organisation and I consider
it should be used for all three brigades.
    Capt Wingate has asked my permission to write privately to the GOC on
the question of training and expanding SNS and 'Police' for the whole country
and as he is Force HQ officer I have given this permission.

It was all in vain. Although Wingate promoted the familiar arguments
about the squads' effectiveness, Haining was already minded to wind up
their operations at the earliest opportunity and to concentrate internal
security operations on the resident infantry battalions. The moment
arrived when Wingate took his extended leave in the middle of October
but before that happened, his men were involved in the tragedy of
Tiberias.

It was an incident which is all too common in protracted terrorist
wars: an unfortunate lapse of concentration by the security forces in the
face of determined action by the terrorist opposition. Taking advantage
of the handover to a fresh British infantry battalion, a large Arab terrorist

gang attacked Tiberias from three sides and entered the Jewish quarter of Kiryat Shemuel. In a brutal assault on the local population nineteen Jews were murdered, ten of whom were children. To add horror to the massacre, the bodies were burned and a synagogue was set alight. There was also a good deal of looting and in the confusion the terrorists were allowed to escape.

Equally distressing was the behaviour of the officers and men of the 1st South Staffordshire regiment which was garrisoned in a nearby Turkish fort. Many of the men were relaxing in Tiberias at the time of the incident but when the firing began in Kiryat Shemuel they failed to take any counter-action. According to Gershon Ritov, the *mukhtar* of Tirat Tsevi, who witnessed the incident, 'the soldiers in the cafés took immediate cover under the tables, and those in the cinema crept under their chairs.' One reason was their inexperience, another the regulation in force at the time that the men's rifles had to be chained to their webbing; but the lack of initiative shown by the battalion was an obvious embarrassment to the British authorities.

It was in the aftermath of the incident that Wingate once more came to the fore. Using information gained from the Arabs captured during the action against Hussein Ali Diab, he had deployed his squads in a counter-insurgency operation in the Tiberias area. While one group proceeded under his command to Kfar Mesha, west of Tiberias, another surrounded the settlement at Sirin, to the south. During the night news filtered through to Wingate from Tiberias. Correctly gauging that the gang would leave by the westward route out of the town to seek refuge in the hills – the other route runs north alongside the Sea of Galilee and is more exposed – Wingate laid an ambush and killed eleven terrorists. As he was able to report, his men were 'the only Armed Forces of the Crown to make successful contact with them [the terrorists] that night'.

Equally importantly from his own point of view, the action allowed him to meet General Sir Edmund Ironside, the Commander-in-Chief-designate Mediterranean Command who happened to be visiting Palestine at that time and who had been taken to Tiberias by Evetts the day after the massacre. Although he was angered by the behaviour of the South Staffords, Ironside was suitably intrigued by his fellow gunner's initiative to congratulate Wingate and spend some time with him at the scene of the ambush. Ironside was in the Middle East at the behest of the War Office, but earlier that year he had already noted in his diary on 10 January 1938 his thoughts on the region's importance in the event of a war which he deemed to be inevitable.

All my thoughts outside the tactical training of the Army are always centred upon the Mediterranean. I cannot help believing that we are taking Mussolini too lightly. Have we anybody who has considered all the aspects of Defence in the Middle East? The Mediterranean is a vital artery to us just as much as the Suez canal. The centre of gravity is changing and so, with the quarrel with Italy, it has shifted again. I hope we are taking stock of the fresh circumstances.

In his subsequent report to the War Office at the end of October Ironside stressed the need to counter Mussolini's territorial gains in Libya and Ethiopia which could threaten Britain's lines of communication to India and the Far East. Although the odds were stacked against Wingate in Jerusalem it seemed as if he had once again found an influential friend in high places.

The next day saw Wingate in action for the last time in Palestine. Travelling back to Ein Harod, his squad came across two taxis speeding towards Dabburiyah and Jenin: they were carrying the terrorist leaders Abu Durra and Naif Zobi; Wingate's men set off in hot pursuit and forced the latter's gang into action on the ridges of Mount Tabor. Although the operation could have turned to disaster when an RAF aircraft mistook the squadsmen for Arabs and started to attack them, Wingate's men inflicted a heavy defeat on Naif Zobi by killing fourteen of his men. As he pointed out to Evetts, it was a satisfactory conclusion: 'There is certainly no force in the country of an equivalent strength that has a tenth part of the fighting or achievement to show ... I do not think that there is a battalion, let alone a company, in Palestine, that can show such a record, even for a whole tour of duty.'

By then Wingate was badly in need of leave. Not only had his wounds debilitated him but he was physically and mentally exhausted after the concentrated effort of commanding the squads and leading them on active service operations. He had already told his mother that he hoped to come home in the autumn and he was able to keep his promise after the Tiberias massacre. In mid-October he travelled back to London where he spent seven weeks' leave with Lorna in a rented apartment in Welbeck Street. True to form, though, he refused to relax and spent much of his leave keeping up his contacts with leading British Zionists and crystallising his thoughts on the creation of Jewish armed forces to fight on Britain's side in a war which he, like Ironside and many others, knew to be not far away.

September had seen the secession of Sudetenland to Hitler's Germany, a crisis so dangerous that a European war seemed imminent and trenches had been dug in London's parks. Although Neville Chamberlain, the

British Prime Minister, had extracted a joint declaration with Hitler renouncing war and accepting consultation and negotiation as a basis for settling future confrontations, the threat of war cast a long shadow over subsequent British foreign and military policy. Following the Munich agreement the government lifted the brakes on rearmament finance and the chiefs of staff and the Foreign Office regained ascendancy over the Treasury in the drive to equip the armed forces and to put the country on a war footing.

While it was true that Chamberlain's diplomacy had given the country a respite, its resources were still dangerously overstretched. This was especially true of Palestine where large numbers of British troops were tied down in labour-intensive counter-insurgency operations: under the circumstances, an imposed settlement seemed to be the only means of protecting British interests, even if it meant offending the Jews. In the event, that is what happened. In April 1938 a commission headed by Sir John Woodhead had arrived in Palestine to take evidence on implementing partition as recommended by the Peel Report. Its findings were published on 9 November 1938 and they were a severe blow to Jewish interests: the bulk of Palestine would be given to the Arabs while the Jews would get a narrow band of territory in the north, measuring only 400 square miles. By a tragic irony the publication of the findings coincided with *Kristallnacht*, an organised pogrom in Nazi Germany during which synagogues were destroyed and 50,000 Jews placed under arrest. A few days later, 10,000 Jewish children from Germany and Austria were refused entry visas to Palestine.

The Woodhead recommendations effectively put paid to British backing for the creation of a Jewish homeland in Palestine. In the immediate aftermath the government announced that it would convene a round table conference in London involving the Jewish Agency, the Palestinian Arab leadership and representatives of the neighbouring Arab countries. If this failed to reach a conclusion, warned Malcolm Mac-Donald, the Colonial Secretary, Britain would have no option but to impose a solution. Needless to say, the leadership of the Jewish Agency and their British supporters were enraged and the decision marked the beginning of the end of the twenty-year-old partnership between the British government and Weizmann's Zionist movement.

Against this troubled political background Wingate arrived back in London and immediately set to work in the Zionist cause by advocating the establishment of a Jewish military force. Amongst his political contacts he met the influential military theorist Captain Basil Liddell Hart to discuss the importance of the Special Night Squads, and he resumed his acquaintance with the Conservative MP Victor Cazalet who had visited Palestine with Blanche Dugdale earlier in the year and who was committed to the cause of a Jewish homeland in Palestine. Through Cousin Rex he was introduced to Malcolm MacDonald, the Colonial Secretary, but the meeting was not a success. At the time MacDonald was under pressure from the chiefs of staff to negotiate an agreement which would ensure Arab support in the event of war and as a result he was careful to distance himself from the Zionist cause. Equally inconclusive were two meetings which Wingate had with the press: neither Geoffrey Dawson, editor of *The Times*, nor Lord Beaverbrook were impressed by his arguments of the importance of keeping faith with the Balfour Declaration.

Inevitably perhaps, he found more congenial company amongst those close to the Jewish Agency. In addition to being a regular visitor of the Weizmanns, he had meetings with Blanche Dugdale, Lewis Namier, Wyndham Deedes, Pinhas Rutenberg, the founder of the Palestine Electric Company, and the banker James de Rothschild. At the end of October there was also a chance meeting with David Ben-Gurion – never a close confidant – and through him he renewed an acquaintance with Lord Lloyd, the chairman of the British Council. Once a highly respected diplomat and High Commissioner of Egypt between 1925 and 1929, differences of opinion with the Foreign Office had blighted his reputation within the government although he was still regarded as an original thinker on the Middle East. Churchill, in particular, had a high opinion of him and was to make him his Colonial Secretary in 1940.

Although Lloyd was outspokenly pro-Arab he was not entirely opposed to the idea of a Jewish homeland, provided that it retained an allegiance to the British Empire. What worried him was the possibility that Jewish refugees from other parts of the world would relinquish those ties which suggested that Britain's interests in the Middle East were best served by the Arabs. None the less, he was prepared to listen to Ben-Gurion's arguments and arranged to discuss them over lunch with him and Weizmann on 27 October. To this meeting, at Lloyd's insistence, Wingate was also invited. According to Ben-Gurion, 'nothing really came of the meeting' at which the main topic of discussion was the possibility of redrawing the Palestine partition map to give the Jews a greater proportion of the south in return for surrendering much of Galilee. However, he also remembered that Wingate used the opportunity to impress upon Lloyd his argument that 'the Jews of Palestine alone constituted a stable force which could be relied on ... [and] that

British policy in the Middle East should be based on friendship with Turkey and with a strong Jewish Palestine.'[1]

As a result Lloyd passed on Wingate's ideas to the recently appointed Chief of the Imperial General Staff, Field Marshal Lord Gort, who replied on 1 November, 'if I can manage it, I will certainly have a talk with him.' The meeting never took place but at least Wingate's ideas were common currency within the War Office's influential Directorate of Military Operations.

In all of Wingate's discussions about the future of Palestine the idea of arming the Jews and creating a properly trained and equipped Jewish army was never far from his mind. Although he had already outlined the broad principles in several papers prepared for Weizmann it was not until this period of leave that he began to put his proposals into a more orderly framework. His first thoughts centred on the creation of a force similar to the Arab Legion in neighbouring Transjordan. It had its origins in a militia force created in 1920 and under the tutelage of its commander Peake Pasha it had grown into a professional Arab army led mainly by British officers who owed their allegiance to the Emir Abdullah. After visiting Transjordan in 1936 Wingate believed that the Arab Legion concept could be translated to Palestine and that the Jews would create the best army in the Middle East, an idea which most British officers in Jerusalem considered to be heresy. When Corporal Thomas asked permission to transfer to a more glamorous-sounding unit like the Transjordan Frontier Force, Wingate told him, 'Oh, don't worry about that. Don't worry about the Arab Legion or the TJFF or the SDF [Sudan Defence Force] because soon you and I will belong to the finest legion of them all. The Jewish Legion.'

How this would have been achieved is contained in a paper entitled 'Jewish State. Internal Security and Frontier Defence – Transition Period'. Written for Weizmann in 1938 it envisaged the implementation of the Peel Commission partition plan which would have given the Jewish state Galilee and a 200-mile-long land frontier. To provide the safety of this frontier and to give the country a powerful army capable of giving 'every Jew living within the State a sense of security from an attack, whether this comes from within or without', Wingate recommended the creation of three different types of armed forces under the generic title of the Jewish Legion.

1. Jewish State Defence Force
A brigade-sized mobile force based at Mount Carmel and reinforced by two

field batteries equipped with 4.5 howitzers and anti-aircraft artillery.
Estimated cost per year: £1 million.

2. Frontier Guards
One regular infantry battalion organised in eight companies of one hundred
strong each distributed along the land frontier. It would be equipped with Ford
trucks and the men would be armed with light automatics and small arms.
Estimated cost per year: £250,000.

3. National Guard
A national militia force for home defence organised in sections of six men and
a section commander equipped with rifles, or, in the larger settlements, in
platoons of four sections.
Estimated cost per year: £70,000.

In the course of his lengthy paper Wingate also made a number of
other recommendations for the defence of the homeland. Some were
straightforward, like the creation of a civil defence system and the
construction of blockhouses and wire fences to defend the exposed
frontier between Kinneret and Metulla. Others were more revolutionary.
Because he had little faith in the work of the Royal Air Force in Air
Control, Wingate could see no reason to create a separate air force:
instead, he recommended that it should come under army command.
He also believed that the new state should encourage civil aviation and
develop its own aviation industry in order to make it less reliant on
imported supplies from other countries. (This aim was eventually realised
in 1975 when the Israeli air force was equipped with Israeli-built Kfir
C-1 ground-attack aircraft.)

Equally radical were his proposals for enlisting women into the armed
forces. Because of the shortage of manpower in the new Jewish state he
recommended that women between the ages of seventeen and forty-five
should be enrolled 'on a voluntary system' as clerks, mechanics or drivers
in peacetime, and in support arms during time of war. To free men for
front-line combat roles he also thought that women could be trained to
fight in anti-aircraft artillery batteries and in home defence militia
companies. Although the employment of women became accepted
practice in the British armed forces during the Second World War – and
became standard practice in the Israeli Defence Forces when they were
formed in 1948 – it was still considered to be a somewhat extreme
concept. Lorna remembered Wingate causing offence by mentioning
the possibility at a dinner party in Haifa at the end of 1936: an elderly

colonel present flushed a dull red and said, 'I think we had better speak of something else.'

Although the paper was shelved after the collapse of the partition plans for Palestine, Wingate never lost sight of the possibility of creating Jewish armed forces both for self-defence and to fight alongside imperial forces in the event of war. Indeed, in the months to come the idea was to become a personal crusade and as a result it was to have a detrimental effect on his career. Being the man he was, Wingate made no secret of his beliefs. He also used all the influence at his disposal and was a regular visitor to the Foreign Office and War Office. Such activity did not go unnoticed and his meeting with MacDonald was considered to be 'bad form' amongst superiors who thought that a relatively junior captain had no business discussing policy with the Colonial Secretary. Inevitably the news filtered back to Palestine where his political opinions were becoming a source of embarrassment to his military masters. When he returned to Palestine on 5 December he found that he had been posted to headquarters in Jerusalem and that the Special Night Squads were in the process of being run down. Ritchie explained that the presence of large numbers made their task unnecessary and that the policy of actively arming members of the Haganah had come to an end for 'political reasons'. This had already been confirmed by MacMichael in a letter to MacDonald on 24 July.

I have discussed with the General Officer Commanding and Inspector-General of Police the general question of defence of Jewish settlements, and we do not favour any increase in numbers, but rather improvement in defence organisations. Unfortunately, each regrettable incident is made material for political propaganda and used as an argument for an increase in the number of Jewish supernumeraries. This particularly applies in the debatable lands of Galilee.[2]

When the letter was passed to the Foreign Office for comment Viscount Halifax concurred with MacMichael's policy and warned against the further employment of the Special Night Squads: 'I am to suggest that the High Commissioner's attention should be drawn in this connexion to the importance on general grounds of avoiding any action which might give the impression in neighbouring countries that Jewish troops are henceforth to be used for offensive purposes.'[3]

Despite making several requests to return to work in the field Wingate was told that his new employment as GSO III (Intelligence) required him to remain at headquarters for the analysis of raw intelligence. Ritchie made his position clear in Wingate's annual report for 1938 which contained the first warnings about official disapproval: 'His judgement, when not obscured by preconceived ideas, is good and he is capable of very hard work when his interest is engaged, but is inclined to be impatient of control if he does not think his views are being accepted.' Ritchie's comments were endorsed by Haining who described Wingate as 'an enthusiast who prefers to travel alone' and ended his summary with the advice that he should 'subordinate self at times to the common good'. After being shown the report, Wingate responded on 30 December claiming that it was unfair because it implied that he was driven by personal ambition. Haining noted the objection on 11 January 1939 and although the matter was allowed to drop, it was obvious that Wingate was now a marked man and that his connection with the Jewish cause had put a question mark over his future employment.

Not unnaturally, Wingate was much aggrieved to find that he had been effectively sidelined from working in the field and that his squads were to be disbanded. But he was not the man to let inaction prevent him from pursuing his goal. The opportunity came on 23 January 1939 when a paper came into his hands from 8th Division minuting a conference on internal security. In Appendix A, Part D, Paragraph II the divisional intelligence officers recommended the abolition of the Special Night Squads in words that Wingate found particularly offensive.

The conference is generally opposed to the dressing up of Jews as British soldiers; in particular it is considered undesirable to have a proportion of Jews in SNS detachments: these should be entirely British . . . In short, if it is desired that we should conciliate the Arab, we should not provoke him by using Jews in offensive action against him.

There was more to this than anti-Semitism or Arabophil enthusiasm, although both were undoubtedly present when the intelligence officers drafted their recommendations. Within Force Headquarters in Jerusalem there was a growing belief that the Jews were primarily interested in defending themselves and were not concerned with protecting British imperial interests. There was also a genuine fear that by arming the Jews and by giving them sound military training the British could be storing up problems for the future. The weapons and tactics could be used against them should the Jews ever rise against British rule in armed insurrection. It was not an idle fear: future Israeli army commanders such as Moshe Dayan were amongst those members of the Haganah who received their first formal military training from the Special Night Squads. With Zvi Brenner, Dayan was arrested and imprisoned in October 1939 for the illegal possession of arms together with forty-three others, some of whom had also served under Wingate. When Bala Bredin returned to Palestine in 1946 with the 6th Airborne Division he was not surprised to find that the terrorists attacking the security forces were 'by and large Jews whom we had trained'.

On reading the paper Wingate's first instinct was to go to Haifa to explain the work of the Special Night Squads to those responsible for writing the paper but as Lord Gort was visiting 8th Division headquarters permission was refused. Undaunted, Wingate wrote a lengthy memorandum to Brigadier Evetts which was intended for a wide circulation. Its intention was to counter the recommendation that the Special Night Squads be closed down and to correct the impression that his men were little more than 'Jews dressed up as British soldiers'. Of particular interest was Wingate's narrative history of the founding of the Special Night Squads and his account of the actions in which they were involved, but he was also at pains to speak up for his men's achievements. Because most of the staff officers in 8th Division were not in Palestine in 1938 they could be excused for knowing nothing about the circumstances which brought the squads into being, but Wingate was unyielding in his criticism of their motives in recommending them down. After stating that he was honour-bound to defend his men Wingate offered an uncompromising conclusion: 'If we in this country pursue a policy of favouring our enemies at the expense of our friends; what fate may properly await us?'

As a result of Wingate's initiative, General Bernard Montgomery, commanding 8th Division, promised to change the offending words and to mark the squads' work with suitable decorations but nothing was done to keep them in existence. (These promises were never kept, much to the chagrin of the men who had served Wingate at Ein Harod.) However right and proper it had been for Wingate to act in that manner, the action only served to remind those in authority of his sympathies towards the Jews. In March he tried again to be released from his desk job but was once more refused permission by Ritchie to leave Force Headquarters. By then Haining was taking steps to post his uncomfortable intelligence officer out of Palestine: there was a strong hint in the final sentence of Ritchie's report which prophesied a rosy future for Wingate, 'provided he finds the correct employment'. The axe fell on 11 May when the War Office wrote to Wingate ordering him to return to England to take up the post of Brigade Major with the newly formed 56th Light Anti-Aircraft Brigade (Territorial Army). Writing on his subordinate's behalf Ritchie replied that Wingate was 'desirous of taking the appointment and will be free to proceed to the UK from 26 May 1939'.

By then the last act was being played out in Britain's troubled relationship with Palestine. The round table conference had already taken place in London but, being in effect two conferences because the Arabs refused to meet the Jews, it had been inconclusive. While Wingate was preparing to leave the country the government published the MacDonald White Paper on 17 May 1939. To all intents and purposes this annulled the Balfour Declaration and ended British mandatory obligations to provide a national home for the Jews. Immigration was restricted to 15,000 per year for the coming five years, after which Palestine would be granted independence with national institutions reflecting the permanent Arab majority and Jewish minority. With war increasingly certain MacDonald had appeased the Arabs while the Jewish Agency was left with little option but to accept it for the time being and to continue supporting British interests.

Because the White Paper was greeted with dismay by the Jewish population in Palestine, Haining asked Wingate to perform one last service by going north to Galilee to act as a moderating influence on the Haganah men who had served under him in the Special Night Squads. The general's gesture also allowed Wingate to take formal farewell of his friends, to remind them that all was not lost and to confirm that the fight for a Jewish homeland would continue. Upset as he was by the outcome of the White Paper, at no time did Wingate succumb to the temptation to advocate the use of force to gain political ends. On the contrary, members of the squads remembered that Wingate counselled caution and used his influence 'to dissuade them from dangerous courses and to convince them that, whatever appearances seemed to show, Great Britain was still their best friend'.

After Wingate's death there were suggestions that he had behaved treacherously during this period by advising Haganah leaders in Haifa to take up arms against the British and to blow up the local oil refinery. These rumours culminated in an article by Leonard Mosley in the *Sunday Express* on 6 March 1954 which concentrated on this period and suggested that Wingate was a security risk who was fortunate to escape prosecution. It was sensational make-believe.

Although Wingate could be intemperate and frequently overstepped the bounds of political correctness in his dealings with the Jews – he was often indiscreet in his dealings with Jews and Dayan admitted that he was both 'mad and maddening' – he was not disloyal. His mistake lay in allying himself so closely to Weizmann and the Jewish Agency and this led to his posting out of Palestine. There was a meeting in Haifa, at the house of Emmanuel Wilenski, where Wingate spoke passionately on the subject of Zionism but when it was suggested that he should raise a Jewish resistance movement in Europe, Wingate refused. 'I can't do it,' he told Lorna on his return. 'I'm a straightforward soldier and I dislike this undercover stuff. If I get mixed up in it I shall be sidetracked and it will be the end of me.' As Lorna noted later, her husband was 'unexpectedly old-fashioned' about the army. (In 1959 Christopher Sykes confirmed there never was any talk of destroying the Iraq Petroleum Company's refinery in Haifa.)

None the less, his promotion of the Jewish cause did tell against Wingate for he had made no secret of the fact that he wanted to see the creation of a Jewish Legion and that he regarded himself as its natural commander. Ideas of that kind not only suggested dangerous ambition but they also hinted that he had identified himself too closely with the Jewish cause to be of continuing use to the British intelligence services. From an operational point of view this was probably correct: it has always been the policy of the British army to transfer officers who identify too strongly with a cause, especially when they are in a position where they have to be neutral. Also, Wingate's public profile and his links with politicians would have told against him. It was considered unseemly for a relatively junior officer to be in the limelight – Wingate never hid his achievements – and there were those in Jerusalem who were jealous of that standing.

Wingate did not see himself in that light. When he came to defend himself later in the year against a further adverse report, he denied that his links with the Jews affected his impartiality and argued that it was 'owing to the fact that my sympathy does not waver with every political tide that I owe my standing and potential usefulness to His Majesty's service'. In other words, he supported a minority but was not prepared to give way unless it could be proved that his bias affected his judgement. In support of that position he pointed to the evidence which he had given to the Woodhead Commission on the question of his own position.

I feel that I lay myself open to the charge of partiality. I repudiate this charge. Nowadays people seem to imagine that impartiality means readiness to treat lies and truth the same, readiness to hold white as bad as black and black as good as white. I, on the contrary, believe that without integrity a man had much better not approach a problem at all.

It was a familiar argument. For Wingate, supporting Jewish claims was an all-or-nothing stance: to compromise was the work of the devil. It certainly did not mean playing one side off against the other as he believed the British to be doing in Palestine. Unfortunately that was not the opinion of his seniors and, honourable though it was, Wingate's unyielding adherence to the Jewish cause was the fundamental reason for his dismissal from the country. He and Lorna left by train for Port Said on 26 May 1939 on the first stage of their journey back to England and an uncertain future.

Eight

MARCHING OFF TO WAR

On arriving at Port Said, the Wingates found that the troopship *Dorsetshire* was scheduled to call at Haifa before proceeding to Southampton, a happy coincidence which allowed Wingate to take an impromptu farewell of the Weizmann family; during his time in Palestine he had become particularly fond of Chaim's brother Chilik and his son Ezer, later to become a distinguished RAF pilot.

Although he was leaving Palestine, Wingate had not put it out of his mind and as the ship crossed the Mediterranean he put the final touches to a paper entitled 'Palestine in Imperial Strategy' which he intended to present to General Ironside in Gibraltar. In this twenty-seven-page-long memorandum Wingate finally crystallised his argument that the best interests of the British Empire in the Middle East would be served by supporting the Jewish cause in Palestine. Shrewdly, Wingate did not immediately promote that case in the opening pages of his paper. Instead, he sketched in the historic reasons for supporting the Arab cause: 'Having regard to our special position as an imperial power with hundreds of millions of Mohammedan subjects we simply cannot afford to adopt in Palestine a policy repugnant to their feelings.'

At the same time, tongue in cheek, he stated the reasons for not supporting the Zionists.

The Jews are a peculiar people whom nobody likes, and for this there must be a good reason. Their manner is unpleasant. We do not trust them. A large number are Bolsheviks and the rest are probably adventurers. Whatever they may have been in the past, today they are not a military race. Their fighting value in war would be small.

Having introduced caricature, Wingate moved on to 'Some Facts' and to his own interpretation of recent British policy in the Middle East. In his view, the average Arab was 'lazy, ignorant, feckless and, without being particularly cowardly, sees no point in really losing his life'. Far too many myths had surrounded his name, due largely to T. E. Lawrence's *Seven Pillars of Wisdom*, 'that unfortunate masterpiece'. Furthermore, British fears of a *jihad*, or holy war, which would affect the Muslims in India, were largely exaggerated. In his view Arab military support counted for nothing and the wartime actions undertaken under Lawrence and Feisal were little more than irritants to the Turks. He also pointed out that the Arabs in Palestine had, in fact, fought in the ranks of the Turkish army until its eventual defeat in 1918.

Compared to the mixture of romanticism and wishful thinking which underpinned the British view of the Arab world in the Middle East, there was a moral obligation under the Balfour Declaration and the League of Nations mandate to fulfil the promise of a Jewish homeland. With the world drifting towards war Wingate recommended that this claim should be fulfilled by scrapping the White Paper and supporting the Jews so that their manpower and energy could be used in the support of the British Empire. While the Arabs in neighbouring Transjordan and Syria would be bound to waver until they had evidence that Britain was capable of maintaining its global power, the Jews of Palestine were already committed to the British side against Hitler's Germany. In the latter case the work of the Special Night Squads could be revived, re-inforced and expanded as the basis of a substantial Jewish contribution to the British war effort. Wingate also thought it would be possible to develop the country's industrial potential, using the knowledge and experience of immigrant businessmen from Europe. This would involve ending the ban on immigration, allowing Jewish capital to be invested in Palestine and encouraging the growth of industry in a country which would 'of course become a member of the British Commonwealth of Nations'.

It was not an original argument – the supporters of the Balfour Declaration had hoped to see a Jewish Palestine fully integrated into the empire and it had been given an intellectual gloss by Lewis Namier in his book *The Margin of History* – but it flew in the face of British strategic thinking in 1939 when both the Foreign Office and the War Office wanted to preserve Arab support throughout the Middle East. The mood was articulated in July 1939 by Major John Bagot Glubb, the new commander of the Arab Legion, in his monthly report from Transjordan: 'The theory that the presence of the Jews is a strategic asset to the British is now completely exploded. To begin with if the Jews were not there, the Arabs would be friendly, a much greater strategic advantage. If the Jews arrive the Arabs become hostile."[1]

Palestine and Transjordan were already aligned to Britain through the mandate, Egypt and Iraq through treaty, as was Syria to France, Britain's European ally. That left Saudi Arabia as the only country lacking a commitment but, despite Nazi blandishments, including a gift of 4,000 modern rifles, Ibn Saud remained neutral throughout the war. Given the need to maintain that situation, both the Colonial Office and the Foreign Office were determined not to push the Arabs into the arms of the axis powers by overtly supporting the Jews. As a result, despite the eloquence and passion of Wingate's arguments, his theories fell on deaf ears.

Not that Wingate did not do his best to advance them. When the *Dorsetshire* arrived in Gibraltar he contrived to get ashore, despite being ordered not to do so, and managed to deliver his paper to Ironside at Government House. The general replied a few days later, sending the letter to Wingate via the War Office to the headquarters of the 1st Anti-Aircraft Division (TA) at Uxbridge. In it he agreed with Wingate's summary of the myth surrounding the Arab revolt and the part played by 'that unfortunate charlatan Lawrence'. He also praised Wingate's handling of the Special Night Squads and, quite unexpectedly, confirmed that it had been his intention as Commander-in-Chief 'to arm the Jews and to withdraw most of the [British] troops'. Although Ironside was wary about supporting the Jews too fully – he admitted to being 'a little frightened of the strength and sincerity of Zionism' – and doubted if Palestine could become fully industrialised, he was intrigued by the strength of Wingate's arguments. He ended the letter by inviting Wingate to discuss the matter further with him when both men were back in London.

By then Ironside knew that he would not be taking up the position of Commander-in-Chief Mediterranean: the post went to Wavell who was appointed General Officer Commanding in Chief of the newly formed Middle East Command. Instead he was ordered to return to London by Secretary of State for War Leslie Hore-Belisha who intended to make him the commander of the British Expeditionary Force (BEF) earmarked for service in France. However, in one of the many games of musical chairs played in the War Office in the crucial days before the outbreak of war with Germany in September 1939, Hore-Belisha changed his mind once more and, acting on the advice of Liddell Hart, promoted Ironside to the vital position of Chief of the Imperial General

Staff (CIGS) while Gort was given command of the BEF.

It was a great mistake. Ironside, a soldier's soldier, had little experience of military administration and none at all of politics and within a year he had been replaced by Field Marshal Sir John Dill. (Although he made his mark with two Chiefs of the Imperial General Staff, Wingate had little luck with them: Deverell, whom he had impressed at Catterick, lasted twenty months in the job, Ironside nine months.) None the less, it suited Wingate's purposes to have a friend in high places at the War Office for, shortly after arriving in London on 13 June, he was to need all the help he could get.

Having reported to the headquarters of the 56th Light Anti-Aircraft Brigade at Duke of York's Barracks in Chelsea, Wingate moved into his club, the Army and Navy, while Lorna went north to Aberdeenshire. (They spent a few days together at the Kensington Palace Hotel and later that summer moved into rented accommodation in the King's Road, Chelsea.) No sooner had he arrived at his new headquarters than on 22 June Wingate received the confidential report which Ritchie had prepared on his departure from Jerusalem. Like every other army report it allowed the immediate commander to comment on the officer's personality, characteristics and technical and military qualities and once written it was then shown to him. Because he had left Palestine before it was written on 9 June Wingate had not been given that opportunity: it is not difficult to understand why Wingate exploded when he finally read Ritchie's assessment.

Captain Wingate possesses many exceptional qualities; however his ardent nature which gives him the power to pursue an objective enthusiastically often obscures his judgement and distorts his sense of proportion.

He has a first-class brain, is exceptionally well read and has great mental energy but he is liable to employ these gifts for the furtherance of some idea which he has adopted because of its emotional appeal. While he has been in Palestine he has given his sympathy so wholeheartedly to the Jewish cause that his service to the intelligence branch has become valueless.

He is an exceptional linguist, possesses great physical energy and powers of endurance and has proved himself to be a tactician of outstanding ability.

The report concluded with the recommendation that he should return to regimental duties and marked his performance as 'indifferent'. For Wingate, who had been given no reason to expect a bad report, it was a stunning blow and reawakened all his old fears about those in authority using their power to prevent him achieving his aims. Despite Ritchie's fair comments about Wingate's virtues, Wingate felt that he had been damned by the observation that his contacts with the Jews had rendered him 'valueless' to the security forces. His first instinct was to fight back and this he did through an obscure right of any officer to appeal to the sovereign to have the report withdrawn. The privilege is granted under section 42 of the Army Act which allows an officer to make a 'complaint' which is considered first by the generals on the Army Council (today's Army Board) who, having taken further evidence, then recommend a course of action to the Secretary of State. The relevant papers, together with a recommendation, are then passed to the sovereign.

Wingate set to work immediately, noting the main points of his argument, drafting and redrafting the material until he was satisfied with the strength of his case. (The material is contained in a personal file of loose-leafed handwritten and typed manuscripts.) Five days later, on 27 June, he returned the complaint with a covering letter to Ritchie in Jerusalem. It was a strongly worded and meandering document, amounting to fifteen foolscap pages, in which Wingate abandoned caution and passionately defended his role in Palestine. In summary, the complaint referred to the 'contents and manner' of Ritchie's report, the absence of a report from Evetts and the 'absence of any recognition of services' since the award of the DSO in July 1938.

Although Wingate was within his rights to contest Ritchie's assessment, the second and third elements of the complaint cannot stand close examination. During the period of Ritchie's report, 1 October 1938 until 30 April 1939, Wingate was under Ritchie's direct command at Force Headquarters in Jerusalem and there was no need to take into account Evetts's opinion. (In any case, he had been posted to India.) As to further recognition, Wingate had been mentioned in despatches in April 1939. Everything hinged on Ritchie's assessment of his indifferent performance, an opinion which was directly related to Wingate's 'sympathy ... to the Jewish cause'.

Wingate based his counter-attack on three main arguments. First, he denied that his support for the Jews interfered in any way with his work as an intelligence officer; on the contrary he believed that it was an asset.

I would be judged by results, not opinions. My public and private support of the Jews was obligatory. They have always been loyal to me and to Great Britain. I would state here that neither I nor my wife, nor any member of either of our families has a drop of Jewish blood in their veins. Experience has taught me that one gets better results, to drop it on no higher ground, by consistency than by trimming one's sails to suit the wind. Is it 'emotional' to have a sense of honour and to defend your men when they are attacked?

Second, Wingate reiterated his belief that support of the Jews would be in Britain's best interests. This did not mean that he was anti-Arab: Wingate explained that his 'natural sympathy for the Arabs and [my] understanding of their position' convinced him that British, Arab and Jewish interests would be best served by creating a Jewish homeland within the Commonwealth.

I have never made the slightest secret of my views from my superiors. Persons who have not served in Palestine will not readily believe the extent of the indiscretion, the violence and partisanship even in official circles. It is unwise to forget that during the past three years to sympathise with Arabs was to side with rebels, to sympathise with Jews was to side with our friends.

Finally, he made a passionate defence of his own abilities, basing his case on the fact that on three occasions in his career the value of his opinions had been put to an acid test and had received 'triumphant vindication': his independent command in the Sudan; the desert expedition; and the creation of the Special Night Squads ('a case par excellence where my judgement was vindicated and my theories justified').

I submit that where acid tests exist opinions are of no value unless in accordance with the results of those tests. I claim that I have given proof of the abilities and qualities of a commander. I state and can prove that in Palestine I was fairly generally viewed with distaste purely owing to my connection with the Jews, that by creating and maintaining this connection I performed an important service to the Crown, that by my work in the field I performed important service, and that the bulk of these services have been unrecognised. I further claim that future developments are likely to render my services in Palestine as again of great use and that they should be employed there.

This was a direct challenge not only to Ritchie's report but also to his standing as a senior intelligence officer. He responded on 22 July, stating that he had received Wingate's complaint and that it had been forwarded to Haining. By way of riposte he enclosed a copy of Haining's own assessment which had been made on Army Form B194. Its contents only infuriated Wingate further. Although Haining praised Wingate's energy and drive, the report also complained that his tendency 'to play for his own ends and likings instead of playing for the side' had become 'a matter of such general comment as to render his services in the Intelligence Branch nugatory and embarrassing'. In other words, Wingate's support for the Jewish cause meant that he could no longer remain in Palestine.

Because he was unsure if the comments were a reply to his complaint or part of his confidential report – Wingate believed them to be the latter – he replied to Ritchie on 29 July enclosing an 'annexure' to his original complaint, answering the general's criticisms. The main thrust of this eight-page document is a rebuttal of the charges that he was pro-Jewish to the extent of damaging British interests and a renewal of his belief that those interests were best served by supporting the Jews. Once the documents had been received by the Army Council they requested comments from both Ritchie and Haining. The latter stuck to his comments in Army Form B194 which had already been shown to Wingate, but Ritchie replied separately. Although he underlined his admiration for Wingate's drive and courage, he reiterated his belief that the Special Night Squads were as much political as military in origin and that Wingate had overstepped the bounds of professional propriety by disclosing information to the Jews. 'Although in so doing he was ostensibly acting in a private capacity, I consider that in view of his official position and known access to official information and opinions Captain Wingate's action was not merely indiscreet, but definitely improper, whatever the nature of his advice.'

Under the circumstances he could see no reason to withdraw his report and there the matter rested until September when the Army Council agreed that the reports should stand and that the complaint should go directly to King George VI without ministerial advice, a course of action which would have led to failure. And there it might have ended, with Wingate's hopes in tatters, had not Ironside intervened with a personal memo to Hore-Belisha on 3 November suggesting that Wingate had been badly handled in Palestine and that the problem had partly arisen because he was under the command of an RAF officer. Noting that Wingate was 'a very valuable officer' he suggested that there was nothing in the substance of the report 'which prevents Captain Wingate being employed for the good of the Army', and that the matter therefore be dropped.

This was also Hore-Belisha's inclination and after consultation the Army Council wrote to Wingate on 25 December informing him that his appeal had failed. The letter also stressed that there was nothing in Ritchie's report which would adversely affect his future career and he could 'rest assured' that his merits were known and noted. It ended by asking if Wingate still wished to pursue his complaint. Realising that to do so would risk disaster, Wingate replied tersely on 28 December: 'Under the circumstances I do not wish to pursue my appeal to His Majesty the King.' By then the country was at war with Germany and would soon be fighting for its very survival.

The affair of the complaint to the sovereign is a curious episode in Wingate's career. On the one hand it provides evidence of his passionate concern for the Jewish cause; on the other, it underlines his inclination to be paranoid when faced by official disapproval of his actions. This tendency would resurface again during the war when he believed that those in authority either devalued his actions or were deliberately attempting to stymie them. While it is not unusual for ambitious officers to be mistrustful of their commanders if their careers are checked, Wingate was taking a considerable risk by insisting that his request for redress be laid before the sovereign. Not only was he on shaky ground – despite its eloquence his complaint contained no fresh evidence to rebut Ritchie's report – but its failure would have ruined him.

That he was persuaded from taking that course was due entirely to the 'protection' which Ironside was able to offer within the War Office. Quite apart from intervening with a memo to Hore-Belisha, Ironside met Wingate privately on 12 December at a dinner party at the Dorchester Hotel which was hosted by Victor Cazalet and attended by, amongst others, two prominent supporters of Winston Churchill: Leo Amery and Robert Boothby. During the course of the meal Ironside launched a bitter attack on Hore-Belisha whom he accused of being unable to understand official documents and who had 'put all the generals' backs up'. While this was true – Hore-Belisha never enjoyed a comfortable relationship with his chiefs of staff – it was heady gossip, and Ironside must have had sufficient confidence in Wingate to make his criticisms in front of a relatively junior officer.

Wingate's position at the table was due to two related circumstances. First, he had met Cazalet in Palestine in 1938 and had maintained contact with him; second, Cazalet, a well-connected Tory MP, commanded the 83rd Light Anti-Aircraft Battery (Territorial Army) which was part of the 56th Light Anti-Aircraft Brigade. In his position as Brigade Major – the brigade's senior operations officer – Wingate kept in close touch with Cazalet and through him was able to advance his interests in the creation of a Jewish force to fight alongside the Allies in the war against Nazi Germany. During the first week of October Cazalet had decided to take the idea a stage further by inviting a group of supporters to meet once a week in the Dorchester Hotel where he and Weizmann had suites of rooms. The meetings took place every Wednesday at 6.00 p.m. and were followed by dinner.

Amongst those who attended regularly were Wingate, Weizmann, Blanche Dugdale and Leo Amery. Other visitors were equally distinguished and influential and included Lord Halifax, the Foreign Secretary; Wilfred Greene, the Master of the Rolls; Admiral John Godfrey, the Director of Naval Intelligence; and Walter Monckton, chairman of the Aliens Advisory Committee. Cazalet's country house, Great Swifts near Sissinghurst in Kent, was also a periodic meeting place and Wingate was a regular visitor: on 10 December he met Eduard Beneš, the leader of the Czech government-in-exile.

It was a heady period in Wingate's affairs and amongst those who met him he cut a dashing and forceful figure. Edgar Dugdale saw a likeness to T. E. Lawrence and, according to his wife Blanche, was 'rather scared by his fanatical earnestness'; the writer Harold Nicolson who served in Cazalet's battery also saw the comparison and was equally troubled by it. Later, Wingate's supporters were to be alarmed by his obsession with the Jewish cause and were to distance themselves from his increasingly intemperate behaviour but in that first winter of the war it seemed that he was in the centre of great events.

Another reason for his enthusiasm was the nature of his job. Although Wingate was kept busy at brigade headquarters first at the Duke of York's Barracks and then at Sidcup in Kent, the work was not arduous. Even so, he took the work seriously and wrote a number of discussion papers recommending changes in the brigade's organisation. These ranged from proposals to eliminate needless personnel at brigade headquarters to a new set of rules for using the telephone. ('I submit that the true way to regard the telephone is not as a means of exchanging remarks with someone at the other end, but as a means of conveying intelligence rapidly.')

He was also interested in more weighty matters. On 1 April 1940, before the fall of France, Wingate advanced his own ideas of air defence and concluded that as enemy bombers would arrive over their target in a stream but at differing altitudes it should be possible for anti-aircraft guns to attack them and inflict considerable losses, provided that they were sited properly. The purpose must not be to prevent the bomber attacking – 'a ridiculous presumption' – but to inflict damage on the attacking air force. Although Wingate had met Arthur 'Bomber' Harris in Palestine (later Commander-in-Chief, RAF Bomber Command), he was sceptical about the value of strategic bombing in winning a war.

A great deal of nonsense upon the effect of aerial bombardment has been spoken – the consequence has been, and will be, that the biggest effect caused thereby is panic. In actual fact a bomber should be looked upon as a very expensive and vulnerable heavy gun with a limited amount of rounds. These rounds or bombs are no more dangerous than shells, and few of them dropped about an average VA [Vital Area] are likely to cause very serious damage. In such cases as the oil depot at Purfleet etc it is, of course, obvious that the enemy can destroy the bulk of the oil. It only remains to punish him for so doing as heavily as possible.

Anti-Aircraft Command was still regarded as a Cinderella organisation, largely because it was composed almost entirely of Territorial Army units which were undermanned and poorly equipped. Following two investigations in the 1930s – the Brooke-Popham Report in 1935 and the Dowding Report in 1937 – the nation's air defences had been revamped to provide minimum numbers of anti-aircraft batteries and searchlight companies and by April 1939 five divisions had been established with two more in the process of formation. Even so, these were only at 60 per cent of their establishment and many of the TA infantry battalions earmarked as anti-aircraft units were still in the process of conversion. There was also a shortage of equipment and it was not until 1943 that planned gun strength was reached.

Something of the state of unpreparedness can be seen in the case of Cazalet's own battery which was manned largely by friends and people who lived near his country home: according to Elwyn Jones, a future Lord Chancellor, it consisted of 'a remarkable collection of publishers, lawyers, actors, stockbrokers, landowners, grooms, bus-drivers, clerks, labourers – indeed a cross-section of the Sevenoaks area'.[2] Amongst those who served with Cazalet were the artist Ben Nicholson, the author Hammond Innes, the architect Denys Lasdun and the publisher Mark Longman. The arrangement was not unique – landowners serving in yeomanry regiments often took their grooms and household servants to war with them – but it does give an idea of the light-hearted approach which characterised the period known as the 'phoney war'. For Wingate it was certainly a great change after Palestine, but at least the atmosphere of heightened unreality allowed him the time to concentrate once more on the possibility of raising a Jewish fighting force. During the winter he and Lorna moved into an apartment at 49 Hill Street, Mayfair, which was to be their home for the rest of the war.

In the midst of Wingate's scheming for the creation of Jewish forces France fell, the British Expeditionary Force was evacuated at Dunkirk and by 20 May 1940 a Ministry of Information survey admitted that 'many people have envisaged the possibility of invasion'. Although the German forces lacked the equipment and capability in combined operations to mount a seaborne invasion across the Channel, the threat of invasion was real enough and British planners worked hard at contingency plans to contain the threat. With his customary zeal, Wingate threw himself into the effort and proposed that units similar to the Special Night Squads could be assembled and trained to mount guerrilla operations against any invading force.

It was not a new idea. General Andrew Thorne, commanding XII Corps, had applied to the War Office for the establishment of 'stay behind' groups who would emerge from hiding to inflict as much damage as possible on the enemy before being captured or killed. The idea was refined by Brigadier Colin Gubbins, a gunner officer whose previous service included fighting on the Western Front and post-war operations in northern Russia and southern Ireland. An admirer of the Irish republican leader Michael Collins, Gubbins wrote two influential pamphlets on low-intensity operations – *The Art of Guerrilla Warfare* and *The Partisan Leaders' Handbook* – both of which were translated into many other languages and later distributed to underground networks in Nazi-occupied Europe and Japanese-occupied South-East Asia. Under Gubbins's direction a network of underground hideouts for cells of 'stay behind parties' or 'auxiliary units' came into being, guerrilla specialists trained in sabotage and low-intensity operations. About twenty of these units were founded and they soon became a magnet for the more eccentric or unconventional type of soldier.

During the first half of 1940 the plans for the stay behind parties and the need to raise independent groups for action behind enemy lines led to the establishment of Special Operations Executive (SOE) which co-ordinated undercover operations in enemy territory under the direction of Hugh Dalton's Ministry of Economic Warfare. Faced by a German threat Ironside, now Commander-in-Chief Home Forces, did all that he could to encourage the development of small guerrilla forces. His own solution was the creation of mobile columns and 'Ironside' units equipped with bren gun carriers and commanded by young officers. With his experience of guerrilla-type operations in Palestine Wingate was an obvious candidate and Ironside interviewed him on 2 June. At this stage he did not want to replicate the Special

Night Squads but suggested that Wingate raise an 'Ironside' unit from his anti-aircraft brigade. This was music to Wingate's ears and within twenty-four hours he had found 150 men and ten officers with Cazalet as his second-in-command.

However, perhaps inevitably in those confused days, Wingate ran into difficulties in finding the equipment and the necessary support to raise the unit. A plan to base it in Northern Ireland was quashed because it was felt that guerrilla training could upset the neutral Irish government or provoke attacks by the IRA. Wingate believed that auxiliary units could help to keep the peace on the border and prevent the possibility of incursions from Eire; in the previous year, 1938, Britain had modified its 1921 treaty by surrendering the clause which permitted it to use Irish military and naval bases. When Wingate returned to London on 7 June he was told that his methods might smack too much of the Black and Tans, the brutal irregular auxiliaries who served alongside the Royal Irish Constabulary in 1919 and 1920. Knowing little about recent Irish history, Wingate saw the hand of General Haining at work but, as Cazalet noted on 4 June, his outbursts against authority did not help his cause.

He, Wingate, has seen Ironside several times, but there seems considerable difficulty in getting authority to start up such a unit. Wingate, although very remarkable, with, in this case, a very good idea, is not very tactful in the method he employs to get it started. He put all the Colonels' backs up and then hoped to get 150 men out of them.[3]

Although nothing came of the idea Wingate's name had been brought to the attention of SOE and it was to prove a turning point in his career. A month later, Wingate was posted to Northern Command in York under General Sir Ronald Forbes Adam and as the threat of invasion receded plans for the creation of various types of guerrilla groups were quietly shelved. In Wingate's case additional obstacles were put in his way by staff officers at GHQ Home Forces who constantly demanded 'full and exact details of the proposed establishment'. ('It was not thus that nations win wars,' Wingate noted in his diary on 21 June.) By then too, Cazalet had been appointed elsewhere, as liaison officer to the Polish General Wladyslaw Sikorski. With the crisis over Wingate had more time to visit London where he continued to bend his efforts towards the creation of a Jewish army.

It must not be thought that Wingate was alone in promoting this concept – Lewis Namier was more deeply involved in the lobbying process – or that the Jewish proposal for an independent fighting force was unique. Independent Polish and Czech squadrons flew with the Royal Air Force and the 1st Polish Armoured Division and 2nd Free French Armoured Division were amongst the war's great fighting formations. After the fall of France in 1940 when Britain stood alone against Germany the need for using friendly forces was unanswerable but, after years of neglect, the army was rapidly expanding and re-equipping itself. It was to be a lengthy and worrying process and in the midst of the battle for survival the émigré formations were the last to benefit. Fully equipped mass armies do not spring into being overnight. (After escaping from Poland and France, Sikorski's Polish forces were based in Scotland where they were employed in coastal defence duties or as makeshift agricultural labourers.)

However, the question of arms and equipment was not the only reason for the government's tardiness in dealing with the question of an independent Jewish force. The mood had been set by Neville Chamberlain who sent a curt note to Weizmann in reply to his immediate offer to pledge 'Jewish manpower, technical ability, resources at the disposal of the British government': 'You will not expect me to say more at this stage than that your public-spirited assurances are welcome and will be kept in mind.' In Palestine the new GOC, Lieutenant-General M. G. H. Barker, had made it clear to Ben-Gurion that the Haganah was an illegal organisation and Wavell, too, was worried about the long-term repercussions of arming the Jews. The impasse highlighted the problem facing the Jewish Agency. To share in the common aim of defeating Hitler they had to support Britain; yet a British victory would leave it the paramount power in the Middle East and British current policy had dropped the concept of a Jewish homeland in Palestine and was directed at appeasing Arab opinion. Because the British government held the whip hand it was not in any hurry to raise a Jewish army whose men and weapons could be used against it after the war. An indication of the new change of mood came as early as October with the arrest and imprisonment of forty-three former Special Night Squad members for the illegal possession of arms. In London the government's policy was outlined in a letter written by Lloyd to Churchill on 27 June 1940.

The precarious state of public opinion in Egypt, and amongst the Arab peoples of Iraq, Syria and Palestine is well known to you. It needs little to tilt the scale against us and, in the light of our experience of the intensity of Arab feeling during the past four years, and of the extravagant claims that have been asserted from time to time by Zionist leaders, the arming of the Jewish community in

Palestine under British auspices would undoubtedly be interpreted by Arab and Moslem opinion, not only in the Middle East, but in India, as a step towards the subjection of Palestine to Jewish domination.[4]

If the Jews wanted to fight Germany, added Lloyd, there was nothing to stop them joining the British armed forces as individuals.

The fight to create an identifiable Jewish force was not to be won until the autumn of 1944 and was to endure several painful setbacks but, from the outset, Wingate was determined to make a substantial contribution to the cause. It is also clear that he saw himself as the force's natural commander: although not stated in his three main discussion papers, 'Palestine 1940', 'Appreciation of the Use of Jewish Forces in the Prosecution of the War' and 'Desert Force for Palestine', he made this point clear to Weizmann and Namier and the information was also widely known at the War Office. On 14 September 1940 Blanche Dugdale heard Wingate tell Namier and Weizmann 'without conceit that no-one could carry out these ideas, except himself, failing himself General Evetts'.

By then Jewish hopes had been raised by the fall of Chamberlain and the introduction of the wartime coalition government headed by Churchill who had opposed the 1939 White Paper. He had already seen Wingate's preliminary paper on the use of Jewish forces which had been passed to him by Victor Cazalet; Brendan Bracken, Churchill's confidant, replied on 31 October that 'My Lord and Master wants me to tell you that Wingate's Memorandum has not been neglected and that he hopes to have a talk with you very soon.' To Churchill, Bracken was more enthusiastic: 'I know this is a daring, not to say, mad, scheme, but we live in such an ill-contrived world that it might well work.'[5] Like the later papers, Wingate's proposals trod familiar ground: that the Jews in Palestine and international Jewry were an untapped resource but were unavailable due to Britain's concerns about supporting Arab interests. Churchill was interested but not sufficiently so as to break ranks once he became Prime Minister.

In all three papers Wingate prophesied that war would soon come to the Middle East and that Britain's main base, Egypt, would be threatened. He also believed that Iraq's oilfields in the Mosul Province would be attacked or fall into unfriendly hands: if so, Britain would be 'fools to fight another campaign in that country'. Given those predictions, Britain's best hope was to concentrate its Middle East resources in Palestine and raise either a Jewish home defence force of 20,000 or a force of 15,000 troops to serve alongside the British at divisional strength. Both would require a cadre of 1,000 officers who would be trained in England by the British army. (In the event Wingate was correct about the war in the Middle East: Egypt was attacked by Italian forces in September 1940 and the North African desert remained a principal theatre of war until the end of 1942. In May 1941 a Nazi-inspired revolt in Iraq was quickly put down by British, Indian and Arab Legion troops.)

Wingate prepared the papers for Weizmann and the revised 'Appreciation' formed the basis of an offer made to Ironside in December 1939 to provide 'a Jewish division to be recruited in Palestine and elsewhere for service with the British Forces in the present war wherever required'. The force would be commanded by a 'sympathetic' British officer – Weizmann was thinking of Wingate but did not mention him by name – and, following Wingate's proposal, there would be a cadre of junior officers, most of whom would be Palestinian Jews. Although Ironside was attracted by the idea and agreed with it in principle, it was vetoed by Hore-Belisha on the grounds of shortage of equipment.

While this was true it was also undeniable that Hore-Belisha was following the War Office and Foreign Office line of refusing to provoke Arab hostility by favouring the Jews. Even the arrival in power of Churchill did nothing to improve matters and a fresh approach on 29 May 1940 was also rebuffed. By then Wingate was becoming increasingly impatient with the lack of progress and had written his final paper, 'Palestine 1940', which he sent privately to Churchill. Although an interesting analysis of Britain's current position in the Middle East, it was an intemperate document which caused much offence. It castigated the lack of understanding shown by the administration in Palestine and seemed to include it in the 'Jewish world persecution', and it poured scorn on the Arab countries of the Middle East. The Iraqi army was 'contemptible', Syria was a 'squalid desperately poor semi-desert', the Egyptians were a 'decadent cowardly people' and Islam was 'in a state of decadence'.

Far from helping the Jewish cause the paper gave rise to a rumour that Wingate had accused the British administration in Palestine of being fascists. The news alarmed Blanche Dugdale who heard it from Vera Weizmann and in her diary on 25 March 1940 she confided her first doubts about Wingate's methods: 'Wingate is an able man, but an irresponsible lunatic, and I only hope Lewis [Namier] is right in saying that such action will do no harm to anyone but himself.' Weizmann had also come to that conclusion and had firmly rebutted Wingate's suggestion that he should march into Churchill's office, bang on the table and demand a Jewish army.

Despite the faux pas – which helped to put paid to his hopes of ever commanding a Jewish force – Wingate was involved one more time in the lobbying process. On 3 September 1940 Weizmann wrote to Churchill proposing the creation of Jewish battalions in Palestine, the establishment of a Jewish officer cadre, the formation of Jewish military units in England and the establishment of a Jewish desert force to fight in North Africa. This latter idea was based on Wingate's paper and it called for the creation of a special force, based on the Special Night Squads, and similar to Glubb's Arab Legion, which would attack the Italians in Libya from the south. On this occasion, mindful of Britain's worsening strategic position, Churchill gave the idea his blessing and ten days later Weizmann was assured by the Foreign Secretary Anthony Eden and the Colonial Secretary Lord Lloyd that there were now no objections to the creation of a Jewish fighting force composed of 10,000 men, 4,000 of whom would be recruited in Palestine.

The walls of Jericho have fallen, fallen [wrote Blanche Dugdale in her diary]! I looked in at the Dorchester about 5 p.m. and found Chaim just back from this interview, elated and solemn. He said: 'It is almost as great a day as the Balfour Declaration.' Orde Wingate was there too, radiant. It may be the beginning of a great future for him too.

Despite that fond hope, it was the beginning of the end of Wingate's part in the drive to found a Jewish army. Throughout the negotiations Weizmann had been careful not to mention Wingate's name in con- nection with the force and this failing led to a furious row on the following day. While Wingate was discussing his outline for raising the force with Namier, Weizmann and Blanche Dugdale, it became apparent that Weizmann had made no arrangements to discuss the command structure with General Sir John Dill, the new CIGS (Ironside had been replaced on 27 May). Blanche Dugdale was shocked to see that Wingate, taking this as an affront, 'lost his temper very badly . . . and nearly smashed the teacups. Afterwards he apologised, but he is a most ungovernable character.'

As it turned out, the question of Wingate leading Jewish forces had never been considered by the War Office. During a meeting of the Middle East Committee of the cabinet in July 1940 Leo Amery had suggested to General Haining, by that time the new Vice-Chief of the Imperial General Staff, that Wingate was ideally suited to lead insurgent forces in Ethiopia as part of Wavell's planned operations against Italian East Africa. (Italy had declared war on 10 June.) The suggestion was passed to Wavell who gave his approval and on 18 September Wingate received orders to proceed to General Headquarters Middle East Command in Cairo where he would take up a staff post with G(R), the organisation responsible for planning operations in irregular warfare. It was a neat solution: Wingate's talents would be utilised but he would be sidelined from the question of leading a Jewish fighting force. That much was made clear by his orders which included an instruction preventing him from entering Palestine during his posting in Cairo.

Even had he stayed in the fray it is doubtful if Wingate would have been able to play a role in the creation of a Jewish army. On 17 October Lloyd wrote cautiously to Weizmann confirming the decision 'in principle' to recruit 10,000 Jewish recruits 'for incorporation in Jewish units in the British Army' but adding the proviso that 'no guarantee can be given as to the theatre of war in which the force, once trained and equipped, will be employed. Equipment will be provided by His Majesty's Government as and when their resources allow.'[6] To balance the general hesitancy the War Office appointed a liaison officer, Brigadier Alec Lee, and announced that the commander of the proposed force would be Brigadier Leonard Hawes.

This seemed to settle the matter but following Lloyd's untimely death on 4 February 1941 and the appointment of Lord Moyne as Colonial Secretary, Weizmann and Namier had to face a humiliating series of delays as the British government refused to implement the decision to create a Jewish fighting force. Churchill's note to Moyne on 1 March 1941 set the tone for the prevarications which would last until the autumn of 1944 when the various Jewish units were welded into an identifiable brigade with its own Star of David badge: 'Dr Weizmann should be told that the Jewish Army project must be put off for six months, but may be considered again in four months. The sole reason given should be lack of equipment.'[7]

In public Weizmann was prepared to accept this explanation but to his closest friends he admitted that the real reason was the British need to appease the Arabs. However, he was not prepared to take the attack to the British government and to some observers in Zionist circles, Weizmann's diplomacy was a sign of weakness. Amongst his fiercest critics was Lorna Wingate who accused him of being 'pedestrian' in his dealings with Churchill. After Wingate had left for Cairo on 19 September she kept up the pressure on Weizmann to push for a Jewish force commanded by her husband and was a constant visitor at the Dorchester Hotel. Although Weizmann admitted that he was fond of Lorna and Ivy Paterson and counted them amongst his closest friends, he, too, began to be concerned about the fanaticism she brought to her arguments about raising a Jewish army.

On 23 January 1941 Lorna subjected Weizmann to angry criticism for his failure to support her husband and accused him of preferring heroic failure to constructive effort. Stung by her criticism, Weizmann replied later in the day, explaining that as Lorna was not a Jew she could not understand the centuries-old patience which he brought to bear on any problem and that his people were '*doyens du martyr*'. The 'dry' letter also made it clear that Wingate would never command a Jewish force during the war, not because the Jewish Agency did not desire it, but because the War Office would never allow it.

As much as you and I regret it that Orde is not with us and will not organise the Jewish force ab initio, need I repeat it that I have tried my best to secure his presence here, but the failure to achieve it is due partly to the attitude of the WO [War Office] towards the whole problem and partly to Orde's differences with some of the high and mighty in that office. I realise that these differences are mainly caused by Orde's personal belief in our cause which is not shared by the others and that brings us up to the crux of the problem – the real disparity between our views and those of the people with whom we have to deal and who are in control. You and Orde are suffering from it as you put it for four years. I can boast of fifty years' work, disappointment, frustration and achievement and those fifty years are merely a tiny fraction of the age-long suffering of my people.

And there the matter rested. Despite her difference of opinion with Weizmann Lorna continued to work for the Jewish Agency in London and her mother Ivy Paterson was also a staunch supporter. But Wingate was never to succeed in his ambition of leading Jewish forces in battle. There is, however, sufficient evidence from fellow soldiers such as Bredin, Evetts and Abraham Akavia that he intended to resign his commission in the British army in order to devote himself to the Jewish cause in Palestine once the war was over. Had he done so, he would inevitably have been one of the commanders in the Arab–Israeli war of 1948; this distinction belonged to Colonel David Marcus of the US army who led an Israeli formation against the Arab Legion at the Battle of Latrun.

Although this dream was never achieved – and it makes little sense to ponder what might have happened had Wingate led Israeli forces in battle – his work with the Special Night Squads left an indelible impression on those who served under him. When the Palmach, a mobile Jewish force of regular soldiers, was formed in 1941 its members included Moshe Dayan, Zvi Brenner and Yigal Allon (a member of the Jewish Settlement Police) and its guerrilla tactics owed much to their training under Wingate. More than anything else, perhaps, Wingate had taught his men to think like soldiers, an important consideration at a time when the Jews were starved of military theory. According to the veteran Haganah leader Yitzhak Sadeh, his men admired Wingate because he advocated the use of counter-offensive operations. This was an essential consideration for small forces unable to engage in a lengthy war of attrition.

I have learned from Wingate that a soldier has to think and not to act like sheep. We could hardly say that we learned from him a certain system, because he always found a new system that fitted in with the situation. You can learn from a textbook how to lay an ambush, but from Wingate we learned how to lay an ambush that suited best the particular conditions under which it had to be laid. As we had neither artillery nor tanks we could not afford to attack fortified enemy positions, and we had to make up for it by night engagements and surprise raids. You cannot learn how to surprise someone, you have to think about it.

Other Israeli military commanders who later expressed their gratitude to Wingate were Major-General Avraham Joffe and the later Prime Minister Yitzhak Rabin who attended Yigael Yadin's secret officers' course in a kibbutz near Mount Carmel. All have testified that, after Liddell Hart, Wingate was the greatest influence on the evolution of Israeli military theory and practice. Not only did he advocate the concept of offensive operations in low-intensity wars which were to become such an integral part of Israeli tactics in the later wars against the Arab states but he refuted the idea that the Jews were not a martial race. By giving the self-confidence and the initial training to the Special Night Squads there is little doubt that Wingate helped to lay the foundations of the future Israeli Defence Forces.

Other influences included Wingate's reluctance to pay too much attention to uniform or to insist on the privilege of rank: in the modern Israeli forces there are few distinctions between officers and men and considerable insistence is placed on the importance of leading from the front. The country also has substantial reserve forces, another concept which Wingate promoted in his papers to Weizmann. Just as he encouraged the notion of a nation in uniform in his paper on 'Internal Security and Frontier Defence', so too do the Israeli Defence Forces rely on their reservists: as Yigael Yadin, put it, 'Every citizen is a soldier on eleven months' annual leave.' (Many of these commanders expressed their indebtedness to Wingate's theories at a conference held by the Institute for Strategic Studies in Oxford in 1975 and summarised in Brian Bond's important essay on Liddell Hart's influence on Israeli military theory.[8])

It must not be thought that Wingate's posting to Egypt was in any way a demotion or a sign of official displeasure. While it was true that the War Office was not unhappy to have him removed from the lobby to create a Jewish fighting force, he still enjoyed Wavell's patronage and was being sent to a theatre where there was considerable scope for his unorthodox approach to low-intensity warfare. Wavell's command stretched over a large area – Egypt, the Sudan, Palestine and Transjordan and Cyprus – and he was also responsible for the deployment of forces in British Somaliland, Aden, Iraq and the shores of the Persian Gulf. By the middle of 1940 he was prosecuting the war over an even larger area, from Libya in the west, to Italian East Africa (Italian Somaliland, Eritrea and Ethiopia) and to Syria and the Balkans in the north. With that in mind Wingate left England for Egypt on 19 September, travelling by ship to Cape Town and then by rail on to Cairo which he reached on 17 October.

Two days after Wingate's arrival in Cairo the Italian air force bombed the suburb of Maadi and it was hard to avoid the impression of defeatism which existed amongst the Egyptian population. (By way of contrast, most of the British residents continued to enjoy a pampered and unhurried style of life.) To the west in Cyrenaica superior Italian forces under Marshal Graziani threatened the frontier with Libya while in Italian East Africa equally strong forces threatened the possibility of a massive two-pronged attack on the Suez Canal, Britain's lifeline with India and the Far East. This threat had been given added impetus by a successful Italian attack on Kassala and Gallabat on 4 July and by the inequality of the Italian and British forces in the southern area. According to Wavell's intelligence sources the Italians had an army consisting of 225,000 troops equipped with 400 artillery pieces, 200 light tanks and 100 armoured cars. Opposing them were three British infantry battalions, twenty companies of the Sudan Defence Force and three companies of the Somaliland Camel Corps.

To combat the threat Wavell had put two plans in place in the summer of 1940. The first called for the fomentation of a rebellion in the western province of Gojjam which the Italians had been unable to suppress. Led by Colonel D. A. Sandford, DSO and bar, late Royal Artillery, and known as Mission 101, it had been raised in September 1939 and had already been successful in making contact with the local tribal chiefs. Having lived in Ethiopia for many years as a farmer and consul in Addis Ababa, Sandford was well placed to understand both the country and its people. Also, as the local director of the Special Operations Executive (SOE) in Ethiopia he advised Wavell to rally the support of the disaffected members of the community around the deposed Emperor Haile Selassie and by supplying them with weapons to encourage a popular revolt. The second plan, 'Operations against Italian East Africa', envisaged an offensive against Kassala and an advance on Kismayu, 'to maintain pressure from as many directions as possible, thus forcing the Italians to use up their resources'. Because this latter operation depended on the availability of increased numbers of men and equipment – which would not be ready until January 1941 at the earliest – Wavell had given his blessing for Sandford to begin 'the first phase of the revolt – the isolation of outlying Italian garrisons by small patriot parties'. However, there were initial problems in getting this started, caused mainly by the rivalry of the principal chieftains in Gojjam, Dejesmach Mangasha and Dejesmach Nagash. It took time and much diplomatic persuasion before Sandford was able to bring them together and to secure their agreement to act in concert as a focus for the Patriot forces.

On his arrival in Cairo Wingate was still uncertain about his future employment because the plans for implementing Wavell's tactics were still being finalised. Until that time he was forced to kick his heels at General Headquarters which had rapidly expanded to employ 1,061 officers and men. Before leaving London he had been approached by Admiral Godfrey of Naval Intelligence to consider the possibility of forming a small subversive group to operate behind enemy lines but Wingate was not at first tempted. As he told Lorna, it was one thing to form specialist units for fighting low-intensity wars; quite another to participate in the kind of guerrilla warfare perfected by SOE, an organisation he never completely trusted. One was soldierly, the other too clandestine to be gentlemanly; however sloppy his uniform was at times Wingate took great pride in being an officer and refused to be seen carrying a parcel or case while wearing uniform.

Ironically, for all his distrust of SOE he was drawn indirectly into its activities because he had been posted to the G(R) branch of GHQ Middle East Command. Ostensibly responsible for irregular warfare in the area, this was the local cover for the irregular MI(R) (military intelligence, research) department which had come into prominence in the summer of 1940 to develop guerrilla warfare techniques using regular army officers. Its activities in the Sudan were directed by Lieutenant-Colonel (later Lieutenant-General Sir) Terence Airey, Durham Light Infantry, who had moved to Khartoum as the staff officer in charge of the forthcoming operations.

During this period he also revived the idea of striking at the Italian army from the south of Libya using mobile forces but this was made redundant by the plans being laid for Lieutenant-General Richard O'Connor's assault on the Italian chain of defences in Libya. At the same time Wavell was finalising his plans for Italian East Africa at a conference held in Khartoum on 28 and 30 October; the other participants included Foreign Secretary Anthony Eden, South Africa's Prime Minister Jan Smuts and Haile Selassie. Taking heed of Eden's proposal that offensive operations should begin as soon as practicable, the conference agreed to begin the campaign in November by first driving the Italians out of Gallabat and then attacking the Kassala region to gain control of the approaches to the Eritrean plateau. It was also agreed to invade Italian Somaliland from Kenya, both to recapture British Somaliland which had fallen to the Italians in July and to gain control of the ports of Kismayu and Mogadishu for a southern offensive on Addis Ababa.

At the same time it was agreed to transform Sandford's mission into a war of liberation and to use Haile Selassie as a focal point for a rebellion of Patriots, those Ethiopians still loyal to their emperor. To this end it was agreed to provide these forces with modern rifles and bren guns and to establish 'operational centres', run by British officers and NCOs, which would be responsible for training the Patriots and leading them in operations against the Italian forces in Ethiopia. Although the Foreign Office had advised against instigating a general uprising in support of the emperor, Eden was persuaded by Haile Selassie who had arrived in Khartoum with the expectation of winning back his lost kingdom. Emboldened by the emperor's arrival, Wingate met Wavell and told him that he considered it 'vital to support Haile Selassie 100% and that the revolt could be made the vital factor in the coming campaign'.

This timely intervention paved the way for his employment in Ethiopia and he left Cairo for Khartoum just as the Gallabat operation was due to begin under the direction of Lieutenant-General Sir William Platt, the commander of the Sudan Defence Force. Wingate's initial task was to act as one of the liaison officers to co-ordinate the arming and training of the Patriot forces and with him he carried credit for 1 million Maria Theresa dollars, Ethiopia's currency. Under the cover of an administrative role as a GSO (2), Wingate was now determined to transform it into an operational command using Ethiopian soldiers to effect the restoration of the emperor. That he regarded himself as a key player can be seen in his notes after meeting Haile Selassie shortly after his arrival in Khartoum on 6 November.

I told him that the liberation of Ethiopia was an indispensable part of the British war aims; that it was also of the greatest importance that the Ethiopians themselves should play a leading role in the coming campaign, and, finally, that he should take as his motto an ancient proverb found in Gese: 'If I am not for myself, who will be for me?'

Once again in his life Wingate had found a cause to fight for and the subsequent fighting in Ethiopia was to be as much a personal crusade as a military campaign.

Nine

WITH THE LION OF JUDAH

By the time that Wingate arrived in Khartoum Wavell had taken steps to strengthen his forces for the forthcoming campaign in Ethiopia. The 5th Indian Division had arrived in the Sudan to reinforce the existing British brigade and the Sudan Defence Force. A South African Division had been formed in Kenya to reinforce the local battalions of the King's African Rifles and, by December, following the success of O'Connor's counter-offensive, he felt confident enough of the British position in Egypt to transfer the 4th Indian Division to the Sudan. By January 1941 the GOC East Africa, General Sir Alan Cunningham, would have sufficiently strong forces to pursue the war into Ethiopia with the intention of defeating the larger Italian army led by the Duke of Aosta and restoring Haile Selassie to the throne he had lost in 1936–37. Cunningham also had the strategic advantage of being able to use the East African ports to reinforce and resupply his forces from India and South Africa, whereas the Italians' lines of communication were badly protected and open to attack.

As it turned out, though, the initial stages of the operation to defeat the Italians in Ethiopia experienced mixed fortunes. The attack on Gallabat began on 6 November but the 10th Indian Infantry Brigade, commanded by Brigadier William Slim, soon got into difficulties: the light tanks of the 6th Royal Tank Regiment were plagued by mechanical breakdowns and, following Italian aerial bombardment, some elements of the 1st Essex Regiment panicked and ran from the battlefield. Although Gallabat was captured, Slim was forced to retire; his brigade suffered considerable casualties and its difficulties were compounded by a failure of morale. More successful were the activities of Gazelle Force, a mobile column formed from elements of the 5th Indian Division, including the mechanised Skinner's Horse and the Sudan Defence Force's 1st

Machine-Gun Regiment. Commanded by Colonel (later General Sir) Frank Messervy, its role was to harass Italian forces in Kassala and, according to its commander, to 'make his life absolute hell ... I want it to be so that they [the Italians] are afraid to move by day or sleep by night.'[1] In this respect Gazelle Force was similar to the Long Range Desert Groups which were used later against the German forces in North Africa.

At the same time Sandford had begun the task of fermenting the Patriot revolt on 18 September and had formed his forward headquarters at Faguta in a mountainous area south of Lake Tana. With him he had taken Captain Ronald Critchley, 13th/18th Hussars, Major D. H. Nott, Worcestershire Regiment, Captain R. E. Foley, Royal Engineers and Lieutenant Clifford Drew as medical officer; and in Khartoum he also had the services of Major Robert Cheeseman, the former consul in Gojjam, who had a detailed knowledge of the territory. Another element of the mission, led by Major Count A. W. D. Bentinck, Coldstream Guards, set up camp north of Lake Tana at Armachaho. Central to the mission's philosophy was the need to return Haile Selassie to his throne and Sandford believed that this aim could only be achieved with the help of friendly Ethiopian tribal forces in Gojjam. The presence of the emperor in Khartoum was an added bonus but Sandford realised that there was little point in him re-entering Ethiopia until he had built up and armed the Patriot forces and that was taking time. As Wingate noted when he arrived in Khartoum, the promised weapons and transport had failed to materialise, 'which left the Emperor sitting alone and dispirited in a Khartoum villa, with a distant and gallant Sandford in occasional contact with us'.

At the conclusion of his service in the country Wingate wrote a series of spirited papers on the Ethiopian campaign; in his appreciation of the military situation between June and November 1940 he was severely critical of Platt's handling of the early stages of the revolt.

No attempt had been or was made to provide transport to service the Mission. No aircraft was made available to support it, and the occasional plane that did answer a summons [for assistance] dared fly only by night when the difficult and dangerous topography made finding the target almost impossible ... To sum up it is fair to say that the conduct of the revolt at this stage shewed poverty of invention combined with an intention to limit its scope below what was possible and from every point of view desirable.

Although this was unfair – Platt was heavily involved in directing the

Gallabat operations and the aircraft flown by the resident 47 Squadron were obsolescent Wellesleys and Vincents which still managed to attack the main Italian garrisons and lines of communication – Wingate understood that his needs would never be granted unless he fought for them. After waiting in Khartoum for several days, on 10 November he was granted an interview with Platt who told him to meet Sandford and to draw up plans for the extension of the Patriot revolt. As he had done in Palestine, he set to work quickly, in rapid succession drawing up a number of discussion papers, both handwritten and typed, in which he evolved the doctrine for the coming campaign. The notes and the eventual 'appreciation' ran to several hundred pages but the general guiding principle remained constant: 'I laid down as an essential point for propaganda that it should follow the lines of David versus Goliath, the strength of the unarmed man versus the man–at–arms.'

Before finalising his plans he had to meet Sandford, at that stage still the overall commander of Mission 101. This was no easy matter. Sandford was at Sakala near Faguta in central Gojjam, an area surrounded on three sides by the canyon of the River Nile and on the fourth by an escarpment falling 4,000 feet to the low–lying forests of the west. Wingate thought it 'an earthly paradise with every kind of produce in abundance', but it was a remote mountain fastness where the ethnic aristocracy of Ethiopia, the Amhara, had managed to hold out against the Italians. To get there Wingate would have to fly in by plane, a difficult undertaking given the unyielding local topography: the landing ground at Sakala was a narrow strip surrounded by deep ravines. Although the aircraft used for the flight, an elderly Vickers Vincent of 430 Flight flown by Flight-Lieutenant Collis RAF, possessed wheel brakes for landing on small fields, it was still a dangerous undertaking which was made worse by the local rainy weather.

With him Wingate took two Ethiopian liaison officers to assist Sandford and the party left Khartoum during the morning of 20 November. Although he was still a nervous flyer, Wingate used the flight to plan the route which the emperor would take when the time came to bring him back into Ethiopia. Having mastered cross-country marching during his Sudan days and having perfected the art of dead-reckoning by compass in Palestine, Wingate felt that his small guerrilla forces would have little difficulty plotting a route into Gojjam through the low re-entrant of forest lying to the west of the escarpment. Not only was this mosquito-ridden country and therefore avoided by the Italians but it appeared to provide easy access to the Gojjam escarpment at Matakal near the prominent feature of Mount Belaya. As Wingate was to discover later, though, the view from the air was to prove deceptive.

Wingate's aircraft arrived at Sakala shortly after 2.00 p.m. and he and Sandford, aged fifty-eight and described by the historian William Allen as 'spectacled and bald but honest with the air of a vigorous schoolboy', spent the next forty-eight hours discussing the planned Patriot revolt. Both men were entirely different in character and outlook but both were committed to the cause of restoring Haile Selassie to his throne; and Wingate was much impressed by the determination which Sandford had shown in pursuing the aims of the lightly armed Mission 101 while working in isolation and with little encouragement from the authorities in Khartoum. However, it is clear from Wingate's notes that even at this early stage he regarded himself as the military commander of the revolt and considered that Sandford should play a purely political role: 'His [Sandford's] presence there made it possible for me to plan the campaign and convince others that it would succeed.'

Later, the blurring of the two men's responsibilities would lead to a serious rift but at that first meeting Sandford was happy to accept the tenor of Wingate's plans; after all, he had been working in isolation and his younger colleague brought news about a fresh impetus to begin the revolt. It is also true to say that Sandford's lifelong concern for Ethiopia made it easier for him to fall in with Wingate's general principles. According to these, the wrong method was to enter an area and offer payment in exchange for serving Britain's interests, just as Lawrence had done with the Arabs during the First World War. Not only did Wingate believe that this was ineffectual but he also thought it was psychologically damaging as the local leader then believed that he was being used as a last resort by a commander in a weak position. Far better, reasoned Wingate, to enter an area with a small well-equipped force and demonstrate to the local population that the commander means business, in this case the restoration of the emperor. Recruitment should only take place once the force has carried out a successful attack on the enemy and can prove that it is capable of succeeding.

Now the essence of this lesson is that to raise a real fighting revolt you must send in a corps d'elite to do exploits and not peddlers of war material and cash. Appeal to the better nature; not the worse. After all what is the best we can hope for from any fifth column?

We can hope that the rare occasional brave man will be stirred to come to us and risk his life to help our cause. This is what is of value to us. All the rest – the rush of the tribesmen, the peasants with billhooks, is hugaboo. If you have a just cause you will get support only by appealing to the best in human nature; down at heel spies and pretentious levies are worse than useless.

While it was one thing to teach self-sacrifice by example instead of precept, Wingate realised that it was also necessary to have the funds and organisation to train the men who would form the nucleus of the revolt. Just as he had done in Palestine with the Haganah training sessions at Ein Harod, Wingate planned a military course in Khartoum for the instruction of Ethiopian regimental and staff officers. The operational centres would be increased to ten and their activities expanded to training Patriots in guerrilla warfare and operations of the type undertaken earlier by the Special Night Squads.

On the operational side, Wingate planned to use two Ethiopian 'refugee' battalions from Kenya as well as the Frontier Battalion of the Sudan Defence Force. It was hoped that these regular forces, numbering 1,000 Ethiopians, 1,000 Sudanese, 40 British NCOs and 50 British officers, would be able to raise equal numbers of Patriot forces. The 1st Ethiopian Battalion was designated as the emperor's 'bodyguard' and both men agreed that Haile Selassie should re-enter his country as soon as it was safe and practicable to do so. To supply them and to provide all logistical requirements, Wingate decided against using motor transport which was in short supply and unreliable and decided instead to purchase up to 20,000 camels and 5,000 mules. The force would have no artillery or armoured cars which Wingate believed to be 'the most useless of weapons; easily detected; confined to roads, and vulnerable to nothing more powerful than a Boys [anti-tank] rifle'.

(Intriguingly, in the same 'Appreciation' of the campaign Wingate put forward the case for a tracked armoured fighting vehicle capable of carrying infantry across difficult terrain: these were eventually introduced to the British army from the 1960s onwards, first as the FV432 and then as the Warrior equipped with a 30 mm Rarden cannon.)

The one sticking-point was the control of the Q stores and equipment which Wingate wanted to be dispersed at the operational centres while Sandford argued for the continuation of the centralised system for the good reason that he had established a safe haven in his fortress base at Sakala. As an immediate decision was unnecessary Wingate left Sakala on 22 November to finalise the plans for a forthcoming conference in Cairo which would decide Wavell's plans for the operations in Italian East Africa. There was a moment of drama when Collis failed twice to get the Vincent airborne and only succeeded by taking off over a steep ravine, a feat which won him the Distinguished Flying Cross. With a top speed of 142 mph the twin-winged single-engined Vincent had entered RAF service in 1935 as a general-purpose fighter-bomber: although somewhat out of date its low take-off speed and rugged construction made it a useful machine for using short and primitive airstrips. For Wingate, though, it must have been a nerve-racking experience and underlined the wartime dangers of using aircraft to transport senior commanders: minor crashes, aborted take-offs, engine failures and tyre bursts were common and few passengers escaped the cold, tedium and fear of wartime flying.

On his return to Khartoum Wingate stayed at the Grand Hotel and spent the next week finalising his plans before attending a conference in Cairo on 2 December to discuss future strategy in East Africa. The main participants were the senior commanders – Platt, Cunningham, General H. M. 'Jumbo' Wilson (commander British troops in Egypt) and Air Marshal Arthur Longmore (Air Officer Commanding in Chief, Middle East) – but other officers were also allowed to speak, including Wingate and Colonel Frank Theron of the South African army. Given ten minutes to introduce his plans, Wingate took half an hour but he used the extra time to good effect and as a result it was agreed to concentrate the tribal revolt on Gojjam using the SDF Frontier Battalion, two Ethiopian battalions and the two operational centres already in existence. At Platt's suggestion it was also agreed to seize a stronghold in Gojjam at Dangila and to install the emperor at the earliest opportunity.

On a broader front the plan for driving the Italians out of East Africa called for a pincered attack: Platt's 4th and 5th Indian Divisions to strike Eritrea from the Sudan while Cunningham's African force was to overrun Italian Somaliland before entering Ethiopia through Dolo and Dagabur. The two armies would then converge on the Italian stronghold at Amba Alagi. In addition another Indian army force from the Aden garrison would land at Berbera and recapture British Somaliland.

On 7 December Wingate returned to Khartoum and set up his planning office at Gordon College (HQ British Troops in the Sudan) and took a room at the Grand Hotel. By that time Platt had formed the Frontier Battalion by drawing a company from each of the corps of the Sudan Defence Force and command of this fine fighting force had been given to Hugh Boustead with Kaimakam J. L. Maxwell Bey, Royal Scots Fusiliers, as his second-in-command. Boustead and Wingate had first met during Wingate's period of service in the SDF but since then they had pursued very different careers. After commanding the Sudan Camel

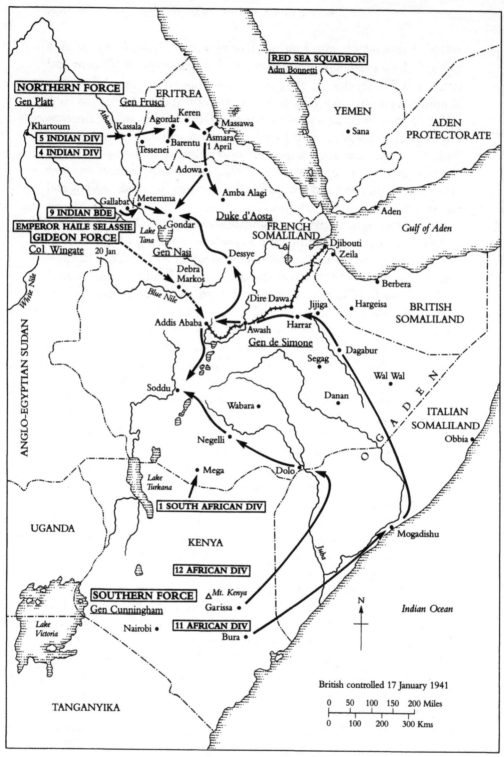

The British East African Campaign

Corps, Boustead had retired in 1935 to join the Sudan Political Service as a District Commissioner in Darfur; following the outbreak of war he returned to serve with the SDF. Eight years older than Wingate, he had fought with the South Africa Brigade during the First World War and served later with The Gordon Highlanders before joining the SDF in 1924. Not only was he a seasoned soldier but he knew Sudan and Ethiopia intimately and as an experienced mountaineer he was well versed in the problems of fighting over difficult terrain.

A strong character and powerful athlete, Boustead was determined that he should retain the independence of his command of the Frontier Battalion and, inevitably, his singularity of purpose led to 'violent alter-cations' with Wingate. From their first meeting in the Grand Hotel – Wingate was lying in a cold bath reading *Pride and Prejudice* – it was obvious that the two men were going to experience difficulties working together. While Boustead conceded that Wingate's 'strategic conception for the type of operation which lay ahead was arresting and brilliant', he believed that his tactics were naïve 'taking into account the topography and means of supply'.

This was a major sticking-point. Seen from the air Wingate's chosen route into Gojjam seemed reasonable enough but Boustead knew that the reality was very different. Although it seemed ideal territory for the kind of compass-marching Wingate had perfected in Palestine, Boustead cautioned that the stony ribs and escarpments of the Shamballa wilderness to the north-west of Belaya were 'quite impassable to motor transport without months of preparation and an army of labourers'. Rather than risk taking the emperor by this route he advised Wingate to follow a southern approach from Roseires which had already been blazed by a company of Western Sudanese from his Frontier Battalion. Although the two men argued 'for several hours', Wingate refused to give way, confident that his camels would have little difficulty coping with the terrain.

Although the two men gradually entered into an uneasy alliance, other problems lay ahead, largely because Boustead was also concerned about Wingate's lack of experience in command.

His previous experience of commanding troops was limited to the command of a battery, of a company of the Eastern Arab Corps, and of small groups of Jews in the Jewish-Arab operations in Palestine in the 1930s. In these latter operations he had distinguished himself. Our relationship during the coming campaign was rendered more difficult from my point of view by his acute lack of experience at this stage of dealing with anything but small bodies to whom he could give personal commands.

The disagreements were also fuelled by what might be called a problem of style. Boustead was not just an older and more experienced man who knew the region better than Wingate, he also believed that war was too serious a business to be taken too seriously. This amateurish attachment to soldiering is peculiarly British – Boustead always made sure that he ate his meals in comfort and, by his own admission, kept a good table – but to the Cromwellian Wingate it was anathema and he was scornful about most of the officers under his command. On more than one occasion during the campaign he complained bitterly that he was being served by 'the scum of the Cavalry Division', an allusion to the fact that many of the officers assigned to the operational centres came from the 1st Cavalry Division which was in the process of being mechanised, thus allowing some commanding officers to purge their regiments of officers and men who would not fit the new order or who were looking for adventure elsewhere. Amongst these was the historian and traveller William Allen, a Life Guards officer employed by SOE, whose account of the campaign accurately summarises the combination of professional guerrilla tactics and amateur sportsmanship which helped to win the campaign.

Others simply knew more about the country and its people and resented the fact that Wingate had arrived in the Sudan to take over responsibility for the operations. Peter Acland, another District Commissioner turned soldier, had served in the Sudan since 1925 and Wilfred Thesiger had been born in Addis Ababa and had a lifelong attachment to the country. Ten years earlier he had watched Haile Selassie being crowned emperor and six years after that he had seen him at Victoria Station in London as he went into exile following the Italian conquest. Not only did he regard the emperor's restoration as a personal mission but he had already seen action with the SDF Gallabat garrison and as a noted explorer of the dangerous Danakil country he had an unrivalled knowledge of the conditions which Wingate's force would have to face. (For that reason he was dubious about Wingate's plans for using the stars and dead-reckoning to cross terrain known to be virtually impassable.) As a company commander in the SDF he was to play a signal role in the coming campaign and should have been a natural ally but he soon found himself being thoroughly exasperated by Wingate's rude behaviour. On meeting him in Khartoum he remembered being taken round Platt's headquarters and immediately sensed the 'irritation and resentment he left in his wake'.

In many respects as ascetic and high-minded as Wingate, Thesiger none the less soon found himself at odds with a man whom he believed to be 'ruthless and uncompromising, an Old Testament figure; brutal, arrogant and assertive'. He was not the only officer to feel that way: in a note to Boustead Captain Peter Upcher of the SDF said that Wingate was 'a scruffy, uncouth, unsoldierly eccentric'. While it can be claimed that a wartime commander has to be relentless in his pursuit of success and that it is generally a mistake for him to court popularity, Wingate did not do himself any favours by his appearance and behaviour in Khartoum. His uniform, complete with Wolseley helmet, was constantly dishevelled; he used an alarm clock instead of a wristwatch – which he did not possess until Akavia presented him with one in Addis Ababa – and he carried a large compass case over his shoulder. On meeting him for the first time in the Grand Hotel, Ken Muir of the SDF exclaimed, 'You're obviously taking no chances of being late for your next appointment or losing your way getting there.'[2]

Platt, too, found Wingate an eccentric and uncomfortable subordinate and confided to Thesiger that he disliked Wingate 'more than the devil himself'. Although he was prepared to implement the plans agreed in Cairo and was keen to see the emperor re-established, Platt had little faith in irregular warfare and on more than one occasion was heard to remark, 'The curse of this war is Lawrence in the last.' By voicing his distrust of private armies and irregular operations Platt was articulating a fear held by many regular officers during the Second World War and he did have a point. Wingate's plans were very different from those undertaken by his distant kinsman but the fact remained that the offensive penetration of Ethiopia depended on his ability to create a revolt by the Patriot forces. As Wingate explained in his 'Appreciation' of the Ethiopian campaign, 18 June 1941: 'Given a population favourable to penetration, a thousand resolute and well-armed men can paralyse, for an indefinite period, the operations of a hundred thousand.' While the means were different, this was certainly an argument which Lawrence would have understood.

Wingate's behaviour and appearance in Khartoum were the subject of much adverse comment but his rudeness and deliberate eccentricity were perhaps understandable. Following his exclusion from the debate about the creation of a Jewish fighting force he was still suffering from damaged pride and – shades of Woolwich – he was convinced that all men in authority were against him. Lack of promotion also weighed heavily on his mind for although he enjoyed Wavell's patronage he remained a major. Never one to insist on rank for its own sake Wingate realised that it conferred the necessary status to get things done and that a relatively junior staff officer was less likely to get his way than a more senior officer. Like any other ambitious officer Wingate was determined to do well and saw his chance to make a name for himself in the coming campaign.

It is also true to say that he never felt at ease with men who seemed to him to enjoy privilege without responsibility and he disliked the relaxed, even convivial, ambience he found in Khartoum. (For similar reasons he was to feel the same antipathy towards the British officers of the Indian Army.) Allen came close to the mark when he saw in Wingate's craggy appearance not so much the bearded Old Testament prophet but the 'Norse blood soured through Covenanting centuries'.

Not that Wingate was completely without personal allies. With Wavell's help he had managed to secure the services of Abraham Akavia as his secretary and his old friend Major Tony Simonds had arrived to take command of the Patriot forces on the northern flank. He also enjoyed a good relationship with two fellow G(R) staff officers, Captain Muchu Chaudhuri and Captain Douglas Dodds-Parker, a tall Grenadier Guards officer and former member of the Sudan Civil Service. They paid little attention to Wingate's occasional tantrums and Dodds-Parker was always prepared to stand up to him. 'Perhaps I lived too close to him to take him entirely seriously,' he remembered in his memoirs of that period. 'When he became specially aloof, Muchu [Chaudhuri] or I would say, "Come on, Orde, you are not Napoleon yet, nor even T. E. Lawrence."'

While Wingate was completing his preparations for beginning the Patriot campaign, events elsewhere conspired to speed up his timetable. In the Western Desert the success of Operation Compass lowered the general estimation of the fighting qualities of the Italian forces and permitted the transfer of the 4th Indian Division to Platt's command. With Italian morale in Ethiopia at its lowest ebb, due to the news from Libya and the threat posed by Gazelle Force and Mission 101, Churchill and Smuts both urged Wavell to begin the campaign in Italian East Africa as soon as practicable. The chance came on 18 January 1941 when the Italians began to withdraw from Kassala; Wavell ordered Platt to begin his attack into Eritrea and on the following day Wingate crossed over the frontier with Haile Selassie on the first part of the journey to take him to Belaya.

In front of him had gone Boustead's Frontier Battalion and the main camel convoy. It took them two weeks to reach their destination, the great horseshoe valley on the north-east side of Belaya which provided their first headquarters. As Boustead had forecast it was a dreadful undertaking and he lost several hundred beasts, usually under the most pitiable circumstances: 'Uncomplainingly they fell in mid-stride, unable to breast one more ascent; in minutes the eyes glazed and with a pitiful gurgle the animal was dead.' Unused to the appalling terrain after the soft sands of the Sudanese plains, the camels simply could not cope with the conditions and of the 17,000 purchased by Wingate few survived the campaign. Pat Lindsay, the Assistant District Commissioner at Sennar, bought 10,000 beasts but fewer than 200 were returned to Roseires later that summer.[3]

Similar difficulties were encountered by the emperor's entourage under Wingate's command. The first stage was easy enough. Haile Selassie's party was flown to Umm Idlaa in an ancient Valentia transport, escorted by two equally elderly Gauntlet fighters. With them went a party of war correspondents and the emperor's re-entry into Ethiopia was widely reported in the British press. The ceremony over – there was a guard of honour and speeches of congratulation – Haile Selassie and his 'bodyguard' and the Ethiopian battalion set off by truck on the difficult cross-country route which Wingate had prepared for them.

Within a week Wingate, scouting ahead on horseback, had discovered that the route was virtually impassable for the motor transport: as predicted the rocky ground and sharp escarpments provided a daunting barrier. To his cost Wingate also found that the maps were wildly inaccurate – Thesiger had already warned him that they had been drawn from imprecise aerial reconnaissance photographs – and he was forced to make his own way to the camp at Belaya which he reached on 31 January. His arrival left an indelible impression on Boustead and the other members of the Frontier Battalion.

On the last day in January Wingate rode into the valley, bearded, dishevelled, filthy and worn, on a dropping horse. The party had been on the way for a fortnight, and the route had been indescribable; he had left the Emperor ditched in a ravine, sitting dejectedly among some dead camels beside the overturned remains of the last lorry.

In his subsequent report on the campaign, Wingate merely noted: 'All went well.' He could hardly have done otherwise. At that stage in the campaign it was essential to maintain morale and it would have caused untold damage if the expedition's leader had admitted to making a major blunder. Besides, with Wingate's assistance, the emperor arrived on 6 February and immediately accepted the loyalty of the Patriot chiefs who had assembled to support him. Watching them in front of their leader, Boustead was instinctively reminded of the arrival of Prince Charles Edward Stewart at the beginning of the 1745 Jacobite uprising and the raising of the Stewart standard at Glenfinnan. As the next stage of the operation was due to begin, it was a good omen.

Boustead's men had already begun work clearing the ground for an airstrip and had moved the mission's headquarters into the horseshoe valley where a bombproof shelter had been constructed for the emperor's use. It was a necessary precaution: alerted by the movements around Belaya the Italians had started flying over the area and it did not take them long to begin a series of raids by Caproni bombers. This had been one of Wingate's objectives – he wanted the Italians to divert their air power away from Platt's attack into Eritrea – but the deployment of the aircraft had a useful side effect. Harried by fierce ground fire from the Patriot forces the pilots believed that it was of divisional size and the deception was given further credence by the construction of a decoy camp higher up the valley.

Following the emperor's arrival at Belaya Wingate and Sandford left for Khartoum for final orders from Platt. It was also necessary to redefine the roles played by the two men and the decision was taken to appoint Wingate as 'Commander, British and Ethiopian Forces' in the temporary rank of lieutenant-colonel and local rank of colonel; while Sandford was promoted brigadier and given overall responsibility for handling the political side of the operation with Edwin Chapman-Andrews, an experienced diplomat, as his principal assistant. Confirming the arrangement in a letter to Haile Selassie, Wavell also made it clear that Sandford was to be considered the emperor's 'principal personal adviser on military and political matters'.

In that way Platt hoped to keep the two elements, military and political, quite separate, with each man reporting to him directly, but it proved to be an unworkable arrangement. Not only did it increase the paperwork – itself a dubious ingredient in what was essentially a guerrilla operation – but it also led to a duplication of effort with the result that the relationship between the two men became increasingly bitter as the campaign progressed. Wingate never quite reconciled himself to the fact that he was subordinate to Sandford and had to communicate through him on any political questions.

The main result of the Khartoum conference, though, was to finalise the operation's objectives. The immediate task was to clear Italian forces from Dangila and Burye so that a suitable headquarters could be secured for the emperor in Gojjam. This would also give the Patriot forces a stronghold for conducting guerrilla operations on the main Italian lines of communication from Gondar and the capital 'which would cause enemy to retain as many troops as possible for the defence of Addis Ababa'. This would have an obviously beneficial effect on the British–Indian drive into Eritrea which had begun on 19 January with the capture of Kassala. Details of the operations were to be left to Wingate who returned to Belaya at ten o'clock in the morning on 14 February, flying in the rear gunner's seat of a single-engined Wellesley bomber, with Akavia in the photographer's seat aft of the main cockpit. Due to problems in locating the airstrip the flight lasted four and a half hours instead of the normal three but, although shaken by the experience, Wingate lost no time in holding a conference with the officers of the Frontier Battalion and informing them of his immediate intentions.

Always an inspired lecturer – his sand-model lecture notes for the Ethiopian campaign still survive – Wingate spent the first period reminding them that they were about to take part in an irregular war and that they had to forgo many of the recommendations contained in their soldier's *Field Service Pocket Book*.

One of the commonest means of obtaining surprise in war is by the use of unexpected boldness, as for example the passage of a small body of troops through the middle of an enemy position. To sum up, it may be said that surprise is the greatest weapon of the guerrilla; that it is far easier for him to obtain surprise against the enemy than vice-versa; that to obtain value for the surprise achieved the commander must think out carefully beforehand how he will exploit the enemy's confusion.

To achieve these aims, Wingate then listed the tactics to be used by his guerrilla squads: never stick to a predictable route, never retrace a route, wear muted uniforms and cover all polished surfaces, develop hand signals for routine orders, create recognition signs for friendly aircraft, maintain fire discipline to prevent shooting at a fellow unit and, lastly, always try to imagine the enemy's intentions.

Having outlined the general principles Wingate rehearsed the problems facing his force. North of their position at Bahardar were some 14,000 Italian troops, while to the south at Burye, Debra Markos and Mota there were 17,000, the whole area being under the command of

Lieutenant-General Nasi at Gondar. Because the primary objective was to drive the Italians out of Gojjam Wingate's first intention was to wreck the lines of communication between these two forces by cutting the road between Gondar and Dessye. Surprise was already on their side. From his intelligence sources Sandford had learned that the Italians had over-estimated the size of the British–Ethiopian force and were making preparations to evacuate Dangila, a key garrison on the route towards Addis Ababa. Luck also helped when news reached Wingate that one of Boustead's officers, Bimbashi T. C. Johnson, had discovered a forgotten route out of the valley on to the 3,000-foot-high escarpment at Matakal; this natural obstacle had to be traversed before the next stage of the operation began.

With these facts in mind I made the following plan [wrote Wingate in his 'Appreciation'], I would divide my force into two parts, in the proportion of one to three. The weaker force should contain the Northern Italian Force until reinforced and strong enough to go on and cut the Dessye–Gondar road. The stronger force, under my own immediate command I would direct upon the Nile bridge at Safartak, thus cutting the enemy's retreat, and then proceed by a process of night attack plus fifth column penetration to reduce the various garrisons.

Before launching the operation Wingate made three sonorous announcements. Bowing to the example of one of his Old Testament heroes he decided to call his little army 'Gideon Force' ('There is nothing else save the sword of Gideon the son of Joash, a man of Israel.' Judges 7:14). Then, with the same feeling of gnosis, he issued an order of the day to his Ethiopian Patriots which reminded them not just of the righteousness of their mission but also of their own role in meeting their destiny.

If I am not for myself who is for me? Do you want to owe all the liberties, which the friends of humanity who are fighting the totalitarian powers in land, sea and air, have promised you, to their helping hands only? Rouse yourselves and put an end to these bickerings and disputes, which will disgrace your Ethiopian names amongst future generations.

To his own men he was more prosaic – 'I expect that every Officer will put his courage and endurance to the severest tests during the coming decisive weeks' – but there is no doubting the idea of crusade which he brought to the operation. As he reminded Akavia, the coming campaign was a war of liberation for a suppressed nation. 'Everyone who is a friend of Abyssinia is at the same time a friend of the Jews. If I shall succeed here, I can be of more help to the Jews later on and you are here for the sake of Zion.' Unable to raise his Jewish army, in Wingate's mind the creation of Gideon Force and the restoration of the emperor were obviously the next best thing.

The first stage was to proceed to Mission 101's original headquarters at Sakala, a time-consuming journey which took six days. In his eagerness, Wingate went ahead of the main party on 20 February and Akavia noted approvingly in his war diary: 'With the Ethiopian colours on his topee and totally unarmed, raising his hat every now and then and saying "Ingliz" (English) and "Tena Yistaliyie" (Health may God give you) Col Wingate went a distance of some 25 miles in "enemy territory".' On arrival he ordered Simonds and his men to proceed north to join an SDF company under the command of Bimbashi Jarvis and this new unit was given the title of Beghemder Force. At the same time he made preparations for the move towards Burye and the investment of the Italian garrisons at Mankusa and Dambacha. On Platt's orders, only after these had fallen would the emperor and his party be permitted to leave Belaya.

Although the terrain and the conditions on the escarpment had improved dramatically – Akavia described it as a 'land of milk and honey' with plenty of 'bread, honey, figs and meat' – Wingate decided to move his force forward at night to prevent interception by Italian aircraft. As he had discovered in Palestine this was not an easy task and during the first night's march on 24 February far too many men lost their way in the darkness and failed to keep the silence demanded by Wingate. The SDF officers received nothing more than his withering scorn – even the loyal Simonds complained of his leader's 'unjustness' – but the Ethiopian Patriots were just as likely to receive a punch in the face. During the campaign Wingate was consumed with remorse when one of his victims, Ombashi Ajawanil, was burned to death as a result of dropping a lighted match into a tin of petrol. Thesiger remembered that before the man died he called for Wingate who said, 'Oh God, this does make me feel such a shit.' This violent trait was to lose Wingate the later sympathy of many of the SDF officers who detested behaviour of that kind and saw it as a betrayal of their men's trust in white officers.

Before setting out for Burye, Wingate issued detailed notes for his company commanders, stressing the importance of undermining Italian morale by concentrating their attacks on white regular soldiers, thereby encouraging the Ethiopian contingent to come across to the emperor's side. He also issued strict orders for the fair treatment of the local

inhabitants and the need to encourage the armed *banda* to join the revolt.
Hard he might have been on his own men but throughout the campaign
in the Gojjam Wingate was well aware that his propaganda efforts should
concentrate on the idea that it was an Ethiopian war of liberation, not a
British imperial war of conquest.

In this war we shall find that our propaganda is cumulative. It will be no use
urging some other patriots to fight for their freedom if they can point to a
dissatisfied Ethiopia. Nor is the enemy at all ignorant of this aspect, or unable
to profit from it.

The reasons we give to induce populations to fight for us must be honest
reasons, and we must be prepared to stand by the implications. In this connection
it is a matter of great importance that the other party should understand that a
contract without consideration is void. There can be no unconditional promises,
and the decision as to whether the condition is unfulfilled or not must be made
by us. But we shall be judged by our decisions.

Writing about the lessons and mistakes of the campaign in his later
'Appreciation' Wingate was discussing the action in Ethiopia but his
mind was still centred on his experiences in Palestine and on the rejection
of his plans for a Jewish fighting force. So similar are many of his concepts,
so insistent his ideas for the creation of small forces capable of disrupting
a larger enemy by employing guerrilla tactics that 'Ethiopian' and 'Jewish'
were almost interchangeable in his thinking. It is certainly true that
between March and May 1941 he led Gideon Force with the same
intensity and fervour he had brought to the Special Night Squads.

Despite the problems of marching at night Wingate's men succeeded
in convincing Colonel Natale, the Italian commander in Burye and
Mankusa, that his 10,000-strong brigade faced a substantial threat and
on 4 March they started withdrawing towards Debra Markos. Before
that happened Gideon Force was involved in several spirited actions.
The investment of the fort at Burye began on 27 February with three
platoons of the Frontier Battalion attacking it with mortars and anti-
tank rifles. During the engagement the Italians replied with rifle and
artillery fire and at one point their cavalry charged – without success –
a mortar position held by Bimbashi Harris. On the following day the
defenders' lives were made more miserable when three RAF Wellesleys
bombed the fort: having tied down the enemy Wingate was free to begin
the attack on the neighbouring Mankusa fort using the bulk of Boustead's
battalion.

These were fast-moving and frequently confusing operations and both

Akavia's war diary and the messages from the platoon commanders indicate the speed of movement. At one point a Sudanese platoon 'got excited' in the heat of battle and, as Wingate feared, started firing on another: 'The fire was very heavy and bullets passed through Colonel Wingate's HQ at the foot of the hill,' noted Akavia on 27 February. Later, on 1 March, Thesiger arrived with a band of Patriots led by Zalleka Desta and their covering fire prevented the two Italian garrisons from making contact. Then, on 2 March, Wingate ordered his propaganda section to use a loudspeaker to call on the native soldiers to join the emperor's cause.

Inevitably mistakes were made. When the Italians began to pull out of Burye on 4 March with the intention of clearing the way for a general retreat, Wingate was caught with divided forces: Boustead's to the north-east of Mankusa and his (three platoons) to the west on a redoubt known as Church Hill. The idea was to combine to harass the Italians as they approached from Burye but the plan broke down when Wingate was persuaded by Azazh Kabbada, the emperor's liaison officer, to take the Mankusa fort as a show of strength to the local natives. As a result Boustead believed that he was isolated when the Italians began their mass retreat and had to retire to prevent his small force from being overwhelmed. Because no signal got through to him Boustead blamed Wingate for failing to keep to the plan and thereby endangering his own forces. Not for the last time in the campaign he accused Wingate of 'interfering in the chain and details of command' and of losing the initiative. Matters were not improved when news came through on 6 March that the 2nd Ethiopian Battalion had engaged the retreating Italians on the road to Dambacha and in the ensuing fire-fight had lost 100 men and many more camels.

However, the first moves in the campaign had been successful in that much of western Gojjam had been cleared, thus allowing the emperor to move out of Belaya on to the Matakal escarpment on 12 March and from there on to the captured position at Burye. To consolidate his position Wingate ordered Boustead to take his force forward to Dambacha while he went back to Burye on 5 March to confer with Sandford. It was at this stage in the campaign that the relationship between Wingate and Sandford started to go sour and cracks began to appear in the chain of command between them. Although their messages had been mutually supportive during the advance on Burye–Mankusa the tenor began to change and by the month's end their correspondence was dominated by scorn and frustration.

One of the sticking-points was Wingate's control of his logistics and lines of communication. Sandford might not have been an experienced soldier but he was a sound administrator and he was critical of the way in which Wingate had failed to ensure a workable chain of supply from Roseires through Belaya to the front line. As this was essentially Sandford's responsibility he suggested a change in command. Because Simonds was a qualified staff officer Sandford ordered Wingate to release him from Beghemder Force to join him at headquarters. The experienced Critchley would take over from him. All might have been well if Sandford had simply requested Simonds but in his notes of the meeting he made it clear that he did not rate him highly as a column commander; these doubts were shared by Thesiger who thought that Simonds was 'a thoroughly bogus individual'.

However, when the notes of the meeting reached Wingate on 9 March he was enraged and leapt to Simonds's defence. There had been occasions early in the campaign when he had criticised his friend – 'I was exposed in front of you as an incompetent CO who couldn't control his affairs,' Simonds had complained after a dressing-down on 22 February – but Wingate was nothing if not loyal to his friends. In reply he reminded Sandford that Critchley was unwell and that in any case Beghemder Force needed an experienced staff officer. Later in the month he took the matter to Airey and Simonds remained with the force, which scored a signal success by cutting the road between Gondar and Dessye and successfully besieging the Italian garrison at Debra Tabor. After the campaign Simonds was phlegmatic about the command and control problems. In his 'brief narrative' he merely stated: 'During the period March 10–28, I received innumerable orders and counter-orders which only tended to confuse the issue. As I had received clear and concise orders originally from Colonel Wingate, I continued to obey these.'

There was also a clash, almost proprietorial in its intensity, over the men's relationship with the emperor. As an old friend with a deep knowledge of Ethiopia, Sandford obviously knew more about Haile Selassie's hopes for the future and he resented Wingate's interference in political affairs. After Wingate had threatened to resign on 1 April because he felt that Haile Selassie had lost faith in him, Sandford reminded him in a sharp note that 'The emperor will, I have little doubt, continue to express his views upon military and political matters in Ethiopia whether you or I agree with them or not.'

However, it was over future tactics that the two men disagreed most severely. Wingate preferred leading from the front and in the latter stages this propensity was to pay dividends but it meant that he and Sandford were regularly out of touch. Wireless communications were poor, messages had to be sent by runner and there were frequent delays in relaying new information with the result that both men had to act independently. All too frequently this involved issuing contradictory orders, another major cause of disagreement.

They also differed in matters of strategy. Sandford wanted to stick to Gideon Force's original plan and feared that pursuit of the Italian forces would drive them out of Gojjam where they could reinforce the armies facing Platt or Cunningham. Wingate was more bullish and believed that the successes at Burye–Mankusa could be repeated at Debra Markos, the main garrison guarding the route to Addis Ababa; once captured this would allow Gideon Force to cross the Blue Nile at Safartak and the road to the capital would be open. Although the Italians were concentrated in large numbers at Debra Markos under a new commander, Colonel of Brigade Maraventano, Wingate was convinced that he could still cause alarm in Italian ranks by dividing his men and moving them rapidly around Debra Markos to give the impression that they were a larger force. 'It is no longer a problem of how to maintain small scattered forces in enemy occupied territory,' he noted to Sandford on 11 March. 'It is a problem of how to realise to the full the power we possess of producing great results with small means through bluff and propaganda.'

That same day Airey arrived in Burye to confer with the two men and their disagreements were temporarily patched up. Once again it was underlined that in addition to his political responsibilities Sandford would concentrate on organising the supplies and lines of communication while Wingate conducted the military operations. In a subsequent operational instruction (Number 19, 14 March 1941), Airey also gave his consent to Gideon Force concentrating its effort on the axis between Debra Markos and Safartak provided that they could neutralise or avoid contact with the powerful army of Ras Hailu, the hereditary governor of Gojjam who had thrown in his lot with the Italians.

Although Airey's intervention concentrated both men's minds on the campaign their quarrel was not over and their correspondence reveals the unedifying spectacle of two senior commanders in deep disagreement with each other. At times Sandford's irritation with Wingate forced him to write tetchy, almost schoolmasterly, letters rebuking him for his frequent silences: 'I am going to be quite frank with you and tell you that I think it is a fair criticism of your show that you do not keep

anything like adequate touch with me, the patriot forces or your units'
(21 March). This was unfair – Wingate's correspondence books reveal
the extent of his detailed instructions to commanders such as Boustead,
Thesiger and Simonds and they in turn maintained close contact with
him – and Sandford's criticisms provoked Wingate into a hasty and ill-
tempered response. In reply he said that the letter had made him 'sick at
heart': 'I suggest that if my instructions were followed and my advice
were taken, matters would be greatly expedited.'

To complicate matters Wingate relayed his objections about Sandford's
'enormities' to Airey. These were kept on file at headquarters in Khartoum and were read by Platt who became increasingly irritated by the
quarrel and by Wingate's frequently intemperate language. 'It is no
exaggeration to say that this incompetent and disloyal direction from the
rear has already cost men's lives and will do so increasingly if allowed to
continue,' he wrote on 28 March. 'There are a hundred and one particular
instances of interference and muddle which I will produce if required to
do so.' Eventually Platt wrote to Wingate on 31 March after the defeat
of the Italian forces at Keren, warning him to stop the quarrel and to
concentrate on the war: 'While I have every confidence in your allotted
role I expect you to take every step to avoid further friction and to realise
that, however much the fault is not with you, it is your duty to go out
of your way to put things right.'

As it turned out, in spite of the provocative correspondence between
the two men, Wingate's tactics were the correct response to the overall
strategic situation in Ethiopia and by using them he revealed himself as
a daring and audacious guerrilla commander. By that point in the
campaign the tide was slowly turning to the Allies' advantage. Platt was
engaged in the final battle for Keren, the 11th African Division had
taken Mogadishu and had swept into Ethiopia covering 744 miles in
seventeen days and the Royal Navy and Fleet Air Arm had destroyed
the Italian navy's Red Sea Squadron. Although aware that Maraventano
had superior forces ranged against him at Debra Markos, Wingate knew
that he still possessed the initiative and was determined to make use of
it to his best advantage. Even while the Italians were preparing to launch
a counter-attack on Burye with the support of Ras Hailu's army, Wingate
was planning a fresh offensive.

His idea was to divide his force in two parts to besiege Debra Markos
while another force led by Thesiger and Foley cut the road between
Debra Markos and Safartak. Although his force was tiny compared to
the Italian garrison – 300 against 12,000 – Wingate decided to confuse

the enemy by making a number of hit-and-run attacks on the enemy positions, quickly moving his men and mortar teams from one position to the next to give the impression of a much larger investing force. There was also some air support when a single Blenheim bomber attacked Debra Markos on 15 and 17 March. As a result of these attacks the Italians abandoned their forward defensive positions overlooking the Gullit River to the west of Debra Markos during the night of 31 March.

In all the operations around Debra Markos Wingate was helped immeasurably by the professionalism of the men of the SDF Frontier Battalion and their British officers. In taking the battle to the enemy Bimbashis Johnson and Harris displayed particular élan, although the latter was badly wounded by machine-gun fire and had to be evacuated, while Boustead was a tower of strength after assuming command of Gideon Force on 13 March and Wingate took pains to congratulate him for 'pushing the night attacks so hard'. (Wingate himself remained overall commander of British and Ethiopian forces with two SDF platoons and an Ethiopian platoon at his disposal.) In fighting of this kind the commanders had to display flexibility of mind and rapidity of response: although Wingate issued regular operational orders their interpretation was usually decided by local circumstances.

Wingate also played a signal role in the front-line fighting. Because so few of his officers had any experience of firing mortars Wingate frequently had to act as a mortar layer and took part in some of the fiercest fighting around Debra Markos. On the night of 20 March he led a successful assault on the Addis fort occupying the Gullit position. After the first mortar bombs landed his men attacked with hand grenades, forcing the Italians to evacuate the post 'at the double'. Three nights later the operation was repeated and Akavia reported that it left the Italians with 'many casualties and a lot of confusion'. Only Wingate's enforced removal from the battlefield prevented his further involvement in this kind of close-quarter fighting which characterised the battle for Debra Markos: on 26 March he left for Burye for a conference with Sandford and on 31 March he established his new headquarters at Dambacha.

During the conference he had another violent row with Sandford who had disregarded his orders by attaching an operational centre to the Beghemder Force instead of sending it to Gideon Force. Sandford had also given four Hotchkiss guns and 561 Springfield rifles to Patriots whom Wingate considered unreliable. Once more the quarrel was patched up but it underlined the problems of combining dual command with the necessity of leading from the front. Whereas in conventional operations the grouping of forces can be arranged in advance, in low-intensity operations they have to be adjusted according to the changing tactical situation. Wingate's plans insisted on mobility and speed of thought so that his little force could be concentrated rapidly at decisive places and times.

He was also aware that in guerrilla-type actions the successful commander has to be visible to his men. Even though Thesiger could never warm to Wingate as a man he admitted that his self-confidence attracted 'a lasting respect'. While he was harassing an Italian force on the left flank of Debra Markos Thesiger found that his men had run out of ammunition and the situation seemed hopeless. 'Suddenly Wingate appeared on a horse with a patriot carrying the Ethiopian banner and about thirty ragged men with him. Instantly the whole outlook changed – the confidence was restored – and the operation carried out successfully. It was quite uncanny, this refusal to accept anything but a complete victory.' However, this inspirational leadership at the sharp end put him at the mercy of officers in the rear area who were not always aware of his movements and, as a result, frequently disregarded his instructions. Throughout the campaign this dichotomy of interests was never resolved.

While Wingate was establishing his new headquarters at Dambacha Gideon Force was completing the investment of Debra Markos. By 1 April, following a spirited night attack by Boustead's men, the Italians retired from the Gullit position and Bimbashi Johnson moved two platoons to cut off the enemy's retreat. The game of cat and mouse continued around the main fort and on the following day Wingate ordered Boustead to begin negotiations for an Italian surrender 'on pain of heavy bombing'. He also insisted that the Italian commanders should be reminded that 'they are surrendering to Colonel Wingate, who, in addition to being a Colonel in the British Army, is commander of the Emperor's forces'. Although contact with the Italians was lost, the retreat began during the night of 3 April and at 12.30 p.m. on Friday 4 April the first Gideon Force units under Bimbashi Hayes entered the main fort at Debra Markos. It had been a cheap victory: over 200 Italian and Colonial troops killed and 800 wounded compared to 10 SDF men killed and 17 wounded.

The way was now open to bring the emperor up the line and he entered Debra Markos on 6 April to be greeted by an honour guard drawn from the 2nd Ethiopian and Frontier Battalions as thousands more followers of the Nagash and Mangasha paid homage to him. The victory was crowned by the surrender of Ras Hailu's *banda* on 7 April, an extraordinary event which completed the Patriots' victory; throughout the latter stages of the campaign Wingate had been rightly concerned about the intentions of Ras Hailu's powerful force. Not everything had gone to plan – although Johnson's men had destroyed a retreating Italian column fifteen miles to the east of Debra Markos, Thesiger had been unable to prevent the Italians destroying the bridge at Safartak because Ras Hailu had bribed the local Patriot leader and had virtually been held prisoner – but the end of the campaign was in sight.

Everywhere Italian resistance was crumbling. On the same day that Haile Selassie entered Debra Markos, Addis Ababa surrendered to the 11th African Division and two days later Massawa, the last remaining stronghold in Eritrea, was captured by Platt's Indian Divisions. Some idea of the scale of the Italians' loss of morale can be seen in a bizarre incident on 5 April when Wingate secured the retreat of enemy forces on the Blue Nile by a ludicrous ruse. Learning that the telephone line to Dejin was still open he asked Edmund Stevens, an Italian-speaking war correspondent with the *Christian Science Monitor*, to speak to the enemy. As he told Airey that same day, the effect was startling.

It went across very well. He said he was Dr Digrofino, who is a prisoner of ours, and that he was taking his life in his hands to tell them that a British division had just arrived in Burye and that a terrible fate was in preparation for the Italians on the Abbai. The man at the other end said 'What do you want me to do about it?' in a very agitated voice. Stevens replied, 'Get out of course, as quickly as you can.'

With the end of the campaign in sight there was time to relax and Wingate began to think about his future employment. On 14 April, at the end of a letter to Airey, he reminded him that he should not 'neglect the duty of getting me out of this hole as soon as possible in any capacity'; and on 19 April he wrote formally to Lieutenant-General N. M. de la P. Beresford-Peirse, the new Western Desert Force commander, to ask him 'most earnestly to consider whether you cannot use my services. I am not needed here now. I am of course prepared to serve in any capacity. I do not want to be left to rot on a mountain in Ethiopia. I would like to wish you the very best of luck in your responsible and most trying task.'

Wingate had also been unsettled by the arrival in the Middle East of John Evetts, his old commander from Palestine days who was now a major-general. Suddenly it seemed to him that the war was gaining momentum and he was in danger of being overlooked. His fretful condition was not helped by being laid low by chigoe fleas in his feet – a painful condition caused by the insects laying eggs in the skin – and he was effectively out of action until 20 April. A week later matters were not improved when he was told that Gideon Force had been transferred to the command of Cunningham's African forces. According to the official historian, 'Colonel Wingate disliked this turn of events for he was always happier giving orders than receiving them', but there was more to his dismay than a change in command. From this point onwards he came to believe that the British, through Cunningham, were delaying Haile Selassie's return for their own purposes. Added to the doubts about his future employment, Wingate came to believe that, just as Palestine became a British mandate in 1919 following its occupation by Allenby's forces, so too did a similar fate await Ethiopia. This would not only tie down a British or imperial division at a crucial stage in the war, but it would also be an abnegation of the promises which Wingate (and others) had made to Haile Selassie about returning him to power.

Once again Wingate found facts to fuel his concerns: the absence of sustained air support, the delay in entering Addis Ababa, Cunningham's caution and the dispersal of Gideon Force in mopping-up operations. Even though he was to be instrumental in arranging the emperor's triumphal return into his capital and even though he was to command the forces which finally drove the Italians out of Gojjam at the month's end, Wingate continued to harbour suspicions about British motives towards Ethiopia. Coupled to what he felt was a lack of recognition for his own efforts, these were to prey on his mind long after the campaign had come to an end and he had left the country.

Ten

WATERSHED

While Wingate fretted about the delays in moving the emperor into Addis Ababa, his original forces were still gainfully employed in attacking the Italians. To the north, Simonds's Beghemder Force had cut the main road through Debra Tabor and by raising large numbers of Patriots had succeeded in tying down the Italians in Dessye and Gondar. Johnson's platoons were busy harrying the Italians retreating from Debra Markos and on 23 April they were reinforced by East African units, including some much-needed light artillery. Overall control for this Safartak operation was given to Major Donald Nott of the original Mission 101. At the same time Boustead's men were engaged in an operation to reduce the Italian garrison at Mota in the mountains north of Debra Markos. Despite the atrocious wintry conditions Boustead was successful in persuading the larger Italian force to surrender to his tiny force.

Gratifying though these further successes were, Wingate was anxious to see the emperor returned to Addis Ababa at the earliest opportunity. He had made his feelings public on 19 April when he invited Haile Selassie and his entourage to a cocktail party in Debra Markos and proposed a fulsome toast, 'drunk in the wine of the discomfited aggressor':

Myself [sic] and the British officers under my command have borne their part with the patriot Ethiopian forces in this campaign in the knowledge that, in so doing, they were supporting that same cause for which England is fighting throughout the world. The right of the individual to liberty of conscience, the right of the small nation to a just decision at the tribunal of nations: these are the causes for which we fight ... It is the earnest wish of myself and the British officers here that Your Majesty will enter at once into the full discharge of your sovereignty in Ethiopia and that no assaults of the adversary will be able to

disturb the peace of your dominions until the final settlement is, by the mercy
of God, accomplished.

The emperor, too, was anxious to return to his capital, but Cunningham had made it clear that he could not welcome Haile Selassie
until Addis Ababa and its approaches had been completely secured. He
was particularly worried about an outbreak of reprisals against the
defeated Italian garrison, a concern which Wingate felt was preposterous.
For that reason Wingate was told in no uncertain terms on 22 April that
'The Emperor will be delayed from starting by persuasion and every
means short of force, until 11 Div confirm that the road is safe, which
they will do.' However, Airey's top-secret telegram also contained an
escape clause which Wingate was happy enough to use: 'If the Emperor
starts in spite of your efforts you will keep E. A. [East African] Forces
informed and provide adequate protection, i.e. 2nd Ethiopians and
bodyguard.'

Two days later, having arranged for Boustead to transfer two companies
from Mota, Wingate issued Field Operation No. 7, 'Move of the Emperor
D. M. – Addis Ababa' which outlined the arrangements to take Haile
Selassie and his party to Ghartisan on the north side of the Blue Nile.
Aware of the continuing dangers of Italian attack, Wingate issued detailed
orders for the emperor's protection: three SDF bren gun platoons
strengthened his personal escort and the men of the 2nd Ethiopians were
sent ahead to guard the road. Travelling in a motorised convoy the party
left Debra Markos on 27 April, crossed the Blue Nile the following day
and on 3 May reached Fiche to the north of the capital where they were
met by Cunningham's representatives. There the final arrangements were
made for what Akavia described as the 'Triumphal Entry into Addis
Ababa'.

Shrewdly, Wingate had ensured that Gideon Force would have pride
of place in the procession. The men of the 2nd Ethiopian Battalion led
the parade with Akavia and a Captain Luyt at the head and the SDF
Frontier Battalion was headed by Maxwell Bey mounted on a horse; the
emperor himself drove in an open Ford car, nine other cars carried the
rest of his party and the whole parade was headed by Wingate riding on
a white horse. Once before in his life he had told Peggy that his ambition
was to return a king to his throne; now he was doing it in reality. Wearing
his Wolseley helmet and service dress with long shorts – not ideal clothes
for riding – he cut a fine figure at the head of the marching Ethiopian
soldiers. The streets were thronged with cheering crowds who were kept

in order by a loudspeaker lorry giving instructions in Amharic. At the royal palace a Nigerian guard of honour was drawn up to allow Cunningham to receive the emperor, a royal salute was fired and speeches made.

Whatever else Wingate would achieve, and as a soldier he still had a long way to go, this was by any standards a high point in his life. A difficult guerrilla campaign had been won, a numerically superior enemy had been defeated and he had shown himself to be a skilful leader of irregular forces. To crown the achievement the operation had culminated in the emperor's triumphal return to his capital. It could never be as grand as Horse Guards or the Mall but it was still a moment to be cherished: in Wingate's mind the refusal to help Haile Selassie in 1935 had been corrected and a leader had been returned to his rightful throne. In the midst of the understandable euphoria, though, Wingate was anxious to return to fighting but his hopes for employment in the desert were dashed when Beresford-Peirse wrote on 7 May to tell him that he had no room for him in any capacity: 'Personally I feel your use should be thro' "irregular soldier" channels – because individuality gets swamped in too close conjunction with normal formations.'

It was a prophetic comment but at that stage in his career Wingate was anxious to disabuse senior officers of the notion that he was only suited to irregular operations. The British experience of using irregular forces in conjunction with its regular fighting formations went back to the eighteenth century and commanders such as Lieutenant-General Sir Banastre Tarleton had won fame for raising the irregular force known as Tarleton's Legion which along with Simcoe's Rangers was amongst the more successful British fighting units during the American War of Independence. In the same campaign Scottish Highlanders fought along-side Hessian and Hanoverian mercenaries as skirmishers or scouts and later Kitchener had raised a so-called Scallywag Corps of irregular mounted infantry in the latter stages of the Boer War. Irregular formations, sometimes disparaged as 'private armies', were still an accepted part of the British army and were destined to play a signal role in the Second World War – Popski's Private Army, the Long Range Desert Group, the army's commando forces and David Stirling's Special Air Service, for example – but lengthy service in them was generally held to blight an ambitious soldier's long-term career prospects.

None the less, at that stage in the war, Wingate was regarded as an ideal leader of irregular forces and that is certainly how he was viewed by Wavell, hence his employment by G(R). Although the emperor had been returned to Addis Ababa, the campaign in Ethiopia was not over and there was still gainful employment for Gideon Force. Significant numbers of Italian forces remained at large, especially in the north of the country where the Duke of Aosta commanded the garrison at Amba Alagi. Once again a pincer move was put in train with Cunningham's African forces moving north from Addis Ababa while the 5th Indian Division pushed south from Asmara. There was also a need to clear the Italians from Soddu in the south and Gondar to the north of Lake Tana. As these required the continued deployment of the regular forces, Wingate was left to complete the clearance of the Italians from the Gojjam. Having escaped from Debra Markos, they were making their way north-west to join General Nasi's Gondar garrison. According to Akavia, the Italian column, commanded by Colonel Maraventano, consisted of 12,000 men, women and children as well as some 4,000 animals. Their fighting strength was judged to be 8,000 combatants. Against them, Wingate hoped to pit 140 men of Gideon Force plus an unknown number of Patriots.

On 10 May, accompanied by Akavia and a small section of Sudanese, Wingate left Addis Ababa for the Italian position at Addis Derra and took over command from Nott. Helped by 500 Patriots under Ras Kassa, the Viceroy of Ethiopia, they drove the Italians from the fort in a series of day and night attacks on 15 and 16 May. Just before the battle commenced, Wingate received a signal from East African Headquarters at Harrar ordering him to call off the pursuit and to use his remaining men to reinforce Beghemder Force and to assist the South Africans in the investment of Dessye. As Thesiger noted approvingly, Wingate disregarded the orders 'on the Nelsonic principle that it cannot be wrong to engage the enemy'; he simply sidestepped the problem by questioning the codes used in the orders, thereby gaining much-needed time.

Once again in the campaign the Italians were misled by the size of the force attacking them and after a sustained battle they withdrew from Addis Derra towards another fort at Agibar, with Wingate's men in hot pursuit. This time Wingate divided his forces into two columns, one led by Thesiger to cut the enemy's lines of retreat to the north and the second led by himself to pursue the enemy towards Agibar. Thesiger's force consisted of one platoon of 2nd Ethiopians (forty-three men under Lieutenant Rowe), No. 3 Operational Centre (forty-three Ethiopians and four sergeants under Lieutenant Naylor) and 300 Patriots. Wingate's force was made up of one company of the Frontier Battalion (thirty-seven men under Bimbashi Johnson), an Ethiopian mortar section and nearly 2,000 Patriots under Ras Kassa. It was hardly a huge force but, following Wingate's arrival, morale was high and the operation was to present Wingate with his most spectacular and colourful military success. As he admitted in his 'Appreciation', he knew he possessed the initiative and he was determined not to lose it.

By now I understood the enemy's mentality. The essential was to maintain the momentum of surprise. Within two days of my arrival the enemy evacuated Addis Derra. From the summit of the fort I watched his column, nearly 18 miles long, disappear into the 5,000-foot canyon and climb the far side. He was en route for Agibar, where were many of his supplies. He had orders to go to Magdala where he would be based on Gondar and threaten Dessye. Great rewards were promised him if he could hold out. He had ample animal transport. He could fight across country. We had no troops able at that time to follow but those under my command.

It should have been no contest. The Italians possessed superior forces and were retreating into territory where the largely Muslim population had proved staunch allies in the past. If they could make good their escape north towards Agibar, Wingate's pursuing forces would be subject to attack by tribesmen still friendly to the Italians. However, to do this, they had to cross a high ridge, or panhandle, which offered both a means of escape and a useful rearguard defensive position.

Wingate's first move was to capture the ridge and at 3.00 a.m. on 17 May Thesiger's column was ordered to push along the right flank towards the ridge and to take the small fort at Uoggidu which covered it. Then at first light Wingate moved forwards with Johnson's men on to the plateau to engage the main Italian force. It was no easy matter. The little force came under fierce Italian fire, during which forty Patriots were killed and one hundred wounded, and they experienced problems crossing the lunar landscape of dried river beds and steep ravines. Despite the losses which were caused mainly by the Patriots' enthusiasm to join battle, Wingate's direction of the fighting was equal to the task. After Johnson's Sudanese had borne the brunt of the Italian counter-attack on the west flank he pulled them out of battle and kept the Patriots in the line to continue harassing the enemy. By nightfall on 18 May he heard from Thesiger that the fort at Uoggidu had fallen and that by skilful negotiation 1,200 Galla *banda* had agreed to join the Patriot cause. Although he had to withdraw on 20 May, following an Italian counter-attack, Thesiger was still able to retain a strong defensive position to the north of the fort.

With the ridge under threat on the eastern flank and with Wingate's forces attacking from the south the Italians began evacuating their positions on 20 May. Seizing the moment, Wingate ordered the Patriots to press home their attack, both to cause further confusion and to prevent exposure of his own weakness. Astutely, he kept the more experienced Sudanese in reserve in case of an enemy counter-attack but by mid-afternoon it was obvious that the battle was going his way. The Italians had retreated eastwards towards Uoggidu where they took up a horseshoe defensive position with their rear towards the fort. As Akavia noted in the war diary, the Italians' position was 'entirely flanked by precipices, except where it confronted Col W's forces. The enemy was thus caught in a trap, the weakness of which must have been apparent.' The Italian forces were estimated at 7,000 and facing them were 1,000 Patriots with 500 in reserve.

Wingate had already made his first attempt to persuade Maraventano to surrender. A day earlier, on 19 May, he had informed him that he would withdraw all British personnel within twenty-four hours 'leaving the conduct of the operations against you to the very considerable guerrilla forces under Ras Kassa and the Crown Prince, which are now assembling around you'. On receiving the reply that the Italian commander had to refer the matter of surrender to the higher command and that he would continue to fight to the last round, Wingate retorted on 20 May that 'commonsense [however] must be applied' and that there was no disgrace in surrender.

By the following evening it was all over. Having gained the necessary permission from his superior officer, Maraventano agreed to stop fighting 'in order to avoid further shedding of blood on either side'. Negotiations were left in the capable hands of Nott and although the ceasefire was broken by the Italians destroying some of their ammunition, it was agreed that Maraventano and his staff would present themselves to Wingate at midday on 23 May at a position marked by eucalyptus trees within the Patriots' lines. Behind them, the Italian forces with their colonial battalions would be lined up without arms in review order on the open tableland. At the same time Thesiger began negotiations for the surrender of 100 Italian and 1,200 Colonial troops in the Agibar fort to the north. As Wingate noted in his 'Appreciation', it was a moment to savour.

When the moment came for us to receive the vanquished army, I felt more alarm than at any time during the battle. Across a level plain sloping towards a hidden valley, the Italian commander and his staff of thirty officers advanced on horseback. Behind them came eight hundred fascisti, and then phalanx

upon phalanx of Colonial troops (who did not want to surrender) with their
250 Italian officers, guns, mortars, machine guns and three million rounds of
SAA. [small arms ammunition]. Altogether 14,000 men marched in order of
battle, while to receive them stood 36 Sudanese. These formed five lanes
through which the enemy poured laying down his arms in heaps, reformed in
units, and passed on over the edge to the valley where they expected to find
the army that had beaten them. Instead they found myself with Ras Kassa and
a few patriots; but their arms already lay piled up under guard of our Brens.

   More prosaically Akavia noted that 'the surrender went according to
plan.' His figures were also more accurate than Wingate's: only 7,000
Colonial troops surrendered but most of the 1,100 Italians who layed
down their arms were trained soldiers from regular 'Blackshirt' battalions.
None the less, it was still a startling achievement. A numerically superior
Italian force had been out-fought and then out-thought. Throughout
the running battle as the Italians retreated towards Agibar, Wingate had
deployed his forces with skill and vision, pressing home Patriot attacks
to suggest that his forces were stronger and concentrating his defences
on his well-trained Sudanese troops. With the battle still in the balance
he was then able to put Maraventano under psychological pressure by
suggesting to him that, with the rainy season almost upon them, the
British officers were about to withdraw to leave the Italians to an
uncertain fate at the hands of the growing numbers of Patriots. By this
use of deception – one of the principles of war – Wingate was able to
achieve results out of all proportion to the size and equipment of the
force under his command. This point was acknowledged in the *Official
History*: 'The combined effort of Gideon and the Patriots cannot be
precisely assessed, but there is no doubt that it was considerable and that
it reached its climax at exactly the right moment.'
   The remaining problems lay with the prisoners of war. With such a
large contingent to guard it was not surprising that Wingate's men were
unable to prevent desertions. Large numbers of Colonial troops simply
melted away from the line of march and went back to their villages as
the column made its way back to Fiche – which was reached on 29
May – but to the lasting credit of all concerned there were no serious
reprisals. As Wingate told the emperor on 26 May this did not bother
him unduly as he thought that those who remained were 'likely to make
good soldiers in Your Majesty's forces'. By the end of the month Wingate
had returned to Addis Ababa where he was ordered to report to General
Cunningham in Harrar to the east. Now that its task was over, Gideon
Force was disbanded and Wingate was relieved of its command, a decision

which he described with natural sadness in his report.

A successful military force partakes of the nature of an animal organism. It grows together. Command, Staff and fighting troops build up a relationship and technique. The whole is greater than the sum of its parts. It was unfortunate that at this moment while the need for my force still existed, that conditions elsewhere necessitated the dispersion of my troops and staff.

At this point Wingate was prepared to accept the decision. There was little else for him to do in Ethiopia and as he had already written to other British commanders offering his services, it is fair to say that he had no quarrel with Cunningham's orders. (Boustead had also written to him on 31 May urging him to leave 'the mountain fastnesses' so that he could rejoin the battle against the enemy in another theatre of war.) Before leaving Addis Ababa Wingate did not have time to take his leave of Haile Selassie but, later, when he was back in Cairo, Akavia brought Wingate a letter containing the emperor's thanks together with a number of gifts; an autographed photograph, an inscribed gold watch and four gold rings. By that time, though, a rot had set in, and Wingate had begun to take a jaundiced view of the treatment meted out to Gideon Force by the general staff in Middle East Command.

One reason for his dismay was the lack of interest taken in his exploits with Gideon Force. According to Christopher Sykes, the staff at GHQ had other more pressing matters on their mind at the time and were relatively unimpressed by a campaign which they considered to be a 'side-show'. By then the focus had shifted once more to the western desert where General Erwin Rommel had arrived to take command of the German forces. Crete had fallen following the disastrous allied intervention in Greece and the strategic situation was complicated by a pro-axis revolt in Iraq and the threat of German intervention in Syria. Because Wavell and his staff were obviously under extreme pressure it is quite possible that events in East Africa were put to one side.

Sykes was in a good position to observe the passing scene in Cairo. He worked for SOE and with his wife Camilla – the daughter of the chief of police Sir Thomas Russell Pasha – he was part of the wartime social set which gave the Egyptian capital a curiously raffish and hothouse atmosphere. Through his social connections there was little that Sykes did not know about the people who passed through the city and he was especially critical about the standard of staff officer serving at GHQ. Indeed, so strong were his feelings and so lasting his impressions of wartime intrigues that he later wrote two revealing and thinly disguised novels about his experiences: *High Minded Murder* (1944) and *A Song of a Shirt* (1953). Both books satirised the rivalries between the organisations responsible for irregular and clandestine operations, of which Wingate's G(R) was a part, and both have hard words to say about the low levels of competence displayed by many of the participants.

Changes were also afoot in the organisation of SOE in Cairo. Sir George Pollock was about to be replaced as Head of Mission by Terence Maxwell, a barrister and merchant banker, who had been sent to Cairo to put an end to what his assistant Bickham Sweet-Escott called an 'atmosphere of jealousy, suspicion and intrigue which embittered the relations between the various secret and semi-secret departments in Cairo that summer of 1941'.[1] Under the reorganisation three new directorates were created: psychological warfare, political subversion and operations. Command of the latter group was given to Airey who also became Maxwell's chief of staff. Under this new dispensation G(R) became the Operations Directorate of SOE (SO2) although it continued to be manned mainly by army officers, a compromise which meant that its activities had to be sanctioned by the GOC. As Wavell put it, 'SOE think they've taken over G(R) and G(R) think they've taken over SOE, so everybody's happy.'

With the direction of the war reflecting that muddled progress Wingate returned to Cairo to find that there was no job for him and that no one seemed too interested in his presence at GHQ. His growing despondency was not helped by the onset of malaria and when Simonds arrived in Cairo in the middle of June he found an unhappy Wingate who had come to the conclusion that those in authority were once more plotting against him. It is also probable that Simonds himself was a further cause of depression: he had been summoned from Beghemder Force to take over a staff job in Cairo only to discover on his arrival that it had been filled by another officer. On top of that disappointment he was suffering from jaundice and nursed a grievance that his removal from command had cost his Patriots victory at Debra Tabor.

With time hanging on their hands and with no immediate prospect of employment, the two men began to suspect that they were being sidelined. The reaction to their exploits and the subsequent high-handed treatment of the men under their commands only seemed to confirm this dismal diagnosis. Although neither man had been asked to write a report both did so as a matter of routine but the reception accorded to these documents only compounded the problem. Wingate's report, 'Appreciation of the Ethiopian Campaign', was not written to influence conventionally minded senior commanders, to whom it must have seemed opinionated, overlong and intemperate. (To the non-conformist it is a brilliant, exhilarating and contentious view of the usefulness of guerrilla-type operations in regular warfare.) In comparison, Simond's ten-page 'Brief Narrative of Beghemder Force' is a model of its kind, concise, logical and factual. Only on the muddle concerning his own command did he raise any criticism and on the question of his posting, he confined himself to observing: 'This succession of orders coming in the middle of a large scale battle for Debra Tabor was unfortunate, to say the least of it, and it did untold harm.' Simonds completed his report on 23 June and it was attached as appendix C to Wingate's report which was sent direct to Wavell, at that time wrestling with the problems thrown up by the failure of the Battleaxe operation in the western desert.

It is not difficult to understand Wavell's feelings on receiving the report. Indeed, he admitted later that, from any other officer, its contents 'would almost have justified my placing him under arrest for insubordination'. A major sticking-point was Wingate's immoderate language. On the manpower allotted to Gideon Force – 'the scum of an army' – he complained that the officers were 'mediocre or inferior' and that 'the standard of the NCOs was so low that they were almost a nuisance.' His signallers were 'lazy, ill-trained and sometimes cowardly'. He accused the staff officers in Khartoum of mistaking ends for means and said that this was hardly surprising in an army 'whose commanders learn most of their art in dummy operations which are in war what dummy operations would be in medicine – fruitful sources of false doctrine and orthodoxy'.

There were other complaints about lack of equipment, most of which were justified as the Gideon Force letter books reveal acute shortages of trucks and wireless sets and the necessary spares to keep them fully operational. Less convincing were his criticisms about air support. The RAF had few aircraft at its disposal and the available Wellesley and Blenheim bombers had to be deployed in force at Keren. In the early stages of the war it was natural for ground forces to believe that the RAF was failing in its duty whenever aircraft were not flying in support of their own operations but, according to the war diary of the Ethiopian Patriot Force, there were daily bombing raids against various Italian targets.

None of this might have mattered, but for one paragraph which criticised the direction of the East African campaign in terms which most relatively junior officers would have shunned if they valued their future employment. In a direct reference to the decision to wind up

Returning a king to his throne: a victorious Orde Wingate leads his Patriots in Addis Ababa, May 1941.

The ships of the desert find it hard going in the scrublands of the Gojjam. Few of the 20,000 beasts purchased by Wingate survived the campaign.

The Emperor Haile Selassie re-enters his kingdom, January 1941. Looking suspiciously like his kinsman T. E. Lawrence, Wingate stands to attention by the emperor's side.

Wingate and Colonel Dan Sandford discuss the Patriot campaign. Their early understanding gave way to bitterness and distrust.

A job well done: Wingate with
the emperor in Addis Ababa.

Inspecting the 2nd Ethiopian
battalion at Dambacha: 'The
right of the individual to liberty
of conscience, the right of the
small nation to a just decision at
the tribunal of nations: these are
the causes for which we fight.'

Assam 1944: Wingate with Derek Tulloch, his Brigadier General Staff and right-hand man in Operation Thursday.

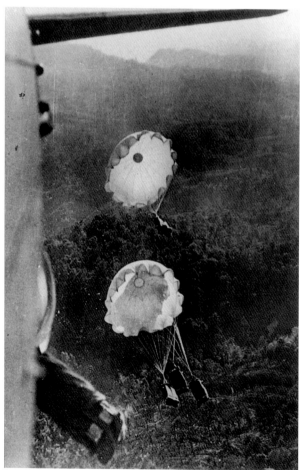

The sinews of war: Chindit forces in Burma depended on airdrops to keep them fighting the Japanese forces in Burma.

Briefing the aircrew of 1st Air Commando at Hailakandi, March 1944. Wingate's ADC Lieutenant George Borrow stands on the left.

Operation Thursday: the key moment. Wingate contemplates the findings of the air photographs of the blocked landing zones which are being shown to Lt-Col Walter Scott by Colonel John Alison. Brigadier Mike Calvert, in peaked cap with mapcase, was 'prepared to be bullish and agreed to be flown into Broadway.'

above: The avuncular commander of the 14th Army in Burma: Field Marshal Lord Slim.

left: A meet of true minds: Wingate with Colonel Philip Cochrane, commander of the 1st Air Commando.

An uneasy relationship: Admiral Lord Louis Mountbatten with his deputy, General 'Vinegar Joe' Stilwell, US Army.

Planning for victory,
Assam, 1944: the floors of
Wingate's headquarters
were always covered with
maps.

Mules shared the same
discomforts and dangers as
the soldiers. Wingate on
board a mule-carrying
Dakota transport.

'There was a man of genius who might well have become a man of destiny.'
The last photograph of Major-General Orde Charles Wingate, Assam,
March 1944.

Gideon Force at the end of the campaign, Wingate wrote: 'To dissipate such a military organism after it has been created and while the need still exists or to suppose that you get equal results from employment of equal numbers in sporadic operations, is the mark of a military ape.'

It was one thing to say this in private – throughout the campaign he had referred to Cunningham, Platt and others as 'military apes' and had used equally immoderate language about Sandford – but it was another to use the expression in a report which would have a wide circulation in GHQ Cairo. Inevitably, in a Cairo which was always awash with rumours, it was not long before Wingate's report had become a matter of gossip and its author reviled for his lack of tact. This was a pity, for in its raw form, the original 'Appreciation' has much good sense to offer about the direction of irregular operations. Instead of relying on guerrilla raids or fifth column attacks, Wingate believed that the time had come for the British army to form its own corps d'élite for irregular operations. Properly manned, equipped and trained, and led by first-rate commanders, such a force would have an independent role while acting in unison with other regular forces operating in the same theatre. It would also enjoy close air support for attacking enemy positions and resupply and it would use propaganda methods to win the support of the local population. Here were the beginnings of an idea which would later come to fruition with the Chindit columns in Burma.

To sum up it is proposed to assemble and employ a force of the highest fighting qualities capable of employment in widely separated columns; that it should employ the friendly portion of the population for cover and support; that it should perform exploits and depend on the effect of these to bring to its support waverers and paralyse hostility; that it should be allotted an objective behind the enemy's lines, the gaining of which will decisively affect the campaign; and that to enable it to carry out its task it must be given a political doctrine consonant with our war aims.

It was not a unique concept – a Middle East Commando (51 and 52) had served in Eritrea and Ethiopia and at the same time, in a Cairo hospital, a Scots Guards officer called David Stirling was writing the memorandum which would lead eventually to the formation of the Special Air Service regiment – but it was rigorously expressed. According to SOE's biographer, the historian M. R. D. Foot, by training and using local forces, Wingate planted the seed of 'what became one of SOE's leading ideas: that patriot forces – however named, however organised – could be given a sharper cutting edge by the presence of small groups of officers and NCOs trained in tactics, especially the tactics of sabotage and attack'. Unfortunately, Wingate's report, together with the official comments, seems to have been destroyed along with other sensitive documents in July 1942 when the fall of Egypt to Rommel's army seemed imminent. (Happily, however, Wingate preserved several copies amongst his own private papers.)

Once again, Wingate's 'protection' must have stood him in good stead because Wavell merely sent for him and rehearsed the main grievances voice in the report which was then quietly filed. His removal from office on 2 July and subsequent replacement by General Sir Claude Auchinleck effectively killed off the report and put paid to Wingate's hopes that it might be acted upon. After all, Auchinleck had more pressing concerns than the campaign in East Africa and a letter of advice from the CIGS Sir John Dill made no mention of it. Wingate, though, did not forget and the report went through several more drafts before it was finally abandoned on his transfer to Burma the following year.

Bad though the reaction to his report had been, worse was to follow as Wingate finalised the administrative details for Gideon Force. As the unit's commanding officer he was entitled to make a number of recommendations for awards and he had produced two comprehensive lists on 10 April, through HQ Sudan, and on 30 June, through 11 Division, which included Distinguished Service Orders (DSO) for Boustead, Nott, Simonds, Johnson, Harris and Thesiger and Military Crosses (MC) for Thesiger, Acland, Rowe (died of wounds at Agibar) and Brown (Australian Infantry, Number 1 Operational Centre). He also recommended the award of an MBE to Akavia who had served him so well throughout the campaign. Of these members of the mission only Simonds and Akavia did not receive the decorations for which they were recommended; Wingate received a bar to his DSO and Sandford was awarded a CBE. Not unnaturally Wingate was outraged. Akavia did not receive an award because he was not officially serving in the British army even though he had carried out the staff duties of a brigade major. Eventually he was mentioned in despatches and admitted to being 'treated very nicely' when he arrived in Cairo but Simonds received nothing, a bewildering omission, given his leadership of Beghemder Force and its successes around Lake Tana.

Equally infuriating was GHQ's treatment of Wingate's request for special 'hardship allowances' to be paid to seven officers and eleven NCOs who had served with the Patriot forces in the period between 1 December 1940 and 1 June 1941. This amounted to a small sum – £227

8s 8d – but they were refused on the administrative nicety that allowances could only be paid to regular soldiers in the field, not to men who came under the control of G(R). Although Wingate complained that 'these neglects have a demoralising effect when the same personnel go to fight again,' and that 'special cases should receive special treatment,' the allowances were not paid. There were also problems in accounting for the Maria Theresa dollars which had been allotted to the mission but this was dropped because the coins had been specially made by the Royal Mint out of silver provided by SOE.

About this time, too, Wingate became convinced that Britain was being disingenuous in its relations with Haile Selassie and meant to use its military success to bring Ethiopia into the empire. His misgivings had already been fuelled by an earlier SOE attempt to create an uprising amongst the Galla people of southern Ethiopia with the intention of ousting the Italians and creating a British protectorate. Led by Courtenay Brocklehurst of the Secret Intelligence Service's Section D – responsible for undercover sabotage work behind enemy lines – the Galla operation would have compromised everything that Sandford was trying to achieve and on Eden's insistence it had been withdrawn. This enabled SOE to concentrate on the priority of making Haile Selassie the focus of the Patriot revolt.

Despite the fact that nothing had come of the Brocklehurst initiative Wingate continued to harbour doubts about British intentions towards Ethiopia. Not only did he feel a personal obligation towards the emperor but he also seems to have transferred to the people of Ethiopia, albeit temporarily, the sense of compassion and companionship he felt for the Jews. In Harrar he had met white East African officers who had belittled the achievements of his Patriot forces and could not believe that black Africans could make professional soldiers. Their racist comments seemed to be little different in tone to the anti-Semitic remarks which had peppered British conversation in Palestine and Wingate was equally enraged by them. All told, it seemed to him as if the authorities were keen to dismiss the role of the Patriots, not because they had been unsuccessful but because small numbers of them, led by British officers, had inflicted a heavy defeat on a white European army. Wingate was not alone. When Douglas Dodds-Parker returned to Britain he, too, was asked to discontinue private talks on the Ethiopian campaign: 'Later I found out that South African pressure had been brought to play down the victory of mainly non-white troops over a largely white army.'

When Wingate returned to London later in the year Ethiopia's position was to become as burning an issue as Palestine had ever been but at the beginning of July he was not in any position to take the matter further. He was seriously ill with malaria but had refused to take medical advice, other than to see an Egyptian doctor. He had prescribed the drug atebrin, or mepacrine, which controls fever but has the side effect of acting as a depressant; hardly the best treatment for a man in Wingate's state of mind. At the time he feared that, were he to report sick to the army's medical services, he might forfeit his position with G(R) and would be returned to general staff duties as a pool officer. The use of the drug was therefore a last straw for Wingate was rapidly approaching a critical moment when he believed that he had been so forsaken that life was no longer worth living. During the afternoon of 4 July he attempted, unsuccessfully, to kill himself in his room in Cairo's Continental Hotel, along with Shepheard's a smart, officers-only establishment.

As with the other key moments in his life it is difficult to gauge the precise reasons for his actions. Much has been written about his suicide attempt and arguments still rage within the medical profession about why he tried to kill himself by the singularly horrible method of stabbing himself to death in the throat. At the time the matter was hushed up by SOE's representatives in Cairo and not even Lorna was told what had happened until he returned to Britain in November. She had merely been told that he had been seriously ill and had injured himself further during a fall.

While it is impossible to understand the conflicting emotions which must jumble through the suicide's mind at the point of self-destruction, it was relatively easy to piece together the sequence of events which led to Wingate's attempt to take his own life. Staying in the room next door to him at the Continental Hotel was Colonel Cudbert Thornhill, a veteran intelligence officer employed by SOE, who was a mute witness to the incident. Also, according to an account drawn up later by Ivy Paterson, there was a logical progression to Wingate's movements. Finding that his temperature was 104°F he left the hotel to get some more supplies of atebrin but in his befuddled state he was unable to locate the doctor who had originally prescribed it. In despair, he returned to his room and, 'trembling with fever and hardly able to stand', prepared to end his life.

Before his resolve ebbed, he took out a hunter's Bowie knife – presented to him in Ethiopia by an American war correspondent called Hiram B. Blauveldt – and walked over to the mirror above the wash-basin. Looking at himself, almost as if he were shaving, he plunged the blade into the right-hand side of his neck in an attempt to strike his carotid artery. Had he done so, death would have been quick – the artery is a primary vascular supply for the brain and the blood pumped out would have hit the ceiling – but he missed his target. Then, with blood dripping into the sink, Wingate suddenly remembered that he had forgotten to lock the door because a floor waiter had been working on the landing outside and he had not wanted to arouse his suspicions.

With the blade still jammed in his neck, Wingate crossed the room, locked the door and returned to the sink to set about his neck once more. With failing strength he plunged the knife into his throat for a second time but the effort was too much for him. He fell heavily to the floor and the noise was enough to rouse Thornhill from his afternoon slumbers. When he got no response from Wingate's room, he ran to the hotel manager's office for help and they succeeded in getting into Wingate's room before life ebbed away from him. 'I think nothing when I hear a door being locked and I think nothing when I hear a fall,' explained Thornhill later. 'But when I hear a door being locked and then I hear a fall, something has to be done.'

If Thornhill had not been in his room and had not acted promptly Wingate would surely have bled slowly to death. By miraculously missing his carotid artery he had given himself a chance of survival and the odds had been lengthened by the blood vessels moving back as he craned his neck at the moment of striking it. Even so, he was in a desperate state and on being rushed to the 15th General (Scottish) Hospital he was admitted 'having stabbed his throat while suffering from depression during the course of malaria, being treated by a civilian. Wounds of pharynx, both exterior jugular and interior jugular.' There he was given an immediate blood transfusion by Lieutenant-Colonel Gladwin Buttle, a pioneer in the technique of using plasma for battlefield casualties who had been dining at the Turf Club with another doctor, Surgeon-Captain Frank Ellis, RN, informed that there was an unconscious man lying in the operating theatre, he told Ellis: 'Give him some O blood, while I find out who he is.' After three pints Wingate was sufficiently restored, and the haemorrhage controlled, to allow two surgeons to operate on his dreadful wounds.

Following a difficult operation – a bout of vomiting reopened the wounds – Wingate was given a further fourteen pints of blood and in his delirium he shouted out that he was dead and must be in hell. Ministrations by a Church of England padre and Church of Scotland minister failed to console him and it was not until a Catholic priest told him that God would forgive him that Wingate was comforted.

The British in Cairo being a tightly knit and gossip-loving community, the story of Wingate's attempted suicide spread quickly and it was impossible to keep the matter secret. (It is untrue that he had failed to use his revolver because it was so filthy: when he left for Harrar Wingate had given his Enfield service revolver to Akavia.) Attempting suicide was a court-martial offence – it remained a criminal matter until 1961 – and rumours were rife that Wingate would either be arrested and charged or condemned to a lunatic asylum. The reasons given for his action ranged from a rumour that he had 'committed hara-kiri' in despair at being passed over for promotion, to a belief that he had done little more than orchestrate a 'publicity stunt' for his operations in Ethiopia.

Although the affable and gregarious Thornhill joined in much of the tittle-tattle and enjoyed being at the centre of attention, his intervention had also helped by involving SOE and through Airey's good offices Wingate was provided with a degree of protection. (All the doctors treating Wingate were ordered not to discuss the incident.) Not that Wingate helped his case much: he confided to visitors, including Simonds and Chapman-Andrews, that he had attempted suicide to draw attention to his grievances about Ethiopia and that the failure of the undertaking meant that he was 'destined for great things'. On 22 July he was fit enough to be examined by Brigadier G. W. B. James, the army's chief alienist, or expert in mental disorders. His diagnosis was that Wingate had suffered from 'a wound of the neck (non-battle)' and 'acute depression' caused by an overdose of atebrin. Added to Airey's support, James's examination cleared Wingate from facing a court-martial; on 18 August he was listed grade D and it was recommended that, once fit, he should return to recuperate in England. Three weeks after entering hospital he lost his local rank of colonel and reduced to his substantive rank of major. This was not an unusual occurrence in wartime when men were given local rank to suit the circumstances of their command but, added to his problems, the demotion seemed like a further slight.

Why then had the normally strong-minded Wingate decided to attempt suicide? Depression was certainly one reason. The lack of interest taken in Gideon Force, the difficulties over payments and awards and the subsequent administrative difficulties all combined to dishearten him. As he told Ivy later, 'Things had often been difficult in the past, but I always believed that nothing could blot out real achievement, and that good work done in a spirit of truth could never utterly be cast away.' Given his cyclothymic personality and the earlier depressions which had made life difficult for him in the Sudan, it is quite possible that he felt so cast down by events that suicide seemed to be the only way out of his predicament. A letter written to Peggy ten years earlier, in April 1931, gives a clue to Wingate's feelings about the importance of hanging on to reality in the midst of any mental torment.

I must learn to love God's creation wherever I am and not shut myself up in a world of dreams that the world of reality can so easily shatter.

Not that the opposite creed of complete avoidance of dreams will hold water. Not to dream is to slip back. The present is in this sense a dream, as is the future and the past – to live rightly is to achieve a proper blending of the three, or rather two, for the present in this sense does not exist.

Perhaps, on coming back to the 'real world' in Cairo, the impingement of too much actuality crushed the dream of perfection which he had created in Ethiopia. There was also a strong feeling inside him that God had withdrawn his love from him and that he had been found unworthy of carrying out the great work for which he had prepared himself. For Wingate, imbued with the belief that he was one of the elect, that every mortal matter was clear-cut and that to compromise was to invite damnation, this must have tipped the balance of his mind.

The physical conditions in Cairo would not have given him any relief. In the summer heat of July it was only possible to work in the morning and early evening and the enervating conditions meant that even a slight illness took its toll on the physical constitution. Although malaria was not yet a problem in Egypt it had created difficulties for the troops serving in the East African campaign, many of whom suffered from recurrences over a period of several months. This was the case with Wingate who had contracted malaria on first arriving in Africa in September 1940 and had been treated with quinine. On its recurrence in Cairo he started taking mepacrine which had been introduced in 1932 under the name of atebrin and, according to James, overuse of this drug had exacerbated his depression. However, atebrin poisoning by itself was not the main cause. As Buttle discovered when he looked at his patient's blood film – taken from his head – it was swarming with malarial parasites. Wingate had cerebral malaria, an acute illness complicated by cerebral symptoms including dementia, drowsiness and eventual coma.[2] Suffering from fever and dislocated by the heat of a Cairo afternoon Wingate would have been at a very low physical ebb and, added to his mental depression, he was literally not in his right mind.

For Wingate the time in hospital in Cairo was doubly beneficial. The Scottish doctors cured his malaria and the period of recuperation allowed him to put his life back into perspective. Visits from friends helped. Akavia arrived in Cairo the day after Wingate's suicide attempt and was one of his first visitors. Later both Shertok and Ben-Gurion paid visits, although the latter was careful not to mention what had really happened when he wrote to Lorna. ('He has had some trouble with malaria – apparently picked up in Abyssinia – but when I saw him seemed completely recovered and in good health.') In fact, Lorna knew nothing about the suicide attempt until her husband returned home later in the year. In September she wrote to her mother-in-law to say that although Wingate appeared despondent, his wounds were far from serious and that the wound in the neck had a simple cause.

The relief is very great, and from all medical opinions I have been able to gather wounds in the neck are not too painful, nor do they usually leave ill effects. You will by now have heard that my secret source of information [probably Ben-Gurion] cabled that Orde had had a fainting fit, fallen and cut himself. That he had had several blood transfusions, and that he was getting on well. He must have been run down after the Abyssinian campaign, because fainting fits don't sound at all like him. Let's hope that the rest does him good, and that he gets a decent holiday.

That last hope was granted. Once recovered – and reimbued with the belief that his life had meaning – Wingate turned again to his report on the Ethiopian operation. Not only did he want to promote the achievements of Gideon Force but he was anxious to advocate the use of small professionally trained guerrilla forces behind enemy lines.

Here he was helped by one of the most colourful characters in Cairo's wartime expatriate community, 'Pistol-Packing' Mary Newall who was in the same hospital suffering from duodenal ulcers. The commandant of No. 11 Convoy, a motorised ambulance unit staffed by fashionable female volunteers, Mary Newall was a tall striking woman who knew everyone worth knowing in Cairo society. (Later she caused one of Cairo's many wartime scandals by leaving her husband and having an affair with Sir Walter Monckton, the British Minister of State in Egypt. She was called 'Pistol-Packing' because she always appeared in uniform wearing her father's revolver in a huge holster.) Suitably intrigued by her fellow patient she made a point of befriending him and, on hearing about his exploits in Ethiopia, sent a copy of his report to Oliver Lyttelton whom Churchill had appointed Minister of State in the Middle East.

It was an unusual arrangement. Lyttelton, formerly President of the Board of Trade, had been sent to Cairo as a member of the cabinet with authority to co-ordinate the war efforts of the various governmental and service departments and to be the 'highest authority on the spot'. Although the appointment was fraught with problems created by rivalries between the various bodies, Lyttelton had Churchill's ear and, once again, Wingate made full use of the unexpected connection. Invited to dinner with the Lytteltons at their exotic villa on the Mena Road – lent to them by the millionaire industrialist Chester Beatty – Wingate used the opportunity to hold forth on the Ethiopian campaign and on his own ideas about guerrilla warfare. Just as he had held Victor Cazalet and Blanche Dugdale spellbound in London by his ability to speak passionately and coherently about the need for a Jewish fighting force, so too were the Lytteltons and their guests captivated by Wingate's performance in Cairo. It did not yield immediate results but in the longer term Churchill was made aware of Wingate's achievements in Ethiopia: an important consideration given the Prime Minister's interest in guerrilla warfare and 'scallywag' operations.

At the beginning of September Wingate was given orders for his passage home. He had hoped for a place on an aeroplane but, being a low priority, he had to travel by troopship, first by the *Llandovery Castle* from Ismailia to Durban in South Africa and then by the *Empress of Australia* from Cape Town to Glasgow which he finally reached on 14 November. Of his closest associates from Gideon Force, Dan Sandford stayed on in Ethiopia as an adviser to the emperor while Tony Simonds and Douglas Dodds-Parker continued to work for the SOE and ended the war as mission commanders. Abraham Akavia almost became embroiled too – he was offered employment by Simonds – but on Wingate's suggestion he returned to Haifa. 'I am obeying your orders and eagerly awaiting your return,' he wrote to Wingate on 30 October. Later he was sent by G(R) to Haifa as instructor to 102 Special Training Centre for Yugoslav and Greek agents. Of the others Boustead went on to command an SDF brigade in Eritrea, Thesiger joined the Special Air Service regiment (SAS) and Allen became the British press attaché in Beirut. Platt went on to command the forces which defeated the Vichy French in Madagascar but his moment in history had already come at the Battle of Keren which was one of the hardest fought allied victories of the war. The other theatre commander was less fortunate. Cunningham took over command of the 8th Army in North Africa but was sacked after the fall of Tobruk.

Although the journey back to Britain was long and arduous – he was forced to spend three weeks at a transit camp in Orubi near Durban – a transformed Wingate began to emerge from the chrysalis of despair. Having taken himself to the brink of destruction his beliefs seemed to be more secure, his actions more controlled. The black dog did not leave him altogether but he was more aware of its presence and understood that it could be kept on the leash. Not that all his old habits died. He was as opinionated and ambitious as ever and his temper still had a short fuse – he kicked a cavalry officer called Brian Franks who made a derogatory remark about the Jews – and he chafed constantly about the restrictions of shipboard and transit camp life. But, if anything, he was tougher physically and mentally. Having rid himself of the debilitating fevers of malaria, he could face the future with greater confidence and the final clinical notes made by the senior medical officer on HMT *Empress of Australia* on 13 November reveal a changed man.

The patient is now an officer of full mental and physical vigour, and determined to get back to the firing line as quickly as possible ... I believe that the unusual experiences and achievements of this officer, joined to his resolute character and marked ability, make his return to combatant duty in the field most desirable from a national viewpoint.

To achieve this aim the doctor recommended that Wingate should be given six months' leave with permission to apply to a medical board for regrading at any time after the first period of three months. He also felt that Wingate would be sensible to consult a good psychiatrist with a view to convincing the military authorities that he was fully cured and ready to be regraded category A.

The first step was to tell Lorna and his immediate family, none of whom knew the real cause of his period in hospital and still believed that he had wounded himself accidentally. They all took the news well. Lorna reminded him that other great men had attempted suicide and mentioned the example of Clive with whom, paradoxically, Wingate came to be compared by Churchill. (It was, perhaps, an unfortunate comparison. Although Clive survived a suicide attempt as a young man when his pistol failed, he eventually succeeded in cutting his throat in 1774.) The notion that he might still be meant for great things certainly helped Wingate through this period and his family became fiercely protective about the incident. Rachel took copies of the medical reports and kept them under lock and key and long after the war, in 1984, Granville was instrumental in making public Buttle's diagnosis about the effect of cerebral malaria on Wingate's psychotic state in July 1941.

With time on his hands in London, Wingate was not idle. Taking his medical report at face value he set about getting a professional opinion from a psychiatrist. Here he was helped by a Jewish doctor, Ben Zion Kounine, whom he had first met in London in 1938. Through his good offices Wingate was able to consult Lord Horder, physician to King George VI and one of the most eminent medical practitioners of his day. Chaim Weizmann also interceded on Wingate's behalf with the result that, following two consultations, Horder felt sufficiently confident to support his patient's case for a return to full-time service. The key moment came on 30 December when Wingate appeared before a War Office medical board which decided that as there was no evidence of a relapse the way was open to reclassify him grade A.

While the necessary process of consultation was being completed, Wingate threw himself back into London's social life and, through Lorna's continuing links with the Jewish Agency, met up again with many of his old friends and supporters. The day after returning to London, on 20 November, he was back at the Dorchester, dining with the Dugdales and the Weizmanns.

Orde, by our desire, held the floor all night. His description of the Abyssinian campaign, his handling of the natives etc quite brilliant. He is obviously a guerrilla leader of genius. But he is so pro-Abyssinian to be almost anti-British. I suppose it is part of his power to almost identify with the bands he leads.[3]

Blanche Dugdale's observation about Wingate's partiality was not without foundation. A few days later he dined with Cousin Rex and discussed with him Ethiopia's future. While Wingate was still in Cairo his kinsman had written to him on 20 June advocating the creation of a Jewish homeland:

You know better than I do how much traditional connection there is between the two countries and having regard to the fact that recent events have shown that you have joint sympathies with the future of the two countries, you might perhaps be instrumental in sounding Haile Selassie and if he is agreeable, the suggestion might come from him (through you) to HMG and through the latter to the American Zionists with whom Weizmann has close relations.

Although the idea had been bruited by others – Uganda had also been considered a possible Jewish national home – Wingate was not interested in taking Cousin Rex's suggestion any further. However, both men were convinced that Britain was mishandling the situation in Ethiopia and Wingate was persuaded to comment on his kinsman's round-robin letters on the subject. There was never any chance that the ideas would be taken seriously – Cousin Rex advocated a repetition of the 'condominium' arrangement by which the Sudan was ruled by the British through Egypt – but Wingate was generous with his comments. One of the main planks of Cousin Rex's proposal was the provision of experienced officers from the Sudan Civil Service to provide Abyssinia with a first-rate administration before power was handed back to the emperor.

To Wingate the idea smacked of paternalism and in a diplomatic letter of 15 December he suggested that the idea would only work if it was supported by the Ethiopians and only then if it appealed to 'their higher human qualities: humanity, faith and courage'. Perhaps with himself in mind he added the thought that the officials should be 'responsible to the Emperor, giving the Emperor the right to sack them, making sure that officials are of the highest calibre'. He also took the opportunity to criticise the existing officials in Ethiopia whom he claimed provided 'little service of value'.[4]

(Dan Sandford also contributed to the debate, writing to F. R. Wingate as 'My dear master', on 9 December. He confined himself to the hope that with British help Abyssinia would be restored within a year: 'We are going all out for setting up a completely independent state and are asking for no "quid pro quo" in return for the help we are giving.' This was eventually what happened: Britain no longer had any interest in taking on mandated territories.)

All might have been well had Cousin Rex restricted the documents but in his desire to influence events he circulated them to the Foreign Office, Buckingham Palace and 10 Downing Street. While the general response was that the ideas were out of touch it was noted that Wingate's name appeared on the documents and once again it seemed that he was guilty of dabbling in politics.

This view was compounded after Sybil introduced him to Sylvia Pankhurst, the editor of New Times & Ethiopia News, a tabloid publication devoted to promoting Ethiopia's cause which published a series of articles in January 1942 suggesting that Britain was conspiring to keep the country under colonial rule. Written under the heading 'Ethiopian Mystery' the articles contain evidence that could only have been supplied by Wingate: the lack of air support and ground transport and the delays in meeting Wingate's requests for Jewish doctors ('the cloven hoof of anti-semitism!'). While Sandford's role was denigrated, Wingate's 'brilliant leadership' was praised. Although Sylvia Pankhurst's publication did not enjoy a wide circulation her name and her espousal of Ethiopia's cause after 1936 ensured it an influential readership. Within the Foreign

Office, which was responsible for the country's administration, Wingate's involvement could hardly have been missed.

Elsewhere his contacts were more fruitful. Shortly before Christmas he renewed acquaintance with another old patron, Leo Amery at the India Office. To him he sent a copy of the Ethiopian report with a request for suggestions. Although Amery was grappling with the problems of winning the nationalists' support for the war effort by guaranteeing a measure of constitutional progress he found time to read Wingate's paper and to make a number of pertinent points in a letter written on 30 December. Of the notorious 'military apes' comment, he observed that he would be 'inclined to omit' it as it created 'an impression that your normal attitude towards the high military command is one of contempt'. Wingate duly rewrote the document and, more importantly, Amery made arrangements for it to be shown to the CIGS and distributed to the influential Chiefs of Staff Committee. Although an irregular process – the report should have been resubmitted to GHQ Middle East – Amery simply told General Sir Alan Brooke, the new CIGS, that he had asked Wingate to write a separate appreciation for his own use.

In the short term the distribution of Wingate's paper did not yield immediate results but it had been seen by a number of influential service chiefs who would be responsible for the future direction of the war and it did not weaken his immediate prospects. For a major this was support of the highest order. Other excitements during this period included invitations to lecture at the Royal Geographical Society and the Royal African Society and from the United States came a request from the publishers Doubleday and Doran to write an account of his experiences in Ethiopia which they thought would be as successful as T. E. Lawrence's *The Seven Pillars of Wisdom*. He also met up again with Tulloch who was serving as a staff officer at RAF Fighter Command headquarters and, after a lecture on the Ethiopian campaign, was introduced to Air Marshal Sholto Douglas, head of Fighter Command, who also took the trouble to read his report.

For all that Wingate was worried about his prospects, he was kept busy and there was little chance that his name would be forgotten. It was also one of the last times when he enjoyed a protracted period of leave with Lorna; apart from the first two years of their marriage and the long leave of 1938 they had not been able to spend much time together and, according to Monica, the book-lined flat in Hill Street became an important haven for them during this time. Knowing that he would probably be posted abroad again Wingate fretted about what would happen to his wife. In February 1942, following the extension of conscription to women, she was liable to be called up for national service, a possibility which filled Wingate with dread. On 29 December he wrote to Ivy warning that everything possible should be done to prevent Lorna being called up for industrial work as she was 'bad at looking after herself and easily victimised'. Following a medical report Lorna was granted exemption and during her husband's absences she helped her mother with Red Cross work in Aberdeen and kept up her links with the Jewish Agency in London.

Wingate was equally solicitous about his own future and, acting on a suggestion from Amery at the beginning of January 1942, he wrote a lengthy appraisal about his own needs and requirements for future employment. It was not a modest document and in describing Wingate's successes it was economic with the truth.

It must be exceptional, even today, when an officer who has defeated and destroyed nearly forty thousand enemy troops strongly supported by aircraft and artillery, with two thousand troops, without either aircraft or artillery, and in complete isolation from any other operations, who, as scarcely ever happens in war, has not only been in sole command of the forces engaged, but has also planned the whole campaign, organised, trained and equipped the troops, and brought the whole to a satisfactory conclusion, that such an officer on his arrival home should not even be asked to see the men who are responsible for the army's hitherto not highly successful campaign; that as soon as they hear he is fit to fight the only response should be an order to join the regimental depot at Woolwich with the rank of major. Even if it were only for a day, it would be a waste of a day!

Given Amery's patronage and his connections at the War Office this could be said to constitute special pleading! However, the paper is of special interest not because it is a résumé of Wingate's achievements but because it introduces the concept of 'long-range penetration', the tactics he was to perfect with the Chindits in Burma. Much of his thinking is a rehash of his appreciation of the Ethiopian campaign but it contains one important difference. Far from thinking that guerrilla forces had to be manned by elite troops Wingate now believed that ordinary soldiers could be trained intensively to achieve the standards and morale of a corps d'éite: 'If we will now do what we failed to do before the Abyssinian campaign we may confidently expect the same success against a more formidable enemy.'

What happened next was indicative of the confusion of wartime administration. (Fortunately Wingate minuted everything scrupulously in a diary for the period. He referred to himself throughout in the third person.) Having been passed fit for service Wingate received orders on 7 February sending him to a regimental posting with 114 Field Regiment RA at Wimborne in Dorset. Not surprisingly he took this as a grave insult and evidence perhaps of a plot to prevent him being given an operational posting. On the same day, having been advised that Wingate was once more available for service, Wavell sent a signal from Delhi requesting his presence in Rangoon for unspecified staff duties. Unfortunately, this message was sent to East African Command and was not communicated to Wingate until 11 February. By that time Weizmann had asked Sir Harold Laski to intervene with Churchill on his friend's behalf. In his reply Churchill's trusted staff officer General Hastings 'Pug' Ismay confirmed that Wavell had requested Wingate's services and that he would be sent out at the earliest opportunity.

The game of box and cox continued for another fortnight as the date for Wingate's passage came and went. Then on 17 February a new note was sounded when Brigadier Gubbins and Sir Gladwyn Jebb, Chief Executive Officer of SOE, asked to see Wingate at the Ministry of Economic Warfare where a copy of the Ethiopian paper had been sent. A diplomat by training, Jebb had been recruited into SOE by Hugh Dalton and he and Gubbins wanted Wingate to remain within the organisation to train Chinese guerrillas for operations against the Japanese in Burma. Even though Wingate rejected the idea and finally parted company with SOE – he had by then received Wavell's offer of employment – Jebb was suitably impressed by him to drop Lorna a note of encouragement: 'However disappointing things may be just now I feel convinced that Orde's qualities are bound to bring him to the top one day. Indeed, the worse things go with us, the nearer that day is likely to be.'

The main problem was getting out of Britain. It was never easy to secure seats on wartime transport flights but by 19 February Wingate had come to believe that he had been forgotten and was being snubbed. In despair he tried to make an appointment with Brooke to convince him that he would be better employed in the Middle East. Instead, he was seen by his deputy, General Sir Archibald Nye, who told him that his appointment to Burma would include liaison with the Chinese forces of General Chiang Kai-shek but the details had to be vague simply because Wavell had not yet decided how best to use his talents in guerrilla warfare.

Therefore Wingate must go out as an unattached Major without appointment of any kind, and Wavell would fit him when he got there. Was Wingate satisfied with this? Wingate said that to send an officer to the Chinese to organise irregular warfare was like sending coals to Newcastle. The Chinese and the Russians were probably a great deal better at it than we were. To this the general replied that Wingate might very well never get to China but remain in India or Burma. Wingate said there seemed little point in sending an officer who was an expert in the Middle East to Burma or India. He then gave a brief résumé of his thesis on modern war.

What Nye made of the lecture Wingate did not record but when he left the War Office at the end of the interview nothing had changed. He was ordered to stand by for a posting to Rangoon where he would receive his orders on joining Wavell's staff with the temporary rank of colonel. One of his last meetings was with Tulloch who dined with him and Lorna on 20 February and his old friend's lasting memory was of Wingate sitting talking animatedly with a huge globe between his knees, wondering where fate would take him next.

A week later, on 27 February, he had left London for the Far East, a journey by Liberator bomber which was to take three weeks due to a lengthy stopover in Cairo. By then his destination had changed to New Delhi and events had moved on. Rangoon had fallen to the Japanese who were carrying all before them and India itself was threatened by invasion. On meeting Wavell on 19 March his orders were quite simple: instead of co-ordinating Chinese operations he was to proceed to Maymyo to the east of Mandalay where he would assume control of all guerrilla operations against the Japanese in Burma.

Eleven

STEMMING THE TIDE

Britain's war against Japan had begun badly. Hong Kong had fallen on Christmas Day 1941 and this was followed by the rapid collapse of the British defence of Malaya. Although outnumbered two to one the Japanese army had fought with a speed and élan which had confounded the British commanders and overwhelmed the British, Australian and Indian defence forces. On 15 February 1942 allied fortunes reached a nadir when Singapore capitulated to General Tomoyuku Yamashita's 25th Army and 130,000 soldiers went into Japanese captivity. Equally disastrous was the retreat from Burma after it had been invaded by the Japanese 15th Army from Raheng in Thailand on 20 January. Originally, the Japanese had not been interested in occupying the country and believed that their strategic needs would be served by taking the port of Rangoon and the airfields on the Kra isthmus. Their minds were changed by the realisation that Britain could use Burma as a base to threaten Malaya and also by the presence in the country of the Chinese 5th and 6th Armies based on the lines of communication known as the Burma Road.

The Japanese plan called for a three-pronged attack – on Rangoon, the Salween River and the Sittang River – and as in Malaya they relied on speed and aggression. On 11 February they crossed the Salween, the defending 17th Indian Division blew the bridges across the Sittang three days later and by 18 March Rangoon had fallen. Although the British–Indian forces counter-attacked in the Irrawaddy Valley at the end of the month they were outflanked to the east and west where the Japanese were driving Chiang Kai-shek's army back towards the Chinese border. Short of supplies, exhausted and demoralised, the two armies decided to go their separate ways and the British–Indian forces began what came to be known as 'the longest retreat in British military history'. After a march of 900 miles the survivors crossed over the border into India on 19 May: of the original 30,000, 4,000 were dead and another 9,000 were missing. As had happened in Malaya, the Allies had been completely out-fought by the enemy and there was a widespread belief that the Japanese soldier was unbeatable in jungle warfare. Although written a short time later, this unnamed young officer's report of a visit to the border is indicative of the widespread decline in morale.

The troops that I came into contact with, and they were the most forward units and their Commanders, were gutless. That is the only word I can find for them. They were all disinterested [*sic*], indisciplined, untrained in many cases. In all they were gutless. For example, I cannot do better than tell you again of the fellow, the British corporal, who said, 'Don't shoot, sir, they'll only shoot back.'[1]

This was not just an army which had been badly beaten: it did not want to go on the offensive. They needed time to recover their strength and morale and the new units needed to be trained before Wavell and his commanders could take the war back to the Japanese in Burma.

The reconquest of Burma is one of the great sagas in the histories of the British and the Indian armies. It was the longest campaign of the Second World War; it was fought over a harsh terrain which included deep jungle as well as desert and mountain; and it was often war to the knife with opposing soldiers caught in bitter close-quarter combat. It began with a painful retreat and ended with a famous victory which relied as much on the endurance and fortitude of the allied troops as it did on the skill of allied commanders. It involved soldiers from a wide range of allied countries – Britain, India, Burma, China, Nepal, the United States and West Africa – and because the campaign was almost as long as the war itself, it saw the introduction of strategic innovations such as the use of air power and modern radios to provide support for the troops on the ground.

And, like the other great campaigns of the war, it had its own share of controversial military personalities whose role continues to excite controversy, not just amongst survivors of the campaign but also amongst military historians: for example, the rancorous American commander of Chinese forces General 'Vinegar Joe' Stilwell; the youthful allied supremo Admiral Lord Louis Mountbatten; the stoical commander of XV Corps General Philip Christison; the avuncular calm of Field Marshal Slim and Field Marshal Wavell and, of course, Wingate and his controversial long-range penetration tactics.

As more than one commentator on the Burma campaign has pointed out, oceans of ink have been spilled on the role played by Wingate and his two Chindit campaigns of 1943 and 1944. Both have been remarkably well documented by the survivors; indeed, some of the accounts are classics of the literature of war, and the campaign itself has spawned a number of histories. Some of these are highly partisan because they centre on Wingate and the correctness or otherwise of his unorthodox strategic concept of long-range penetration which had the backing of Wavell. At one extreme Wingate is seen as the man who turned the tide of war in Burma by proving that the Japanese soldier could be beaten and introduced revolutionary tactics to bring this about; at the other, his achievements have been disparaged as being no more than expensive side-shows which cost men's lives in return for little strategic gain and much questionable publicity.

This latter view seemed to be sanctioned when the *Official History* of the campaign in Burma was published in 1961. Not only did it question Wingate's direction of the second Chindit expedition but, to the fury of many ex-Chindits, it cast aspersions on Wingate's leadership qualities and, uniquely for such a history, made adverse comments on his personality. Although the *Official History*'s criticisms have been countered and corrected by two of Wingate's most loyal lieutenants, Derek Tulloch and Peter Mead, it is clear that much of the animus against him came, and continues to come, from dislike of his complex personality and his military and social non-conformism. As Louis Allen pointed out in his own history of the Burma campaign, 'Even now, to do him [Wingate] – and his enemies – justice, requires a fair amount of dexterous tight-rope walking.'

In the midst of this continuing turmoil over Wingate and the Chindits one fact has been overlooked: the campaign in Burma was the goal for which he had been subconsciously preparing for most of his military life. From the plans for the Special Night Squads in which he proved that lightly equipped and armed numbers of ordinary men could operate over difficult terrain, to Gideon Force's guerrilla exploits against superior forces in Ethiopia, everything in Wingate's thinking pointed to the development of long-range penetration forces in Burma. Years earlier, in the Libyan desert, he had felt the hand of God guiding his actions and as a boy he had experienced the spiritual security of being one of the elect for whom any compromise was to bargain with the devil. Burma was not only his destiny, it was a culmination of all Wingate's acquired knowledge and experience.

When Wingate arrived in New Delhi on 19 March the full retreat had not yet begun and the army headquarters at Maymyo were still operational. It took Wingate three days to get there and he was met by Lieutenant-General T. J. Hutton, soon to be replaced as Commander-in-Chief Burma by General (later Field Marshal Lord) Harold Alexander, who told him that shortages of men and equipment and the Japanese army's rapid advance left little scope for guerrilla warfare. However, he suggested that Wingate should report to the Bush Warfare School, whose headquarters were also in Maymyo. It had been established in great secrecy as part of Mission 204's role to provide British support and advice for Chiang Kai-shek and its immediate aim was to train British officers to run bands of Chinese guerrillas in special service operations against the Japanese. More of a practical training base than a 'school', its chief instructor was a soldier who was to be of considerable assistance to Wingate's immediate career: Major (later Brigadier) Michael Calvert, Royal Engineers, an army champion at both boxing and swimming, who had fought in the 1940 campaign in Norway and had later been involved in the establishment of the commando training centre at Loch-ailort in Scotland. From the very outset, the two men discovered that they were in tune about the use of guerrilla forces in conventional war. In his autobiography, Calvert made it clear that it was a meeting of true minds and his memories provide an intriguing and attractive picture of Wingate during that period.

He stayed on for a while at Maymyo and I took him around and showed him the type of country in which he would have to operate. We walked for miles and talked for hours and my conviction grew that this was a man I could fight for. He was not the popular type of swashbuckling hero. One of his habits was to dictate letters as he walked up and down stark naked in the heat; and physically he was not very great. But this did not matter in the least. He had a tremendous spirit which drove him on and completely overcame any physical drawbacks. No one could spend long in his company without realising that he had this burning fire inside him. With his thin face, intent eyes and straggly beard he looked like a man of destiny; and he believed he was just that; I am one of those who would agree with his own assessment of himself, and I think the Jews would, too.[2]

The view was shared by the school's military commander Major Peter Lindsay but others at Maymyo were less sure. Mission 204 had attracted some of the men connected with Mission 101 in Ethiopia and they were far from convinced that Wingate was the man to take charge of guerrilla warfare in Burma. Amongst these were Count Bentinck, Courtenay Brocklehurst of the ill-fated Galla initiative and Lieutenant-Colonel John Milman, Highland Light Infantry, who had served with 52 Middle East Commando. They had arrived the previous year and, following Japan's entry into the war, they had formed two Special Service Detachments for commando-type operations for the defence of Burma. Having operated independently it came as something of a surprise when Hutton informed them that Wingate was now in overall command of all irregular operations with the local rank of full colonel. Not surprisingly, Milman took this change of command badly and after getting out of Burma he turned down Wavell's invitation to serve under Wingate. The main point of conflict was not so much over the use of irregular forces – Milman was an expert in guerrilla techniques – but over Wingate's comparison of Burma with Ethiopia. It is also likely that, having experienced warfare in the Burmese jungle, Milman was not impressed by the arrival of a fellow officer who had set ideas about long-range penetration in such a testing environment. (Most of Brocklehurst's Special Service Detachment were killed during the retreat from Burma.)

Fortunately, Calvert did not share his colleagues' views, although the two men's first meeting could have caused problems. Wingate had arrived in Maymyo on 25 March while Calvert was absent on a daring raid on the port of Henzada and when he returned he found the newcomer sitting at his desk. Given Wingate's insistence on rank and the importance he always placed on his own command, a clash of personalities seemed inevitable, but Wingate yielded and the two men set about comparing their ideas and experiences. The result was Wingate's memorandum 'Notes on Penetration Warfare – Burma Command' which proposed the formation of a guerrilla group to act in concert with Mission 204 behind Japanese lines.

Warfare within the enemy's camp, like all other forms of warfare, is Military in character, and results can be achieved only by the attack and destruction of *objectives vital to the enemy*. Effectual sabotage, in actual fact, is only carried out under the aegis of columns acting on the spot, whose presence and activities permit the patriot saboteur to carry out his work, without it being laid to his door and that of his people. All these activities therefore should be carried on under the general direction of the Officer in Command of the Long Range Penetration Group.[3]

Alexander expressed enthusiasm for the idea and referred Wingate to Slim's Burma army (Burcorps) headquarters at Prome where he was

planning a counter-attack to retake Rangoon. Slim had met Wingate in
Ethiopia and admitted that he was in general agreement with his ideas
'on the organisation and practice of guerrilla warfare' but he had no
troops to spare. Prome was under daily attack by Japanese bombers and
the town itself was inundated with thousands of Indian refugees waiting
to cross the Irrawaddy and to flee to the Arakan coast in front of the
advancing Japanese forces.

Wingate attempted to counter Slim's objections about manpower
shortages by proposing the employment of Kachin Levies and recently
enlisted Pathans but the corps commander was not in any position to
offer immediate encouragement: within two days of the visit he was
forced to move his headquarters north to Allanmyo where he was visited
by Wavell and Alexander. Both men were under political pressure to
maintain solidarity with the Chinese and were due to meet Chiang Kai-
shek in Maymyo on 6 April to discuss the co-ordination of the remaining
Chinese divisions with Burcorps. Although the proposed collaboration
was largely abortive, the moves provided Wingate with his next opportunity to promote his ideas about guerrilla warfare. When the Chinese
generalissimo flew back to his headquarters in Chungking, Wingate was
given a seat on the flight so that he could confer with the British officers
attached to Mission 204. It was an eventful flight – the aircraft had to
take evasive action when chased by Japanese fighters – but the visit to
Chungking proved to be less fruitful.

Shortly before Wingate's arrival the mission leader Major-General
L. E. Denys was killed in an air crash and SOE hoped that Wingate
might take his place as Gubbins and Jebb had originally planned: 'I
wonder who will succeed the man who was unfortunate enough to get
himself into a defective plane?' W. E. D. Allen wrote somewhat cryptically
to Lorna on 18 March. The suggestion came to nothing as Wingate's
door to SOE had already been shut – command was given to Major-
General J. M. Bruce – but that was not the main difficulty. Mission 204
lacked the men and equipment to mount long-range penetration attacks
from China and Chiang Kai-shek was already receiving sufficient military
advice from his US chief of staff, General Joseph Stilwell. In fact SOE
had already accepted the position on 2 April when Lindsay signalled
SOE's Oriental Mission chief, Valentine St John Killery, that 'there is
no other source for obtaining troops in this country except through
Slim, and so we had to accept the disappointment and reform our plans.'[4]

On 16 April Wingate returned to Maymyo and with the situation in
Burma deteriorating he spent a few days driving around the Shan states

with Captain George Dunlop, 2nd Royal Scots, who was serving with Calvert at the Bush Warfare School and who had experience of soldiering in Palestine. Then, shortly before the month's end he left by air for New Delhi where he took up residence in Maiden's Hotel. Later, Dunlop recalled that they drove to the landing strip at Lashio where Wingate told him: 'There is only one seat: you shall make your own way to India and report to me there.' Dunlop later served as one of Wingate's column commanders and he noticed that 'he often used the imperative "shall", giving emphasis to what he wanted.'[5]

In the days that followed, much of Wingate's time was spent at GHQ and there he discussed his memorandum with the officers of the Joint Planning Staff who had been given the task of formulating plans for the reconquest of Burma. Although Wavell had decided that an attack down the Arakan towards Akyab offered the most immediate chances of success, his staff officers were encouraged to look at other proposals and this willingness gave Wingate the opportunity to promulgate further his plans for the deployment of long-range penetration groups to go into action in the enemy's rear areas in support of the main offensive. The concept was neatly and trenchantly encapsulated in the opening paragraphs of Wingate's memorandum:

Modern war is war of penetration in almost all of its phases. This may be of two types – tactical or strategical. Penetration is tactical where armed forces carrying it out are directly supported by the operations of the main armies. It is strategical where no such support is possible, e.g. where the penetration group is living and operating 100 miles or more in front of its own armies.

Of the two types, long range penetration pays by far the larger dividend on the forces employed. These forces, operating in small columns, are able, wherever a friendly population exists, to live and move under the enemy's ribs, and thus to deliver fatal blows at his Military organisation by attacking vital objectives, which he is unable to defend from such attacks. In the past, such warfare has been impossible owing to the fact that control over such columns, indispensable both for their safety and their effectual use, was not possible until the age of easily portable wireless sets. Further, the supply of certain indispensable materials such as ammunition, petrol, wireless sets and spare parts, was impossible until the appearance of communication aircraft.

However much Wingate's theory was to be refined in subsequent discussion papers, the theory depended on two factors: training men in jungle warfare so that they could fight the Japanese on equal terms; and using air power to supply them and support them on the ground. Having placed the penetration forces in enemy territory, transport aircraft could drop supplies to them by parachute while fighter-bombers and long-range bombers could take the place of artillery by attacking difficult positions. Because they were no longer dependent on land lines of communication, the ground commanders were given freedom of action to take the battle to the enemy, provided that air support was always forthcoming and correctly employed. By so doing they would surprise the enemy and sow confusion about the force's intentions.

Nothing venture, nothing win. The initiative can be gained only by bold offensive measures. In Burma, although conditions are not ideal, long range penetration appears possible. Its bold application may reverse the position and, in conjunction with short range penetration by the main forces, turn the tables on the Japanese.

As Wingate himself admitted, it was not a particularly profound principle but it had not yet been tried to the extent that he envisaged it. All that remained was to find the necessary men and aircraft and both were in short supply in India during the summer of 1942.

Here he was undoubtedly helped by Wavell's personal support for the project: the Commander-in-Chief was impressed by Wingate's pen-ultimate recommendation that 'Success in this operation will remove most of the obstacles in the way of long range penetration at this moment, and nothing else will do.' Without that assistance he would have been hard pressed to find support from other sources for, as Major Bernard Fergusson, The Black Watch, remembered in his account *Beyond the Chindwin*, during his visits to the Joint Planning Staff Wingate appeared to be 'a broad-shouldered, uncouth, almost simian officer who used to drift gloomily into the office for two or three days at a time, audibly dream dreams, and drift out again'. Not for the first time Wingate did not cut much ice at a headquarters in which presentation was every bit as important as military reality.

However, appearances notwithstanding, he did enough to convince Wavell to back him with a brigade-sized force and a training ground at Saugor, south of Gwalior in the Central Provinces. It was given the cover title of 77th Indian Infantry Brigade and it consisted of 13th King's (Liverpool) Regiment, 3rd/2nd Gurkha Rifles and 2nd Burma Rifles. Also attached to the brigade was 142 Commando Company, the remnants of Calvert's Bush Warfare School who had escaped with him from Burma: Peter Fleming described them as 'a scratch battalion of odds and sods, including several lunatics and deserters'. Wingate's enthusiasm for the project persuaded a number of capable officers to join him, including

Fergusson who quit his comfortable staff job to throw in his lot with the new deep-penetration forces.

The creation of 77th Indian Infantry Brigade was a tremendous concession, given the complexity of the problem facing the military planners. Although the Indian Army was to expand from 189,000 to 2,500,000 troops between 1939 and 1945 and thousands more British troops flooded into the country, it took time to train and equip them. Many of the best soldiers had served in the Middle East and there was a desperate need to train men for jungle warfare in Burma's unforgiving climate and terrain. Airfields had to be constructed in Assam for the transport aircraft which would fly 'over the hump' to take much-needed supplies to China to keep that ally in the war and India's own industrial infrastructure had to be modernised. The advent of the United States of America into the war also meant that steps had to be taken to create a unified operational command to harness both countries' political aims and military methods.

Wavell had also made changes to the command structure by creating new armies in India: Central, Eastern, Northern and Southern. Responsibility for operations in Burma lay with Eastern Army and command was given to Lieutenant-General N. M. S. Irwin. It consisted of two army corps, IV Corps commanded by Lieutenant-General Geoffrey Scoones and XV Corps commanded by Slim as well as a brigade in Assam. However, given the shortages and the lack of experience it was generally agreed that there could be no serious offensive in Burma until after the monsoon in 1943.

Against that unfamiliar and uncertain background Wingate realised that it would be impossible to raise his force with the same decision and élan which had created the Special Night Squads and Gideon Force. (None the less, he remained an unwelcome visitor at GHQ in New Delhi where his constant demands were the cause of much friction. Faced by refusals to grant him equipment, he wrote back: 'Inability is a sign of incapability.') Indeed, the period of training at Saugor was perhaps the happiest period in his life since the days of the Special Night Squads in Palestine. Once again he was in independent command of a small tightly knit force – this time as a brigadier – and once again he was training his men from scratch. He also had subordinate commanders whom he could trust. (Following a series of hair-raising adventures during the retreat from Burma, Calvert and Dunlop joined him in August, the latter after narrowly surviving a bad dose of jaundice.) He had also been given an ideal training area which replicated the conditions of northern Burma and when the actual training began, Wingate threw himself into the task with an energy and commitment which appalled the weaker and less motivated men but which inspired many more. As Calvert noted, 'He believed that the way to beat the Jap was to be tougher than them and he drove himself relentlessly.'

Originally, Wingate had estimated that it would take him eight weeks to train and prepare his force for operational duties in Burma but his calculations had not taken into account the chronic shortages of men and equipment and the time it would take to assemble them. After Ethiopia, he had made it clear that it was possible to train ordinary soldiers for the special forces, but he had demanded elite forces for jungle warfare and he was initially taken aback by the standard of the troops allotted to him. Although he respected the officers and men of the Burma Rifles, many of whom, such as Captain (later Lieutenant-Colonel) D. C. Herring, had worked in teak before the war and knew the jungle intimately, he was not so sanguine about the other two units under his command. The Gurkhas he never grew to trust completely and he was appalled by the low standard of the King's battalion which had been deployed on coastal defence duties in Britain before being sent to India. Most of the men were in their thirties and had been brought up in industrial cities like Liverpool and Glasgow and the rest were raw recruits.

Wingate's reasons for disliking the Gurkhas lay mainly in the distrust he felt for the Indian Army: according to Mountbatten he caused great offence in New Delhi by describing the Indian Army as 'the largest unemployed relief organisation in the world'[6] and made it clear that under no circumstances would he have Indian soldiers under his command. In particular, he was 'pathologically opposed' to the close, almost mystical, family relationship which existed between the officers and men of most Indian regiments. This was particularly true in the Gurkha Rifle regiments. British officers frequently compared their profession to a religious calling and there was a strong bond of affection between them and their men. Wingate failed to comprehend this feeling, just as he never understood that few Gurkhas spoke English and resented the fact that the battalion, which meant home and family to them, was broken up into separate columns. Also, they did not like the way in which Wingate treated their officers in public. Early on, while preparing the training regime, Wingate insisted that all officers should run from one position to the next and angrily berated those who could not keep up with him. To the Gurkha soldiers, schooled in a tradition of mutual respect, this was thoroughly disagreeable as they detested seeing their officers lose face in such a public way.

On the other hand, it is fair to say that the 3rd/2nd Gurkha Rifles was a young wartime battalion and lacked experienced officers to smooth over the inevitable professional difficulties; Calvert noticed that the Gurkhas had a good conceit of their own abilities in jungle warfare and that they were disinclined to accept Wingate's theories. There was also a suspicion that this disdain filtered down from the training depots with the result that none of the Gurkha regiments serving under Wingate ever reconciled themselves to his command. This was underlined long after the war by their historian, Byron Farwell (not a Gurkha officer), who claimed that 'Wingate was the only officer in more than 130 years of service ever to criticise the performance of Gurkha soldiers, characterising them as mentally unsuited for their role as Chindits. Of course, the same might be said of Wingate.'[7]

That is the voice of injured regimental pride. With the 13th King's, Wingate had to face the problem of an almost complete absence of esprit de corps. It was not the fault of the men, who had accustomed themselves to their role as garrison and line of communication guards. Many had low medical categories and as Wingate reported, most 'showed a marked lack of enthusiasm' for the task in hand. Inevitably, given the high standards expected from Wingate's training programme, there was a high casualty rate: around 200 men dropped out or were considered too old, including their commanding officer who was replaced by Lieutenant-Colonel (later Major-General) S. A. 'Sam' Cooke. They were a far cry from the elite volunteers requested originally by Wingate but as Fergusson astutely noted later, 'It is far better in my view to select a unit and say: "You're Chindits: congratulations!" or alternatively: "Bad luck!" and then shape it by trimming off the unsuitable elements.' In fact, as the training progressed younger men were found from other units and Wingate estimated that his brigade eventually consisted of men from forty regiments and corps.

In addition to the infantry element there were eight Royal Air Force sections equipped with powerful radios for calling in air support and a brigade mule company drawn from the Royal Indian Army Service Corps. To give his brigade greater versatility Wingate divided the King's and Gurkha battalions into seven 'columns' each containing 300 men and 100 mules. Equipped with heavy machine-guns, mortars and Boys anti-tank rifles, they would be completely self-sufficient and would be resupplied by air drops, thus obviating the need for lengthy and vulnerable lines of communication. The eventual order of battle for 77th Brigade was:

Commander: Brigadier O. C. Wingate, Royal Artillery
Brigade Major: Major G. M. Anderson, Highland Light Infantry
Staff Captain: Captain H. J. Lord, Border Regiment

Number 1 Group
Commander: Lieutenant-Colonel H. J. Alexander, 3rd/2nd Gurkha Rifles
Adjutant: Captain Birtwhistle, 3rd/2nd Gurkha Rifles
No. 1 Column: Major G. Dunlop, Royal Scots
No. 2 Column: Major A. Emmett, 3rd/2nd Gurkha Rifles
No. 3 Column: Major M. Calvert, Royal Engineers
No. 4 Column: Major R. B. G. Bromhead, Royal Berkshire Regiment

Number 2 Group
Commander: Lieutenant-Colonel S. A. Cooke, Lincolnshire Regiment,
    attached King's
Adjutant: Captain D. Hastings, King's Regiment
No. 5 Column: Major B. E. Fergusson, Black Watch
No. 7 Column: Major K. D. Gilkes, King's Regiment
No. 8 Column: Major W. P. Scott, King's Regiment

2nd Burma Rifles
Commander: Lieutenant-Colonel L. G. Wheeler, Burma Rifles
Adjutant: Captain P. C. Buchanan, Burma Rifles

Realising that the task of training his men for the physical and mental strains which lay ahead would test even the hardiest souls, Wingate insisted that his officers maintain a positive attitude at all times. Everyone had to attend his lectures on the principles of long-range penetration, no difficult task because Wingate proved to be a gifted and spell-binding talker. Few of those who listened to him have forgotten the mixture of military certainty and mystical belief he brought to the planning for the coming campaign. No attempt was made to leaven the problems: instead, Wingate hammered home the fact that it was going to be a difficult and dangerous operation and that there was a good chance that few would survive. A surprised Herring was told that his 'life was of no use to anyone' and many soldiers in the King's were disconcerted when Wingate suddenly arrived in their midst and, with a piercing stare, reminded them that their survival depended on their training. As Major J. C. Long of the Gurkha battalion recalled later, this forthrightness was one of the reasons why he eventually came to admire him.

It was certainly not any kind of charisma on his part – for even on further acquaintance I found him a prickly, rather than an easy, individual. It was not purely his eloquence, for oratory alone (albeit helpful) does not win over the wide cross-section of people who believed so implicitly in Wingate. It was, I am convinced, the way his undoubted ability came over, and the feeling he gave that here was an honest man whom one could trust, and who would not let one down, if one threw one's lot in with him.

The men also respected him because he would not order them to do anything he could not himself do and, as Long also noted, this attribute 'involved tremendous mental guts on his part, for his physique, per se, was certainly not robust enough to match the immense physical demands he made upon it'. Unpredictability, bordering on eccentricity, was another ploy. When Major J. C. Bruce of the Burma Rifles first arrived at the brigade headquarters at Patharia he was ordered to swim thirty yards across the river complete with rifle and boots; and Dunlop remembered a briefing when Wingate took off all his clothes during a heavy rainstorm and encouraged his fellow officers to follow suit. Together with his beloved Wolseley helmet and fly whisk and his habit of munching raw onions, these were oddities which marked him as a true eccentric, a man set apart from the normal run of regular officers.

He was still capable of losing his temper – in a letter to Lorna he owned to pangs of regret for punching a young officer who had made an elementary mistake – and he continued to be a hard taskmaster who insisted on setting and keeping high standards. On the question of health and hygiene he was especially strict. Attending a sick parade without good reason became a punishable offence and platoon officers were ordered to inspect their men's latrines to check if complaints of dysentery attacks were true. They were also trained to look after minor ailments simply because it would be difficult to provide blanket medical cover once the men were deployed in the jungle and it was understood that sick and badly wounded men would have to be abandoned. It took time for the men under his command to come to terms with this draconic approach but once they had done so, few would speak badly of him outside the brigade.

If it was a hard regime it was meant to be, because Wingate was under no illusions about the conditions his men could expect once they were deployed in the jungle behind the Japanese lines. Time was never wasted and, as Fergusson noted, each day the force seemed to get 'smaller and

more sinewy'. The day's training began at six o'clock and continued
until late evening with a midday break to miss the worst of the heat.
Exercises consisted of training in commando-type operations such as
laying ambushes and attacking targets like bridges and airfields. There
were lectures on how to survive in the jungle and how to live off the
land and everyone was expected to be proficient in jungle navigation.
The mules, too, had to be managed, all 1,000 of them: the Gurkhas had
to overcome their traditional dislike of them and the British soldiers had
to learn not to treat them as pets. Above all, as Calvert insisted, the men
were trained to believe in themselves and in their own innate abilities.

Most Europeans do not know what their bodies can stand; it is the mind and
willpower which so often give way first. Most soldiers never realised that they
could do the things they did, and hardly believe it now. One advantage of
exceptionally hard training is that it proves to a man what he can do and suffer.
If you marched thirty miles in a day, you can take twenty-five in your stride.[8]

Not that it was all work and no play. At the day's end Wingate enjoyed
talking to his fellow officers over a glass of whisky. The course of the
war was one topic, military history another, and, as ever, he enjoyed
lengthy discussions on biblical history. On one memorable occasion the
appearance of a large snake in the mess provoked an improbable discussion
about Adam and Eve: Calvert and Dunlop both noted that Wingate
often enjoyed argument for its own sake and would sometimes offer a
bizarre point of view simply to provoke discussion. But for all that he
could be harsh to the point of intolerance, Wingate often showed a
softer and more human side, especially where his men's welfare was
concerned. Once, when Lieutenant J. G. Lockett of 142 Company
accompanied Wingate to Delhi he found that he was obliged to sleep in
a tent in the hotel garden. Wingate insisted that a room be provided and,
inevitably, one was found for Lockett.

That action showed me one thing and that was – hard taskmaster though he
was, if you had served him loyally and well, nothing was good enough for you,
within reason. That I think was one of the main characteristics which gave the
tremendous confidence placed in him both by his officers and men who served
under him.[9]

Other officers simply learned to live with his moods and to avoid
confrontation. The more confident stood up to him, pulled his leg or
proved to his satisfaction that he was following the wrong course and
that his own plans were flawed. For example, Wingate had never been a

good driver yet refused to admit that he was creating a problem. After a number of staff cars had been written off Dunlop was forced to act firmly: 'I had discovered how to stop him driving – just sit firmly in the driver's seat and very politely open the passenger door. He always took the hint with a smile.' Those who wanted to survive and remain on even terms also learned to avoid using words like 'impossible', 'difficult' or 'unreasonable'.

By way of reward the brigade was given special forces status and evolved its own distinctive uniform of standard khaki drill dyed green and an Australian-type bush hat. Eventually, too, it was given its own badge, based on the *chinthe* symbol which appeared in stone carvings outside many Burmese pagodas. Representing a mythical griffin, half lion and half eagle, and symbolising guardianship, it was adopted as a badge for the brigade and in time and in anglicised form provided the unique name by which Wingate's force came to be known: the Chindits.

By September 1942 the brigade was 2,000 strong and it embarked on its first major exercise to test its new techniques before being passed fit for operational duties. It was not a complete success – few military exercises are – but Wavell was sufficiently impressed to encourage Wingate to continue working up his men for their expected deployment as 'strategic cavalry' in support of a planned major offensive in northern Burma, to reopen the Burma Road supply route into China and to bring the Japanese to battle with the intention of eroding their resources. Wavell's plans called for a three-sided offensive from Assam, Ledo and Yunnan, using IV Corps and the Chinese forces under Stilwell's command. At the same time an offensive would be mounted in the Arakan. During the planning Wavell toyed with the idea of using Wingate's force to create a diversion during the amphibious operations to retake Akyab but this was dropped when the attack by 14th Indian Division went in by land.

Ever impatient to prove that his force had a role in Wavell's plans and aware that any setback could give ammunition to his detractors, Wingate was sufficiently depressed by the results of the exercise to drop his usually self-confident guard. However, the subsequent dejection he held to himself, like a shroud. Calvert and others insist that only those closest to him were ever aware of his darker moods. Even though he had managed to control the depressions which had threatened to engulf him in the Sudan and Libya ten years earlier, it would be wrong to think that Wingate was an eternal optimist. Like most other men he nursed private doubts and fears but like other great leaders he knew how to control them and to present a positive face to the men under his command.

Commanding the brigade and preparing it for operational service also involved Wingate in frequent trips to GHQ in Delhi. While Wavell never wavered in his support, other senior staff officers were less inclined to be completely helpful, either because they distrusted the Chindit concept or because they disliked Wingate and his singular approach. On this score, as had often happened in the past, Wingate did not help matters by sturdily refusing to compromise. Often, as Lockett recalled, it was a case of: 'Either you're for me or against me.'

He would have no prevarication from anyone, driving both himself and his staff mercilessly. At one conference on a high level, he made certain demands for the equipment of his force. A very senior officer got up at the conference table and said 'But I have been told nothing about this whatsoever.' Wingate rose, rapped on the table and said, 'Why should you have been? I am telling you now.' After that the conference proceeded on smooth lines.

Behaviour of that kind was unheard of in Delhi and the disapproval and dislike felt by many senior British and Indian army officers was to detract from Wingate's post-war military reputation. Amongst those senior officers was Wavell's Director of Staff Duties, Major-General S. Woodburn Kirby, a Royal Engineer officer who frequently crossed swords with Wingate over the troop levels and equipment for his brigade. When Wingate discovered that there had been delays in supplying smoke grenades he sent an urgent signal to GHQ complaining that his orders had not been followed 'and those responsible should be sacked for iniquitous and unpatriotic conduct'. According to some witnesses of the meetings between the two men, Wingate treated Kirby with an indifference bordering on rudeness, 'as if he were the inefficient manager of a rather unsatisfactory multiple store'.[10] Later, Kirby was to be the principal author of the *Official History* of the war against Japan and many of Wingate's friends and supporters insist that he used the opportunity in volume III to take his revenge on his unruly former colleague.

By November 77th Brigade was at its full battle strength of 3,000 officers and men and Wingate had moved his advance headquarters to Eastern Army Headquarters at Imphal. This was put under the operational command of Major John Jefferies, Royal Irish Rifles, who was one of the Chindit volunteers from 204 Mission. From the very outset Irwin 'supported the whole idea' and the long-range penetration concept was also given an enthusiastic response by Scoones, the commander of IV Corps under whose aegis the operation would be mounted. Added to Wavell's uncompromising backing Wingate was in a strong position but at that point in the campaign the deployment of the Chindits ran into unexpected difficulties. Although it had come through two final exercises in Saugor and a grinding journey to Imphal which included a forced 133-mile march from Dinapur, Wingate's force fell foul of other more pressing strategic considerations.

As we have seen, Wavell had laid plans for a three-pronged assault on northern Burma but, one by one, the points of his trident began to disappear. First, the absence of manpower and transport called a halt to IV Corps's projected attack on the Japanese positions at Sittaung and Kalewa. Second, Chiang Kai-shek decided to withdraw Chinese forces from the plan because of the allies' failure to provide a major naval presence in the Bay of Bengal. (Chiang enjoyed direct contact with President Roosevelt and Stilwell was frequently stymied by the Chinese leader because the *Kwang-Fang*, or seal of office as Commander-in-Chief, had been denied him.) Then, as first proof that Wingate's plans had to fit into a broader united nations' strategy, the allied summit at Casablanca in January 1943 called a halt to all large-scale operations against the Japanese in Burma until the following year's dry season.

Lesser men might have accepted the decision but Wingate had not come so far to be denied at the last moment. He believed that long-range penetration tactics could only be perfected in active military operations against the enemy, otherwise they would only exist in theory and could be dismissed by doubters: as he admitted in the subsequent report on the operation, 'The Brigade had been raised and trained for operations in the winter of 42/43 and the whole tempo, physical and psychological, set to that tune. Not to use was to lose it.' To clinch his case he pointed out that an independent attack could divert Japanese attention from the siege of the small British garrison in Fort Hertz in the extreme north of the country.

It was a telling argument but there were still serious military objections to be overcome before Wavell would agree to the new plans. The most serious came from Irwin who advised Wavell that 'from the operational value and the inevitable disclosure of the whole idea, Wingate should not be used yet'. Although he agreed that there were benefits to be gained from testing the air support system under operational conditions these were outweighed by the absence of any foreseeable strategic gains and by the possibility of needless casualties of well-trained troops. Irwin was not being over-cautious. On the contrary he shared Wavell's desire to get to grips with the Japanese and to restore the shattered morale of

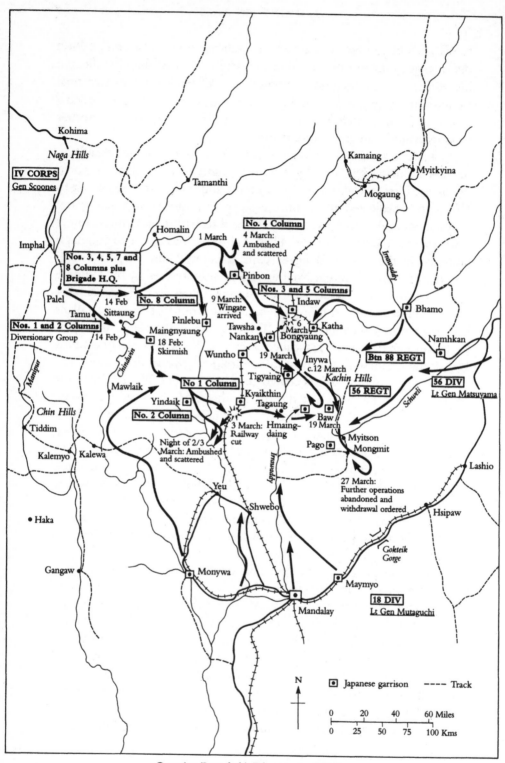

Operation 'Longcloth': February–April 1943

the British and Indian armies. As the commander of IV Corps in early 1942 he had watched the remnants of the Burma army stagger back into India and he had been shocked by their lack of morale and apparent unwillingness to continue the battle.

It was not lack of aggression which made him oppose the independent deployment of 77th Brigade. Because he supported Wingate's concept of using aircraft to supply men in forward areas – on 16 November 1942 he had asked Wavell for 'an Armada of transport planes' – he wanted to conserve the idea until it could be put into practice in conjunction with a major offensive. To his way of thinking the precipitate use of the long-range penetration force would merely warn the Japanese of the allies' intentions in northern Burma. 'I did not feel competent to weigh these alternatives against the bigger issues involved,' he wrote later, 'and so asked Wavell to go up to Assam, see Wingate and Scoones and decide on the spot.'[11]

Wavell's intervention on 5 February 1943 proved to be decisive. Not only did he have a high opinion of Wingate's abilities but he was also interested enough in unconventional warfare to believe that now was the time to test it in Burma. Like Wingate he refused to hold to the view that the Japanese soldier was some kind of superman. Even so, as he admitted in Charles Rolo's account of the operation: 'I had to satisfy myself that Wingate had no doubts and that the enterprise had a good chance of success and would not be a senseless sacrifice: and I went into Wingate's proposals in some detail before giving the sanction to proceed for which he and his brigade were so anxious.' The conference lasted two hours and in Wingate's subsequent report he claimed to have based his case on the following arguments:

Had we not gone in, the following would have happened:

Firstly, the vast majority of staff officers who denied the theory would have continued to deny it. Secondly, the Brigade would at once have gone off colour. Thirdly, our ignorance of Japanese methods and reactions would have remained profound. Fourthly, the Japanese campaign against the Kachin Levies would have been pursued beyond Fort Hertz. Fifthly, the projected Japanese infiltration over the Chindwin would have taken place. Sixthly, the serious interruption of enemy plans and confusion in his military economy throughout Burma, which our penetration caused, would have left him free to develop offensive plans.

The following day Wavell bade a tongue-tied farewell to Wingate's men before the brigade began pulling out from Imphal towards Tamu on the Assam–Burma border to cross the Chindwin. Its task was to cut the Mandalay–Myitkyina railway, to attack Japanese forces in the Schwebo area and, if possible, to cut the Mandalay–Lashio railway. To do this Wingate had divided his forces into two parts: a Northern Group, containing Brigade Headquarters, 3, 4, 5, 7 and 8 columns, would provide the main attack while a Southern Group, containing 1 and 2 columns, would make a diversionary attack to deceive the enemy about Wingate's intentions. (When the group crossed the Chindwin near Auktang, Jefferies was dressed as a brigadier to convince the Japanese that Wingate was directing the main attack on Kalewa to the south.) Later, the two groups would meet up in the Kachin Hills near Mongmit, having crossed some 250 miles of enemy territory. The operation was given the codename Longcloth.

It was the supreme moment in Wingate's life and he rose to the occasion by producing an Order of the Day which must be counted amongst the greatest exhortations a commander has ever produced for his men. Wingate was taking 3,000 soldiers and 1,000 mules deep into an unforgiving landscape where they would face an equally unyielding enemy and his words gave dignity and a sense of purpose to what would be an exceptionally dangerous adventure.

To-day we stand on the threshold of battle. The time of preparation is over, and we are moving on the enemy to prove ourselves and our methods. At this moment we stand beside the soldiers of the United Nations in the front line trenches throughout the world. It is always a minority that occupies the front line. It is a still smaller minority that accepts with a good heart tasks like this that we have chosen to carry out. We need not, therefore, as we go forward into the conflict, suspect ourselves of selfish or interested motives. We have all had the opportunity of withdrawing and we are here because we have chosen to be here; that is, we have chosen to bear the burden and heat of the day. Men who make this choice are above the average in courage. We therefore have no fear for the staunchness and guts of our comrades.

The motive which has led each and all of us to devote ourselves to what lies ahead cannot conceivably have been a bad motive. Comfort and security are not sacrificed voluntarily for the sake of others by ill-disposed people. Our motive, therefore, may be taken to be the desire to serve our day and generation in the way that seems the nearest to our hand. The battle is not always to the strong, nor the race to the swift. Victory in war cannot be counted upon, but what can be counted is that we shall go forward determined to do what we can to bring this war to the end which we believe best for our friends and comrades in arms, without boastfulness or forgetting our duty, resolved to do the right so far as we can see the right.

Our aim is to make possible a Government of the world in which all men can live at peace with equal opportunity of service.

Finally, knowing the vanity of man's effort and the confusion of his purpose, let us pray that God may accept our service and direct our endeavours, so that when we shall have done all we shall see the fruit of our labours and be satisfied.

O. C. Wingate. Commander
77th Indian Infantry Brigade

The Order of the Day was then given to the column commanders who passed it round their men, often with surprising results: Fergusson called it a 'fitting committal to a great enterprise' and even the hard-boiled members of 142 Company were impressed by its sonorous language and the appeal to man's better nature. In the weeks to come they would need all the assistance they could get. On the night of 13 February the first Burma Rifles elements of the Northern Group crossed the Chindwin at Tonhe and they were followed a night later by the Southern Group at Auktang. By the morning of 18 February the entire force and its equipment had crossed the river unopposed: no easy matter given that the operation was conducted by a variety of methods including rafts, rubber boats, towropes and by simply swimming across the river.

Having crossed the Chindwin they had to traverse the two mountain ranges, the Zibyu and the Mangin, each man carrying his sixty-pound pack. Almost immediately, though, the expedition ran into difficulties. On 18 February the Southern Group had its first encounter with the Japanese near Maingnyaung and during the resulting fire-fight vital equipment and supplies were lost. Although this cost three days and the loss of supplies hindered their march, they continued fitfully towards their first target, the Mandalay–Myitkyina railway below Kyaikthin. For both the Northern and the Southern Groups the going was hard but, on the credit side, the first RAF supply drops had worked satisfactorily and apart from the Southern Group's exploits the only contact with the Japanese had been self-induced. Fearing that the Northern Group was becoming complacent and that 'the sooner we had a fight the better, other things being equal, since we were most of us unshot over and untested', Wingate ordered Calvert to pursue an enemy patrol near Tonmakeng on 23 February.

At that stage he admitted that his force still had much to learn and that they needed action to put the training into effect. The opportunity came on the night of 2–3 March when No. 2 column (Southern Group) was ambushed by superior Japanese forces near Kyaikthin and some elements of the Gurkha Rifles panicked. A similar fate befell No. 4

column (Northern Group) on 4 March when they encountered the
enemy in strength near Nyaungwun. Faced by overwhelming odds both
columns had to retire and disperse as best they could. The men of 4
column acted according to Wingate's instructions and eventually made
their way back to the Chindwin. The disaster (Wingate's word) was
compounded by the loss of both units' radio sets and, more importantly,
their cyphers. Equally damaging had been the accidental dropping on a
Japanese position of mailbags containing papers revealing the force's
order of battle. Prisoners were also lost and the intelligence allowed the
Japanese to have a clearer picture of Wingate's movements although it
remained impossible to gauge his intentions.

In fact the Japanese response to the Chindit incursion shows that
Wingate had succeeded in his objective of sowing confusion in the
enemy's mind. They guessed rightly the size and formation of the force
and that it was intent on avoiding detection but its intentions remained
vague. From post-war interrogation reports with senior Japanese commanders it is possible to see the extent of the enemy's concern about the
Chindit operation, which Japanese commanders feared might be the
prelude to an offensive by IV Corps. By the middle of March units
from two experienced divisions – 18th (Lieutenant-General Mutaguchi
Renya) and 56th (Lieutenant-General Matsuyama Yuzo) – were engaged
in countering the threat but it was not until the end of the month that
they succeeded in breaking up the force into smaller units.

Inevitably, though, the most accurate Japanese intelligence came from
encounters with the Chindit columns. Although he had lost Bromhead's
and Emmett's columns Wingate was determined that the remaining five
columns should continue their assault and on 6 March Fergusson's and
Calvert's men demolished three railway bridges near Bongyaung and
Nankan. At this point in the operation Wingate had lost contact with
the Southern Group and was unsure if the remnants had crossed the
Irrawaddy: accordingly he sent a signal to Fergusson advising him to
think twice about continuing the raid and giving him carte blanche to
'make safe bivouac in Gangaw Hills to harass construction railway'.
Realising that the Japanese would expect him to withdraw, Fergusson
decided to keep to the plan and made his crossing of the Irrawaddy at
Tigyaing between 7 and 12 March.

On 9 March Wingate arrived at Tawsha, some fifteen miles west of
Bongyaung, where he learned that the Southern Group had already
crossed the Irrawaddy. He had considered the possibility of concentrating
his force in the hills north of Wuntho which could be turned into a

stronghold for mounting attacks on the Japanese lines of communications, but the crossing of the Irrawaddy left him with little option but to follow suit. Once over he acted decisively by ordering Fergusson and Calvert to destroy the strategically important Gokteik viaduct which carried the Mandalay–Lashio road. This would have been a fitting culmination to the operation but it proved difficult to execute. First, Wingate had to withdraw Fergusson's column from the attack to use it as his advance guard for his proposed movement into the safety of the Kachin Hills. Then, on 24 March, Scoones ordered Wingate to abandon the operation because his new deployment would take him beyond the reach of air resupply.

By then the Chindits were facing all manner of problems. Not only was the hot and arid plain on the east bank of the river unsuited to their type of operations but they found themselves caught in a triangle bounded by two rivers, the Irrawaddy and the Schweli with the Japanese closing in on them from the north and south of the Kachin Hills. In the *Official History* Wingate was criticised for crossing the Irrawaddy and leading his men into a trap but, as a commander, he had little option but to stick to his original plans. While it is true that he under-estimated the physical conditions on the other side of the river he also knew that long-range penetration would only be accepted if it was seen to work, whatever the difficulties. As Wingate himself admitted in his report, there was no substitute for experience:

In view of the inevitable lack of follow up, the main value of our operation was plainly demonstrative and experimental. I have learned by experience that one never knows enough and that unless one continually subjects oneself to acid tests one becomes bogus. I thought I could take the Brigade across the Irrawaddy, but I didn't know I could. I learned much in taking it across that I need to know.

It is also true that Wingate had succeeded in most of his objectives. The air supply and signals systems had worked well and the Mandalay–Myitkyina railway had been cut. His men had proved that they could survive in the jungle and beat the Japanese: on 23 March Calvert's column successfully ambushed an enemy patrol on the Nam Mit River, killing around one hundred for the loss of a Gurkha NCO. He also thought that it would be safe to recross the Irrawaddy at Inywa, reasoning that the Japanese would be unlikely to guard the place where his men had originally crossed the river. Here he was mistaken: 7 column met determined opposition when it attempted the crossing on 28 March and Wingate was forced to rethink his options. The following day he con-

vened 'a short and sad meeting' of column commanders and the decision
was taken to break the force up into small dispersal groups which would
attempt to break out of Burma on a broad front.

Fergusson still believed that it would be possible to retreat north into
the safety of the Hukawng Valley but Wingate disagreed because the
force would be beyond the limit of air support and the men were already
exhausted.

[Wingate] described the extreme lassitude and lethargy of the troops which had
been with him and blamed the climate of the jungle in the area to the east of
the Irrawaddy. He said further that he had reason to believe that we had brought
into play enemy reserves on a scale greater than we could cope with. He believed
that his correct course of action was to abandon all mules and equipment and
save our most valuable asset, i.e., the experience we had gained.[12]

The retreat was no less heroic than the assault – Wingate's subsequent
report described it as 'the second and more fruitful phase' – and it
spawned two classics of war literature in Fergusson's *Beyond the Chindwin*
and Calvert's *Fighting Mad*. Both provide graphic descriptions of the
desperate conditions faced by the survivors: of the difficulties in crossing
rivers like the Schweli, of the hardships caused by lack of food, of the
debilitating effects of dysentery and malaria and of the ever-present fear
of contact with the Japanese. On 14 April Calvert's men crossed the
Chindwin to safety and Wingate's headquarters group followed suit a
fortnight later. Others had different fortunes. Two groups reached Fort
Hertz to the north, 7 column crossed the Kachin Hills to reach Paoshan
in China and many of the Burma riflemen simply returned to their
villages.

Wingate was heavily involved right until the last minute. His dispersal
group consisted of forty-three men and their adventures were as remarkable as any encountered by the other Chindit columns. The story of the
retreat also shows the true measure of Wingate's leadership. As he had
done in Palestine and Ethiopia he led from the front: according to one
survivor, Private Mercer of the 13th King's, 'he marched at the head of
his column with his revolver, a rifle and jungle knife, just like the rest of
us.' He also showed unexpected moments of compassion. At one point
in the retreat he broke all the rules about abandoning the sick and the
wounded when he rested up for forty-eight hours to enable his signals
officer Lieutenant Spurlock to recover from dysentery. The pause did
nothing to help Spurlock who had to be left behind – he was taken
prisoner and survived the war – but the incident does balance the side

of Wingate's nature which was dominated by the need to be a hard taskmaster.

To the very end of the operation he remained to the fore. When his breakout group reached the Chindwin he and five others (Jefferies, Aung Thin, his Burmese interpreter, and three other ranks) swam across the river while Major Anderson remained with the non-swimmers. It was a terrible crossing, especially for Wingate who was not a strong swimmer, and it had to be carried out in daylight but by that stage the risks were outweighed by the group's exhaustion. On the other side Wingate found a Burmese fisherman who took them to a Gurkha outpost four miles upstream. That night Anderson and his party were picked up by boat and despite coming under heavy Japanese mortar and machine-gun fire managed a safe crossing. Of the original group of forty-three only thirty-four survived the ordeal.

The figures for the rest of the Chindit force were equally dispiriting. Of the 3,000 men of 77th Indian Infantry Brigade, only 2,182 came back from Burma. Around 450 had been killed in action and the rest of the missing were either lost for ever or in Japanese hands. The 13th King's alone had lost one-third of their complement of 721 men. Worse, only 600 of the original force ever regained full fitness for active soldiering: the rest had fought their last battle. So shocked was Wingate by the high losses that he returned to Imphal convinced that he would face court-martial. That men did get over the ordeal depended largely on the excellence of the nursing services of the 19th Casualty Clearing Station at Imphal which were under the direction of the legendary Matron Agnes McGeary. Using a mixture of devoted medical care and strict discipline she and her team were responsible not only for nursing wounded and sick Chindits back to life again but also for giving many of the worst cases the will to survive.

This was an important consideration because the Chindits had faced one of the toughest campaigns of the Second World War, during which the force commanders had to impose a strict level of discipline. Before the operation Wingate had ruled that injured and wounded men would have to be left behind and the order was generally obeyed; much to his anguish Fergusson had to abandon men during the crossing of the Shweli and Lockett remembered a member of his commando section who 'just disappeared into thin air' during the retreat. According to Calvert the men accepted the regime because they had been well trained beforehand and understood that 'true sympathy was not to stop and tend one dying man when by losing command of a battle a lot of men would die'. The other reason for this acceptance was the draconic standard of discipline imposed by the column commanders. Even the medical officer Captain F. W. Faulkner advocated firmness in dealing with men who wanted to give up: 'Laggards disappear on getting into enemy country and reappear on getting out. They are more the job of an energetic combatant officer. I usually give him a hand at the rear of the column aided by a stout stick.'

During the retreat Fergusson discovered that one of his outermost sentries had left his post and had gone back to sleep with the rest of his section, thereby endangering the rest of the column. All morning he pondered on how to deal with the matter and eventually decided to court-martial the offender who was then given the choice of a flogging or making his own way back to India. He chose the former and was given six strokes by the company sergeant-major but the victim was allowed to wear his trousers because any broken skin would have invited infection and endangered his life. According to Fergusson's description, the man took the punishment well: 'He straightened up, gulping, and said – "You won't have any further cause to complain of me, sir." Or words to that effect.'[13] The man was killed in action a few days later and Fergusson always insisted that he 'never had the slightest compunction concerning the incident, bearing in mind how exceptional were the circumstances'.

Lockett, too, admitted to flogging his men and it was widely rumoured in the brigade that Wingate had been given special powers to punish men in the field, including permission to execute offenders. This was not true – on the question of punishment he recommended Field Punishment Number 1, tying up a man for a short period – but it added to Wingate's reputation as an unyielding and brutal commander. For his own part, although free with his fists and his boot, Wingate only punished once when he reduced an officer to the ranks and sent him to Fergusson's column because against his orders he shot a Japanese sentry and revealed the Chindits' presence at the village of Baw during the breakout. On the other hand Calvert never flogged and maintained discipline through his personal example and by weeding out potential backsliders during training. Given the severity of the conditions the incidence of field punishments is remarkably low and survivors insisted long after the war that discipline had to be tough if the operation were to have any chance of succeeding in its objectives.

By way of reply, though, the Chindits seemed at first to have accomplished little. The Japanese had only lost 204 casualties in combat and the Mandalay–Myitkyina railway was only out of action for four weeks, having been quickly repaired by the Japanese army's fine engineers. True, both Calvert and Fergusson had directed RAF bombers on to sizeable enemy troop positions and throughout the operation Japanese commanders had been puzzled by Wingate's intentions, but all these gains seemed to be nullified by the high casualties and the loss of expensive equipment. Even the loyal Fergusson was moved to state that the Chindits had accomplished 'not much that was tangible'; and fiercer critics claimed that the operation was of no strategic value other than as an expensive publicity stunt.

To accept that point of view, though, is to see military operations only in terms of numerical profit and loss. Operation Longcloth did cost men's lives but they were not wasted: just as the Dieppe raid in August 1942 had taught the Allies many important lessons about commando operations so too did the Chindits correct many misapprehensions about jungle warfare in Burma. It was possible for ordinary infantrymen to be trained and equipped to fight the Japanese on equal terms in the jungle; the system of air drops worked satisfactorily and ground troops had been able to direct strike aircraft on to their targets by using powerful wireless sets. While agreeing that 'the strategical value of the campaign was negative', Wingate argued in his report that he had finally proved the value of long-range penetration operations in Burma:

Thus the great value of the campaign is that it has demonstrated the power of the Columns to penetrate as far as they please into enemy occupied Burma. In this case the Columns were not of high fighting calibre and were not supported. They were none the less able to traverse the immense tract of Burma [shown on the accompanying sketch map]. The enemy did his utmost to arrest the penetration. He did not succeed at any time. It ceased because enough had been done and the force had only sufficient strength left to get out.

To sum up, when Long Range Penetration is used again, it must be on the greatest scale possible and must play an essential role in the reconquest. It is the one method in which we are superior to the Japanese. The possibilities have been demonstrated. Do not let us throw away the harvest by Lilliputian thinking or piecemeal squandering of resources.

Other gains were less tangible but equally important. At the time the Chindits were coming out of Burma the campaign in the Arakan was coming to an unsuccessful conclusion. Not only had the Japanese retained possession of Akyab but during the counter-attack they had pushed the demoralised 14th Indian Division back to its startline north of Maungdaw.

In the aftermath Irwin was sacked and replaced by General Sir George Giffard, and Slim was promoted to command the troops in Arakan. Although these changes were to have long-term effects for the reconquest of Burma, the real hero of the hour was Wingate who rapidly became the best-known soldier of the day. With British and Indian morale dented by another heavy defeat in the Arakan where the Japanese seemed to have reinforced their image as military supermen, the Chindits had provided a wonderful fillip. As Slim grudgingly admitted in his account of the campaign, *Defeat into Victory*: 'For this reason alone, Wingate's raid was worth all the hardship and sacrifice his men endured, and by every means in our power we exploited its propaganda value to the full.'

For the first time in the war in Burma the tide of war seemed to be turning in the Allies' favour and at the time it all appeared to be Wingate's doing.

Twelve

PLANNING FOR VICTORY

No sooner had Wingate reported to Scoones at IV Corps headquarters in Imphal than the high command in India turned its attention to making capital out of the expedition's success. Indeed, as the exhausted and emaciated Chindits continued to come out of the jungle it was impossible to keep quiet about their exploits: the problem lay in managing the story once the true facts of the expedition had become clear. From Scoones's initial communiqué, based on his interview with Wingate, headquarters in Delhi knew that the operation had been a success but they needed more facts before the story could be released to the press. They were also keen to milk the story for all it was worth. Following the retreat from Burma it had seemed that the British Empire in India was about to collapse and the military authorities had exercised a strict press censorship. All the British journalists were ordered out of Burma and from then onwards they had to rely on official – and frequently misleading – communiqués from Delhi and Chungking. Any report which smacked of defeatism was rigorously edited out by the authorities.

Wingate changed all that. Here was an irregular force, led by an eccentric-looking commander, which had out-fought and outwitted the Japanese in the depths of the jungle and had thereby provided the British with their only success of arms against a seemingly unbeatable enemy. Carefully managed it would provide a thrilling story of British guts and derring-do and as a morale-booster it had no equal at the time. From everyone's point of view – the government's, the army's and the press's – Wingate and the Chindits came as a godsend.

Management of the story began on 6 May when Irwin arrived in Imphal to interview Wingate before taking him back to Delhi for a fuller debriefing. Four days later the Viceroy of India Lord Linlithgow arrived in Imphal to meet the survivors and the Chindits got their first taste of being marketable personalities. Once Wingate had been debriefed in Delhi and the facts of the operation had become better known, arrangements were made for a party of journalists and broadcasters to visit Imphal on 12 May. Instead of the usual restrictions they were given full rein to interview the men in the hospital and the brigade lines and censorship was kept to a minimum. Arrangements were also made for two Chindit officers, Major J. B. Jefferies of 142 Company and Squadron Leader R. G. K. Thompson, a column air liaison officer, to return to Britain for propaganda and publicity purposes.

This was a story which had its own momentum and when it was made public on 21 May it captured the headlines in the British press and on BBC radio. *The Times* spoke admiringly of 'British mastery in the jungle' and the *Daily Mail* hailed Wingate as 'the Clive of Burma'. Much was made of the fact that these were not supermen but 'ordinary family men from Liverpool and Manchester' who had restored the morale of the British army in Burma. Back home in Britain where he was serving at the School of Artillery, Larkhill, Tulloch noted approvingly that 'Everyone was thrilled to the core', and his wife told Lorna, 'we bask in the reflected glory of knowing Orde.' (In one of her first letters to Wingate in May Lorna astutely reminded her husband that the news of the Chindits had come as a much-needed tonic after the failure of the Arakan campaign.)

Later, in the first week of July, photographs of bush-shirted soldiers in Australian slouch hats became a motif for the operation's romantic success. Wingate, too, became a vital ingredient in promoting the Chindits: a gaunt and bearded figure, casually dressed and wearing a Wolseley helmet, he became a hero overnight and one of the best-known British soldiers of the day. It was at this stage, too, that the word 'Chindit' came into common usage to describe Wingate's force.

Although Wingate did not actively court publicity he knew the value of press support and, like other successful wartime commanders, took selected and trusted correspondents into his confidence. In Ethiopia he provided a good story for Stevens of the *Christian Science Monitor* with the result that the campaign was widely reported in the American press, whereas it remained something of a side-show in Britain. He also had the happy attribute – which he shared with Montgomery – of being a lucky yet unorthodox hero-figure. Wherever he was things seemed to happen. Reporters also admired him for his informality and lack of military pomposity; above all, they sensed that he could provide good copy and Wingate repaid that interest with striking biblical phrases which spoke of destiny and man's endeavour. Like Lawrence of Arabia, Wingate proved to be adept at 'backing into the limelight'.

Welcome though the public interest in the Chindits had been, Wingate realised that his military future would not just be decided by the press. To convince his superiors about the necessity of building on his experiences he set to work on a lengthy official report which had to be written quickly because changes were afoot in the army's command structure in India. On his arrival in Delhi Wingate discovered that his patron Wavell had been summoned back to London to discuss the strategic situation in the Far East with Churchill and, later in Washington, with the Americans. It was rumoured that he would be replaced as Commander-in-Chief, but before leaving India he had repaid Wingate's success by ordering the formation of another long-range penetration group: 111th Brigade under the command of a Gurkha Rifles officer, Brigadier William 'Joe' Lentaigne. To capitalise on his success Wingate produced the sixty-one-page typescript – plus seventeen appendices – within three weeks and the result is an invigorating and lively account of the entire Chindit operation.

The work began almost immediately. On 29 May he returned to Imphal to oversee the dispersal of his brigade: the Gurkhas returned to their regimental depot at Dehra Dun, the 13th King's were sent to Bombay and the Burma Rifles to Hoshiarpur and Karachi. Everyone was granted five weeks' leave but Wingate decided to stay in Imphal to write his report in one of the spare rooms at the 19th Casualty Clearing Station. The arrangement was doubly beneficial because it allowed Matron McGeary to supervise Wingate's recuperation. It was not surprising that a close and loyal relationship quickly built up between them: both had Scottish blood (hers Glasgow-Irish), both had an iconoclastic attitude towards military authority and both shared a determination to get things done to the best of their ability. Like Wingate, too, she had developed her own ideas about dealing with casualties and she had a healthy belief in her own abilities. Something of that determination can be seen in an order she gave to Wingate's stenographer: every Monday he had to place an air letter in front of him and to remain there until Wingate had written to Lorna.

The stenographer's main object, though, was to transcribe and type up Wingate's report which was finished on 17 June. Because it had been shown to Scoones for his approval as it was being completed, Wingate thought that he had been given permission to produce the report without further reference to Delhi. Here he was mistaken and the misunderstanding was to lead to another exasperating – and unneces-

sary – confrontation with his military superiors. Scoones had advised
Wingate to be careful with his wording because the report would be
read by Britain's allies but Wingate ignored his warning. While it was
not as immoderate as his Ethiopian report, it did contain a number of
hot-headed personal comments both about his subordinates and also
about some of the departments in the higher command in Delhi.

When the report was published on 6 July it was immediately withdrawn from circulation so that the offending passages could be censored.
In all, fifteen excisions were made and although none of them altered
his argument in any way, they seemed to Wingate to represent once
more the dead hand of an authority bent on damaging his career. There
were other portents. During his journey back to Delhi from Imphal he
had been refused a seat on an RAF transport at Calcutta, even though
there were spare seats, and after arriving a day late he found little
enthusiasm for the Chindits at General Headquarters. Also, his first
meeting with Lentaigne was not wholly successful.

His suspicions were confirmed when the report was eventually published in a censored version with the offending comments blacked out.
In some instances it is not difficult to understand why cuts had to be
made. On page 7 he accused the Military Training Directorate of taking
'not the slightest interest' in his brigade; on page 8 he criticised 'the
prejudices of the clerical soldier'; on page 29 he charged most of his
officers of 'abysmal ignorance' and he claimed that one column commander had an 'excellent knowledge of Gurkhali but [was] unfit to
command men'. The most damaging reference concerned the whole
force: '90% of the personnel were in any case unfit for this type of
operation and should not therefore be used again. Most of the priceless
10% are among the 70% who are back in India.' While it is one thing
for a commander to make strictures about his men in a private report,
this would have a wide currency and, as Scoones hinted, it would be
read by the Americans including Stilwell, who was always suspicious
about British intentions.

Despite Wingate's criticisms the report is a sober and thought-pro-
voking document which did not attempt to minimise the lessons which
had been learned during the planning and execution of the expedition.
The main findings were:

1. Long-range penetration is an offensive weapon and should be employed as
'a vital part of the major plan of conquest'.
2. The men should be suitably equipped and trained: 'Training is more important
than physical hardness.' On this point more thought had to be given to basic

jungle fighting including ambushes and close-quarter combat.

3. RAF liaison officers must work in tandem with column commanders to co-ordinate supply drops and air strikes.

4. There was room for improvement in wireless operations.

5. Columns need better training in river crossing, otherwise 'the operation easily becomes a shimozzle'.

Commanders such as Fergusson had complained that the ration scale was inadequate – this was borne out by the men's gaunt state – but Wingate stuck to his belief that 'hardship is an indispensable part of Long Range Penetration.' (He also added that the biscuits in the rations were both nutritious and healthy: 'The roughage in it is a great element in promoting healthy action of the bowel. Personally I have never passed better stools.') He was, though, prepared to concede that a future diet should contain more fats and bulk. Equally, on the medical side he argued that by weeding out malingerers and by forcing men to resist hypochondria, they felt the benefit during the operation. While admitting to prior apprehension about the marginal levels of food and medical supplies, Faulkner recommended only a number of additions, including snake venom and anti-anthrax serum, to the basic medical supplies. On the treatment of wounded, Wingate acknowledged that leaving men behind had a bad effect on morale, particularly during the withdrawal, and recommended that steps should be taken for evacuation by air.

Wingate was not tardy with his praise. He had kind words to say about the support he had received from IV Corps and 23rd Division and he singled out for commendation the leadership of Calvert and Fergusson, the professionalism of the officers and men of the 2nd Burma Rifles and the co-operation of the 'indefatigable RAF officers attached to the Brigade'. However, given his previous brushes with authority and his knowledge that not everyone in Delhi supported his theories, Wingate was reckless to imagine that the report would be published uncensored. Two years earlier, in Cairo, a similar setback forced him to sulk in his tent and had almost unhinged him. In Delhi he simply counter-attacked. A copy of the original uncensored version was given to, amongst others, Colin Mackenzie, head of SOE Missions in India, and another was sent back to London to his old patron Leo Amery at the India Office. The first step ensured that an uncut version survived in the public records, but the second step was to be the more fruitful. As he had done before, Amery acted on his protégé's behalf and sent a copy of the report to Churchill with an accompanying memorandum which recommended that it was time 'to keep the Japanese as busy as we can in North Burma by a vigorous expansion of the guerrilla war as waged by Wingate's brigade'.

The report reached Churchill at a stage in the war when he was having to reconcile Britain's strategic aims with those of his American ally. Although he and Roosevelt had agreed the priority of Hitler's downfall in Europe before the defeat of Japan and that every effort should be made to achieve this aim, the Allies differed sharply over their policy in Burma. To the Americans, the country provided a route to supply Chiang Kai-shek's nationalist forces, which they wanted to keep in the war. For that reason they supported the idea of a British initiative in upper Burma in conjunction with a Chinese thrust westward from Yunnan and south from Ledo as a first step in opening a land route to China. While the British shared the need to keep China in the war they also wanted to liberate all of Burma, hence their belief that amphibious operations would eventually be needed to clear the Arakan. Two other factors intruded: as the providers of the larger air transport fleet in India and Burma the Americans were able to dictate their use; and they were also suspicious of Britain's continuing imperial aspirations in the region.

Against that background – which had been agreed at the Allies' Casablanca conference in January 1943 – Churchill had also been greatly disappointed by the failure of the offensive in the Arakan. On Wavell's return to Britain Churchill had made it clear that the operation was a 'complete failure' and during a visit to Washington for the Trident conference in May he compounded his disgust by criticising Wavell in front of Roosevelt and arguing for more rigorous prosecution of the war against Japan. During the visit Churchill proposed the creation of a Supreme Commander for South-East Asia to co-ordinate allied strategy and, somewhat naïvely, Wavell hoped that the post might be given to him. It was never on the cards – Churchill described him as 'a busted flush' – and Wavell returned to India in the post of Governor-General in succession to Linlithgow. His place as Commander-in-Chief India was taken by General Sir Claude Auchinleck.

It was at that moment that Wingate's report reached Churchill. Its recommendations – dependence on air supply to put men behind Japanese lines – offered an attractive solution to the problems of creating effective lines of communication in northern Burma and of carrying out Churchill's order 'to engage the Japanese in force wherever possible'.[1] Always attracted to the possibilities thrown up by the unconventional in warfare, Churchill was excited enough by Wingate's report to bring his name to the notice of the Chiefs of Staff Committee on 24 July.

After proposing the appointment of General Oliver Leese as land forces commander, he turned his attention to his latest protégé.

I consider Wingate should command the army against Burma. He is a man of genius and audacity, and has rightly been discerned by all eyes as a figure quite above the ordinary level. The expression 'the Clive of Burma' has already gained currency. There is no doubt that in the welter of inefficiency and lassitude which has characterised our operations, this man, his force and his achievements stand out; and no more question of seniority must obstruct the advance of real personalities to their proper stations in war. He too should come home for discussion at an early date.[2]

The recommendation was made following receipt of a paper by Auchinleck which argued for the postponement of further operations until 1944 and 1945, a proposal which Churchill derided because it would only create 'the deepest suspicions in the United States that we are only playing and dawdling with the war in this theatre'.[3] In the same minute, written on 26 July, he returned to the need to employ commanders capable of infusing 'vigour and audacity into the operations'. By then Wingate had already received a signal ordering his immediate return to London. He left Delhi by air for Cairo on 30 July and arrived in England on 4 August. During his short stay in Egypt he met his old friend and colleague Abraham Akavia and reminded him that he fully intended to carry out his promise of working for the creation of a Jewish state in Palestine once the war was over. During Wingate's journey home a second bar was gazetted to his DSO.

Immediately on his arrival Wingate was taken by car to the War Office where he was interviewed by Brooke who was finalising preparations for the next round of talks with the Americans due to be held in Quebec later in the month under the codename Quadrant. The main thrust of the discussion was taken up with Wingate's recommendation for the expansion of long-range penetration groups and the need to provide them with the best available men and equipment. While that is the wish of every commander Brooke was sufficiently impressed to offer him 'backing with reason' and promised to meet him again on his return from Canada. Once the interview was over he told Wingate to report to 10 Downing Street where Churchill was expecting him. Before going there Wingate telephoned Lorna at Monymusk and she immediately made arrangements to travel to London by the overnight train from Aberdeen.

When Wingate arrived at the Prime Minister's residence he cut an unusual figure: Churchill's private secretary John Martin described him arriving 'with little but a bush shirt and a toothbrush – an interesting and striking person, not unlike my idea of T. E. Lawrence.' Typically, and perhaps in accordance with his belief that he had to be unconventional to be remembered, Wingate had not troubled to change into service dress while he was in Cairo despite the fact that he had time to do so. The sartorial blunder was of no consequence. Churchill invited Wingate to dine with him, his wife and his daughter Mary and, according to his history of the war, 'we had not talked for half an hour before I felt myself in the presence of the highest quality.' The reason was not hard to find. Never averse to propounding his theories in front of an audience Wingate used the opportunity to talk at length about jungle fighting and his theories for the development of long-range penetration warfare.

Churchill was suitably captivated and 'decided at once' to take Wingate with him to the Quebec conference so that he could explain his theories to President Roosevelt. As the 300-strong party was due to leave by train at midnight to meet the *Queen Mary* at Faslane on the Gare Loch, Wingate would have to travel as he had arrived in England earlier in the day. While he was prepared to obey the Prime Minister's order Wingate was moved to express his regret that he would miss seeing Lorna. This, too, proved to be no problem. Churchill decided that she too should accompany the party to Quebec and arrangements were made to get her off the train in Edinburgh. As the official train was due to use the east coast route north to Scotland there would be difficulty in picking her up the following morning. And so it proved. A bemused Lorna met the train at Edinburgh's Waverley Station and by 2.30 p.m. on 5 August she was with her husband on board the SS *Maid of Orleans*, an old cross-Channel steamer, which took the Prime Minister and his party out to the waiting *Queen Mary*.

Although this episode must rank as one of the war's most quixotic moments, it was not just serendipity which prompted Churchill to include Wingate in his party. That he admired him as a military commander is beyond doubt but he also believed that his presence in Quebec could be important when Burma came to be raised with the Americans. Following the acrimonious discussions during the Trident conference about the policy for the invasion of Europe Churchill also realised that there was a need to restore harmony. Not that it would be an easy matter. As they travelled westwards Italy was falling to the Allies and Churchill still advocated a further push into southern Europe as an alternative to the proposed Overlord cross-Channel invasion. This was not to the

Americans' liking and according to the history of the Chiefs of Staff: 'Both sides, indeed, approached this fourth wartime summit, code-named "Quadrant", in an exasperated mood, verging upon outright mistrust of each other.'

That the conference was not a disaster was due largely to Brooke's statesmanship and to the careful diplomacy of Field Marshal Sir John Dill, Head of the British Joint Staff Mission in Washington. As Churchill anticipated, Wingate, too, was to play a vital role by selling to the Americans his plans for the operation of long-range penetration forces to attack the Japanese in northern Burma. During the voyage Wingate had discussed his plans with Churchill, Brooke and Mountbatten's combined operations team but he was not called to present them officially until 8 August while the Chiefs of Staff were perfecting their tactics for the forthcoming summit. At the first meeting of the Chiefs of Staff Committee on the evening of 7 August Brooke had warned that long-range penetration would have to be 'backed up by the main advance to make good what he [Wingate] had gained'[4] and this concept was included in Wingate's presentation which envisaged the use of six (originally eight) brigades:

One, starting out from China, against enemy communications in the Mandalay–Lashio–Bhamo triangle.

One, from India, against the railway Schwebo–Myitkyina.

One, from the Chin Hills, against the Japanese communications to Kalewa.

These operations would be supported by conventional formations advancing from the east, north and west to occupy, respectively, Bhamo and Lashio, Myitkyina, and the area Katha–Indaw including the latter's main airfield.

Three further LRP brigades should be trained and ready in case the Japanese struck at our regular forces before their advance started.[5]

If successful, these operations would provide the Allies with a base in northern Burma for continuing offensive operations against the Japanese and the capture of the airfields would provide greater protection for the aircraft flying much-needed supplies to the Chinese. The LRP brigades would operate in advance of an attack by the Chinese army from Yunnan, Stilwell's forces from Ledo and a British attack of divisional strength from Imphal. Churchill was sufficiently impressed with Wingate's performance to send a telegram to his deputy Clement Attlee describing Wingate as 'a remarkable man' who would produce 'vigour and inventiveness in this decayed Indian scene'.

The plan was adopted by the Chiefs of Staff Committee – Brooke admitted that it 'gave shape to our plans for Upper Burma' – and Wingate was ordered to produce a memorandum for the forthcoming Quebec conference. After arriving at Halifax, Nova Scotia, on 9 August the British delegation proceeded by train to Quebec where they were lodged in the Frontenac Hotel. (Churchill stayed at the Citadel, the summer residence of the Governor-General, before crossing over to the United States for preliminary discussions with Roosevelt.) No sooner had Wingate arrived in Quebec than he had produced his memorandum and recommendations for the future employment of long-range forces in Burma. It was a masterly document, couched in firm and aggressive language; Brooke had warned him that it would be seen by the Americans who expected a positive response. The object, as Wingate delineated it, was 'the conquest of Burma north of the 23rd parallel'; the means would be the deployment of long-range penetration forces in advance of the main assault:

Long Range Penetration affords greater opportunity of mystifying and mis-leading the enemy than any other form of warfare. It provides the ideal opportunity for the use of airborne and parachutist troops without risking their loss. This calls for the use of the best troops available. RAF sections operating with columns are in a position to direct our aircraft with great accuracy on targets invisible and undetectable from the air. Such is the description of the vast majority of enemy targets in South Eastern Asia. To sum up, LRGs should be used as an essential part of the plan of conquest to create a situation leading to the advance of our main forces.[6]

Later, after discussions with the Americans, the concept would be refined further: instead of walking into Burma, the Chindits would be flown in by transport aircraft and gliders to create a line of fortified positions and airstrips in Burma's main river valleys. The paper requested the provision of 26,500 officers and men – almost two divisions – and ended with the following recommendations:

(a) Accept plan.
(b) Authorise the organisation briefly outlined to be finalised as and when the forces are available.
(c) Arrange the provision of the elements mentioned in the accompanying list from the UK.
(d) Warn GHQ India to take immediate steps for the provision of the troops required. Time and place of reception to be arranged with Force HQ.
    These steps cannot be completed until the return of the commander of the force to India. This should therefore take place at an early date.

The memorandum was accepted by the Joint Planning Staff on 12 August when it was considered 'promising' and steps were taken to consult Auchinleck about the availability of eight brigades of suitable troops. At that stage Wingate envisaged the creation of an LRP Force Headquarters to control two 'wings' consisting of four brigades with each brigade consisting of eight Chindit columns. (In their signal the planners requested the immediate formation of six brigades with two more to follow.) Although the chiefs of staff realised that there would be problems in supplying the suitable manpower they left Auchinleck in little doubt that they fully supported the concept: 'Irrespective of Wingate's plans for Northern Burma in coming dry season we feel that value of LRP forces in Japanese war has been proved and that expansion in considerable scale is desirable.'[7] While Auchinleck considered his response, Wingate presented his plans to the Americans on the afternoon of 17 August and Brooke was sufficiently satisfied with his performance to note in his diary that it had been 'a first-class talk'.

In fact, as he was to remain throughout the Quadrant conference, Wingate was in sparkling form and his performance in presentation and debate impressed everyone who watched him. (Once on board Wingate had been kitted out with a dark blue naval battledress which he wore without any insignia except for his DSO ribbon.)

Although friends such as Tulloch always denied that there was anything of the actor in him – meaning that he was always sincere in his beliefs and was not putting on a show for effect – at his best, Wingate obviously had a commanding presence. He spoke well and persuasively, had a good speaking voice and he possessed the ability to hold his audience. Because he felt so strongly about his subject, he rarely used notes and argued his case with a conviction which bordered on obsession. He was also supremely confident and in the presence of important men was able to exert a good deal of charm. The following day he repeated the performance in front of a small audience consisting of Churchill, Roosevelt and Mountbatten and received an accolade from the Prime Minister: 'You have expounded a large and very complex subject with exemplary lucidity.' Wingate's reply was short and to the point: 'Such is always my practice, sir.'

However, no sooner had Wingate taken the opportunity to shine on this important world stage than he was forced to confront familiar setbacks. Although Auchinleck was not opposed to the concept of long-range penetration forces – in Egypt he had sanctioned the creation of David Stirling's SAS regiment – and had discussed the subject with

Wingate before he left Delhi the previous month, he replied on 19 August questioning the value of using the Chindits against 'a first-class enemy'. The plan could only work in conjunction with an airborne advance by the main force but this was unlikely to take place before March 1944 and four additional squadrons of transport aircraft would be needed. In his view, Wingate's role was not to engage the enemy in pitched battle but to harass them with guerrilla tactics. 'Therefore, in my opinion the proposal is unsound and uneconomical as it would break up divisions which will certainly be required for prosecution of the main campaign in 1944/45.'[8]

It was on this latter point that Auchinleck had strongest reservations. To achieve Wingate's needs he would have to break up two of his best formations, the 70th British Division and the animal and motor transport elements of the 1st Indian Division, a move which would leave the 14th Army without any reserve. It would also be necessary to find 3,600 British troops from other arms, including 600 from the Royal Corps of Signals. The telegram concluded that 'The Commander in Chief adds that he considers it would be a grave mistake to set about a reorganisation of the Army in India on these lines, because it is only settling down to another reorganisation which has been launched in the last two months.' As a compromise he offered a brigade from 81st West African Division to join the existing 77th and 111th Indian Brigades. Two days later Auchinleck sent another signal modifying his offer by offering all three brigades from the West African Division and retaining their headquarters and command and control system. Should additional LRP brigades be required these could be drawn from the 82nd West African Division which was due to arrive in India some time between March and May 1944. Not surprisingly, Wingate said that the offer was 'quite unacceptable'.

On this occasion it is possible to understand both parties' point of view. Wingate's plan had been accepted by the Chiefs of Staff and was about to attract American backing: to have reneged on the creation of an LRP force for operations in northern Burma would have invited a fresh rift between the Allies by renewing American suspicions that the British lacked an aggressive attitude in the Burma theatre. On the other hand, although Auchinleck was represented in Quebec by Major-General Walter Mallaby, his Director of Military Operations, he was obviously not privy to the Quadrant decisions and, as requested, had merely offered his views on the implementation of Wingate's plans. As the Commander-in-Chief India it was his responsibility to plan the deployment and use of British and Indian forces for operations in Burma in the dry season of 1944. He also had to balance the available resources: most of the new troops were untrained and under-equipped and both he and Wavell had been forced to deploy up to fifty infantry battalions to meet the problems caused by the Congress Party's campaign of civil disobedience. Faced by a plan which called for the creation of what amounted to a new corps manned and equipped with the best of everything, Auchinleck was right to be cautious.

Given his previous brushes with authority Wingate did not see matters in that light. True to form he wrote an eight-page memorandum on Auchinleck's response and this effectively demolished the Indian Commander-in-Chief's argument. Much of the criticism is robustly expressed: 'Everywhere, except in one instance [i.e. the Chindits], the troops given the task of fighting the enemy have been worsted and made a fool of.' However, on this occasion, he was not just concerned with scoring points: he wanted his plan to be implemented and he offered a compelling counter-argument which was summarised by the war cabinet Joint Staff on 23 August:

(a) If these Groups are really to be effective, they must consist mainly of British troops. The West Africans, and particularly their officers, have not been tried in battle, and it would be a mistake now to base the whole plan on their being a success in this role.

(b) The retention of the battalion and brigade organisation cuts across the whole conception of the reorganisation that is necessary. He proposes a complete reorganisation into columns, and feels that he must start afresh and do the thing on his own lines if he is to make a success of it.

(c) Provided he is given a free hand in their organisation and training, he would be prepared to accept one West African Brigade as an experiment on the clear understanding that any further expansion by using these troops would be subject to results, and that he is not committed to the use of West African troops for the coming campaign in February/May 1944.

(d) With regard to the scale of air transport proposed, Brigadier Wingate considers that the Commander-in-Chief's requirement of 4 to 5 squadrons is greatly overestimated.

(e) With regard to the formation of a Force Headquarters, this is essential not only for the early period when the force is being organised and trained but also during operations.[9]

The Joint Staff recommended, therefore, that eight LRP groups be formed immediately and that the 70th Division be broken up for this purpose with one brigade coming from the 81st West African Division.

They also backed Wingate's proposal for the creation of a separate Force Headquarters for organisation and training. The new formation would be numbered 3rd Indian Division but it would be known as Special Force and it would be commanded by Wingate in the rank of major-general.

In a sense Wingate had been knocking on an open door. As Kirby noted during the preparation of the *Official History* after the war, Wingate had been in the right place at the right time in the war. 'Perhaps the reason the Chiefs of Staff accepted Wingate so readily and created Special Force was the semi-political one, that, at the very difficult Quadrant Conference, Wingate's proposal for the advance into northern Burma was the only point of agreement with the Americans.'[10]

He enjoyed the absolute support of the Prime Minister and would return to India with the promise of further personal backing should problems be placed in his way. His star had also been hitched to Mountbatten's and he involved himself in the outline plans for Operation Culverin, a more ambitious concept to attack the Japanese in northern Sumatra, thereby cutting their links with Burma. On 25 August it was confirmed that the youthful naval captain and member of the royal family would become supreme commander of the allied forces in South-East Asia with the responsibility of waging the war against Japan in all theatres in the region, including Burma. Auchinleck retained the responsibility for administration but operational command went to Mountbatten. According to Oliver Harvey, secretary to Foreign Secretary Anthony Eden, Wingate had also been a candidate but the outcome was still a dream ticket: 'People here are doubtful of Mountbatten being up to this but the PM and the Americans are het up on it. Mountbatten–Wingate is at least a refreshing contrast to Wavell–Auchinleck.'

This latter point was important as the successful operation of Wingate's plans would depend on co-operation with the Americans. At the end of the conference Wingate and Mountbatten travelled to Washington to discuss further the possibility of raising an American LRP formation and the provision of American transport and strike aircraft to support Special Force's operations. This, too, was successful. The US army agreed to send to India 5307th Composite Unit (Provisional) which became better known as Merrill's Marauders after its commander Brigadier F. D. Merrill and, following discussions with General 'Hap' Arnold, the US air force agreed to provide the special air unit known as No. 1 Air Commando which would fly in the Chindits and provide close air support throughout the operation. Thus, within the space of a month,

Wingate had not only seen the fulfilment of his dreams but he had created the equivalent of a private army and air force. What is more, he also had a direct line of communication to Churchill and Mountbatten: from being considered an eccentric, even undesirable, soldier and unruly subordinate he had become one of the most powerful figures in the war against Japan in the Burma theatre.

It would have gone against all human nature if his dramatic rise to power and prominence had not generated jealousies amongst the staff officers at GHQ in Delhi, many of whom were senior to him both in age and rank. These differences were to surface when Wingate returned to India, and the task of creating and equipping Special Force was often carried out in an atmosphere of tension, rivalry and bitterness. Auchinleck himself tried to be sympathetic but there is little doubt that an unbridgeable gulf had been created by the decisions taken in Quebec where his own ideas had been quashed and Wingate had been given command of the equivalent of an army corps. The dilemma was encapsulated after the war in a private memorandum on Wingate for the *Official History*.

Forcefulness and determination made Wingate many enemies. His consuming fire of earnestness was such that, in a theatre where resources were extremely limited, he had energy only to grab tools to get on with the job and none to conciliate his professional rivals who found themselves the beaten bidders.[11]

However, to anticipate the difficulties involved in creating Special Force and Wingate's 'forceful' method of solving them is to jump ahead of his story. While Lorna travelled back on the *Queen Mary* Wingate flew from Washington to London to begin preparations for the establishment of his new command. During the eleven-day visit he stayed at 49 Hill Street with Monica and established an office at Combined Operations Headquarters in Richmond Terrace where officers were interviewed and equipment ordered. Wingate reckoned that he would need at least thirty first-class staff officers and his first move was to recruit Derek Tulloch, first as a second-in-command of one of his brigades and then, as he proved his worth as an organiser, as his Brigadier General Staff (BGS). At the time he was beginning a fortnight's leave at his home in Formby, Lancashire, but he answered the call and found 'a very different man to the one to whom I had bid God speed on his departure for India. No indecision here. Clear cut purpose, a firm plan and in a tearing hurry to put the plan into operation.'

On one level it was an unusual choice. Tulloch was a good regimental officer with little staff training but that very deficiency, added to the ties of friendship, commended him to Wingate as his principal staff officer. Certainly, as Special Force's BGS, Tulloch was to prove a loyal subordinate and occasional peacemaker who understood and tolerated Wingate's many moods. For that reason it was a good decision. Tulloch was told in no uncertain terms that a battle royal lay ahead, not just against the Japanese in Burma but also against the General Staff in Delhi who, Wingate suspected, would attempt to thwart his plans. As an antidote to these forebodings, Wingate also had three meetings with Colonel Philip Cochran, US air force, who would command the American air commando force. At their first encounter Cochran suspected that Wingate might just be another English blimp with an impenetrable plummy accent but he, too, was captivated by Wingate's enthusiasm and promised to provide solutions to any problem that the Chindits might 'dream up'.

SOE's Baker Street headquarters were also visited, not to renew old contacts but to get the latest information on powerful wireless receivers. Wingate was particularly interested in the S-phone suitcase sets which were used by SOE operatives in Europe and by the new Australian sten guns but by this stage in his planning Wingate did not want to divulge his plans to John Keswick, Director of Operations, Area C, which included India and the Far East. At the time SOE's Force 136 was involved in operations to arm the Kachins and, as their agents would be operating behind enemy lines, there was a good argument for co-operation with the Chindits. Shortly before departing from London Wingate left a minute at Combined Operations Headquarters that 'the time seems to have arrived for full co-operation in the field with this department' but the message failed to get through to Delhi and was the cause of considerable friction between GHQ India and SOE.

A visit to the army's petroleum warfare department introduced him to a new type of weapon, the infantry flame-thrower which was known as a Lifebuoy due to the shape of the petrol container. Wingate placed great importance on these weapons for close-quarter combat in the jungle and had ordered 10,000 to be supplied immediately. Before leaving Washington he had requested supplies of Ranger river-crossing boats and hoped to re-equip his force with the American Garand .30 M1 rifle which was the first self-loader to be adopted by any army as a standard weapon. Delays in the supply of this type of scarce specialist equipment was to be a constant bugbear in the months to come.

Equally distressing was the matter of rank. There was a slight delay over his promotion to temporary major-general and it took time to convince the Military Secretary's department that officers appointed to superior rank in Special Force had to travel with the new rank otherwise there would be delays once they reached India. Once again, as he explained to Mountbatten in a private memorandum before he himself left, this was not a question of privilege but of common sense:

I cannot emphasise too strongly that projected operations will be made wellnigh impossible if every officer must wait until his appointment is through before assuming the rank. It is a matter of days now, and we shall only be able to carry out our programmes if officers can go flat out from the moment they arrive. It is quite impossible to do the work of one rank while holding another rank.

Mountbatten eventually agreed to a compromise by which an officer would leave Britain with his original rank but would assume his new rank during the journey out to India.

During that busy period Wingate found time to be with Monica and Sybil – both Nigel and Granville were serving with the Royal Artillery – and they were made aware of the importance of their brother's plans and of the problems which he might face from a jealous establishment in India. He also managed to pay visits to Cousin Rex, the Weizmanns and his patron Leo Amery. Sadly, his mother had died while he had been away – after a short illness on 8 August – and it was a matter of keen regret that he had not been able to see her for one last time. Still, it was an invigorating moment: few other commanders of the Second World War had been granted such powers and as Tulloch noted, his friend was 'keyed up for action'.

In his original plans Tulloch was to have remained behind in London to complete the necessary staff work but such was the pace of their progress that both men and four staff officers were able to leave Britain together on the night of Saturday 11 September. Before leaving at midnight they dined together at Marlborough and, as Tulloch told his wife later, he and Wingate went for a long walk together on the Downs. Like many other soldiers going off to war both men revelled in this last look at an English countryside which had meant so much to them in past years: carefully stored memories of the endlessly rolling hills could dispel for a few minutes the heat and dust of a foreign land and the horrors of the battlefield.

Their flight by Liberator from Lyneham took them first to Lisbon where they spent the day resting in a hotel and at each stop Tulloch wrote a letter to his wife describing the journey. Somewhat to his surprise Wingate had not brought any shaving kit with him and had to borrow

his. He also caused a good deal of hilarity by using the bidet as a lavatory –
the two men were sharing a room – and Tulloch noted that 'he [Wingate]
has not cleaned his teeth since he started and shows little inclination to
start!' When the party reached Castle Benito in Tripoli they were allowed
to change into uniform and Wingate was still dressed in his blue naval
battledress. It was at that stage in the journey that Wingate foolishly
drank stale water from a vase which had once contained flowers, an
action which was to cost him dear later.

By 14 September they were in Cairo and no sooner had they arrived
at Shepheard's Hotel than Wingate met his brother Nigel who was
recuperating from an attack of jaundice. Although Wingate knew that
he was commanding a light anti-aircraft regiment he did not know of
his whereabouts and was naturally delighted to see him during the two-
day stopover. From there they flew to Basra in Iraq by Sunderland flying-
boat and then on to Karachi before reaching Gwalior on 17 September.
Two days later they were in Delhi for their first meetings with staff
officers to discuss his plans and, as Tulloch noted, the problems began
almost immediately.

The general attitude adopted and made clear by those who attended this
meeting was (a) disapproval of the man, (b) disapproval of the plan, (c) the
realisation that unfortunately this upstart had temporarily got the whip hand,
but that (d) he must be put soundly in his place at the first possible moment,
and be made to realise with due humility his gratitude to them for having
anything to do with the plan at all.

Wingate's response was not calculated to win him friends in high
places but it did win him grudging assistance. He reminded those present
that he enjoyed Churchill's whole-hearted support and would not scruple
to inform him that the operation was being jeopardised by their opposition. It was Tulloch's first experience of Wingate's high-handed attitude
to authority and although he admitted that his behaviour was 'aston-
ishingly and wonderfully rude' it did produce the necessary promises.
Once the air had been cleared Wingate outlined his plans for training
Special Force and listed his requirements with the authority of a man for
whom an order is but a brief prelude to its execution. Even so, as both
men were to find, there were delays in finding him a suitable headquarters
and providing him with stenographers, an official car and a personal
aircraft, all of which had been promised in Quebec.

In addition to these prerequisites Wingate also left orders for the
addition of further staff officers for the headquarters which he intended

to establish at Gwalior and for the immediate secondment of RAF officers to direct air support with his columns. He also wrote to Akavia hinting that he might be able to find a job for him but warning that 'this is not a pleasant part of the world and I do feel that unless there were a Jewish contingent out here, Jewish soldiers are probably happier in the Middle East. As you know, I never forget any of you or your interests.'

Having made clear his requirements he left Delhi for Bangalore to visit the 70th Division whose troops had been allotted to him. With him was the division's commander, the experienced Major-General George Symes, who agreed to serve under Wingate as his second-in-command even though he was more senior to him. Although this could have caused problems Symes behaved with tremendous dignity, partly because it was his soldier's duty and because Auchinleck had asked him to stay on and reconcile his men to the Chindit idea, and partly because he wanted to prevent Wingate from breaking up the division's brigade and regimental structure in order to create new columns for Special Force. (A column was essentially a reinforced rifle company of 250 men consisting of four infantry platoons, a heavy weapons platoon equipped with a Vickers .303 medium machine-gun and a three-inch mortar, a commando platoon, a reconnaissance platoon and a section of Burma Rifles.)

The changeover to the new order of battle could have caused difficulties because the 70th Division contained regiments which were a roll-call of the British army and, as Symes pointed out, many of their histories and traditions went back two centuries. Curiously, perhaps because his own career had included little regimental soldiering, Wingate was not alert to the upset he caused by breaking up the system and Symes fought 'a battle royal' to retain individual identities 'by allotting column numbers where possible to conform with the old regimental numbers of the regular battalions'.[12] (For example, in 14th Brigade, nos 42 and 73 columns consisted of the 2nd Black Watch.)

The regimental system lies at the heart of the British army. A man might join the army and swear his soldier's oath of allegiance to the sovereign but he will belong to a regiment which he will also find is as much a home as a military formation. As a creator of morale, the alliance between the man and his regiment has no equal: it has been claimed that it will stiffen a man's courage in time of war and offer a sense of belonging in time of peace. Wingate was therefore risking much by breaking up the division and to Symes and his senior officers he was also betraying a lack of knowledge about the British soldier. Of course, as Special Force grew it evolved its own morale and esprit de corps and to be a Chindit was to be a member of a corps d'élite; but at the outset Wingate's roughshod methods caused unnecessary offence and Symes played a vital role in placating those officers who disliked the sudden change of command.

Wingate was also helped by inheriting the division's headquarters and by employing a number of first-class staff officers including Lieutenant-Colonel F. J. C. Piggott who had flown out to India with him and Lieutenant-Colonel R. F. N. Marks, Indian Army, who became his principal quartermaster. Veterans of Longcloth had also been called up: both Calvert and Fergusson were given brigades, Lockett commanded a column and in Lentaigne he had another regular officer with experience of jungle combat. From Bangalore Wingate flew up to Imphal to discuss the situation with Scoones and Lieutenant-General G. E. Stratemeyer, the American commander of Eastern Air Command which controlled the integrated allied air operations against the Japanese in Burma.

It was a busy and concentrated period and the fact that Special Force took only twenty weeks to be raised and trained speaks volumes both for Wingate's vision and dynamism and for the skill and professionalism of his senior staff officers. Although Wingate at the time, and Tulloch in his numerous writings, complained bitterly and contemptuously about the lack of support they received from the staff at GHQ India they were not justified in claiming that it was a complete uphill struggle. Just as the training period for Longcloth helped to weed out unsuitable troops, so too were many men in the 70th Division found wanting. To meet the need for replacements, Auchinleck provided two additional infantry battalions, 7th Leicesters and 2nd Duke of Wellington's, two armoured regiments, 26th Hussars and 163rd Royal Armoured Corps, and two artillery regiments to serve as infantry. Men were also allowed to volunteer from other formations and 400 specialists were flown out from Britain.

Also assigned to the force was the American LRP unit and Cochran's Air Commando which consisted of 30 P-51 Mustang fighter-bombers, 12 B-25 Mitchell medium bombers, 13 C47 Dakota transporters, 12 C46 Commando transporters, 100 Stinson L1 and L5 light aircraft, 6 Sikorsky R-4B helicopters and 225 Waco CG-4A gliders. Air supply would also be the responsibility of the RAF and the close air support would be augmented by 84 Squadron RAF flying American-built Consolidated Vultee Vengeance dive-bombers.

True, Wingate had to fight long and hard to get these forces assigned to him and there is little doubt that some staff officers did obstruct him, either through incompetence or lack of sympathy or, simply, because the resources were not immediately available. No doubt others disliked his unorthodox behaviour and kicked against his blatant rudeness. As the *Official History* noted, 'his brusque manner often bordering on rudeness and even insubordination and his reiterated complaints that his plans were being deliberately baulked, tended to make enemies of those who were doing their best to co-operate with him.' Few people who worked with him during this period have failed to comment on Wingate's bluntness and acerbity and on his unwillingness to compromise. Even loyal supporters such as his chief signals officer Colonel C. B. Fairweather thought him 'a rude person' on first meeting him and, while recognising his 'energy, drive, ruthlessness, vision, duplicity and his touch of genius', the long-suffering Symes was forced to admit after the war that 'he [Wingate] was an egomaniac and he revelled in offending others and creating difficulties for the sheer joy of overcoming them.' Mountbatten, too, was exasperated by Wingate's 'amazing success' in getting himself disliked by people who might otherwise have supported him.

While many of the criticisms were justified – Wingate in full flow at conference was an awesome and, for some officers on the receiving end, a terrifying spectacle – it is also true that Wingate was a man in a hurry. Powerfully supported by Churchill and Mountbatten he had big political guns behind him but, as a soldier, he also realised that his continuing success could only be justified by results in the field and that meant getting the Chindits into action early in 1944. There were other personal factors: his ambition and impatience to succeed, his unerring belief in the rectitude of his plans, his aggressiveness in debate and, of course, a lifelong inability to suffer fools gladly. It is also true that while Wingate might have upset the generals, his uncompromising attitudes and refusal to be awed by the 'top brass' won plaudits from his own junior officers. Soldiers always warm to a commander who has their best interests at heart: Wingate might have been an uncomfortable presence amongst the staff at GHQ in Delhi but his cold rages and tantrums were always directed towards ends which would benefit his men.

This propensity became even clearer during the training period when Wingate was a constant presence, cajoling here, inspiring there. Another survivor of Longcloth, Lieutenant-Colonel D. C. Herring of the Burma Rifles, had returned for the second Chindit operation to lead a commando-type raiding group called Dah Force, whose role was to raise a

Kachin revolt north of Bhamo and he noted that the men 'felt compelled to follow' their messianic leader.

General Wingate was not an easy man to follow. By regular army standards, he was obviously eccentric, but he possessed that prized ability to inspire confidence in the minds of his subordinates. He was a hard taskmaster and, at times, appeared to be downright unreasonable. Notwithstanding this, things got done and, after a while as confidence built up, many of us came to regard him with a strange sort of affection.

The expansion of the Chindit force from brigade strength meant that much of its cohesion had to be sacrificed. However, Wingate still did his best to visit the various units during the intense period of training and few Chindits failed to be impressed and inspired by his leadership qualities. Not only were his lectures inspirational – he constantly stressed the need for bold measures and was free with his quotations from the scriptures – but his very presence with beard, soiled bush shirt and the familiar Wolseley helmet made him instantly recognisable. Like Napoleon's Marshal Lannes at Ratisbon in 1809 – and others before and after him – Wingate understood the value of bold personal leadership.

Unfortunately, at the very moment when he was needed to provide a focus for the establishment of his force's headquarters at Gwalior and the training of the Special Force columns, Wingate became unwell when he returned to Delhi at the beginning of October. At first it was thought that he had a recurrence of malaria and Tulloch was 'shocked by his appearance, he was obviously very ill indeed'. Distressed though he was, Wingate refused to go into hospital immediately because Mountbatten was due to arrive on 6 October and he wanted to present him with a hard-hitting report outlining his problems with GHQ India. Although not invited to the official reception at the airport Wingate made sure that he was there and made brief contact with the new supremo. Having explained his health problems and made arrangements for Tulloch to represent him, Wingate allowed himself to be taken into hospital. Eight days later he was found to be suffering from typhoid as a result of drinking the unboiled water in Tripoli.

It was a crippling blow which would keep him out of action for at least two months but once again in his hour of need Wingate was helped by having friends in high places. When Lorna heard about his illness she immediately contacted Major-General Charles Haydon at Combined Operations Headquarters in London and asked him to make a request for Matron McGeary to look after Wingate. At the time she was living in Aberdeen and, three months' pregnant, had been ill herself. Even though that message never got through Tulloch had acted on his own initiative by contacting Mountbatten who gave him carte blanche to arrange for McGeary to be brought to Delhi to tend Wingate. On 21 October, in what he told his wife was 'a classic in good organisation for ever', Tulloch contrived for her to be flown from Imphal to Delhi in a specially diverted RAF Dakota transport. (In his own account Tulloch insisted, somewhat self-deprecatingly, that Lorna had telegrammed Mountbatten directly but this was not the case as she acknowledged in a letter to her husband on 7 November.) None the less it was a sensible move because McGeary was one of the few medical people who could control Wingate: as Tulloch told his wife on 22 October, 'she has transformed his room and his meals and he now feels satisfied that he will be treated well.'

There were other tonics to help him on his road to recovery. As soon as it was known in London that Wingate was ill he received a most secret cipher signal on 17 October from Churchill wishing him a speedy recovery and telling him: 'Please do not, repeat not, hurry your convalescence.' Not surprisingly perhaps, the concern shown by Churchill in Wingate's health further compounded the disgust which many staff officers in Delhi already felt about the special relationship he enjoyed with the Prime Minister. It was followed on 12 November by a further signal from the Prime Minister to Mountbatten asking him and Auchinleck personally to ensure that Wingate did not return to work too quickly. Mountbatten passed on the message to Wingate with the warning that he would not 'agree to your going back to full duty until the doctor and Sister [sic] McGeary agree'. By then Wingate had begun his first stage of convalescence at Viceregal Lodge where he was a guest of the Wavells and, although touched by the interest taken in him, he stressed on 22 November that the danger of any relapse would have passed and that he intended to get back to work as soon as was sensible. 'After all [he wrote on 14 November] I have lived 40 years, and most of what I have accomplished has been accomplished in the face of a certain amount of disease here and there. I know my body, and assure you that I am fitter for work at this moment than I have frequently been in the past in the midst of campaigns.'

With his belief in the ability of his mind to control his body and his paranoia about anything which suggested hypochondria, Wingate stressed that he was putting on weight at the rate of two and a half pounds a day and that he expected to have reached 'complete normality'

by 1 December. Before then he intended to accept Mountbatten's
invitation to stay at his residence at Faridkot House in Delhi before
moving south to stay with Humphrey Trevelyan, the political agent at
Nowgong in the Central Provinces whom he had met during the
preparations for Longcloth. Because Trevelyan had made provision for a
stenographer to stay in the residency rest-house Wingate was able to get
back to work immediately and was also able to visit his brigades while
they completed their training programmes in the area.

On the day that Wingate left Nowgong, Trevelyan walked around the
airfield with him as they waited for the RAF transport aircraft. In his
memoirs he recalled the moment:

'Do you know the story of the Italian captain in the first war in the trenches,
waiting to attack with his eyes intent on his wrist-watch?' he asked. 'Five
seconds, four, three, two, one, zero. Avanti. He leapt out of the trench and
immediately fell under a hail of bullets. His men stayed in the trenches, clapping
vigorously and crying, "Bravo, il capitano!" That is how I feel about this
campaign.'

In fact, although Special Force had been bedevilled by delays in
supplying equipment Symes and Tulloch had worked hard to ensure that
the first three brigades, 16th, 77th and 111th, had kept to their schedules
and would be ready for operations by 15 January 1944. (The remaining
brigades, 14th, 23rd and 3rd West African, were due to have completed
their programmes by the middle of April.) Co-operation with Cochran's
Air Commando was also being perfected. As air support was vital, these
meetings were particularly important and Fergusson never forgot the
moment when Cochran first addressed the Special Force commanders:
'I've hurd about yew boys an' all your waalkin',' he said. 'I feel real bad
about all that waalkin'; maybe yew think I'm kiddin'; well, we can always
dream, cann't we?'

Quite apart from the benefits of removing the wounded – a service
much admired by Fergusson – Cochran's Air Commando offered the
opportunity of flying in the Chindits by air. Wingate was not slow to
grasp the possibilities. Although he had never been keen on the use of
parachute troops he could see that airborne tactics would allow him to
land his brigades behind enemy lines. Once deployed they would con-
struct landing strips for transport aircraft to keep them supplied and to
fly out the sick and wounded. From this understanding came the concept
which is indelibly associated with Wingate's name: the 'stronghold', a
well-defended safe haven which would provide a secure garrison from

which his columns could attack and harry the Japanese forces. This was the basis on which his plans were refined in January 1944.

By the end of 1943 the Chindit columns had almost completed the gruelling training schedule and a full-scale exercise was successfully held in the Central Provinces before Wingate moved his forward headquarters up to Imphal. Needless to say, Wingate was a constant presence during the exercise and many of the younger soldiers were struck by his uncanny ability to have all the facts at his fingertips. Lieutenant J. E. D. Wilcox, South Staffordshire Regiment, remembered meeting Wingate in the middle of a paddy field at dusk and being 'profoundly grateful and relieved that I knew exactly where column HQ was, and could point it out to him'. Once the exercise was over Wingate addressed his officers in a packed cinema in Gwalior and kept them spellbound with a riveting analysis of the recently completed exercises. He spoke without notes and as Tulloch remembered: 'That was the first close contact many of his officers had with him. They came away very deeply impressed. I have never heard a more powerful address.'

As had happened so often in the past, though, there was a darker side to Wingate's mercurial brilliance. He still had a ferocious temper and many of his younger staff officers were terrified of him. While it is not unusual for generals to develop fire-eating reputations, Wingate was a class apart when he was in a foul temper. Although he claimed that his criticisms were never personal, the loyal Tulloch frequently had to smooth ruffled feathers and restore confidence to nervous or frightened younger officers. When Peter Mead, a gunner major and former colleague from Larkhill days, applied to join the Chindits, he was told by Wingate, 'Are you that so-and-so who used to argue with me in Larkhill? If you aren't, don't bother. If you are, come on up here.' He was appointed a G2 to oversee air operations and his unpublished account, 'Chindit Headquarters', contains revealing insights into his commander's methods. Like Tulloch he was aware of the intensity of application to the task in hand and there is little doubt that, coming after a debilitating attack of typhoid, Wingate's moods were affected by physical and mental exhaustion. There is also a suggestion that he was suffering from an arcus senilis – a white ring at the outer margin of the cornea which indicates premature degenerative changes usually associated with ageing – although this was denied by the Ministry of Defence in 1976 during an investigation made by Dr W. Brockbank into medical conditions for the two Chindit expeditions.[13]

Some of Wingate's tantrums were justified by infuriating delays in the arrival of equipment. GHQ India had cut his order for flame-throwers to 5,000 but fewer than a hundred had arrived by November. There were also delays in providing ammunition for the PIAT anti-tank grenade launchers and the necessary American K rations had not arrived; Wingate argued that at least 3 million would be needed if the problems of malnutrition were to be avoided. With characteristic energy Wingate sent the evidence of shortcomings to Mountbatten with an urgent plea for help in securing the missing items.

These must be hastened from England. Priorities must cease to be given, as they have been given, to such items as the Ceylon–India cable, whose completion is likely only to introduce more confusion into our counsels, instead of the man who has to meet the enemy in battle being given the means to beat him. This has not been done and those responsible should be sacked for iniquitous and unpatriotic conduct.[14]

As ever Wingate insisted that he only had his men's best interests at heart. If each Chindit was being forced to carry seventy pounds of equipment deep into the jungle to fight a tenacious enemy it was not asking too much for them to be properly equipped and fed. Wingate also wanted his force to have a 'respectable code name, and not one produced by some facetious clerk at GHQ'. Originally he had wanted to resurrect the use of Gideon Force but the request was turned down because it could have affected security. Eventually the name Special Force was adopted but on 13 November Wingate successfully argued for the forthcoming operation to be known as Thursday.

As the year came to an end Wingate still believed that the Quebec plans remained intact and that his brigades would be deployed as originally agreed. In fact the planning staff in Delhi had already produced fourteen different plans and sub-plans which examined different options for implementing the Quadrant decisions. Amongst these were Buccaneer (an amphibious attack on the Andaman Islands), Dracula (an amphibious attack on Rangoon), Toreador (an airborne invasion of Burma) and Tarzan, a plan based on Wingate's LRP groups which would be followed by the fly-in of 26th Division to hold the strategically important airfield at Indaw. To work, Tarzan would also depend on: a Chinese attack from Yunnan to Bhamo and Lashio, Stilwell's forces advancing down the Hukawng Valley from Myitkyina to Katha—Bhamo, the capture of Indaw and limited advances by IV Corps over the Chindwin and by XV Corps in the Arakan.

Tulloch and Mead insist that Tarzan met Wingate's objectives and that 'the plan for the 1944 Long Range Penetration operations, though it suffered many alterations in details before being put finally into effect, did not change in its original object at any time until Wingate's death.' However, its implementation did suffer from problems which were beyond Wingate's control. First, it would require large numbers of scarce transport aircraft and amphibious landing craft: most of the latter were earmarked for the forthcoming Overlord operation to invade in Europe and the aircraft for carrying supplies over 'the Hump' to Chiang Kai-shek's forces in China. Second, it was by no means certain that the Chinese would agree to the plan: China had been at war for seven years and Chiang Kai-shek was loath to squander his divisions in rash offensive actions. Third, there were still formidable obstacles to be overcome in agreeing the overall allied strategy for prosecuting the war against Germany and Japan.

All these limitations were to play their part in deciding the Chindits' role in 1944. Although Wingate was aware of them and wrote acutely about the strategic situation in his many papers, he was not always privy to the decisions taken by the politicians and there were occasions when Mountbatten failed to keep him informed, either because he did not want to pass on the information to a subordinate commander, or because there simply was not enough time. 'Wingate worried me,' Mountbatten wrote in his diary on 5 January 1944, 'heaven knows I have a big load these days.'

Thirteen

OPERATION THURSDAY

By the end of 1943 it was becoming increasingly difficult for the British to decide on the employment of Special Force in the reconquest of Burma. In the interval between the heady days of Quebec when Wingate's star was in the ascendant the political and strategic situation had changed dramatically. One reason was the unwillingness of the Chinese to agree to allied plans for Burma, another was Stalin's demand for the creation of a second front in Europe. To compound the difficulties, the Americans and the British were still at odds over the correct policy to pursue against the Japanese. This was a distinct problem as the Americans were suspicious about British imperial intentions in South-East Asia and feared that they were obsessed by the need to recapture Malaya and Singapore, while their war aims in the China-Burma-India theatre were governed by the need to keep China in the war. Indeed, Stilwell had already told the British Chiefs of Staff that the final battle to defeat the Japanese would be fought on land in China.

Although he was a thorn in the side of the British military planners in India, Stilwell makes an interesting comparison with Wingate. Both were paranoid about the higher command, both had sharp tongues and excoriated those who failed to meet their high standards, both were personally brave and led from the front, both demanded offensive operations against the Japanese, both understood the value of publicity and both were true eccentrics in an army of conformists. Fergusson, no bad judge of character, saw immediate comparisons between the two men when Wingate arrived to meet Stilwell at Ledo before 16th Brigade began its operation.

When at last I was summoned, I sat for ten minutes and discussed our plans with these two very forceful characters. Wingate, heavy-browed, broad and powerful; Stilwell, with his steel-rimmed spectacles, tallish, wiry and gaunt. Both had determined faces, with deep furrows about their mouths; both could display atrocious manners, and were not prepared to be thwarted by anybody. Both looked like prophets, and both had many of the characteristics of prophets: vision, intolerance, energy, ruthlessness, courage and powers of denunciation to scorch like a forest fire.

Much has been written about Stilwell and his infamous Anglophobia. 'The more I see of Limeys the worse I hate them,' was one of his more temperate criticisms; Mountbatten was 'a fatuous ass', Wingate an 'exhibitionist' and British soldiers 'pig-fuckers'. Yet it would be a mistake to see him simply as an oddball who hid his soldierly qualities behind a mask of publicity-seeking intemperance. Like Wingate, Stilwell believed that he had a personal mission to crush the Japanese and he intended to achieve his objective by advancing towards Myitkyina, a northern offensive which would free northern Burma and protect the supply route from Assam into China. This move provided Wingate's Chindits with a realisable military role at a time when the possibility of any British action in Burma in 1944 had been questioned by outside events.

Two allied conferences in November and December had almost put paid to any initiative in Burma. At the first, codenamed Sextant, which was held in Cairo on 23 and 24 November 1943, the Allies confirmed the following plans:

Stilwell's forces to advance towards Myitkyina.
Chinese forces to advance from Yunnan towards Bhamo.
British IV Corps to advance from Imphal.
Special Force to disrupt Japanese lines of communication.
An airborne attack on the airfield at Indaw.

The operations would depend on a British amphibious assault on the Andaman Islands, the price demanded by the Chinese for their participation in the north Burma operations. However, at the following Tehran summit Stalin was successful in demanding an allied invasion of Europe by May 1944 to relieve pressure on the eastern front. As every available landing craft would be needed for the invasion of Europe, this put paid to Buccaneer and with it the hope of any Chinese advance from Yunnan. Culverin, the invasion of Sumatra, was also postponed, as were the airborne attack on Indaw and the Chinese advance towards Bhamo. The decisions effectively killed off Operation Tarzan and with it any hope of deploying the Chindits.

Although Wingate was not in a position to comprehend fully the reasons for the changes in allied policy, he was aware of the doubts hanging over the employment of Special Force. As early as 11 November 1943 he expressed his anxiety about Chinese co-operation to Giffard and warned that the early deployment of Special Force in northern Burma was essential for maintaining allied solidarity: 'It is highly desirable, if not necessary, for the Chinese army to SEE the British brigade land and enter Burma. This more than any other thing will secure the active follow-up and co-operation.' Later, as it became clearer that the Chinese were unwilling to support an offensive in northern Burma Wingate realised that, as a result, his own forces would be isolated and left without reinforcements. An earlier request to Slim to use 26th Division as follow-up troops had failed but on 27 December he drafted a letter to Mountbatten outlining his fears and requesting the employment of garrison and follow-up troops to exploit his hoped-for success.

Although strongly opposed to the flying in of a full division, with the enormous commitments that implies, I am strongly in favour of small bodies of garrison troops holding nodal points captured by LRP brigades. Not many are required for this purpose, and since a great saving in SD [supply drop] aircraft has been effected by the change of plan, there should be ample for this very profitable object.

The truth, however, is that the Army and the Air Force Commanders are proposing to use their reserves of SD aircraft on other operations. I do not ask that they be kept on ice, I do ask that you will personally intervene to see that measures necessary to clinch it (such as flying in a battalion here and there) are taken on my recommendation.

Although the letter was never sent – it is headed 'not submitted, keep on file at present' – its contents were made known to Mountbatten who adopted them in a personal minute the following day. The document also underlined Mountbatten's determination to keep up the momentum by deploying a British brigade to strengthen Stilwell's Ledo force and by taking full advantage 'of the action of the LRPGs, such as by flying in troops to hold an airfield captured by the LRPGs until reinforcements arrive from Yunnan, Ledo and the Chindwin.' At the same time he decided to send Wingate to Chungking in a last-ditch attempt to persuade Chiang Kai-shek to change his mind. Wingate left on 29 December and had two meetings with the Chinese generalissimo who made it clear that there would be no advance into northern Burma until November 1944 at the very earliest.

Before returning to India Wingate took the opportunity to visit

Stilwell whom he had first met in Delhi in November. Although he was impressed by the American general's plan to take Myitkyina and realised that Special Force could play a helpful role, he argued that it would be risky to commit three brigades on an unsupported raid against Japanese lines of communication. To avoid that danger, Stilwell's Ledo force should be strengthened by one British brigade and IV Corps should move across the Chindwin to take advantage of the attack on the powerful Japanese 18th Division in northern Burma. However, when Wingate arrived at 14th Army's headquarters at Comilla in Bengal he was presented with a disappointing memorandum written by Giffard in response to Mountbatten's paper. Briefly stated, the commander of 11 Army Group was against reinforcing Stilwell with a British brigade, because none could be spared from 2nd or 36th Divisions and he did not consider that it was a feasible operation to fly in troops until all-weather airfields had been built. Even so, a brigade was unlikely to be available for this specialised role.

The following day, 4 January 1944, Wingate repeated his requests for reinforcements at an army commanders' conference at Headquarters 14th Army only to have them rejected. Instead it was agreed that IV Corps would provide a battalion to cross the Chindwin to exploit any Special Force success and that 26th Division would provide a battalion to garrison a landing ground once one had been captured. These decisions were confirmed in 14th Army's Operation Instruction Number 51 on 9 January.

Stung by the refusal to back his forces and alarmed about the consequences of deploying them in an unsupported advance into enemy territory, Wingate wrote a lengthy memorandum to Giffard on 5 and 9 January and requested that it be sent to Mountbatten.

In view of the fact that the plan submitted by me at Quebec has now been abandoned, and that the Force under my command is at the moment committed to an operation which is not one for which it was designed, I desire to place on permanent record, both for my own protection and for the benefit of the Army, the reasons why the operation proposed by me has become impossible.

Entitled 'Considerations affecting the employment of LRP Forces, Spring 1944', the nine-page memorandum recorded Wingate's 'firm conviction, firstly, that the Quadrant plan was the only possible plan of operations for Northern Burma in the Spring of 1944: secondly, that it was perfectly feasible had the local authorities concerned been willing: thirdly and lastly, that it has now become impossible by the inaction of

those same authorities.' Having rehearsed the difficulties he had faced –
from getting adequate air support from the RAF to the delays in
providing reinforcements and equipment – Wingate offered three alternatives:

(a) Go ahead with the present plan with the indispensable air and ground
support.
(b) Substitute another plan for immediate adoption.
(c) Dissolve the Force and use the Brigades as ordinary infantry (because this
Force must not be kept idling about or it will lose its high morale).

He also recommended handing over the Merrill's Marauders force to
Stilwell – a proposal which was soon accepted – and offered his own
resignation if Special Force were to be disbanded. It was almost certainly
a formal protest but it did little to sweeten his relationship with Slim
who now commanded the British 14th Army and who would have the
final word in agreeing the operational planning for Special Force. Indeed,
the complexity of the chain of command in India was hardly helpful to
the smooth running of the campaign in Burma. Although Mountbatten
was the supreme commander, the land forces came under Giffard's
command and the air forces under Air Chief Marshal Sir Richard Peirse,
RAF. Stilwell was Mountbatten's deputy but he refused to take orders
from Giffard whom he did not respect. At the same time he insisted on
retaining control of the 10th US Air Force. However, because he admired
Slim he agreed to come under his operational command, as did Wingate.
To complicate matters, though, Wingate enjoyed direct access to
Mountbatten who felt under a personal obligation to make sure that his
forces were given the backing promised by Churchill. Given the strong
personalities of the main protagonists – Mountbatten, Slim, Stilwell and
Wingate – the intricacies of the system inevitably produced a good deal
of confusion which was to affect the outcome of the forthcoming
operations.

Realising that he would have to concentrate his efforts on both Slim
and Mountbatten if reinforcements were to be made available from
Scoones's IV Corps, Wingate met the supreme commander on 11
January in Delhi and repeated his proposal that 'a direct order must be
given to 14th Army that not less than one brigade of 4th Corps, lightly
equipped will advance across the Chindwin to exploit successes gained
by Special Force.' Two days later he repeated the request in writing
and on 16 January he encapsulated the requirement in his new plan,
'Appreciation of Situation in Northern Burma'. This called for a revision

in the deployment of his brigades in northern Burma: 111th Brigade to fly into an area south of Pinlebu, 77th Brigade to be flown into the Kaukkwe River valley and 16th Brigade to march into northern Burma from Ledo and to attack Indaw. The plan would depend both on a IV Corps attack of brigade strength across the Chindwin and the provision of four additional garrison battalions. These would be used to hold the strongholds which the Chindits would establish at the landing grounds.

In his training notes, Wingate outlined his ideas for the stronghold in language that managed to combine the vocabulary of modern warfare with the sentiments of the Old Testament: 'Turn you to the stronghold, ye prisoners of hope' (Zechariah 9: 12).

The Stronghold is a machan overlooking a kid tied up to entice the Japanese tiger.
The Stronghold is an asylum for Long Range Penetration Group wounded.
The Stronghold is a magazine of stores.
The Stronghold is a defended air-strip.
The Stronghold is an administration centre for loyal inhabitants.
The Stronghold is an orbit round which columns of the Brigade circulate. It is suitably placed with reference to the main objective of the Brigade.
The Stronghold is a base for light planes operating with columns on the main objective.

Wingate envisaged the creation of four strongholds, each of which would be garrisoned by an infantry battalion and a troop of field artillery equipped with light anti-aircraft guns. In addition to its defensive role it would also be a focus for Japanese attack: no easy matter as the strongholds would be sited in positions inaccessible to wheeled transport and the enemy would be denied the use of their heavy weapons. Acting on IV Corps's experience in defending the Imphal region Wingate also planned for the deployment of 'floater' columns and companies which operate in the vicinity of each stronghold and which would attack the enemy in force and cut off their lines of communication. As Wingate described their employment in his training memorandum: 'If we look upon the Stronghold perimeter as the kid tied up to attract the enemy tiger, then we find the ambuscaded hunter in the shape of the floater columns on the grand scale and the floater company on the minor scale. The floater columns are a strategical, the floater company a tactical, ambuscade.'

One other element determined Wingate's ideas for the strongholds. By the end of 1943 British military intelligence had established that

Mutaguchi was planning an attack on Imphal in order to seize Assam to break communications between Slim and Stilwell's forces as a prelude to invading India. This would be preceded by a counter-offensive in the Arakan, known as Ha-Go, or Operation Z. Paradoxically, the Japanese general had first seen the possibilities of making an attack in northern Burma after he had been presented with evidence of the Chindits' activities in the difficult jungle terrain between the Chindwin and Kohima. If the despised British army could operate in those conditions, then surely it would be a simple matter for the Japanese soldiers who had enjoyed such an easy victory in Malaya? In view of this probable attack, known to the Japanese as U-Go (Operation C), Wingate believed that his force would be able to operate behind the Japanese advance and cut their lines of communication. Everything would depend on the strongholds which would allow the force to operate for up to ninety days in comparative security.

This brilliant concept was to lie at the heart of Wingate's revised plans and the thinking behind them shows him at his inventive best. To be successful, though, the stronghold needed garrison troops and as the argument about the provision thundered on during the latter part of January it is easy to understand why Wingate became so frantic in his search for extra troops. To his way of thinking, the obstructions put in his way seemed to be indicative of an uncaring attitude, shared by Slim and Giffard, that Special Force was about to be deployed behind Japanese lines with virtually no support. This question of the additional garrison troops was to be Wingate's final battle with authority and, inevitably perhaps, the episode was not without controversy.

It began amicably enough on 19 January when Wingate met Slim at Ranchi. The 14th Army commander was late in arriving and he remembered Wingate becoming 'uncomfortably angry' when one of his staff officers teased him about his new general's red hat. Then it was down to business. Having accepted the stronghold concept and having agreed to provide the necessary artillery, they discussed the provision of aircraft for the fly-in – Wingate favoured finding the additional aircraft from those allotted to the 50th Indian Parachute Brigade while Slim thought that they could be removed temporarily from the Hump route. The two generals then considered the provision of garrison troops. Slim readily conceded that a battalion could be provided to garrison 77th Brigade's stronghold, once Calvert's men had secured a landing strip. On the matter of three further battalions he agreed that these could be provided by 26th Division but they would only be deployed under his direction to exploit Chindit gains. His orders are contained in a signal sent to 14th Army headquarters the same day.

Have agreed that when Calvert has seized Dakota landing strip I will have ready one Bn to fly in and hold strong centre for Special Bde. In addition require three further battalions trained and ready to take advantage of possible opportunities developing later. 26 Div will provide and intensify air landing training forthwith. I will give decision if and when bns are to be flown in.[1]

The order was repeated to Giffard at 11th Army Group headquarters on 21 January and the signal included the words: 'Wingate realises this.' The trouble was that he had not grasped the implications of the orders. Slim had made it clear that the battalions were only to be used under his direction for exploitation and that their deployment would depend on prevailing circumstances. To Wingate, ever eager to get his own way, the offer was cut and dried and on 20 January he despatched Fairweather to Mountbatten in Delhi with a letter outlining the new position. In the second paragraph he claimed that Slim had 'agreed at once' to the provision of four additional battalions and that the three additional formations would be found from 26th Division. Having secured that agreement Wingate said that he was proceeding to Comilla to discuss their selection with the divisional commander, Major-General C. E. N. Lomax. In due course he hoped that they would be transferred from Chittagong to Silchar so that they could commence training with Special Force.

Wingate then set off on a busy round of visits by air to his three brigades to bring them up to date on developments and was back in Comilla on 24 January for a further meeting with Slim on 26 and 27 January. At this point it became clear that Slim had only promised one battalion to support 77th Brigade's fly-in – it was named as the 3rd/9th Gurkha Rifles – and that the three additional battalions would not be made available as garrison troops. To Wingate this was a betrayal of an earlier promise and, once more, it seemed to smack of a conspiracy against his plans. On the one hand Slim was now unwilling to use battalions from 26th Division as this was his only reserve, while Wingate countered that to deploy Special Force 'with no support whatever from the main British forces is to court disaster'. Faced by an impasse it was agreed that the garrison troops should be found from the 3rd West African Brigade which was currently being trained for LRP operations as part of Special Force. Although Wingate had no option but to accept the situation he made sure that Mountbatten was informed and on 26

January repeated his earlier suggestion that the Army Command should return the Special Force brigades to normal duties and that he should be relieved of his post.

And so I have to tell you very seriously that I believe you should cancel the operation; not because it is inadvisable; on the contrary if it were backed by the military command it would have a chance of great success; not because the Air think it impossible; they're playing; but simply and solely because the commanding British Generals are not at heart for it. That is to say they are opposed to making the minimum contribution necessary to its success. Not only has this already prejudiced the success of the operation but who can tell its deadly effect in the future when at the height of some crisis I shall wish to be able to count on loyal support.

It is a change of heart that is required and I cannot change their hearts.

It was a strong appeal, forceful enough for Mountbatten's Chief of Staff, General Sir Henry Pownall, to note in his diary on 28 January that Wingate might press its acceptance with the Prime Minister, in which case Churchill might be tempted to replace Slim with Wingate: 'which would be a most dangerous affair. Wingate may (or may not) be all right as a specialist but he simply hasn't the knowledge or the balance to be in high command.' The matter was never put to the test, largely because Giffard had promised to supply the required artillery pieces, four twenty-five-pounders and six light anti-aircraft guns per stronghold, and Wingate himself had come reluctantly to the conclusion that the success of the operation need not be prejudiced by the use of the West African Brigade provided that additional British infantry battalions were trained in the LRP role.

Not for the first time in Wingate's career it is possible to understand both sides' point of view. Wingate had worked long and hard for the LRP concept to be accepted and believed that he was working under the remit agreed in Quebec. He also believed that it was disgraceful not to adopt an aggressive policy in northern Burma and that the endless prevarications were having a bad effect on his men's morale; he had already been faced by a threat of resignation from Fergusson who feared that the absence of a forceful follow-up and the possibility of a second withdrawal would be disastrous. Unfortunately, too, in the heat of the moment, Wingate had misinterpreted Slim's orders about the deployment of garrison troops.

Slim, on the other hand, was facing an imminent Japanese attack from Burma and had to marshal his available forces to meet it. His plan envisaged pulling his forward divisions to the Imphal plain to block off their retreat and then unleashing his reserves of infantry and armour. For that reason he needed 26th Division and was not prepared to break up one of its brigades to garrison Wingate's strongholds. As the overall army commander he could not confide his every move with every subordinate general but at the fateful meeting at Comilla he undoubtedly enraged Wingate by failing to give precise reasons for his decision. At the time Slim also knew that Mountbatten was laying plans for a fresh amphibious assault, codenamed Axiom, first against northern Sumatra and then against Malaya, once the war against Germany had been concluded. If that had been accepted, aggressive land operations in Burma would have been suspended and as Slim's biographer, Ronald Lewin, points out, 'Slim's subsequent reputation would then have lacked the full, rounded quality that derives from absolute victory.'

Axiom was rejected in February even though Mountbatten had sent a high-level mission to Washington to attempt to persuade the Americans, but it was obvious to Slim that his future and the future of 14th Army were in the balance. Wingate could not have known this – Mountbatten did not tell him about Axiom until 8 February – but had he done so, he might have had greater sympathy for Slim's position. As it was, the question of the additional battalions was complicated further after the war when Slim claimed in his autobiography that he had threatened Wingate with court-martial unless he acceded to the plans. Although the 14th Army War Diary gives no hint of this disagreement, by the time that Slim published *Defeat into Victory* in 1956 he had radically revised his opinion about Wingate and the Chindits.

Having come to a conclusion about the back-up troops – however unsatisfactory it might have been for his own plans – Wingate wrote to Mountbatten on 27 January saying that he was prepared to accept the situation and that his brigades were 'in great heart', ready for the fray. 'I have seen Stilwell at Shinbwiyaung and established excellent relations. He is all for the operation. The Air are all for it. I have myself made flights over the relevant areas and satisfied myself that the plan is possible.'

A week later, 14th Army headquarters confirmed the deployment of Special Force in northern Burma and gave its orders in Operation Instruction Number 4:

To help the advance of Stilwell's force.
To create a favourable situation for the Chinese to advance from the Yunnan across the Salween River.

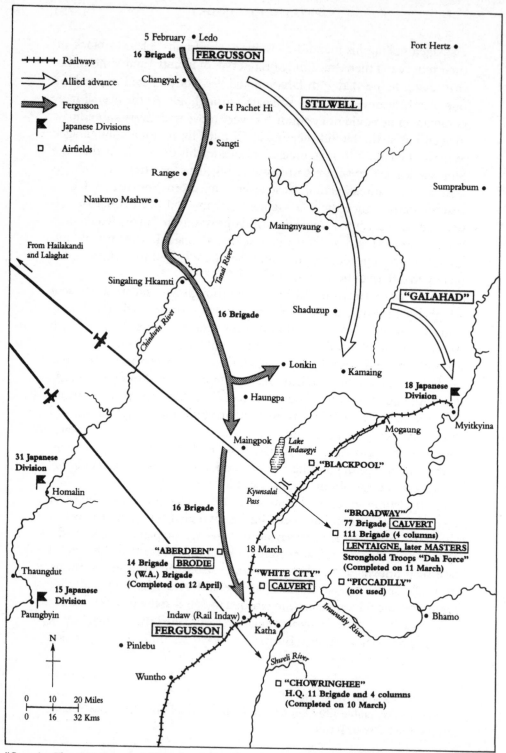

"Operation Thursday": Fergusson's March from Ledo; Fly-in of 3, 14 and 77 Brigades; Stilwell's Advance on Myitkyina

To inflict maximum confusion, damage and loss on the enemy forces in North
  Burma.[2]

The three brigades would all move in separately. 77th Brigade (Calvert)
would be flown in to two landing zones in the Kaukkwe River valley to
be known as Broadway and Piccadilly: their task would be to attack
Japanese road and rail links in the area. 111th Brigade (Lentaigne) would
fly in to Piccadilly to attack Japanese lines of communication south of
Indaw. A Gurkha Rifles element of the brigade would fly in to another
landing strip known as Chowringhee south of the River Schweli: commanded by Brigadier J. R. Morris and known as Morrisforce, its task
was to cut the Bhamo–Myitkyina link. Acting in support was Herring's
Dah Force which was supposed to act in concert with operatives from
SOE's Force 136. Meanwhile 16th Brigade (Fergusson) would march
into Burma from Ledo to establish a stronghold known as Aberdeen on
the River Meza, before capturing the Japanese airfields at Indaw. From
the very outset it was clear that these operations were designed to support
Stilwell's advance although the American general was hardly enthusiastic.
When Slim visited him on 3 March he merely said, 'That'll be fine if
Wingate does it and stays there; if he goes in for real fighting and not
shadow boxing like last time.'

The following day, 5 February, Operation Thursday began when the
men of 16th Brigade began pulling out of Ledo to begin the long haul
over the Patkai Hills towards the Chindwin, an epic journey which was
brilliantly described in Fergusson's book *The Wild Green Earth*. Its
garrison battalion was to be the 12th Nigerian which would be flown in
once the airstrip at Aberdeen had been secured. Wingate shared the first
day's march with the brigade and visited it by air once they had crossed
the Chindwin to lend encouragement to the weary men and to present
Fergusson with his operational orders for the stronghold. During the visit
he expressed surprise that Fergusson, a Presbyterian, did not recognise the
source of the strongholds quotation and mischievously told him that it
came from Isaiah.

In his own accounts of the campaign Calvert, too, has described the
fierce sense of joy and impishness which Wingate brought to the planning
and execution of Operation Thursday. With his own men he felt at ease
and the feeling was reciprocated. Major A. E. L. E. Noble of the 2nd
Burma Rifles noted the mixture of determination, energy and humour
which he brought to the task. No visit to a unit failed to inspire them
and although some men smiled behind his back at his beard and his long

bamboo staff, both of which added to the image of the patriarch, Noble recognised that 'he was the right man – an utterly honest man in the right place at the right time, and he loved and admired him immensely, and would willingly face death for him.' While this is the voice of a loyal subordinate, it speaks volumes for Wingate's ability to inspire that his Chindits were willing to go on supporting his memory long after his death.

Inevitably, perhaps, there continued to be a distaff side to his personality. After flying back from Ledo to Comilla he was enraged to discover that his transport was not waiting for him. As the Dakota taxied towards the dispersal pen he assaulted Piggott, his G1 (Operations), and kicked him from the open door of the moving aircraft. Later he apologised and claimed that he had acted impulsively – 'I always used to kick my younger brother off moving buses and quite suddenly the old impulse came over me' – but it was a foolish action which could have severely injured Piggott and once again Tulloch was forced to intervene to prevent further trouble.

There were problems, too, with SOE. Wingate had come a long way since he first became involved with the organisation in Ethiopia and he was now distrustful of its war aims in Burma. Mackenzie, head of Force 136, was not told about Operation Thursday until the last minute even though Herring's Dah Force was supposed to work with SOE's operative already with the Kachins, Major L. V. Lovett-Campbell. A last-minute attempt at co-operation was made at the end of February when Force 136's chief of staff Colonel Robert Guinness and head of the Burma Section Ritchie Gardner met Wingate at Sylhet. Because Wingate was disinclined to reveal his plans it was not a fruitful occasion and only resulted in the finalisation of arrangements for Lovett-Campbell to provide a reception committee for Herring who was supposed to be flown in by glider to a landing strip known as Templecombe. When this plan failed – Lovett-Campbell's message did not get through and Herring was forced to be flown in to Broadway and march seventy miles to his destination – Wingate wrote to Guinness on 14 March angrily complaining that it was 'only what I had in the past experienced from your organisation'. The inability of Special Force and Force 136 to co-operate led to some duplication of effort and to the failure to use SOE personnel as 'pathfinders' in advance of the main fly-in.

Mountbatten, too, was frequently driven to despair by Wingate's intransigence. Indeed, on 19 February, following an exchange of angry letters between the two men, Pownall was moved to wonder how long the supremo could afford to deal with Wingate: 'I shouldn't be at all surprised if within the next three months it is proved that Wingate is bogus; at any rate he is a thoroughly nasty piece of work.' However, in the correspondence between the two men Mountbatten managed to keep his temper, in spite of considerable provocation from Wingate, and his responses were little more than wearied reprimands. Even the loyal Tulloch was forced to admit to his wife that his relations with Wingate were '90% delightful and 10% bloody awful!'

One of the reasons was Wingate's restlessness during the final period of training before the first fly-in on 5 March. In his mind's eye he envisaged the extension of LRP operations in Burma to include all British and Indian brigades – an idea he had first bruited in a memorandum on 27 January – and the extension of the stronghold concept across Burma to allow a continental advance to Hanoi in Indo-China. The idea was first put forward at Imphal on 8 February to Scoones and Mountbatten, who was alarmed enough by Wingate's thinking to write to him the following day warning him that 'the Chief of Staff's World Strategy runs counter to your own future hopes.' Not only did Mountbatten not envisage a major land campaign in Burma but he was still holding on to the Culverin amphibious operations which formed part of Axiom. Although Wingate was not privy to the new plans, he knew about Culverin from the Quebec conference and it is easy to understand why he decided to promote the extension of LRP operations. Mountbatten, though, was not prepared to argue and demanded an 'assurance that you are fully prepared to carry on with LRPG operations on the basis of your present directive, which was prepared without any thought or suggestion of continental operations on the scale you now propose'.

Wingate responded by return in a lengthy eight-page letter which is the best summary of his fears for the safety of his force if it were not reinforced once its objectives had been achieved. Having reminded Mountbatten about the decisions taken in Quebec, Wingate insisted that the seizure of land and airstrips in northern Burma and China would be an important adjunct to amphibious operations by providing airfields for long-range bombers. This was not the same as switching all resources to a major land offensive but a means of providing 'another string to our bow and to keep the enemy in play during the long and lengthening period of sea inactivity in this theatre'. However, to accomplish this Wingate argued that he would need reinforcements and an adequate number of support aircraft.

Since writing this letter I have paid a visit to General Slim, and he assures me that he does not intend to impose any restrictions upon the exploitation by 23rd and 14th Bdes [Special Force's reserve], or by the entry of garrisons, should a favourable opportunity arise, but of course he cannot speak for Delhi.

In spite of this microscopic measure of support, I was, and am, prepared to take on the operation provided I am guaranteed of the following: the use of 14th and 23rd Bdes to exploit as and when needed; a guarantee of the necessary SD aircraft and supporting aircraft.

Although Wingate could not resist a dig at what he took to be the pusillanimity of the Delhi planners, the letter is very much a call to arms, that victory could be ensured provided that everyone kept their nerve and granted full support. With the benefit of hindsight it also has astute words to say about the need for reinforcement and the proper supply of aircraft, both of which were to have important effects on the outcome of the operation. On the question of world strategy it is also clear that Wingate was not prescribing 'high-faluting ideas for extending LRP operations into Siam' (Giffard's description to the official historians after the war) but merely postulating how long-range penetration airborne forces could be deployed with heavily armed follow-up brigades to seize and then hold territory.

Nothing came of the bickering over strategy largely because the situation in Burma was rapidly changing. On 6 February the Japanese launched their offensive in the Arakan against 7th Indian Division and despite early successes were held by Christison's forces at Sinzwetya. By 26 February they had called off the offensive, having been held for the first time by British and Indian troops who had stayed put and fought off the attack. Just over a week later, on the night of 7–8 March the Japanese launched their main U-Go offensive in the Tiddim area. By that time Wingate's Chindits were already operating behind their lines to the north.

They had flown in on the night of Sunday 5 March from an airfield at Lalaghat near the Chindits' training base at Silchar. The date had been chosen because it provided the air-landing force with the full moon which was required in such a hazardous venture, the first of its kind in the Second World War. Even so, it had been a close-run thing. Because Wingate did not want to invite the possibility of betraying the landing sites by sending over low-flying reconnaissance aircraft in the prelude to the operation, the sites had not been reconnoitred in the week before the operation, a failing which worried the practical Americans for whom photo-reconnaissance was routine before any mission. Because they did not come directly under Wingate's command – 1st Air Commando answered to 10th US Air Force – Colonel John Alison had ordered a B-25 Mitchell to photograph the landing sites earlier in the day following a routine bombing operation. When the film was processed it revealed the presence of a large number of felled trees on the Piccadilly landing strip.

The information came at the worst possible time, less than an hour before the first of the eighty Waco gliders and their Dakota tugs were due to depart at 5.00 p.m. Not only was there a fair degree of tension at Lalaghat as Calvert's 77th Brigade completed their preparations to embark but, as Mead noted, there was 'an impressive collection of senior officers' assembled to watch them depart. Amongst them were Slim, Stratemeyer, Air Marshal Sir John Baldwin of 3rd Tactical Air Force and Brigadier General W. D. Old, the American commander of Troop Carrier Command. Not unnaturally, the revelation of the photographs came as a shock to Wingate whose first reaction was to fly into a fury because Cochran had disobeyed his orders.

Once he had composed himself and apologised the full implications began to sink in. If the felled logs had been deliberately planted there was a good chance that the operation had been betrayed to the Japanese. If so, then their troops might be present in strength when 77th Brigade landed or they might be present in strength at Broadway and Chowringhee and the result would be a massacre. Even if the strip had been blocked by the Japanese as a routine measure to prevent air landings – a publicity photograph of the same strip had appeared in *Life* magazine following Longcloth – there was still a good chance that the operation had been compromised. Given that uncertainty it is little wonder that Wingate was thrown off balance and appeared agitated to those watching him. After all he was not flying in with Calvert's men and was unhappy about giving an order which might send men to certain death.

Historians such as Louis Allen and Bidwell have both pointed out that the episode could have been avoided if specialist reconnaissance aircraft of the Army Photographic Intelligence Unit had been used to survey the landing strips prior to the operation. This specialist unit used Mosquito PR XVI and Spitfire PR XI photo-reconnaissance aircraft which were capable of flying at up to 20,000 feet, well above the range of Japanese aircraft operating in the Burma theatre. The failure to use these aircraft was a serious planning error which was probably caused by Special Forces' reliance on the Air Commando's low-flying Mitchells for photo-reconnaissance. As for the logs, the most likely explanation is that they had been felled for commercial purposes and laid out to dry by the local Burmese foresters.

With time beginning to run out such considerations could not be taken into account. Instead, Wingate and his planning staff, including Baldwin and Cochran, had to weigh the odds with Calvert. According to Tulloch, Wingate was 'anxious to go on; his only concern was about sending others into a job he was not going [sic] himself.' He was not prepared to order 77th Brigade to go unless Calvert and Lieutenant-Colonel Walter Scott of the 1st King's agreed. True to form Calvert was prepared to be bullish and agreed to be flown into Broadway only; the option of using Chowringhee was rejected because Calvert did not want to split his brigade on both sides of the Irrawaddy. There was another consideration: as had happened with Longcloth, any postponement would have dented morale and, given the Japanese attack on Imphal, ended Special Force's long-range penetration role.

Once Wingate had agreed to the change of tactics he reported to Slim who, as 14th Army commander, had to make the final decision. According to Tulloch's evidence he had remained silent throughout the discussions and having weighed the evidence gave the order to go. Three considerations persuaded him: Calvert's determination, Baldwin's promise of increased air support and his own soldier's instinct that, if cancelled, it would be difficult to restore the men's fighting spirit for such a hazardous enterprise. On any reading Slim gave the final order on the strength of the evidence available to him but unfortunately his own account of the episode in *Defeat into Victory* suggests that Wingate panicked and that he, Slim, had to take him aside to calm him down. Allied to the implication that Slim alone was responsible for giving the order and that Wingate was supplementary to it, the account has caused a good deal of offence amongst former Chindits.

As with any episode on which great events hang, there is a bit of truth in each of the main protagonist's accounts. Wingate was right to claim later that he was instrumental in recommending that the attack go in, once he had received Calvert's and Baldwin's reassurances. (Slim later told the official historians that 'If Calvert had said "no" I am sure Wingate would have attempted to make me cancel my order.') Slim was equally correct to say that the final decision was his and there is no reason to disbelieve his contention that Wingate was in a 'very emotional state'.[3] It would have been surprising had he not been and, true to form in a desperate situation, he was suffering from the old failing of being unable to control his emotions.

Worse was to come. At 6.12 p.m. the Dakota tugs started taking off, each one dragging behind them two heavily laden Waco gliders; this was a last-minute change of plan to allow the men and their equipment to be deployed as quickly as possible. The first to go were the aircraft containing the combat engineers and the forward air controllers whose radio sets and flares would guide the rest of the air armada to the jungle landing strip. That part of the operation went smoothly but as the night wore on things started to go wrong. On the ground at Broadway several gliders crash-landed and jammed the heavily rutted landing strip. Because the fly-in had a tight timetable others landing behind them also crash-landed. Meanwhile in the air, eleven gliders failed to reach Broadway and were posted missing, eight crashed in allied territory and another eight were called back. Only thirty-five out of the original sixty-two landed reasonably safely. Watching the mayhem on the ground in the darkness at Broadway, Calvert was suitably alarmed at 2.30 a.m. to send the signal 'Soya Link'. Although this was the codeword for failure (a soya link was a particularly disgusting artificial sausage), it was the only means at Calvert's disposal to halt the fly-in.

Needless to say the receipt of the message caused dismay at Lalaghat where Slim, Wingate and Tulloch were huddled in the control tent at the end of the airstrip. According to Slim, Wingate 'gave me one long bitter look and walked away'; but Tulloch's account is more credible. 'Well, Derek, it looks as though we've failed,' he said, to which Tulloch replied that there had been a muddle over codewords and that matters would improve overnight. 'Derek, you are an optimist,' said Wingate. 'Good night.' Four hours later the joyful signal 'Pork Sausage' was heard and Tulloch's indomitable optimism had been proved correct, although he did not pass it on immediately to Wingate who was in a deep sleep.

The coming of daylight had helped to settle nerves and the American combat engineers were soon at work clearing the strip with their airportable bulldozers. Even better, the Japanese had not been alerted to the landing and the way was clear to complete the fly-in. By the night of 7–8 March the strip was ready for business and fifty-five Dakotas had landed and returned safely, followed by a further thirty-eight the next day. By 9 March Baldwin was able to report that 'up to daylight today a cumulative total of approximately three thousand men have been landed at Broadway.' At the same time 111th Brigade's fly-in had begun at Chowringhee and 1 Air Commando's P-51s and B-25s had successfully attacked Japanese bases at Schwebo, Onbaik and Anisikan. On 11 March Wingate felt confident enough to report that 'operations of troop carrier command have been a marvel of efficient smooth working, everyone contributing his utmost to the remarkable success achieved.' Even the normally unruffled Baldwin was moved to use colourful language to report the operation's complete success: 'Nobody has seen a transport operation until he has stayed at Broadway in the full light of the Burma full moon and watched Dakotas coming in and taking off in opposite directions on a single strip all night long at the rate of one landing or one taking off every three minutes.'[4]

And a success it undoubtedly was: over 9,000 men, around 1,500 mules and all their equipment and supplies had been landed deep in enemy-held territory or, as Wingate expressed it in his Order of the Day dated 11 March, 'all our columns are inserted in the enemy's guts ... Let us thank God for the great success He has vouchsafed us, and press forward with our sword in the enemy's ribs to expel him from our territory.' The next day he sent a less colourful signal directly to Churchill, through Mountbatten, reporting that both 77th and 111th Brigades were achieving their first objectives, the former by marching towards Mawlu, the latter by crossing the Irrawaddy, and the situation was most promising 'if exploited'.

And that was the rub. Wingate wanted to build on his success by committing his reserve brigades to reinforce the existing strongholds. To Giffard and Slim – and later to the official historians – this smacked of inconsistency as Wingate had always argued that his columns should operate in close co-operation with the main forces, but there were good reasons for his constant requests for reinforcements. First, he had never made any secret of the need to plant garrison troops in the strongholds, thereby freeing his columns to attack the Japanese lines of communication in the Indaw pocket. Second, as is expected of any good commander, he wanted to exploit his force's early success and to continue the operations to support Stilwell and to cut the Japanese lines of communication. Although he still believed that the need had been accepted, the imminence of the Japanese Imphal battle meant that Slim had to reconsider the deployment of his forces and their reserves. On 8 March Slim had arrived at Lalaghat and warned Tulloch that he might have to use 14th and 23rd Brigades as reserves for IV Corps at Imphal. Wingate was so infuriated by the decision that he flew to see Slim at Comilla and offered his resignation because it seemed to countermand the agreement he had reached with Mountbatten on 9 and 10 February. After discussion Slim agreed to release 14th Brigade 'should the situation on the main front develop satisfactorily'.

On that understanding Wingate accepted Slim's decision but it was not to be his last brush with authority. Remembering the successful press coverage given to the first Chindit expedition Mountbatten's headquarters had released the first information about Operation Thursday on 16 March. Unfortunately it only spoke in general terms of a successful airborne operation mounted by the 14th Army and there was no mention of Wingate, the Chindits or the US Air Commando. When it was published in *SEAC*, the daily information newspaper edited by Frank Owen, Wingate exploded. The same day he sent off a furious telegram to Air Chief Marshal Philip Joubert, Mountbatten's head of publicity, cancelling the delivery of *SEAC* to Special Force and telling him in no uncertain terms that he would not be 'answerable for the consequences on the morale of the troops who not only carried out this operation but who are well aware of its background and meaning'.

To Wingate this was not just an affront to his force but a further reminder that the high command was intent on doing everything possible to hinder Operation Thursday and to prevent it succeeding. Unfortunately, Wingate's signal to Joubert was open in that it went through normal channels and was read by cipher and signal staff. Because it was a public attack on Mountbatten's headquarters, the supreme commander felt that he had to respond in kind on 19 March. Having explained that he proposed to release the news in stages and that everyone would be given their full due, he reminded Wingate of his responsibilities.

In future I suggest that when you consider a direct report to me is necessary, that this should be written entirely objectively without any note of bitterness being allowed to creep in. If you wish to let off steam I don't mind your doing so in a covering letter which no-one else sees, but if you mix vituperation and factual accounts it merely means that the factual accounts cannot be circulated.

Your astounding telegram to Joubert has made me realise how you have achieved such amazing success in getting yourself disliked by people who are only too ready to help you.[5]

Mountbatten ended the letter by saying that the decision not to give due prominence to 'Wingate's Special Force' had been taken to confuse the Japanese but that the news would be released gradually as the campaign proceeded. He also told him that Slim and Baldwin were enthusiastic about the operation to date and, more importantly for the immediate future, that 'Slim assured me that he would not use 14th or 23rd brigades without consulting you and certainly not in the defensive role. It may be necessary for them to do a short range penetration job murdering the rear of the Japs but he is anxious to avoid using them even for that.' The employment of these two brigades was to play an important part in Wingate's strategic thinking in the days following the deployment of his Chindit brigades in northern Burma.

By then Wingate was juggling two plans within his head: plan A which was the official one put forward to conceal a plan B in which he would use his reserve forces to attack the rear of the Japanese 15th Army as it attacked IV Corps. From his correspondence with Mountbatten it is also clear that he envisaged using his LRP groups to play a more ambitious role in the operations to reconquer northern Burma: instead of being supplementary to the operations undertaken by the regular forces, they would be the main players. On 13 March he introduced the possibility of expanding his forces' operations south of Katha in tandem with an advance by IV Corps in a paper entitled 'Forecast of Possible Development of Thursday'. However, this was only a theoretical proposition which would depend on the establishment of three strongholds; at that stage only one, at Broadway, was in use by Calvert's 77th Brigade. It would also depend on the immediate deployment of 14th Brigade at Pakkoku followed by 23rd Brigade at Meiktila early in April.

Needless to say, operations may develop in a very different and unexpected manner, and it is more than probable that a hard fight must first be fought before the Japanese will accept this startling measure of defeat. But in any case, the establishment of the three Strongholds and the introduction of 14th Brigade may be regarded as a practical certainty, unless we in turn are prepared to accept defeat.

Although Mead acknowledges that the report would have been 'of academic interest to Scoones, now deeply involved in the Japanese offensive and his Corps' planned withdrawal to the Imphal Plain', it does confirm Wingate's thinking in mid-March. Plans for the expansion of his forces were still unformed: in the immediate future he wanted to use the Chindits in much the same way that Stonewall Jackson had handled his small force of 16,000 men in the Shenandoah Valley, making rapid and unpredictable moves, turning up to attack where least expected and constantly keeping the enemy guessing. Only this time the scene of operations would be the area to the north of Indaw through which ran the railway line to Myitkyina. To the Chindits, this was known as Railway Valley.

The situation which Wingate wanted to exploit was complicated by the need to keep in close touch with his brigades which were enjoying different levels of success. Having secured Broadway Calvert's men had blown up the railway north and south of Henu and had established a new defensive position and landing strip codenamed White City. From there he had sent out offensive patrols to probe Japanese positions south of Mawlu and had engaged the Japanese in some vicious close-quarter fighting at a position called Pagoda Hill. By then the Japanese had begun to realise the extent of the threat posed by the Chindits. Mutaguchi's first reaction had been to use local garrison units but on 10 March his three divisions supplied one battalion each for the defence of Indaw and the railway line.

At that time Lentaigne's 111th Brigade was still reassembling after being flown in at Broadway and Chowringhee, which had to be abandoned because it was too difficult to defend. Delays in the fly-in and the need to cross the Irrawaddy had put him behind schedule and it was not until 26 March that the brigade had reached Wuntho. Fergusson's 16th Brigade was also behind schedule, having endured a long and gruelling march over some of the most inhospitable terrain in northern Burma. In addition, two columns, 51 and 69, had attacked the Japanese at Lonkin following a request from Stilwell and they were ten days behind the main body. Although the brigade was clearly exhausted Wingate gave it fresh orders on 12 March: he was to make for Indaw and attack it directly after establishing a stronghold, codenamed Aberdeen, in the Meza Valley.

By 20 March most of Fergusson's brigade was in the Kalat Valley where their stronghold would be built and Wingate flew in during the afternoon to discuss the next stage of the operation. What happened next has been the subject of a good deal of disagreement amongst former Chindits. Wingate's orders were clear enough: 16th Brigade was to attack Indaw immediately and take possession of its east airfield before the Japanese were able to reinforce the area. This would allow the reserve 14th Brigade to be flown in to support the Chindits' operations. Although it was a risk – Fergusson's request for a breathing space to allow his men to recover from the forced march was denied – Wingate clearly believed that the Japanese were unprepared and that the element of surprise would give Fergusson's brigade a decided edge. In any war commanders have to make unpopular decisions by asking tired men to engage the enemy at critical junctures in a battle and Indaw was no exception. The capture of the airfields made strategic sense in the long term and in the short term the engagement would take pressure off Calvert's brigade at White City.

All this makes sense. The disagreement lies in the role given to 14th

Brigade under the command of Brigadier Tom Brodie. During his discussion with Wingate Fergusson was convinced that the brigade was being flown in to reinforce his attack on Indaw. This was the view he expressed in *The Wild Green Earth* and, later, in *The Trumpet in the Hall*. Although, as a historian, he accepted that personal recollection could never be conclusive evidence Fergusson remained absolutely certain that Wingate had ordered 14th Brigade to support his offensive at Indaw. 'The one thing I am convinced of is that I fought, however incompetently, the Indaw battle expecting 14th Brigade eventually to come to our support from the west and I will go to the stake in defence of my conviction that this is what Orde assured me of at Aberdeen.'[6]

Late in the afternoon Wingate returned to Broadway and the following day, 21 March, he flew to meet Tulloch at Lalaghat. There he received the disquieting information that Slim had told Tulloch that 'the situation in IV Corps area might make it necessary for him to take away Wingate's remaining brigades' (14th and 23rd). Slim had also asked Tulloch not to confide this information to Wingate as it might not be necessary to make the switch. Loyal subordinate that he was, Tulloch told Wingate who immediately flew on to Comilla to confront Slim to request the immediate fly-in of 14th Brigade and 3rd West African Brigade. Once inserted, 14th Brigade would be used to attack the lines of communication through Pyingyaing used by the Japanese 33rd Division and those at Pinlebu which supplied the 15th and 31st Divisions, all three of which were engaged in the attack on Imphal. This is made clear in Wingate's 'Appreciation of Situation' of 21 March.

What it boils down to, therefore, is that if any good is to be done at all (i.e. if the Japanese are first compelled to draw on their own communications and not ours), these communications must be cut at their two nodal points, i.e. Pinlebu and Indaw. The Indaw communications are already cut and the Pinlebu communications can be cut by forces of LRP. The Japanese would with the loss of communications be compelled to withdraw.

Slim agreed because 'the alteration had obvious advantages as it would use Special Force in direct tactical co-ordination with the main battle.' In other words, Wingate's force would be employed to cut the Japanese lines of communication as they advanced on to the Imphal Plain during IV Corps's planned withdrawal. He also agreed to back Wingate's requests for additional transport aircraft as the bulk of those available were busy flying the 5th Indian Division from the Arakan front into Imphal. On 22 March he sent a lengthy signal to Giffard requesting 'as strongly as I can' the provision of four additional RAF transport squadrons for his operations on the Imphal front. These would be used to supply his forces beyond reach of adequate road transport.

The present situation on the 14th Army front, while undoubtedly causing anxiety in the 4 Corps area, holds great possibilities of a major success. The Japanese have committed their main forces across the Chindwin. At the same time, they are being pressed from the north by the advancing Chinese, and 3rd Indian Division [i.e. Chindits] behind them is already striking at their main lines of communication. If, by the use of air transport reinforcement we can, within the next month, smash the enemy forces west of the Chindwin, we shall be presented with an opportunity whose exploitation might easily lead to a really major victory. But, to carry out such exploitation, it is essential to have an adequate pool of air transport by means of which not only can certain portions of our force be maintained without road lines of communication but by which reinforcing formations, eg additional LRP brigades or other formations can be flown in behind the enemy.

Unfortunately, Slim seems not to have told Wingate about his support for the additional aircraft. Fearing that his plans were jeopardised Wingate sent an impassioned telegram to Churchill through Mountbatten claiming that he was on the verge of destroying four Japanese divisions and securing territory which would remove the necessity for the Hump airbridge. 'Get Special Force four transport squadrons now and you have all Burma north of twenty-fourth parallel plus a decisive Japanese defeat. But get us these four squadrons and let the truth be told about what has happened and is happening. General Slim gives me his full backing.'
However, when Slim was confronted with this evidence he accused Wingate of taking his name in vain and in his later correspondence with the official historians spoke of a 'row' on 22 March. Mountbatten, too, was displeased by Wingate's action and although he forwarded the telegram he added the provision 'neither Peirse, Giffard nor I know why Wingate requires these extra squadrons' and that the request had been made 'in principle' only. However, the following day, 23 March, Slim sent another signal to Giffard saying that he supported Wingate's request 'much more strongly than merely in principle. I regard them as a necessity for a major success and an insurance against any reverse demanding air maintenance on a large scale.' Again, his views were not communicated to Wingate who returned to his headquarters on 22 March; instead of operating an advance headquarters at Imphal and a rear headquarters at Sylhet, the two were to be combined at the latter place. Before leaving Comilla Wingate took his farewell of Slim and added the dramatic

afterthought: 'You are the only senior officer in South East Asia who doesn't wish me dead!'

Once back at Sylhet Wingate issued new operational instructions on 23 March: 14th Brigade would begin its fly-in that night and, using Aberdeen as its base, it would then march south to establish a block on the Japanese lines of communication south-east of Pinlebu. None of this was passed to Fergusson – who began the attack on Indaw 'hoping hourly to get news of them' – with the result that the *Official History* accused Wingate of misleading a loyal lieutenant and this charge has been repeated by other historians of the war in Burma.

In fact Fergusson's attack on Indaw did fail but not just because it lacked the support of 14th Brigade. Due to faulty reconnaissance two of his columns pressed home their attack over waterless ground and 45 column encountered stiff opposition from Japanese defensive positions at Thetkegyin to the north of Indaw. Although the Leicesters took Indaw east airfield and held it with close air support from the 1st Air Commando the other columns failed to reinforce them. On 29 March Fergusson gave the order to withdraw to the stronghold at Aberdeen, admitting that he was 'damned angry' that his signals for support from 14th Brigade had been ignored at Chindit headquarters. Later, when he wrote *The Wild Green Earth*, he thought he understood the reason. 'The plan devised at Aberdeen for the use of 14th Brigade had never reached Force Headquarters. Thus none of my signals addressed to Wingate about 14th Brigade had been understood by his staff; and that Brigade's task had remained unconnected in any way with the Indaw battle.'

But later still, when he read Wingate's order to Brodie, Fergusson thought that he had been badly let down by his commander. Although he relented before his death in 1980 and admitted to Shelford Bidwell that he 'didn't like the suggestion that I have done Wingate posthumous dirt', his last published comment in *The Trumpet in the Hall* is uncompromising: 'At times the truth was simply not in him [Wingate].' Tragic though this split is between two such fine fighting soldiers it is possible to see how the misapprehension arose. From the very outset of the operation Fergusson understood Wingate's desire to take Indaw so that reinforcements could be flown in: this was the Tarzan concept. When Wingate ordered him to attack Indaw on 20 March and told him about 14th Brigade's fly-in the two moves seemed to be linked. If Wingate did promise to deploy the brigade in support of Fergusson's attack he probably did mean it at the time. 16th Brigade's attack began on 26 March by which time the first elements of 14th Brigade had begun to arrive at Aberdeen. There was still time to change Brodie's operational orders to support Fergusson should he be experiencing difficulties at Indaw. As it turned out, though, Fergusson was forced to withdraw well before 14th Brigade had completed its fly-in. It remains an academic point, therefore, whether or not its presence would have changed the course of the battle.

The main difficulty over Indaw arises in the lack of written evidence. There is no written record of Wingate's meeting with Fergusson at Aberdeen and as Calvert admitted his commander often forgot the difference between what he had planned and communicated to his staff and what he had merely divulged. Tulloch offered another reason: 'He would not tell Fergusson, as he thought he could capture Indaw without difficulty.'[7]

Communications also proved to be a problem. Not only was the Chindit headquarters in the process of being moved from Imphal to Sylhet but Fergusson was experiencing difficulties with his own wireless contacts both in the field and with his rear headquarters. As Bidwell points out, 'Fergusson was blind for lack of intelligence of the Japanese, and at crucial moments he was also deaf and dumb as well.' The other problem was that Wingate himself was constantly on the move and not always in a position to pass on all his orders.

Ever since the beginning of the operation he had kept up a busy round of flying visits to his column commanders in the field. Although it had been agreed in Quebec that he should be supplied with two Dakota transports for his own use, Wingate had never received an official aircraft and before and during Operation Thursday he had to rely on Cochran's Air Commando. In the frontline positions he was flown in an L1 or L5 but for the longer journeys back to the rear headquarters he was generally flown in a Dakota or a Mitchell bomber. On 13 January he had asked Mountbatten to intervene by allotting him a personal transport but this had come to nothing, even though he had promised that he would not 'abuse the trust placed in me or take unjustifiable risks ... I need hardly say that from now onwards success or failure of the campaign may depend on this.' On this point he added that 'the question of whether fighter escort is required should definitely be MY responsibility.'

Attack by Japanese aircraft was not the only danger. While coming in to land on 12 February Tulloch's aircraft had a narrow escape when it collided with a large kite-hawk which smashed into the cockpit. From that point onwards as Tulloch told his wife, 'we both knew that one of us was bound to take a bender and we had a mutual compact never to

travel together if possible so when he went I stayed and vice-versa.'
Tulloch also worried about Wingate being shot down over enemy
territory and falling into Japanese hands. This was not an idle fear: on
13 March the Japanese air force bombed the Broadway airstrip and the
attack was only beaten off by concentrated anti-aircraft fire and by the
presence of six RAF Spitfires. Four days later the Japanese struck again,
this time with greater success, and the Spitfires were either shot down
or destroyed on the ground. As for Wingate, although he recognised the
usefulness of aircraft to transport him round the battle front, he never
lost his innate dislike of flying.

Tulloch's worst fears were realised on 24 March. The day before
Wingate had flown from Hailakandi into the Katha area by L5 to visit
Aberdeen and to discuss the situation with Calvert. He then returned to
Broadway, again flying in an L5, where he contacted Cochran and asked
for transport to take him back to Imphal. A B-25, under the command
of 1st Lieutenant Brian Hodges, USAAF, already on its way from
Hailakandi, arrived in mid-afternoon. Shortly afterwards it left for Imphal
carrying a crew of five, Wingate and his ADC Captain George Borrow,
Royal Sussex Regiment and two war correspondents who had been
offered a lift, Stanley Willis of the *Daily Herald* and Stuart Emeny of the
News Chronicle. The aircraft reached Imphal at 6.23 p.m. and the crew
and passengers disembarked to allow Wingate to confer with Baldwin
and Air Commodore S. F. Vincent, 221 Group RAF. During its brief
stay the B-25 was under constant guard in the dispersal area.

At 8.00 p.m. the aircraft took off from Imphal and headed west towards
its destination, probably the airfield at Hailakandi or Lalaghat. About
half an hour later it had plunged in flames into a hillside ridge near the
Naga village of Thilon in the hills west of Imphal. Next day, once it had
become clear that Wingate and his party were missing – a C-47 pilot
had reported seeing an aircraft strike the ground and explode in the
Thilon area – Cochran ordered a number of air sorties over the area.
Although the wreckage was eventually discovered it was impossible to
ascertain from the air that it was a B-25 and Cochran asked Special Force
headquarters to send in a foot patrol. That evening a three-man team
led by Captain J. F. F. Barnes left Lalaghat and reached the crash site the
following day at 11.30 in the morning.

They discovered the unmistakable evidence of a high-impact crash: a
large crater, smashed-up pieces of wing and fuselage and the broken
bodies of the crew and passengers. Although it proved impossible to
identify what remained of the bodies the presence of Wingate's Wolseley

helmet and personal papers proved beyond doubt that he had been on board. As he usually sat in the co-pilot's seat and as the B-25 had hit the ground nose first, it was obvious, too, that he had been killed outright and that there were few recognisable physical remains. Having given orders for what was left of the bodies to be buried Barnes and his patrol returned to Lalaghat on 27 March. Wingate was dead and the Chindits would have to cope without him.

At White City, giving vent to a universal feeling of dismay once the news was broken, Calvert put his head in his hands and said, 'Oh, who will look after us now?' For Richard Rhodes James, a cipher officer with 111th Brigade, the feeling was the same: 'Now that Orde Wingate was no more, what would happen to us? Our master was gone and we, his masterpiece, were now ownerless.' Throughout the force the main emotion was disbelief. Wingate had seemed so indestructible that it was impossible to comprehend life without him. Although there is evidence to suggest that some staff officers at Sylhet, those who had been on the receiving end of Wingate's rages, were openly relieved by the news, the overwhelming feeling amongst the Chindits' rank and file was genuine sorrow at the loss of their uncommon leader.

Inevitably, given the sudden death of a notable military commander in an unexplained aircraft accident, a number of myths grew up around Wingate's last flight. At the time news reports spoke of the crash happening in bad weather but all contemporary accounts, including Baldwin's and Vincent's, speak of a clear night with scattered clouds. In his autobiography Slim suggested that the aircraft hit 'one of those local storms of extreme turbulence so frequent in the area', but the C-47 pilot who witnessed the B-25 going down confirmed that visibility was good. It has also been suggested that the aircraft had mechanical trouble and that Wingate pulled rank on Hodges and insisted that he take off but, again, there is no evidence to support the theory. Even so, as Tulloch told his wife in a letter written that evening, the signs had not been propitious.

It is sad to think that on this occasion I pressed him no less than four times not to take this particular trip and he nearly weakened and called it off, he himself had a strong premonition of disaster and before taking off went back to his office on purpose to speak to his stenographer and pat him on the back, telling him that he had worked wonderfully well for him and apologising for having cursed him at times.

This was Tulloch being wise after the event and imagining portents of disaster which would have been dismissed if Wingate had not been killed. Sabotage can be written off as well because the aircraft was either occupied or under guard between the time it left Hailakandi in the afternoon and landed at Broadway and Imphal. In any case because Cochran did not order Hodges to pick up Wingate until his flight was under way it would have been impossible for any 'conspirator' to sabotage the aircraft either by damaging its controls or by hiding a time bomb or pressure bomb on board before take-off.

Like all air accidents the crash of B-25 number 43–4232 was investigated by a board of enquiry which was held by the US authorities between 1 and 9 April. It concluded that the aircraft went into a spin or steep dive due to the failure of one of its engines.[8] Eyewitnesses also confirmed that it was on fire before it hit the ground and as it was fully fuelled and armed with fragmentation cluster bombs it would have exploded on impact. Another theory, put forward by Master-Sergeant Charles N. Baisden in 1962, claimed that the bombs themselves were to blame because the binding wires on the bomb clusters on B-25s were prone to rust and break loose. 'Three or more fragmentation bombs broke away from the cluster either during the landing or in the air turbulence of the weather front. There was always some air currents in the bomb bay which could cause the arming vanes to spin off and the bomb or bombs rolled into the fuselage and detonated.'[9]

This would account for the B-25 being on fire before it crashed but Baisden's theory depends on the weather being bad and the aircraft hitting turbulence. Another possibility is that Hodges was disabled when the B-25's trailing aerial was hit by a lightning strike and the shock stunned him through his headphones. Although the aircraft had two transmitters and a qualified radio operator on board it did not send out a distress signal during its slow descent into the hills.

But fifty years later perhaps it does not matter what caused the B-25 to plough violently into a hillside in Assam. Many thousands of allied aircrew and their passengers had their lives taken from them in equally distressing circumstances. Today most of them rest easy. The same cannot be said of Wingate: in death, as in life, he was destined to remain a controversial figure.

Fourteen

AFTERMATH

In distant London where she was serving in the WRNS Peggy Jelley had a strange premonition that something dreadful had happened to Wingate when she woke from a deep sleep to hear him calling out to her. She had not seen him since their bitter parting in 1935 but the anguished sound of his voice in her half-woken mind was as clear as it had ever been during their long relationship. Instinctively she knew that he was in some kind of trouble but it was not until a week later, when the news of his death was announced, that she understood the reason for his distress.

Following normal practice Lorna had been warned on 25 March that Wingate was missing, presumed dead. The message had come directly by a telegram from Tulloch which was passed by Giffard to Ismay in the Office of the War Cabinet.

Lorna from Derick [*sic*]: Deeply regret Orde missing, feared killed in air crash on 24th March at 8.30 pm. His work goes on. We will strive ceaselessly to achieve his object. This is the most fitting memorial we can build for him. Special Force mourns his loss. It is irreplaceable. I lose my best friend. Be brave. I have so much to tell you.

Shattering though the blow was, Lorna was spared the knowledge that Mountbatten wanted to censor the news of Wingate's death on the grounds that it would be bad for Chindit morale. On 25 March he sent a signal to Churchill announcing the 'shattering news' and requesting permission to keep it from public consumption: as he told Brooke, 'He [Wingate] appears to have such a charmed life that he may well be walking out of the jungle by himself, or at least be brought out by the search party.' At first Churchill was inclined to agree, at least until 'after the battle is decided', but following Barnes's return he decided against a deception plan. When Mountbatten proposed 'a whispering campaign that Wingate is still alive and engaged in secret operations', Churchill replied on 30 March that the Chiefs of Staff disagreed with the proposal because it would lead to 'unnecessary and undesirable complications'. And with that order the matter was dropped.

Official confirmation from the War Office Casualty Branch in Liverpool arrived at Place of Tilliefoure that same day and two days later, on 1 April, the news was announced in the British press. In *The Times* the obituarist described Wingate as a soldier who combined the qualities of the guerrilla leader with the scientist: 'he was a solitary elusive figure, and his disregard for convention fitted ideally into his orthodox military caution.' The *Observer's* obituary was equally flattering: 'His military genius wedded to his humanist sympathies have left their mark on this war but Wingate was one of the men we needed most for the years to come.'

As the news of Wingate's death swept in small waves of grief through London many of his closest friends met to remember him. A memorial service led by Canon A. C. Donn was held in St Margaret's Westminster on 14 April and a week earlier, on 6 April, Chaim Weizmann led a short memorial service at the Jewish Agency which was also addressed by Lewis Namier. Blanche Dugdale was there to record the event but by then she had admitted to herself that she had never liked Wingate and wondered if his influence had ever been as great as his supporters believed. Somewhat tartly she noted that 'the hagiology is already far advanced. He will be a greater inspiration to the Jews now he is dead than if he had lived to take a hand in their politics.'

Dugdale's comments are a curious precursor of the historical revisionism which would set in after Wingate's death. Slim, for example, was to change his mind about Wingate but his immediate response was generous. Writing in a South-East Asia Command pamphlet, *The Chindits, 1944,* he described him as a man of genius who had 'the power to see things more clearly than other men can'.

The number of men of our race in this war who are really irreplaceable can be counted on the fingers of one hand. Wingate is one of them. The force he built is his own; no one else could have produced it. He designed it, he raised it, he trained it, he led it, inspired it and finally placed it where he meant it to be – in the enemy's vitals.

Mountbatten, too, was aware of the sense of personal loss, writing to his wife Edwina that, despite differences of opinion, he would miss

Wingate's larger than life personality: 'Not only had we become personal friends but he was such a fire-eater, and it was such a help to me having a man with a burning desire to fight.' After coming out of the jungle Fergusson wrote to his parents about his lost leader, describing him as 'one of the best soldiers and certainly one of the greatest men I have met'. Wavell was no less generous in his obituary in the *Central Asian Review*, describing Wingate as a man 'of remarkable power and genius', a phrase that was echoed in Churchill's famous encomium in the House of Commons on 2 August 1944: 'There was a man of genius who might well have become a man of destiny.'

At her parents' home in Aberdeenshire Lorna began the task of recalling and commemorating her husband by noting down everything she could remember about him. Letters helped, too, and she was soon surrounded by a huge correspondence from people who had known him well and also from those who believed that their own lives had been enriched by serving under him. Some of those who wrote only knew him by reputation but still felt that they had to record their sense of loss. It was a distressing and dislocating time but life had to go on: a month later, in May, she gave birth to their son and he was christened Orde Jonathan Wingate. Ten years later, in February 1954, she remarried in Edinburgh John Smith, a well-known East Lothian farmer and land-owner.

Life also had to go on in Burma where the Chindits were still engaged in hard fighting at Broadway, White City and the Bhamo road. Obviously a commander had to be found to replace Wingate and Slim first spoke to Tulloch by telephone on 25 March to ask for his advice. In every respect, as Wingate's closest friend and loyal supporter, Tulloch was an obvious choice; indeed, he carried a letter from Wingate authorising him to take over command in the event of his death. Symes, too, thought that he had a claim on the position. Having been a loyal deputy to Wingate and being an experienced major-general he warranted serious consideration and, indeed, on receiving the news of Wingate's death he had hurried from Gwalior to Chindit headquarters at Sylhet. Three brigade commanders were also candidates: Lentaigne because he was the senior brigadier and Fergusson and Calvert because they had served under Wingate during the 1943 operation. It was a difficult choice for Slim and he was within his rights to discuss the matter with Tulloch who had impressed everyone with his common sensical approach to Operation Thursday.

But Tulloch was in a quandary. He ruled himself out because he had not commanded in the field and he realised that the Chindits would expect that experience of any successor to Wingate. The same stricture affected Symes who was bitterly disappointed by the decision which, after the war, he put down to not being 'in the right place at his death' and after making a formal protest he asked to be relieved of his post as deputy commander. That left the three brigade commanders. If sheer military competence and leadership abilities were the sole criteria then Calvert was the obvious choice but he was stymied by the 'Mad Mike' myth and it was widely held that he was just a good fighting soldier and not much else. This was not so. In the fighting at White City he had shown himself to be a sound tactician and his papers on irregular operations reveal a logical and elastic mind. For all that he possessed a Cambridge degree, though, it is unlikely if Slim would have accepted him and he never considered himself a front-runner for the post.

Fergusson was a fine leader who had shown that he understood Wingate's theories but he was not widely experienced in the problems of command. It is possible that Brigadiers Lance Perowne (23rd Brigade) and Tom Brodie (14th Brigade) were also considered but Tulloch's choice finally fell on Lentaigne. On the surface it was entirely logical. Lentaigne was the senior brigadier, he commanded 111th Brigade and he had distinguished himself in the fighting during the retreat from Burma. Like Slim he was also a Gurkha officer and Tulloch may have felt that this added to his acceptability. (Perhaps. According to Bidwell, Slim said that he had appointed Lentaigne, 'Because he was the only one who wasn't mad.') Tulloch also felt that Wingate's death had had 'a tremendous psychological effect on Fergusson and Calvert' and that Lentaigne was the officer closest in spirit to Wingate.

It was a mistake. Good officer though Lentaigne was, by March 1944 he was tired and feeling the strain of command. He was also drinking too much. Worse, he had never felt that he was in tune with Wingate and had made no secret that he despised his methods and style of leadership. In years to come the decision was to weigh heavily on Tulloch's mind and he went to his grave convinced that he had betrayed his friend's trust. As it also turned out, Tulloch lost in other ways. Although he was appointed deputy commander his duties were gradually taken over by Lentaigne's chief of staff Colonel H. T. Alexander and he was left with an empty role. After the operation had come to an end, in July 1944, he was left to regret what might have been:

In every way every follower of Wingate is to be trodden remorselessly into the dust. I shudder to think what my fate will be when I am thrown to the jackals! G2 of some sub-area-district I expect, or some such role to put me thoroughly in my place. I am certainly not going to be allowed to go home and they are about right there!'

Tulloch was gradually sidelined and although he later reached the rank of major-general he always believed that he was under a cloud because he was Wingate's closest friend. While it is true that many senior officers were relieved that Wingate had disappeared from the scene and were unlikely, therefore, to grant favours to his associates, Tulloch did not help his cause by removing and keeping the files relating to Operation Thursday. Later they were shipped home – quite illegally – and many of them found their way into the possession of the Wingate family. As time went by Tulloch became convinced that he owed it to his friend to use those papers to demonstrate Wingate's greatness as a military commander.

Having instituted a new chain of command Slim convened a conference at Comilla on 27 March. With the Imphal battle still being fought he wanted Special Force to concentrate on attacking the Japanese 15th Army's lines of communication. This was impossible for 16th Brigade who were engaged in the fighting at Indaw and for 77th brigade at White City but a compromise was reached whereby 14th Brigade and 111th Brigade would move west towards the Chindwin to carry out this essential task which was based on Wingate's Plan B. The new plans were endorsed at a commanders' meeting at Jorhat on 3 April when it was also decided to remove 23rd Brigade from Special Force and allot it to the defence of Kohima. Throughout the conference Slim was at pains to reassure Stilwell that Special Force was still involved in his advance towards Myitkyina. It was the beginning of the end of Wingate's plans for the forces he had created.

Six days later Slim cancelled the orders and decided to put the Chindits under Stilwell's operational command by the middle of May. Lentaigne moved his forward headquarters up to Shaduzup to be closer to his new commander and Calvert was ordered to abandon White City, despite having fought the Japanese to a standstill. Special Force also pulled out of Broadway and Aberdeen and Fergusson's exhausted 16th Brigade was flown back to India. A new stronghold was built to the north near Hopin and 77th Brigade, 14th Brigade and 3rd West African Brigade pulled out towards it. By moving northwards they would be in a better position to help Stilwell but at a cost to one of the original Chindit concepts.

To the east Morrisforce was operating against Japanese lines of communication between Bhamo and Myitkyina and to the north of him Herring's Dah Force was working with SOE to raise a patriot rebellion amongst the Kachins. Both had enjoyed a fair degree of success operating against the Japanese but both would be compromised by the new deployment of the brigades. Morrisforce had used classic Chindit tactics to ambush Japanese convoys and to destroy supply dumps. Despite friction with his SOE colleagues, Herring had succeeded in raising a small force which he used to harry the Japanese. Lentaigne believed that their success should be supported and was so concerned by the lack of action that he sent off a signal to Mountbatten's headquarters on 28 April requesting that Churchill be told what was happening.

Operation conceived by Wingate successfully completed but lack of follow-up troops makes withdrawal inevitable. This lays whole Kachin population, who have co-operated most loyally, open to severest reprisals. All ranks deeply deplore failure to protect Kachins, and Americans will undoubtedly publicise betrayal of our most loyal subjects. Consider Wingate would have appealed to you for assistance.[2]

It was a good try but Mountbatten refused to budge. Not only had Slim advised him that the Japanese would be unlikely to harry the Kachins but he was in no mood to reopen Special Force's direct channel to the Prime Minister. When his deputy Chief of Staff replied to Lentaigne on 1 May he reminded him that 'the arrangement between the prime minister and Wingate was on a strictly personal basis because they had become friends. SAC [Mountbatten] is not prepared to make the same arrangements with you.' With Wingate dead that source of support had disappeared and Special Force had lost all its friends in high places.

That lack of assistance helped to seal the Chindits' fate. After moving north they lost their long-range penetration role and were deployed in battle as regular infantry formations, but without armoured or artillery support. Fighting in support of Stilwell's forces in the Mogaung–Myitkyina area 77th, 111th and 3rd West African Brigades gave a fine account of themselves in spite of suffering heavy casualties but they were wasted in that role. At the end of August, physically and mentally exhausted, they were finally withdrawn to India. They had been in the field for five months, two more than was originally agreed, and many of the men were totally demoralised. At the beginning of 1945 Special Force was disbanded because as Mountbatten argued, 'there is no need for Chindits. We are all Chindits now.' Eight months later the war in Burma came to a victorious conclusion after Slim's 14th Army had smashed the Japanese army first at Imphal and Kohima and then at Meiktila before advancing on Mandalay and Rangoon.

In the aftermath of the war, as the campaign in Burma was reassessed, the role played by the Chindits underwent several revisions and Wingate's reputation suffered as a result. Before discussing that long-drawn-out argument between Wingate's supporters and those who denigrated his achievements Operation Thursday needs to be put in its proper perspective. Because Wingate died at a crucial juncture in the operation and was unable to influence future events, it is difficult to give a complete estimate of their achievements. They lost 1,034 casualties killed and 2,752 wounded: against that they accounted for over 10,000 Japanese, 5,764 of whom they killed. True, they suffered dreadful privations from illness and lack of food and came out of Burma a much-weakened force but as with the first Chindit expedition the battlefield accountancy should not just be numerical.

Once they had landed in northern Burma on 5 March the Chindits had operated freely against the Japanese lines of communication, cutting railways and destroying dumps. In so doing they sowed confusion in the minds of the Japanese commanders who were never entirely certain of the force's whereabouts or its intentions. As a result a large number of troops were used in countering the threat: one reserve division and two battalions drawn from the divisions attacking Imphal and Kohima. At least half of the available Japanese military aircraft in Burma had to be diverted to deal with the incursion. After the war General Mutaguchi admitted that, more than anything else, this affected the outcome of the battle for Kohima. Later, in 1968, he told Tulloch that on hearing of Wingate's death, he was both relieved and saddened: 'I realised what a loss this was to the British Army and said a prayer for the soul of this man in whom I had found my match.'

At White City they had shown that the enemy's lines of communication could be blocked permanently but only if follow-up forces were sent in to reinforce their lightly armed columns. This had always been Wingate's plan – and it is noteworthy that Lentaigne argued that it should be implemented when he contacted Mountbatten directly on 28 April – but shortage of available troops and the onset of the Japanese moves towards Imphal and Kohima prevented Slim from using Special Force in that way. In the aftermath of Wingate's death Plan B, the use of Special Force to attack the Japanese lines of communication, was executed, but only briefly.

Instead, the Chindits were forced to fight battles for which they were not trained. 111th Brigade's bloody defensive battle at Blackpool was the antithesis of everything which Wingate had preached, even though the Chindits' courage and determination encouraged the Chinese to attack on the Salween front in May. However, if the Chindit columns had continued to harass the Japanese lines of communication, using guerrilla-type tactics, the outcome of their operation would have been very different. But that depended on their leader. 'Had Wingate lived,' argued Mead, 'this, we may be sure, is how Chindit operations would have developed with, possibly, the final destruction of the Fifteenth Army west of the Chindwin.'

Unfortunately, that was not how Operation Thursday was viewed by the *Official History*. When volume III was published in 1961 it contained the unequivocal statement that 'in spite of the fortitude and gallantry of the LRP troops, the results achieved were not commensurate with the resources devoted to it at the expense of 14th Army.' The volume also contained specific charges against Wingate: that he misled Fergusson about the attack on Indaw by promising support from 14th Brigade which he never intended to provide, and that he misled Slim about the future deployment of 14th Brigade. The volume also accused him of misdirecting his forces and attacked the thinking which lay behind the evolution of Special Force.

Unusually for an official history the book contained a three-page assessment of Wingate which included several pejorative references to his unconventional personality. The draft for that section had been written by one of Kirby's assistant historians, Miss R. J. F. Hughes, and her analysis is based largely on the evidence provided by those who knew Wingate. Although she insisted that Wingate was an inspired commander who had 'a flair for the flamboyant in military command' and thereby helped to promote the 14th Army, she also accused him of 'lack of self-control, egoism and megalomania'. Much of Hughes's assessment was used verbatim by the historians who arrived at this conclusion in the *Official History*: 'Wingate had many original and sound ideas. He had the fanaticism and drive to persuade others that they should be carried out, but he had neither the knowledge, stability nor balance to make a great commander.'

The volume was written under the direction of Major-General S. Woodburn Kirby, CB, CMG, CIE, OBE, MC, with the assistance of Captain C. T. Addis, DSO, RN; Brigadier M. R. Roberts, DSO; Colonel G. T. Wards, CMG, OBE and Air Vice-Marshal N. L. Desoer,

CBE. Produced under the guidance of Sir James Butler for the Cabinet Office the official histories were supposed to provide an accurate and impartial account of the direction of the war and the historians and their assistants had full access to the official documents and to evidence provided by the principal commanders. In producing volume III Kirby and his team were provided with a series of straightforward factual military 'narratives' written by Brigadier M. Henry and Lieutenant-Colonel J. E. B. Barton of the Cabinet Office Historical Section. They also took evidence from the main participants in the Burma campaign including those who had most contact with Wingate, amongst whom may be mentioned Slim, Mountbatten, Giffard, Pownall, Tulloch, Symes, Fergusson, Brooke and Baldwin. All had words to say about Wingate which would affect his post-war reputation.

Kirby, it will be remembered, had been Director of Staff Duties in Delhi when Wingate arrived in India after the Quadrant conference and it may be supposed that he was not inclined to like or respect him. Not only was he one of the staff officers who was opposed to the Chindit concept but he also saw Wingate at his arrogant worst and as Bidwell suggests, 'he took his revenge'. This may not have been his original intention, but in the correspondence with the Burma commanders it is obvious from the frequent, and usually disparaging, references to Wingate that there was a degree of animus in Kirby's methods. Indeed, the first drafts produced by 1958 contained lengthy and detailed criticisms of Wingate, many of which were removed at the insistence of those who gave evidence. For example, the original drafts concluded that Wingate was indecisive on 5 March when it became clear that the Piccadilly airstrip had been blocked by felled logs and that the atmosphere of Lalaghat was dominated by 'the deepest gloom'. Both Tulloch and Baldwin, who were present at the time, took exception to these comments with the result that a more sober account was published. Baldwin also took the opportunity to take Kirby to task on 29 June 1958 for being 'very definitely unfair to Wingate'.

Chapter XII left a very disagreeable taste. I felt we had gone right back to the original position in which the official account of the fly-in had shaken both Tulloch and myself. There appears to be a deliberate desire to belittle Wingate. Admittedly he was a difficult and obstinate man, but he was a personality and did achieve success.

Kirby's reply on 8 July indicates that he was aware that he was skating on thin ice when he and his team dealt with Wingate.

I must now turn to your remarks on Wingate. I should have thought that you had gathered from our conversations and previous correspondence that we are trying to do our duty properly and assess Wingate without any bias. If, however, we are to sum up Wingate properly we must bring out to the reader his very odd character and the way in which he fought against every authority but his own.

After dealing with specific points about the events surrounding the fly-in Kirby ended the letter by saying: 'It is quite clear that whatever we say about Wingate will not meet with everyone's approval because he was a man who either had admirers or enemies, but what we eventually say will be as fair as we can make it, but we have no intention of whitewashing his very obvious faults.'

Certainly, that was a fair indication of what Kirby hoped to achieve and throughout the correspondence about the drafts he insists on the need to treat Wingate and the Chindits fairly and extensively. However, the tone adopted by some of the generals adds to the impression held by Baldwin that Wingate's 'failings were considerably more stressed than any of his virtues'. With the exception of Slim who described Wingate as 'one of the only two picturesque and puzzling figures in Burma (Stilwell was the other)', most comments were disparaging:

Giffard: 'Wingate's expedition was in my opinion a great waste of effort.'
Pownall: 'I hope you won't devote too much space to that contentious figure. His vivid personality was important largely because of the attention it drew and its impact on his subordinates; but I know of quite a few people in this history who were better soldiers and better men.'
Symes: 'He was an egomaniac, and he revelled in offending others and creating difficulties for the sheer joy of overcoming them.'

Although these were personal comments of the kind which do not appear in official histories Kirby must have been influenced by them, especially because he had decided at an early stage to investigate the relationship between Wingate's character and personality and his actions. It is also clear that he was affected by the antagonism which many of the generals felt for the long-range penetration concept and he soon came to the conclusion, voiced by Slim in a letter written on 22 October 1958, that 'the contribution of Special Force was [n]either great in effect or commensurate with the resources it absorbed.' He confirmed his own beliefs in his reply of 1 December.

I propose to say so in the final chapter of the volume, but I must include sufficient detail in the text to enable the reader to follow how the historians arrived at the view they expressed. Otherwise we shall be dubbed as biased from the start: for all Wingate's supporters (and there are many) always consider orthodox generals are automatically prejudiced against them.

Kirby voiced similar sentiments to other correspondents who believed that he was being unfair to Wingate but by 1958, as the volume neared the end of production, the argument was clear. In general the long-range operations of Spécial Force had a comparatively limited effect compared to the effort and resources they employed and Wingate was a difficult, overbearing and inexperienced commander who owed every-thing to the political influence of Wavell and Churchill. A year later, on 14 December 1959, Slim wrote once more to Kirby congratulating him on his treatment of Wingate.

Your summing up of the effectiveness of Special Force is clear and fair. If the experienced 70th British Division which I had first trained in jungle fighting at Ranchi had been used as a division in the main theatre it would have been worth three times its number in Special Force. We are always inclined in the British Army to devise private armies and scratch forces for jobs which our ordinary formations with proper training could do and do better.

In time this axiom became generally accepted in the British army. Just as Platt had once complained about Lawrence's legacy in the field of unconventional warfare so, too, was Wingate regarded as a malign influ-ence. Calvert later told Mead that while working at the War Office in 1948 he had come across papers playing down the role of the Chindits on the grounds that the army did not want to encourage soldiers like Wingate. Two years later, while raising the Malayan Scouts (SAS) for counter-insurgency operations against Chinese terrorists in Malaya Calvert was also disconcerted to discover that the Chindits' experience of jungle warfare had been lost or disregarded. After the force had been raised he was then told that there was to be 'no talk about Burma'.

Unfortunately, Slim did not just confine his thoughts to his private correspondence with Kirby: he committed many of them to print in his fine account of the war in Burma, *Defeat into Victory*. When it was published in 1956 many Chindits were angered to find that Slim's view of Wingate had altered over the years. Although he retained his respect for him – his comparison of Wingate with Peter the Hermit is a brilliant analogy – he was now prepared to be critical about the man and his methods. Instead of being the man of genius he described in 1944 Wingate had become 'difficult' and 'strangely naive when it came to the business of actually fighting the Japanese'.

With him, contact had too often been collision, for few could meet so stark a character without being either violently attracted or repelled. To most he was either prophet or adventurer. Very few could regard him dispassionately; nor did he care to be so regarded. I once likened him to Peter the Hermit preaching his Crusade. I am sure that many of the knights and princes that Peter so fiercely exhorted did not like him very much – but they went crusading all the same. The trouble was, I think, that Wingate regarded *himself* as a prophet, and that always leads to a single-centredness that verges on fanaticism, with all its faults. Yet had he not done so, his leadership could not have been so dynamic, nor his personal magnetism so striking.

Slim also had some gruff words to say about Wingate's threats to contact Churchill when his plans were thwarted but like the above assessment his criticism is not without foundation. Wingate was junior to Slim and it was tempting fate to behave in such a discourteous manner by appealing to 'higher authorities'. Fortunately, Slim was not known as 'Uncle Bill' for nothing and was well able to handle and understand his unruly subordinate. As his biographer Ronald Lewin makes clear, it was not Slim's style to denigrate former colleagues and he 'throttled his feelings' about Wingate and in his generosity was less outspoken than he might have been.

However, it was not so much the minor personal criticisms which upset former Chindits. Good book though *Defeat into Victory* undoubt-edly is – the first edition of 20,000 sold out immediately – it does contain a number of errors about Operation Thursday, including, most notably, the account of the fly-in and the use of follow-up troops to exploit its success. None of these might have mattered had Slim written the book unaided but during its composition he was in touch with one of the official historians, Brigadier Michael Roberts, a fellow Gurkha officer, who helped him greatly by making suggestions for improvements to the original manuscript. At the time Slim was Governor-General of Australia and was unable to check original sources. Lewin insists that Roberts's help was invaluable: 'Pages of courteous but ruthless criticism passed continuously from London to Canberra.'

In the writing of any historical account there has to be a fair degree of cross-fertilisation and it is not unusual for drafts to be discussed and criticised before publication. Slim was only being sensible in conscripting Roberts's services but in so doing he was also able to draw on the findings of the official historians. At the same time Kirby and his team were able to draw on Slim's own work and in the personal assessment of Wingate there are several references to Slim's book. More than anything else this has convinced Wingate's supporters that there was a conspiracy to denigrate their former leader. This was the view taken by Tulloch and Mead, and, more recently, by the historian David Rooney.

While it is unlikely that the official historians set out deliberately to blacken Wingate's name or to belittle his achievements – Kirby insisted throughout that he was unbiased and that his findings were backed by evidence – it is clear that there had been a sea-change in the appreciation of the Chindits. In 1945 the campaign in Burma had been won by Slim's Indian divisions and the operations in northern Burma were increasingly viewed as a side-show, important at the time for engaging the Japanese but strategically unnecessary and costly in the long term. Although there was admiration for the men's courage and resilience, many commentators had come to Slim's conclusion that their gains were outweighed by the levels of support and resources they received. Against that background the historians put the Chindit operations into a different perspective, one which would most certainly have been challenged by Wingate had he lived.

Inevitably the reaction brought a counter-reaction and by 1962 Tulloch had become convinced that he should write his own account about Wingate's military career. Partly his decision was formed by his correspondence with Kirby and his inability to persuade him that he was wrong on several points, including the matter of Slim's backing for the additional transport squadrons. Partly it was a matter of honour – he believed that he had failed Wingate by suggesting Lentaigne's appointment – and partly too he wanted to get across his point of view, not least for the family's sake.

In this he was helped by his acquisition of the bulk of Wingate's operational papers from Burma. These had been sent back to his home at Formby in Lancashire and they were also shown to Lorna who was thinking about writing her husband's biography. As it was illegal for an officer to remove official papers, Tulloch was rightly dismayed when Lorna herself took away – and retained – a large number of the papers in the spring of 1946. At the time he was still in India suffering from appendicitis and from his sickbed in Secunderabad he wrote an anguished appeal, reminding her of the dangers to himself. 'I hope you realise that you hold my whole future in your hands as long as those papers are in your possession and I would welcome their return at the earliest possible moment. They're not conducive to a quick recovery or a good night's sleep as things are at the moment.'

Lorna replied on 30 April that she was fulfilling her husband's wishes by taking possession of his private papers – when he had been suffering from typhoid Wingate had asked Matron McGeary to ensure that his despatch boxes were returned to his wife – and that by so doing she was protecting Tulloch's interests. Although the matter was resolved when Tulloch returned to England later in the year, the difficulties of writing a book based on these documents began to weigh ever more heavily on his mind. Most were unavailable for inspection in the Public Record Office and he feared that by publishing them he would be punished by the War Office. In 1962 he admitted to Sybil that he would have been court-martialled had Lentaigne not turned a blind eye to his actions. Even so, he was still in danger. On 19 October 1962 he wrote again to Sybil indicating that his project was under threat because he had been interviewed by senior officers at the War Office and reminded that he could be prosecuted under the Official Secrets Act. He described the gist of the conversation:

We don't want any more books on Wingate. The *Official History* has been written by unbiased experts with all the War Diaries etc to their hands and it cannot be challenged. If you write a book challenging the official history it will not be passed by the War Office. At the best they will adopt delaying tactics and will keep your book 'still under revision' for years and years and years and will NEVER pass it. You [Tulloch] are extremely vulnerable. We know that you broke one of the strict rules affecting army officers by abducting Top Secret papers during the war and even at this stage you could be prosecuted for this.

Later letters to Sybil spoke of Tulloch being threatened by imprisonment in the Tower of London and the forfeiture of his pension should he proceed with his book. When *Wingate in Peace and War* was eventually published in 1972, having been edited by the historian Arthur Swinton, no action was taken and it is now regarded as a passionate defence of Wingate and his work. Tulloch never admitted to being a writer and Sybil attempted, unsuccessfully, to enlist the help of, amongst others, Michael Foot and George Fraser. Tulloch died in 1974 – Fergusson believed that his death had been hastened by the strains of writing his book – and the final act in the campaign against the *Official History* was taken in 1977 by Mead and Sir Robert Thompson (an RAF liaison officer in both Chindit operations) who produced for the Cabinet Office a 'Suggested Statement' correcting Wingate's treatment by the official historians. No action was taken.[3]

Lorna, too, considered the possibility of writing a biography. Having committed her memories to paper she produced a lengthy manuscript about life with her husband in England and Palestine which also went into considerable detail about his personality. It was never completed but is still the most reliable guide to Wingate's life before the war. Not unnaturally, given Wingate's career, other writers were also interested in writing about him and the family found themselves answering a large number of requests for access to his papers. Amongst the first was John Masters, a Gurkha officer, who had commanded 111th Brigade in succession to Lentaigne and whose *Road Past Mandalay* (1961) is one of the best personal accounts of the Chindit campaign. In 1951 he wrote to Lorna proposing a book which would counter the 'small spate of war memoirs, the majority rather poorly written', but he failed to reach agreement with the family.

The 'official' biography was eventually written by Christopher Sykes and it was published in 1959. The second son of the diplomat Sir Mark Sykes, he was both a man of letters and a soldier, having served with the SAS during the war and he was a friend and later the biographer of the novelist Evelyn Waugh. At the time he was working for the features department of the BBC. Although Lorna provided him with her husband's papers, including those brought home by Tulloch, and read the manuscript before publication she later distanced herself from the book and was critical of many of Sykes's conclusions.

By then the family had set their face against further books about Orde, having come to the conclusion that anything written about him would only sensationalise or trivialise his life. When the distinguished writer Alan Moorehead visited Lorna in Edinburgh to discuss a film about Wingate to be produced by Jack Le Vien he was rebuffed and a later drama-documentary made by the BBC and written by Don Shaw encountered similar problems during its production in the mid-1970s. Sybil and Rachel also shared Tulloch's belief that there was an official plot to deny their brother's post-war fame: Sybil spoke of 'the whole wicked unscrupulousness of second-rate crooks who dare not allow their malice to be exposed' and Rachel kept many of her brother's papers in heavily sealed envelopes which were only to be opened by her siblings in the event of her death.

The allegations that there was an official campaign against Wingate were given some substance by the treatment of his remains. Shortly after his death, in July 1944, a small party of mourners led by Lieutenant-Colonel Rev Christopher Perowne left Sylhet and made their way to the crash site near Thilon village. On 6 July they conducted a short service there and left behind a cross which carried a simple bronze plaque engraved with the Chindit symbol and listing the names of the dead servicemen. After the war Lorna wrote to Churchill requesting that her husband's remains be brought home but was told that these would be buried in the British war cemetery at Imphal. This was done in April 1947 when a joint US–British team from the Commonwealth War Graves Commission and the US Graves Registration Unit removed some human remains for reburial at Imphal.

There they might have remained but for Washington's insistence that as the majority of the remains were American they should be interred in a US war cemetery in the Philippines. Although the Foreign Office attempted to counter the proposal, which was made under US Public Law, it eventually authorised the removal of the remains from Imphal in March 1949 and these were exhumed in December. The following year it was decided to change the place of reburial from Manila in the Philippines to the Arlington National Cemetery at Fort Meyer, Virginia. The remains were interred there on the afternoon of 10 November 1950 and Lorna was informed at the same time: it was the first official notification that her husband's remains had been removed from Imphal. Despite her and the family's angry and distressed protests, which were followed by complaints in the press and the House of Commons, the government insisted that it had to comply with the agreement that 'the final resting place of intermingled remains in a common grave should be determined by the country whose dead were in the majority in that grave.'[4] And there the matter rested until 1974 when the grave was rededicated with a common headstone listing the names of those men who lost their lives when the USAAF B-25 plunged in flames on to a hillside in distant Assam.

Over fifty years have passed since Wingate's death and, as many of his closest friends and colleagues predicted, he remains a controversial figure in the annals of British military history. First, he was a military innovator who was often ahead of his times; second, he was a genuine eccentric who managed to escape being typecast; and, lastly, because he was considered an outsider he was the cause of equal measures of admiration and loathing amongst those who knew him.

Of his military genius there is little doubt. Even if his untimely death means that it is impossible to do full justice to his experimental long-range penetration theories, he accomplished enough to prove that in an air–land battle they could be used to complement the actions of regular forces. He also understood the value of radio communications to direct his columns behind enemy lines and he could see how air power could be used tactically to support ground forces and operationally to interdict, isolate and destroy enemy positions. In this respect he was unfortunate that the helicopter was still in its infancy. Modern air assault troops no longer have to depend on vulnerable fleets of transport aircraft, gliders or parachutes to reach their targets and airborne forces using helicopters as weapons platforms and transport systems are today's strategic cavalry.

At a time when the Allies feared the Japanese soldier as a military superman he proved that given good leadership, training and equipment ordinary British soldiers could survive and fight a tenacious enemy in even the most difficult conditions. His experiences in Palestine with the Special Night Squads and in Ethiopia with Gideon Force proved to him that men will endure anything if they believe that the cause is right and if they have the confidence of their leaders. Although smaller in scale, his experiences during these campaigns helped to pave the way for the later Chindit operations: within the space of eight years Wingate had developed both as a soldier and as a strategist. Above all, he was an inspired leader who possessed physical and mental energy in abundance and who was blessed with moral courage and self-confidence. Some may not have warmed to him, others have admitted to hating him but no one who served him has ever denied that he was anything but a spirited and highly effective military commander.

Not that he was an easy man. Stories are legion about his extremes of temper and his black rages. He had a rude and abrasive personality and at times he appeared unhinged. If his soldiering had been confined to peacetime it is unlikely that he would have risen to the high rank he achieved during the war. Instead he would probably have been dismissed as an objectionable crank and it is difficult to imagine that after Palestine and his open espousal of the Jews he would have been promoted beyond the rank of major. However, just as the war helped to make Montgomery – another British general who was not always popular with everybody, save the troops who owed him their lives – so too did Wingate's star rise as a result of wartime exigencies. He had a talent to simplify matters and to clarify his strategic objectives and, when it mattered, he was blessed by the ability to communicate his ideas and his enthusiasms to those who mattered. In the company of Churchill he displayed a complete conviction of the rectitude of his opinions and demonstrated that he could not suffer fools gladly.

However this restless creativity was balanced by the complaint known as the black dog, those cyclical bouts of depression which were such a handicap in his earlier years and which had to be controlled or disguised in later life. Faced by acute despondency the world seemed a hostile place and its inhabitants implacable enemies who were determined to destroy him. From his wife's accounts of those bouts of depression it is clear that Wingate did suffer mentally and emotionally and all the evidence points to him being a mild manic-depressive of the kind which is frequently found in Celtic countries. When he was 'up' he was fiercely inventive, displaying a passion and loquaciousness which dazzled those in his company. But when he was 'down', the reverse was true and he was frequently left with the feeling that he was ahead of his time and that the rest of the world was out of step and somewhat mundane.

That zigzag of contradictions in his personality is central to Scottish life and although Wingate was never greatly interested in his Scottish Presbyterian background it did leave a long shadow over his life. In his long poem *A Drunk Man Looks at the Thistle* his fellow countryman, the poet Hugh MacDiarmid, apostrophised that polemical restlessness as:

> I'll hae nae hauf-way hoose, but aye be whaur
> Extremes meet – it's the only way I ken
> To dodge the curst conceit o' bein' richt
> That damns the vast majority o' men.

With Wingate it was no different. For him there could be no middle way and no compromise and throughout his brief life he was always found at the place where the extremes met.

References and Bibliography

The papers of Orde Charles Wingate have never been systematically collected and catalogued. The majority of his personal papers and letters are held by the family and are not open to public inspection. The main collections are held by his son, Lieutenant-Colonel O. J. Wingate, and by Mrs Judy Wingate, widow of Judge Granville Wingate. The first collection contains two important biographical essays: a lengthy book-length manuscript known as the 'Edinburgh Manuscript' written by Lorna Wingate in the early 1950s and an essay entitled 'Orde Wingate', written after the war by his lifelong friend Major-General Derek Tulloch. Lorna Wingate also compiled several handwritten notebooks containing reminiscences of her husband's life and career. Two selections of copies of Wingate's personal Chindit papers were presented to the Public Record Office by Granville Wingate and are listed under CAB 101/184 and CAB 106/170. Both were closed until 1996 but were opened to public inspection in 1993.

Other papers relating to Wingate include three collections in the John Rylands Library, University of Manchester: the Tulloch Papers (Major-General Derek Tulloch), the Hay of Seaton Papers (Ivy Hay of Seaton, formerly Paterson, Wingate's mother-in-law) and the Dunlop Papers (Major G. D. Dunlop, Royal Scots). The papers of Sir F. R(eginald) Wingate, 'Cousin Rex', are held by the Centre for Middle Eastern and Islamic Studies in the University of Durham. The centre also contains several collections of papers relating to the Sudan Defence Force, most notably those collected by Colonel J. H. R. Orlebar.

The official biography is Christopher Sykes, *Orde Wingate* (London: Collins, 1959) and the following books also deal with Wingate's life and career:

Hay, Alice Ivy, *There was a Man of Genius* (London: Neville Spearman, 1963)
Mead, Peter, *Wingate and the Historians* (Braunton: Merlin Books, 1987)
Mosley, Leonard, *Gideon Goes to War* (London: Arthur Barker, 1955)
Tulloch, Derek, *Wingate in Peace and War* (London: Macdonald, 1972)

Mention must also be made of David Rooney, *Wingate and the Chindits:*

Redressing the Balance (Arms and Armour Press, 1994) which was in the press while the present biography was being completed and could not therefore be consulted.

In 1982 members of the Chindits Old Comrades' Association produced for private circulation a typescript collection of comments about Wingate's wartime leadership in Burma: 'An appreciation of the planner and leader of the two Chindit campaigns in 1943 and 1944 behind the Japanese lines during World War II'.

The following manuscript collections have also been consulted:

IMPERIAL WAR MUSEUM
Brigadier Shelford Bidwell
Lieutenant-Colonel C. C. A. Carfrae
General Sir Robert Haining
Lieutenant-General N. M. S. Irwin
General Sir William Platt
Lieutenant-General Renya Mutaguchi
Sir Robert Thompson and Brigadier Peter Mead: memorandum on Wingate and the *Official History*
Department of Sound Records: Middle East: British Military Personnel 1919–1939
Papers collected for the *Official History*
SEATIC Bulletins
ATIS Interrogation Reports
Burma Command Intelligence Summaries

NATIONAL LIBRARY OF SCOTLAND
Brigadier the Rt Hon Lord Ballantrae (Bernard Fergusson)
Walter Elliot

LIDDELL HART CENTRE FOR MILITARY ARCHIVES, KING'S COLLEGE, LONDON
Captain Sir Basil Liddell Hart
General Sir William Platt

PUBLIC RECORD OFFICE, KEW
Palestine
CO 733 Palestine Original Correspondence
CO 814 Palestine Secessional Papers
CO 831 Transjordan Correspondence
FO 371 Palestine 1936–1938
WO 32
WO 106 Directorate of Military Operations and Intelligence

WO 191 War Diaries

Abyssinia
WO 169 HQ and area reports
WO 201 MEF HQ Papers
WO 217 War Diaries
WO 276 East Africa Command

Burma
CAB 101
CAB 106
HSI/27 SOE Papers Burma
HSI/47 SOE Papers Burma
PREM 3 Prime Minister's Private Office, 'Operational' Papers
PREM 4 Prime Minister's Private Office, 'Confidential' Papers
WO 106 C-in-C India
WO 186
WO 187
WO 203 Military HQ Far East
WO 208 Directorate of Military Intelligence
WO 216 Chief of Imperial General Staff Training Papers
WO 231 Directorate of Military Training
WO 235
WO 241 Directorate of Army Psychiatry

In an attempt to keep references to a minimum I have not listed private papers which are not in the public domain although a note on their provenance is given at the beginning of each chapter's source notes.

SOURCE NOTES

Chapter One: Father to the Man (pp. 5–13)
The main source of information about Wingate's childhood comes from a series of private reminiscences written by Sybil and Monica Wingate.

1. Gavin Carlyle, *Life and Work of the Rev William Wingate, Missionary to the Jews* (London and Glasgow: 1900), p.10
2. David McDougall, *In Search of Israel: A Chronicle of the Jewish Missions of the Church of Scotland* (London: Nelson, 1941), pp.20–1
3. Sir Reginald Wingate to Mrs Dalrymple of Gargunnock, 31 August 1911, Wingate Papers, Centre for Middle Eastern and Islamic Studies, Durham, 235/2

Chapter Two: Fighting the Good Fight (pp.14–34)
The main source of information about Wingate's childhood comes from a series of private reminiscences written by Sybil and Monica Wingate and from Lorna Wingate's 'Edinburgh Manuscript' and private notes. Background details about Wingate's time at Charterhouse can be found in W. H. Holden (ed.), *The Charterhouse We Knew* (London: British Technical and General Press, 1950). Tulloch's reminiscences about Woolwich are from his private essay, 'Orde Wingate'.

1. Jossleyn Hennessy, 'I was at school with Orde Wingate', BBC Home Service, 20 April 1959
2. Hay, op. cit., p.24
3. Civil Service Commission: *Army Entrance Exams* (London: HMSO, 1920)
4. K. W. Maurice-Jones, *The Shop Story* (Woolwich: Royal Artillery Institution, 1954), p.65
5. John Bagot Glubb, *Arabian Adventures* (London: Harrap, 1978), p.9

Chapter Three: Officer and Gentleman (pp.35–58)
The main sources of information about Wingate's time at Larkhill come from Tulloch's essay and from N. D. G. James, *Gunners at Larkhill: A History of the Royal Artillery School* (London: Gresham Books, 1983) and J. R. I. Platt, *Three Hundred Years of Fox Hunting in South and West Wilts* (Warminster: Berkewell, 1990). The account of Wingate's time at the School of Oriental Studies and of his mental anguish in the Sudan is taken from the 'Edinburgh Manuscript'. Enid 'Peggy' Jelley provided the author with information about her relationship with Wingate in a private interview.

1. Brigadier C. Childs, *The Gunner*, no. 138 (1982)
2. Claud Fothergill, *A Doctor in Many Countries* (London: Pickering and Inglis, 1945)
3. Mary Jelley to Derek Tulloch, 20 September 1972, Post 1945 Correspondence, Tulloch Papers
4. J. H. R. Orlebar, Sudan Defence Force Papers, Sudan Archive, 740/9/1–72
5. E. A. Balfour, Correspondence, Sudan Archive, 606/316
6. Shelford Bidwell, *The Chindit War* (London: Hodder and Stoughton, 1979), pp.38–9

Chapter Four: Soldiering in the Sudan (pp.59–82)
The main source of information about soldiering with the Sudan Defence Force is J. H. R. Orlebar, *Tales of the Sudan Defence Force* (Durham, 1981) and *The Story of the Sudan Defence Force* (Durham, 1986). Other information comes from the 'Edinburgh Manuscript' and Wingate's private letters to his family and to Enid Jelley.

Other works consulted:

Collins, Robert O., and Francis M. Deng (eds), *The British in the Sudan, 1898–1956* (London: Macmillan, 1984)
Daly, M. W., *Empire on the Nile: The Anglo-Egyptian Sudan, 1898–1934* (Cambridge: Cambridge University Press, 1986)
Kenrick, Rosemary, *Sudan Tales* (Cambridge: Oleander, 1987)

1. J. H. R. Orlebar, 'The Story of the Sudan Defence Force', *The Condominium Remembered: Proceedings of the Durham Sudan Historical Records Conference*, vol. I, ed. Deborah Lavin (Durham: Centre for Middle Eastern and Islamic Studies, 1991)
2. Brigadier G. W. B. James, Presidential Address to the Psychiatric Section, Royal Society of Medicine, *Lancet*, 1945, vol. 2, pp.801–5
3. Hugh Boustead, *The Wind of Morning* (London: Chatto and Windus, 1971), p.78
4. Orde Wingate, 'In Search of Zerzura', *Geographical Magazine*, April 1934
5. Hay, op. cit., pp.21–2
6. Mary Jelley to Tulloch, op. cit.

Chapter Five: In the Land of Beulah (pp.83–103)
The main sources are the 'Edinburgh Manuscript', Tulloch, and Wingate's private correspondence with his family. The paper 'Palestine in Imperial Strategy' was written for Field Marshal Lord Ironside in 1939 and does not exist in the public records.
Other books consulted for this chapter and for Chapters Six and Seven:

Cohen, M. J., *Palestine: Retreat from the Mandate* (London: Elek, 1978)
Connell, John, *Wavell: Scholar and Soldier* (London: Collins, 1964)
Connell, John, *Wavell: Supreme Commander* (London: Collins, 1969)
Lewin, Ronald, *The Chief: Field Marshal Lord Wavell, Commander-in-Chief and Viceroy* (London: Hutchinson, 1980)
Raugh, Harold E., Jnr, *Wavell in the Middle East 1939–1941* (London: Brassey's, 1993)
Rose, Norman, *Lewis Namier and Zionism* (Oxford: Clarendon Press, 1980)
Rose, Norman, *The Gentile Zionists: A Study in Anglo-Zionist Diplomacy 1929–1939* (London: Frank Cass, 1973)
Zweig, R. W., *Britain and Palestine during the Second World War* (London: Royal Historical Society, 1986)

1. *Palestine: Annual Report*, 1931, CO 831/11
2. Chaim Weizmann to Vera Weizmann, November 1937, quoted in Norman Rose, *Chaim Weizmann: A Biography* (London: Weidenfeld and Nicolson, 1986), pp.257–8

Chapter Six: Defender of the Faith (pp.104–26)

Wingate wrote several papers on the need to create Jewish defence forces including 'A Desert Force for Palestine' which advocated a Jewish Legion. None of these are extant in the public records although his memoranda on the Special Night Squads were presented to Captain Sir Basil Liddell Hart and copies exist in the Liddell Hart Centre for Military Archives, King's College, London.

Oral evidence relating to the creation of the Special Night Squads comes from two sources:

(i) Hay of Seaton Papers, John Rylands Library, University of Manchester: Interviews with Dov Yirmiya, Moshe Shertok, Reuven Shiloah.
(ii) Middle East: British Military Personnel, 1919–1939, Imperial War Museum, Department of Sound Records:

004550/05 Major-General H. E. N. 'Bala' Bredin
004463/03 Major Arthur Dove
004451/03 Lieutenant-General Sir John Evetts
004506/03 Lieutenant-Colonel J. E. S. Gratton
004510/03 Lieutenant-Colonel Michael Grove
004619/03 Corporal Fred Howbrook
004486/07 Lieutenant-Colonel Robert 'Rex' King-Clark
004545/04 Colonel Ivor Thomas

1. David Ben-Gurion, *Letters to Paula and the Children* (Tel Aviv, 1968), pp.210–13
2. Norman Rose (ed.), *Baffy: The Diaries of Blanche Dugdale, 1936–1947* (London: Valentine Mitchell), 1973, p.23
3. Chaim Weizmann, quoted in N. A. Rose, *The Gentile Zionists: A Study in Anglo-Zionist Diplomacy 1929–39*, op. cit., p.182
4. Hugh Foot, *A Start in Freedom* (London: Hodder and Stoughton, 1966), p.51
5. Sir John Shuckburgh, memorandum on Jewish defence forces, 26 May 1938, CO/733/367/1
6. MacMichael to MacDonald, 29 July 1938, CO/733/371/1

Chapter Seven: Gideon's Men (pp.127–54)

The same sources have been used as for the previous chapter, with the addition of interviews with Israel Carmi and Nathan Shadni (Hay of Seaton Papers).

A copy of Lieutenant-Colonel Rex King-Clark's diary is held by the Imperial War Museum and the greater part of his interview was published in his memoirs, *Free for a Blast* (London: Grenville Publishing, 1988)

1. David Ben-Gurion (with Moshe Pearlman), *Ben-Gurion Looks Back* (London: Weidenfeld and Nicolson, 1965), pp.92–3
2. MacMichael to MacDonald, 24 July 1938, CO 733/366/4
3. Baxter to MacMichael, 29 July 1938, CO 733/371/1

Chapter Eight: Marching off to War (pp.155–77)
Wing-Commander Ritchie's report and Wingate's papers relating to his complaint to the sovereign are held privately by the family. Blanche Dugdale's diary extracts were published in *Baffy: The Diaries of Blanche Dugdale* (op. cit.).
1. Glubb, *Palestine: Monthly Report*, July 1939, CO 831/51/10
2. Elwyn Jones, quoted in Robert Rhodes James, *Victor Cazalet: A Portrait* (London: Hamish Hamilton, 1976), p.218
3. James, ibid., p.229
4. Lloyd to Churchill, 27 June 1940, PREM 4/51/9
5. Bracken to Churchill, 31 October 1940, ibid.
6. Lloyd to Weizmann, 17 October 1940, CAB 66/12
7. Churchill to Moyne, 4 March 1941, PREM 4/51/9
8. Brian Bond, 'Liddell Hart's Influence on Israeli Military Theory and Practice', *Liddell Hart: A Study of His Military Thought* (London: Cassell, 1977)

Chapter Nine: With the Lion of Judah (pp.178–202)
Wingate's appreciations of the Ethiopian campaign and Gideon Force's letter books are in the private family papers. Accounts by other participants are contained in:

Allen, W. E. D., *Guerrilla War in Abyssinia* (London: Penguin, 1943)
Boustead, Hugh, *The Wind of Morning*, op. cit.
Dodds-Parker, Douglas, *Setting Europe Ablaze* (London: Springwood, 1983)
Thesiger, Wilfred, *The Life of My Choice* (London: Collins, 1987)
Thesiger, Wilfred, interview with Ivy Paterson, Hay of Seaton papers, op. cit.
    The War Diary of Abraham Akavia, WO 217/37
    Mission 101 War Diary, WO 169/2858
    Ethiopian Patriots' War Diary WO 169/2859

1. Henry Maule, *Spearhead General* (London: Odhams, 1961), p.31
2. Upcher's and Muir's comments, Orlebar, Sudan Defence Force papers, op. cit.
3. Lavin (ed.), *Condominium Remembered*, op. cit., pp.124–5

Chapter Ten: Watershed (pp.203–28)
The same sources have been used as for Chapter Nine, with the addition of:

Cooper, Artemis, *Cairo in the War* (London: Hamish Hamilton, 1989)
Foot, M. R. D., *SOE: The Special Operations Executive* (London: BBC Books, 1984)
Macleod, Roderick, and Dennis Kelly (eds), *The Ironside Diaries* (London: Constable, 1962)
Minney, R. J., *The Private Papers of Hore-Belisha* (London: Collins, 1991)
Playfair, I. S. O., et al., *The Mediterranean and Middle East*, vol. I, The Early

Successes against Italy (to May 1941) (London: HMSO, 1954, 1974) (*Official History*)

West, Nigel, *Secret War: The Story of SOE, Britain's Wartime Sabotage Organisation* (London: John Curtis – Hodder and Stoughton, 1992)

The account of Wingate's suicide attempt is taken from a private typescript, 'My account of Wingate's attempted suicide in Cairo – as told to me direct by him in London during the war on his return from Cairo', signed Alice Ivy Paterson, 21 March 1952.

1. Bickham Sweet-Escott, *Baker Street Irregular* (London: Methuen, 1965), pp.74–5
2. Surgeon-Captain F. P. Ellis, obituary of G. A. H. Buttle, *British Medical Journal*, 9 July 1983
3. Dugdale, op. cit., p.189
4. Sir Reginald Wingate to Orde Wingate, 11 November 1941; Orde Wingate to Sir Reginald Wingate, 15 December 1941, Wingate Papers, 243/7/1–151

Chapter Eleven: Stemming the Tide (pp.229–56)
There is an extensive bibliography for Operation Longcloth and the first Chindit expedition of 1943. In addition to the Chindits Old Comrades' Association's 'Appreciation', op. cit., and the records in the Imperial War Museum, the main published personal accounts are:

Burchett, W. G., *Wingate's Phantom Army* (London: Muller, 1946)
Calvert, Michael, *Fighting Mad* (London: Jarrolds, 1952)
Calvert, Michael, *Prisoners of Hope*, rev. ed. (London: Leo Cooper, 1971)
Fergusson, Bernard, *Beyond the Chindwin* (London: Collins, 1945)
Fergusson, Bernard, *The Trumpet in the Hall* (London: Collins, 1970)
MacHorton, Ian, *Safer than a Known Way* (London: Odhams 1958)
Rolo, Charles, *Wingate's Raiders* (London: Harrap, 1944)
Stibbe, Philip, *Return via Rangoon* (London: Newman Wolsey, 1947)

The campaign is also described at length in the following histories:

Allen, Louis, *Burma: The Longest War, 1941–45* (London: J. M. Dent, 1984)
Kirby, S. W., et al., *The War Against Japan*, vol. II (London: HMSO, 1958)
Prasad, B., (ed.), *Official History of the Indian Armed Forces in the Second World War (1939–1945) Reconquest of Burma 1942–45* (Calcutta: Orient Longmans, 1954)
Wingate, Brigadier Orde, *Report on Operations of 77th Indian Infantry Brigade in Burma, February to March 1943* (New Delhi, printed by the Manager, Government of India Press, 1943)

A censored version of this report is contained in CAB 106/51. The original typescript version is in WO 231/13 but this is closed until 2043: however

SOE's version of the same typescript report is open to inspection in HSI/27. The Tulloch Papers include a photocopied version with Tulloch's annotations and both his and Mead's books (op. cit.) provide detailed commentaries on Operation Longcloth.

1. Report on Visit to the Maungdaw Front, 4–9 May 1943, Irwin Papers
2. Calvert, *Fighting Mad*, op. cit., p.76
3. 'Notes on Penetration Warfare – Burma Command', 25 March 1934, HSI/27
4. Lindsay to St J. Killery, 2 April 1943, HSI/27
5. Notes of Major G. D. Dunlop, 1st Chindit Expedition, Dunlop Papers
6. Mountbatten to Kirby, 26 October 1958, CAB 101/181
7. Byron Farwell, *The Gurkhas* (London: Allen Lane, 1984), p.217
8. Calvert, *Prisoners of Hope*, op. cit., p.12
9. Major J. G. Lockett, Narrative, Tulloch Papers, op. cit.
10. Bidwell, op. cit., p.40
11. Irwin to Kirby, 4 January 1956, Irwin Papers
12. Major B. E. Fergusson, No. 5 column, 77 Ind. Inf. Bde, Operations in Burma, February–April 1943, Preliminary Outline Report, 1 May 1943, Ballantrae Papers
13. Ballantrae (Bernard Fergusson) to Bidwell, 13 January 1978, Ballantrae Papers

Chapter Twelve: Planning for Victory (pp.257–83)
Both Peter Mead and Derek Tulloch wrote lengthy manuscript essays on the Chindit campaign. A copy of Mead's 'Chindit Headquarters' is kept in the Tulloch Papers, op. cit., and Tulloch's account of the operation is held by the Wingate family. Many of Wingate's Chindit papers are also held by the family.

There is an extensive bibliography for Operation Thursday and the second Chindit expedition of 1944. In addition to the Chindits Old Comrades' Association's 'Appreciation', op. cit., the books cited for Chapter Eleven and the records in the Imperial War Museum, the main published personal accounts are:

Carfrae, Charles, *Chindit Column* (London: William Kimber, 1985)
Fergusson, Bernard, *The Wild Green Earth* (London: Collins, 1946)
Masters, John, *The Road Past Mandalay* (London: Michael Joseph, 1961)
O'Brien, Terence, *Out of the Blue* (London: Collins, 1984)
Ogburn, Charlton, *The Marauders* (London: Hodder and Stoughton, 1960)
Rhodes James, Richard, *Chindit* (London: John Murray, 1980)
Thompson, Robert, *Make for the Hills* (London: Leo Cooper, 1989)

In addition to Allen, Bidwell, Mead, Prasad and Tulloch, op. cit., the campaign and Wingate's role are described at length in the following studies:

Bond, Brian (ed.), *Chief of Staff: The Diaries of Lieutenant-General Sir Henry Pownall*, vol. II (London: Leo Cooper, 1974)

Churchill, Winston S., *The Second World War*, vol. V (London: Cassell, 1952)

Collier, Basil, *The War in the Far East* (London: Heinemann, 1969)

Connell, John, *Auchinleck: A Critical Biography* (London: Cassell, 1959)

Elliott-Bateman, Michael, *Defeat in the East* (London: Oxford University Press, 1967)

Gilbert, Martin, *Churchill*, vol. VII, 1941–1945, *Road to Victory* (London: Heinemann, 1986)

Hickey, Michael, *The Unforgettable Army* (Tunbridge Wells: Spellmount, 1992)

Keegan, John (ed.), *Churchill's Generals* (London: Weidenfeld and Nicolson, 1991)

Kirby, S. W., et al., *The War Against Japan*, vol. III (London: HMSO, 1961)

Larrabee, Eric, *Commander-in-Chief: Franklin Delano Roosevelt, His Lieutenants and Their War* (London: André Deutsch, 1987)

Lewin, Ronald, *Slim the Standard Bearer* (London: Leo Cooper, 1976)

Lunt, James, *A Hell of a Licking* (London: Collins, 1986)

Martin, Sir John, *Downing Street: The War Years* (London: Bloomsbury, 1991)

Matthews, Geoffrey, *The Reconquest of Burma* (Aldershot: Gale and Polden, 1961)

Romanus, Charles F., and Riley Sunderland, *The United States in World War II, China, Burma and India Theater*, vols I and II (Washington DC: Department of the Army, 1953, 1956)

Rooney, David, *Burma Victory* (London: Arms and Armour Press, 1992)

Slim, William, *Defeat into Victory* (London: Cassell, 1956)

Smith, E. D., *The Battle for Burma* (London: Batsford, 1979)

Swinson, Arthur, *Kohima* (London: Hutchinson, 1968)

Tuchman, Barbara, *Sand Against the Wind: Stilwell and the American Experience in China 1911–1945* (New York: Macmillan, 1970)

Warner, Philip, *Auchinleck: The Lonely Soldier* (London: Buchan and Enright, 1981)

Ziegler, Philip, *Mountbatten* (London: Collins, 1985)

1. Minutes of war cabinet, 28 July 1943, PREM 3/143/8
2. Prime Minister's personal minute, General Ismay for COS Committee, 24 July 1943, ibid.
3. Prime Minister's personal minute, General Ismay for COS Committee, 26 July 1943, ibid.
4. Chiefs of Staff Committee (Quadrant), 4th meeting, 8 August 1943, PREM 3/366/3
5. Chiefs of Staff Committee (Quadrant), 5th meeting, 8 August 1943, ibid.
6. 'Forces of Long Range Penetration: Future Development and Employment in Burma', memorandum by Brigadier Wingate, 10 August 1943, WO 203/5213
7. Quadrant to Auchinleck, 12 August 1943, ibid.
8. Auchinleck to Quadrant, 19 August 1943, WO 203/5214

9. 'Long Range Penetration Groups', report by the Joint Planning Staff, 23 August 1943, WO 203/5213
10. Kirby to Alanbrooke, 3 April 1959, CAB 101/182
11. 'Wingate as a Man and a Commander', memorandum by Miss R. J. F. Hughes, undated, CAB 101/202
12. Symes to Kirby, February 1958, CAB 101/182
13. Dr W. Brockbank to Sir Richard Drew, 11 February 1976; Ministry of Defence comment, 5 April 1976, Correspondence Box 2, Tulloch Papers
14. Notes for Supreme Commander by Commander Special Force, 13 January 1944, WO 203/5218

Chapter Thirteen: Operation Thursday (pp.284–312)
Copies of Wingate's correspondence with Mountbatten, Giffard and Slim during the planning stages of Operation Thursday are contained in the Wingate Papers held by the Public Record Office in CAB 101/184.

The British file on the circumstances surrounding his death is also held by the Public Record Office in WO 203/4881/7033. The definitive account of the crash of the USAAF B-25 and the reburial is Dennis Hawley's *The Death of Wingate* (Braunton: Merlin Books, 1994). Sources for Operation Thursday are as for the previous chapter.

1. 'Support for Special Forces December 1943–January 1944', CAB 101/202
2. 'Fourteenth Army and Eastern Command Operation Instruction No. 4', WO 172/4164
3. Slim to Kirby, 22 October 1958, CAB 101/185
4. LRPG Air Sortie Signals between CAS and AAC-in-C SEA, WO 203/5220
5. Mountbatten to Wingate, 17 March 1944, WO 203/5215
6. Ballantrae to Bidwell, 4 January 1977, Ballantrae Papers, Acc. 9259/99
7. 'Notes on an Interview with Major-General Tulloch', 20 November 1957, CAB 101/182
8. The full report and comments are contained in Hawtrey, op. cit., pp.66–76
9. Baisden to Slim, 1 August 1962, CAB 101/182

Chapter Fourteen: Aftermath (pp.313–30)
The correspondence concerning the writing of the *Official History* is contained in the Public Record Office in CAB 101/181–185.

1. Tulloch diary, 25 July 1944, CAB 101/184
2. Lentaigne to Lushington, 28 April 1944, WO 203/5221
3. The full text is contained in Mead, op. cit., pp.195–6
4. Crocker to Churchill, 27 November 1950, WO 32/12967

Index

Brigades and divisions are grouped under those headings, except for Artillery brigades which are under Royal Artillery. OW stands for Orde Wingate.